Supervision

Second Edition

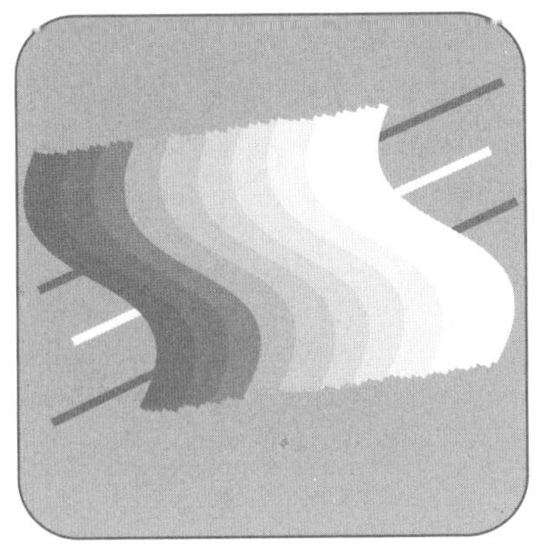

Stan Kossen

SUPERVISION

Second Edition

Stan Kossen

West Publishing Company
St. Paul New York San Francisco Los Angeles

To Marilena—
A person who assisted me
far more than she realizes

Copy Editor: *Gale Miller*
Illustrations: *John Foster*
Chapter Opener and Intext
Photography: *David Hanover, Hanover Photography*
Cover Image: *The Image Bank / West / Jim Salvati © 1990*
Compositor: *Parkwood Composition*

50 W. Kellogg Boulevard
P.O. Box 64526
St. Paul, MN 55164-0526

Printed in the United States of America
98 97 96 95 94 93 92 91 8 7 6 5 4 3 2 1 0

Library of Congress Cataloging-in-Publication Data

Kossen, Stan, 1931-
Supervision / Stan Kossen.—2nd ed.
p. cm.
Includes index.
ISBN 0-314-76552-2 (hard)
1. Supervision of employees. I. Title.
HF5549.K665 1991
658.3′02—dc20

90-21284
CIP

Contents in Brief

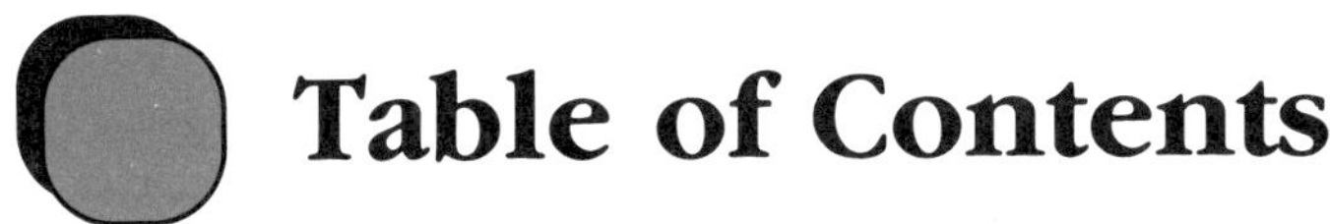

Table of Contents

Supervision

Second Edition

Stan Kossen

SUPERVISION

Second Edition

Stan Kossen

West Publishing Company
St. Paul New York San Francisco Los Angeles

To Marilena—
A person who assisted me
far more than she realizes

Copy Editor: *Gale Miller*
Illustrations: *John Foster*
Chapter Opener and Intext
Photography: *David Hanover, Hanover Photography*
Cover Image: *The Image Bank / West / Jim Salvati © 1990*
Compositor: *Parkwood Composition*

50 W. Kellogg Boulevard
P.O. Box 64526
St. Paul, MN 55164-0526

Printed in the United States of America
98 97 96 95 94 93 92 91 8 7 6 5 4 3 2 1 0

Library of Congress Cataloging-in-Publication Data

Kossen, Stan, 1931-
Supervision / Stan Kossen.—2nd ed.
p. cm.
Includes index.
ISBN 0-314-76552-2 (hard)
1. Supervision of employees. I. Title.
HF5549.K665 1991 90-21284
658.3'02—dc20  CIP

Contents in Brief

Table of Contents

3 Problem Solving and Making the Right Decisions–39

Part 2 Supervisory Roles in Planning and Controlling–65

Planning Work Activities–67

Controlling Work Activities–89

Part 6 Special Employment Concerns–449

Special Employment Concerns—Equal Employment Opportunities–451

Special Employment Concerns—Disabilities, AIDS and Substance Abuse in the Workplace–473

Special Employment Concerns—Organizational Health and Safety–493

Preface

To the Reader

What is it that a reader like you personally wants out of a textbook? I first began to search for an answer to this question when I began training people for management positions almost two decades ago.

Any textbook should, in my opinion, be tailored to the needs of its readers. A significant challenge for most authors, however, is to know precisely what the specific needs of each reader actually are, since every reader is a unique individual with his or her own interests, desires, and requirements.

I've been lucky enough over the years not only to have received direct feedback from the graduate and undergraduate students whom I've taught at Idaho State University, Merritt College, Golden Gate University, and St. Mary's College, but also to have worked directly with employees—managers and those aspiring to become managers—who are on the front lines of organizational activity. My direct contact with organizations as a consultant and seminar leader has helped to substantiate my belief that most readers want a textbook that is both understandable and practical. The thousands of employees who have attended my management seminars have stressed that one of their primary concerns is to be exposed to materials that can help them perform their responsibilities and tasks more effectively. They've indicated a preference to avoid the types of materials that are written in an excessively theoretical and so-called scholarly manner.

Who Can Benefit from This Text?

I've discovered that there tend to be at least three different types of readers of texts like this. The *practitioner* is one type—the person already involved in a supervisory position who wants to gain additional knowledge and skill in order to perform his or her tasks more effectively.

A second category of reader is *one who aspires to become a manager*. This type of person wants to be prepared and ready for a supervisory position when the opportunity for promotion arises.

A third type of reader is the *curious*—the person who is exploring the field of management as a way of deciding whether he or she is really interested in becoming a manager one day.

What's in It for You?

SUPERVISION is logically organized into six main sections intended to enhance your understanding of concepts related to your job as a supervisor.

- Part I—The Supervisory Process
- Part II—Supervisory Roles in Planning and Controlling

- Part III–The Management of Human Resources
- Part IV–Giving Employees Direction
- Part V–Problems, Challenges, and the Supervisor
- Part VI–Special Employment Concerns

Take a careful look at the table of contents. You'll find that it not only focuses on the basic functions and activities common to most supervisory positions, but it also includes up-to-date topics that have become highly critical in recent years—in some cases, burning issues—for supervisors to understand and be able to apply. These important topics include:

- How to manage stress and other difficult situations both on and off the job.
- How to manage time and self more effectively.
- How to manage your own manager.
- How to improve your perception, problem-solving, and communication skills.
- How to supervise special employment groups, such as minorities, women, individuals with disabilities, older workers, and those with alcohol and drug abuse problems.
- How to avoid problems related to sexual harassment.

Anything to Make It Easier . . .

There are a number of aids found in the text that are designed to make learning the material easier for you. For example, each chapter begins with a set of *learning objectives.* These items tell you the key points of the chapter and indicate what you should be able to understand or do after you've studied it.

Each chapter also includes *margin definitions* that briefly explain major terms that are located in the sections nearby. There also is a *Glossary* situated in the back of the text where terms are listed in alphabetical order.

Each chapter concludes with *summaries* of its main points, along with *questions for discussion* and a listing of significant *chapter terms,* all intended to enhance your understanding of the presented materials. There is also a *Supervision in Action* section at the end of each chapter, with exercises and incidents that enable you to make direct application of the concepts you've learned.

Acknowledgments

I am especially grateful for the patience and editorial assistance provided to me by the staff of West Educational Publishing. Writing college textbooks is a pressure-laden activity, and not once did I feel pushed—only guided—by such highly qualified people as Rex Jeschke, Clyde Perlee, Denise Simon, Mario Rodriguez, Stephen Schonebaum, and Sarah Bennett, an impressive lineup indeed.

Special appreciation is extended to the following professors who provided me with excellent suggestions and assistance during the manuscript-development phases of *SUPERVISION.*

- Raymond F. Balcerzak, Jr. Ferris State University
- Charles Beavin, Miami-Dade Community College
- Barrett R. Burns, Houston Community College
- James W. Cox, Lane Community College
- Suresh Gopalan, Louisiana Tech University
- Carl M. Guelzo, Catonsville Community College
- Donald E. Harris, Oakton Community College
- Karen Heuer, Des Moines Area Community College
- Carl F. Jenks, Purdue University, Calumet
- Edward L. Jones, Tidewater Community College
- John B. Maloney, College of Du Page
- Edwin F. Minor, Phoenix College
- Jean Nelson, Austin Technical College
- Kristi Newton, Chemeketa Community College
- Forrest W. Price, Stephen F. Austin State University
- Jennie M. Rucker, Community College of Denver
- Wendy M. Smith, Seattle Central Community College
- Jeff Stauffer, Ventura College
- Verna Teasdale, Prince Georges Community College
- Rick Webb, Johnson County Community College
- W. J. Waters, Central Piedmont Community College
- Charles H. Wetmore, California State University, Fresno
- Sam White, Portland State University

Special words of gratitude are in order for Marilena, without whose consistent encouragement and expressions of endearment the monumental task of completing another textbook would have been extremely difficult indeed.

Stan Kossen

Part One

The Supervisory Process

Chapter 1

The Nature of Supervision

Supervisors are, so to speak, the ligaments, the tendons and sinews of an organization. They provide the articulation. Without them, no joint can move.

—Peter F. Drucker, Management Philosopher

Learning Objectives

When you finish this chapter, you should be able to:

1. Identify the supervisor's role in the organizational hierarchy.
2. Express the distinction between a manager and other employees.
3. Relate the various relationships that supervisors have with other organizational members.

"What, me a manager? You've got to be kidding! I'm the low person on the totem pole. I get it from the bosses upstairs, and I get it from my people below. I'm just a supervisor, nothing more. I've got lots of responsibilities, and that's about all."

What is your reaction to those words? Are supervisors considered separate from, or are they also a part of, management? Do they merely have responsibility, or is there much more inherent in their positions? Precisely what is a supervisor? Are supervisors managers? What are the principal differences between a supervisor's and a worker's positions? What are the relationships that a supervisor has with others in the organization?

You've just been bombarded with a lot of important questions. Now let's turn to their answers, which is the main thrust of this chapter.

Is Supervision a Part of Management?

Are supervisors truly managers? Or, instead, are they really just workers with a desk, a telephone, possibly a desktop computer, and one heck of a lot more responsibility than they had as ordinary **operating employees**?

Operating employees: *Employees other than those placed in management positions.*

A Case of Role Confusion?

Some supervisors aren't sure whether or not they're managers. They continually find themselves in awkward positions. Frequently, as a result of having risen through the worker ranks, they still strongly identify with their fellow workers. Yet their relationships have changed so that they are now responsible for overseeing and directing the activities of these workers.

How Do Higher Managers Perceive Supervisors?

Unfortunately, some middle and senior managers have contributed toward this role confusion. They seem to regard supervisors as something not much removed in status from a pencil sharpener or a fax machine, and fail to recognize the true importance of the supervisory position to the organization.

Fortunately, however, most middle and senior managers seem to have become increasingly aware of the importance of first-line supervisors. They recognize that unless first-line supervisors understand them and are convinced of their merits, policies, rules, and organizational philosophies, which usually originate at the higher levels of an organization, are unlikely to be carried out successfully by operating employees.

Is a Supervisor a Manager?

Let's return to that burning question, "Is a first-line supervisor of a department really a manager?" The answer to this question is emphatically *"Yes!"* To elaborate, let's look at how management can be described. **Management** has been aptly explained as "the art of getting things done." **Managers** are individuals who get things done by *blending resources*—human, material, and financial—in a manner that achieves predetermined organizational objectives. In this sense, the president of a multinational corporation, a plant manager, and a supervisor in an office or on an assembly line are all managers. All three have the responsibility to maintain organizational standards and to achieve results with and through people and things. A principal difference among the various levels of management is that the supervisor is typically the only manager who does not supervise other managers.

Management: *The process of combining resources to achieve organizational goals.*

Managers: *Individuals who blend resources—human, material, and financial to achieve organizational goals.*

Will You Assume the Role of Supervisor?

It's probably fairly safe to assume that you—the reader—already have some interest in the area of supervision, or you probably wouldn't be reading this book. Perhaps you've already attained a supervisory position and want *to sharpen your leadership skills* and *expand your knowledge of the subject.* Or maybe you have no immediate aspirations to become a supervisor, but are merely *exploring the subject* to see if you might one day be interested. Possibly *your boss has encouraged,* or even *required,* you to further develop your supervisory skills. Or maybe your interest is mostly academic—that is, you have a desire *to develop an understanding of the role and importance of supervisors to organizations.*

Regardless of your own personal motives for studying this book, your interest in the subject of supervision is all to the good. Learning is usually a lot easier when you can relate to the subject matter. To make your learning experience even easier and more meaningful, as you read the material that follows try to assume that you currently *are* a supervisor. This assumption should make you feel more like an insider than an outsider when studying the concepts.

What Is Supervision?

An examination of the meaning of the term *supervision* and its *functions* can aid in reinforcing our awareness that supervisors are truly managers.

How Is Supervision Defined?

Supervision: *The art of motivating and coordinating people and resources to accomplish organizational goals.*

The term **supervision,** for our purposes, is defined as *the art of motivating and coordinating people and resources for the purpose of accomplishing organizational missions, goals, and ob-*

Supervisors are responsible for results, which are accomplished by coordinating people and resources.

jectives. In effect, every manager in a company—*senior, middle,* or *first-line*—is typically involved with some sort of supervisory activities, although the title **supervisor** usually applies to first-line managers. The term *executive* typically applies to the senior, or top, level of management.

Supervisor: *Similar to other managers but generally applied to the first-level of management.*

The Taft-Hartley Act more specifically defines a supervisor as a person who has the formal authority to:

> *... hire, transfer, suspend, lay off, recall, promote, discharge, assign, reward, or discipline other employees or responsibility to direct them, or to adjust their grievances, or effectively to recommend such action, if in connection with the foregoing the exercise of such authority is not a merely routine or clerical in nature, but requires the use of independent judgment.*[1]

Federal legislation also considers employees supervisors "if they spend no more than 20 percent of their time performing the same kind of work that their employees do and if they are paid a salary with no compensation for overtime."[2]

What Is the Organizational Hierarchy?

Take a look at Figure 1–1. As you can see, there are traditionally three levels of management in the hierarchy of an organization: first-line, middle, and senior (or top) management. Supervisors are typically considered to be **first-line managers.** In some organizations—mainly in the *goods-producing industries*—the traditional term *foreman* is still used, although much less frequently than in the past. As we'll see shortly, supervisors are responsible for performing a wide variety of activities.

First-line managers: *The first level of management; generally referred to as supervisors or, in some goods-producing organizations, foremen.*

The next level of management is considered **middle management.** Managers on this level may be known by such titles as plant manager, superintendent, or department head. Middle managers are responsible for translating senior management decisions into action. They typically depend on supervisors to carry out senior management directives.

Middle management: *The next level of management above the supervisory level.*

Senior (top) management is the level of management that determines objectives and basic policies for the entire organization and has the ultimate responsibility for the company's success or failure. Senior management includes various top *executives,* such as vice-presidents, president, chief executive officer (CEO), and chief operating officer (COO). In governmental organizations, managers at the middle and senior levels are often considered to be *administrators.*

Senior (top) management: *The top of the management hierarchy; individuals who determine the broad objectives and basic policies of the organization.*

Where Will You Work? In Service-Producing or Goods-Producing Industries?

As a supervisor, you'll typically be involved in either the **service-producing industries** or the **goods-producing industries.** Both

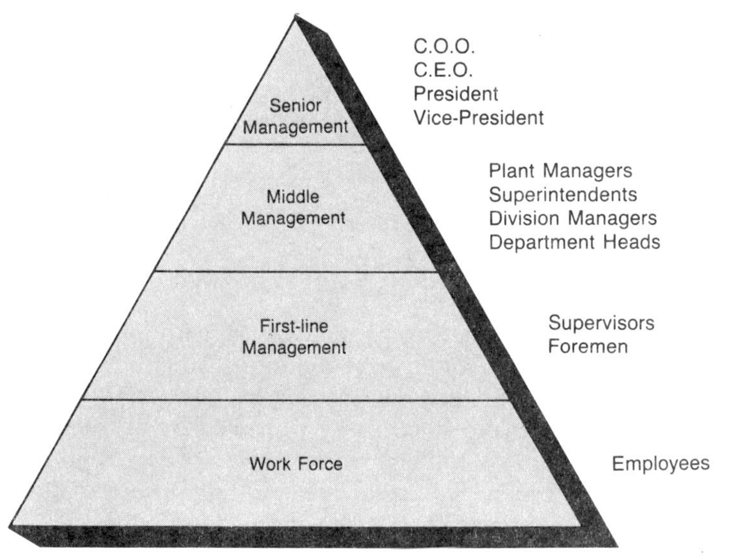

FIGURE 1–1
The Organizational Hierarchy

Service-producing industries: *Groups of firms or organizations* not *directly involved in the manufacturing of products.*

Goods-producing industries: *Firms directly involved with the production of tangible products.*

areas offer a multitude of opportunities for skilled leadership. The Bureau of Labor Statistics includes the following industries within the *service-producing* category:

1. Transportation
2. Public utilities
3. Wholesale and retail trade
4. Finance, insurance, and real estate
5. Services
6. Government

Included in the *goods-producing* industries are:

1. Manufacturing
2. Construction
3. Mining
4. Agriculture, forestry, and fishing

Although manufacturing industries shrank during the 1980s, they are a significant employer of workers and will continue to require qualified supervisors. The *service* and *government* subcategories of service producers will continue to need large numbers of supervisors. Services in item 5 above that are not included in the other service-producing subcategories include hotels, motels, restaurants, car washes, and picture-framing and shoe-repair shops, to name but a few. Government includes all levels—local, state, and federal.

What Are the Differences Between a Manager and a Worker?

Recognition of the significant differences between being an operating employee and a supervisor can aid you in adapting to a newly acquired first-line management position. The major differences include:

1. Perspective of the future
2. Relationship to others in the organization
3. The need for team building over competitiveness
4. Relative level in the organization

These differences are briefly discussed below.

Why Must Supervisors Look to the Future?

Although many workers do look to the future regarding their own personal careers, in general they have traditionally operated mostly in the present—the here and now—from the standpoint of their positions. Workers have tended to be primarily concerned with the details associated with their current tasks. This viewpoint is somewhat natural when employees are not encouraged to think beyond their presently assigned duties and responsibilities.

Managerial functions: *Activities that include planning, organizing, communicating, decision making, coordinating, leading, and controlling.*

Supervisors, on the other hand, *must* look beyond their immediate duties and responsibilities. **Managerial functions,** such as planning, require looking to the future and conceptualizing in more general terms (i.e., visualizing the "whole picture"). Managerial tasks, such as forecasting labor needs and scheduling work assignments, can't be left to chance; they must be carefully thought out in advance. A supervisor's current departmental activities do not exist in a vacuum; they must relate to the long-term goals and overall mission of the enterprise. They also relate the organization as a whole. And finally, a supervisor should always look to the future to anticipate the likely effects of any decisions or changes that are made.

Referring once again to operating employees, an interesting countertrend has developed in recent years in some organizations: Employees are expected to be actively involved in both planning and carrying out organizational objectives; hence, they are as concerned with the future as their managers.

How Do Relationships Differ?

As a supervisor, you now find yourself having a significantly different set of relationships, some of which may seem a bit awkward and stressful at first. Figure 1–2 illustrates graphically the principal relationships that supervisors have with other organizational members, including:

1. Employees (former peers)
2. Other supervisors
3. Higher management
4. Staff specialists
5. Union representatives

Relationship with Employees and Former Coworkers. In your initial period as supervisor, you may develop the belief that your employees and former peers—those with whom you used to work—now perceive you as having "sold out to the bosses upstairs." You may even find it difficult, at first, to give orders to former peers, especially those who were close friends. You may feel somewhat caught in the middle between your employees and higher management. Your former peers may even try to test you at first. It is very natural during this initial phase for many supervisors to develop excessive sensitivity toward employee behavior and comments.

If you do find yourself developing oversensitivity, try to put yourself into your employees' shoes. If one of your former peers had been promoted and became your boss, would you really be surprised or upset when that person gave you directives? Wouldn't you *expect* orders to be given by your new boss, even if a former peer? Once you are able to shake off your hypersensitivity and accept your new role as boss, you should find that your relationships with former peers will feel more comfortable. To achieve this comfortable feeling, however, requires that you treat each of your employees fairly, plus provide them with adequate training, direction, and a decent working environment.

FIGURE 1–2
Principal Relationships of Supervisor to Other Organizational Members

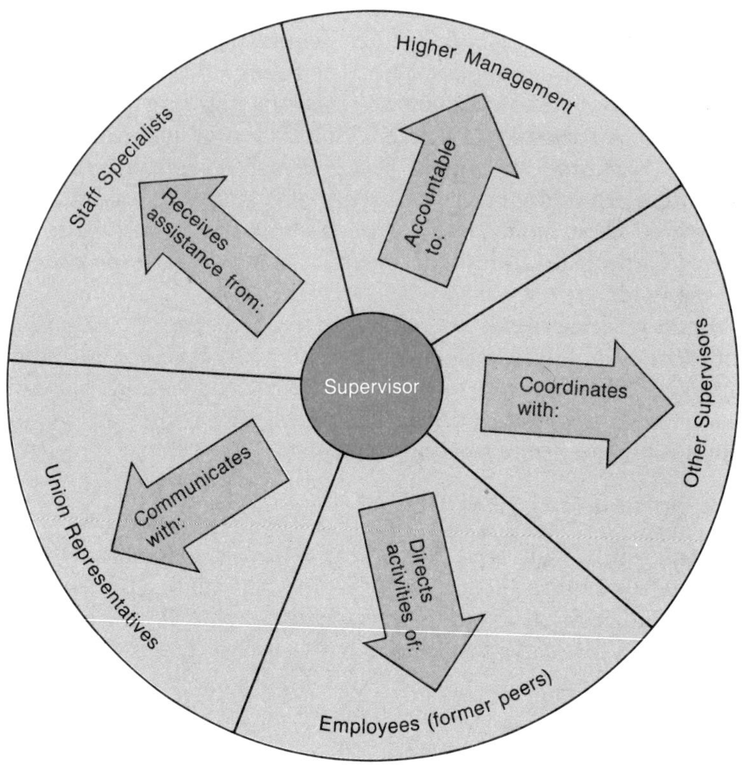

Relationship to Other Supervisors. In your new role as supervisor, you now find that people on the same organizational level as you are no longer coworkers per se—they, too, are managers. You now have the responsibility of keeping supervisors in other departments informed about activities that affect their operations. Likewise, you should seek out information that affects your department. Coordination of your department's activities so that they harmonize, rather than conflict, with those of other departments is essential if the organization as a whole is to achieve its goals and accomplish its mission. Less-successful organizations tend to lack effective communication and coordination among the various departments.

Relationship to Higher Management. As a new supervisor, you will also discover that you have a new type of relationship with management. Your own boss, for example, now shares information with you that is of primary concern to management, information to which you weren't privy in the past. You also find that you are an important link between the higher managers who develop organizational goals and policies and your own employees. You now have the responsibility for directing others in a manner that helps achieve the objectives of senior management.

Relationship with Staff Specialists. Chapter 8 discusses the activities of **staff specialists,** such as members of a personnel or human resources department, and their relationship to others in the organization. The primary responsibility of staff people is to *assist and serve* the **line organization.** Line managers are directly, rather than indirectly, responsible for doing what is necessary for the achievement of the organization's principal goal of generating a profit or surplus. As a line supervisor, you will frequently find staff specialists providing you with advice, requesting data, and requiring that you maintain records and document employee performance. You must guard against developing the attitude that staff people are outsiders simply meddling in your affairs. Staff and line individuals should continually remind themselves that they are all members of the same organization and should be working toward common objectives.

Staff specialists: *Those whose responsibility is to assist the basic line organization.*

Line organization: *A structure in which individuals are engaged in activities intended to directly accomplish the primary goals of the organization.*

Relationship with the Union. In organizations where a union represents the employees, you—as a supervisor—will find yourself in a new relationship to the union. For example, when a conflict arises, you may find yourself dealing with the **shop steward,** who is both an employee and a representative of the union. This person

Shop steward: *A union representative who is also employed by the firm.*

Supervisors are expected to be team builders. Skills developed as operating employees do not always transfer to management positions.

meets with you—the supervisor—to negotiate any grievances or conflicts that develop between you and employees. The supervisor's role related to unions and collective bargaining will be discussed in greater depth in Chapter 15.

Competition or Teamwork? Another difference in your new role as supervisor relates to ways in which you apply your skills. Let's assume, for example, that you were an outstandingly productive, high-volume salesperson with your company for about five years. You were considered one of the best producers of sales volume in your division. Let's further assume that because of your exemplary past performance, you were promoted to the position of sales supervisor. Will success naturally follow in your new supervisory position? You may prove to be successful, but it's unlikely that this success will come about naturally.

Some of the skills and traits that you developed as a salesperson could actually work to your detriment in your new position, at least in the short run. For example, when you were an individual salesperson, you often found yourself competing with your fellow coworkers—other salespeople in your company—especially during sales contests in which you were pitted against them. As a sales supervisor, however, you are now expected to be a ***team builder,*** rather than a competitor. Your responsibility is to assist and guide your employees in becoming winners, not attempt to surpass them. Instead of competing with your associates, that is, employees, you are now responsible for their performance.

Is It *We* versus *Them*?

Another significant difference between operating employees and supervisors relates to their relative positions, or levels, in the organizational hierarchy. Some employees do not identify with management; they may be caught up in a "we-versus-them" syndrome. Supervisors, on the other hand, *are* one of "them," but they are likewise not far removed from the "we" group. As a result, supervisors, as mentioned earlier, sometimes feel squeezed between their bosses and their workgroups. To illustrate this attitude, this author once overheard a supervisor moan, "As supervisor, I get it from both sides. I'm not supposed to get too friendly with the workers, but yet the managers don't really accept me as a part of management, either."

Summary

Supervisors sometimes find themselves in confusing roles, especially when they have risen through the operating-employee ranks. Supervisors sometimes feel caught in the middle, sort of squeezed and tugged between their workgroups and higher management. This feeling is due in part to higher management's attitude toward supervisors and in part to the attitudes of some supervisors themselves. However, supervisors are key links in any organization, responsible for carrying out and enforcing the policies, rules, and organizational philosophies that originate with senior management. Supervisors, as with managers in general, achieve organizational objectives with and through people and things.

Supervisors, of course, are managers. They are typically included in the first managerial level of the *organizational hierarchy,* which also includes the middle- and senior-management levels. Supervisors are typically involved in either service-producing or goods-producing industries.

There are differences between the focus of operating employees and that of supervisors, which can include concern for the future, different sets of relationships, and the need for *developing teams* rather than competing with fellow workers.

Questions for Discussion

(The questions in this and subsequent chapters are intended primarily to reenforce your learning of certain key areas of each chapter. Most of the answers can be found within the chapter or, in some cases, may require an expression of your opinion.)

1. Is a supervisor truly a manager? Explain.
2. Why do some supervisors have a hard time perceiving that they actually are managers?
3. What are the principal reasons discussed in the text for studying the field of supervision?
4. Evaluate the following statement: "In a sense, virtually *every* manager in an organization is a supervisor."
5. What three general levels of management typically exist in the *hierarchy of management*? What are some of the managerial titles that exist at each level?
6. Describe four major differences between being a first-line supervisor and an operating employee.
7. Describe the principal relationships that supervisors have with other organizational members.
8. Do people who perform well as operating employees automatically make good supervisors? Explain.
9. Why do some supervisors feel caught in the middle between their workgroups and higher management? What can you do as a supervisor if you develop this feeling?

Can You Define These Terms?

Instructions: Write a definition for each of the following terms. You may check your definitions with those provided in the end-of-text glossary.

operating employees
management
managers
supervision
first-line managers
foreman
middle management
senior (top) management
executives
administrators
service-producing industries
goods-producing industries
managerial functions
staff specialists
line organization
shop steward

Supervision In Action

1–1 Up through the Ranks

Dennison Framingham has been a sales representative during the past five years for the Euphrates Eco-System Corporation, a company that specializes in the marketing of toxic waste disposal systems.

Dennison's sales success has consistently been phenomenal. He has finished first in sales volume in every sales campaign except one since starting with Euphrates. He has exceeded his sales quota by an average of 18 percent in four of the past five years. Even during his worst year, Dennison exceeded his sales quota by 6 percent (a year in which companywide sales volume declined by 15 percent).

Henry Spinks, sales supervisor of the Catsonville branch, recently submitted his resignation to Euphrates. After considering three other candidates for the position (all average sales representatives) Laura Williams, the regional sales manager, has decided to offer the sales supervisor's position to Dennison.

Questions

1. To what extent might Dennison's outstanding past performance *assist* him in fulfilling the sales supervisor's responsibilities? In what ways might it be a *detriment*?
2. What are some of the significant differences between the activities Dennison engaged in as a sales representative and those that he will be expected to carry out as a sales supervisor?

1–2 "But What Are Friends For?"

Jenny Fitch, an employee with the Bumstead Brewery Company for six years, was promoted two months ago to supervisor of her department. Jenny had always been close friends with most of the department members, who generally had a high degree of respect for her working ability. Jenny's peers were quite supportive when they learned of her promotion.

Shortly after her promotion, Jenny said to herself, "I've got it made because of the past friendly relationships I've had with my employees. I really shouldn't have any serious problems with them since I'm an insider—not an outsider. And I already have their respect."

By now, however, Jenny is having second thoughts about her earlier comments of "having it made." Bert and Bobbie, two of Jenny's employees, had always been punctual before her promotion. Things have changed, however. Each of them has been about 30 minutes late on three different occasions during the past six weeks. When questioned by Jenny as to the reason for their lateness, they simply responded, "Don't sweat it, Jenny." An additional incident occurred when Hildegard, another of Jenny's employees, departed from work two hours early, failing to either request or notify Jenny of her departure. Jenny now believes that her employees are taking advantage of their past friendships with her.

Questions

1. What seems to be the principal problem in the above case incident?
2. Should individuals promoted from within an organization continue to be friends with their employees? Explain.
3. If you were Jenny, what would you do about this problem?

Endnotes

1. As defined by the Labor Management Act (Taft-Hartley Act) of 1947.
2. As defined by the Fair Labor Standards Act of 1938.

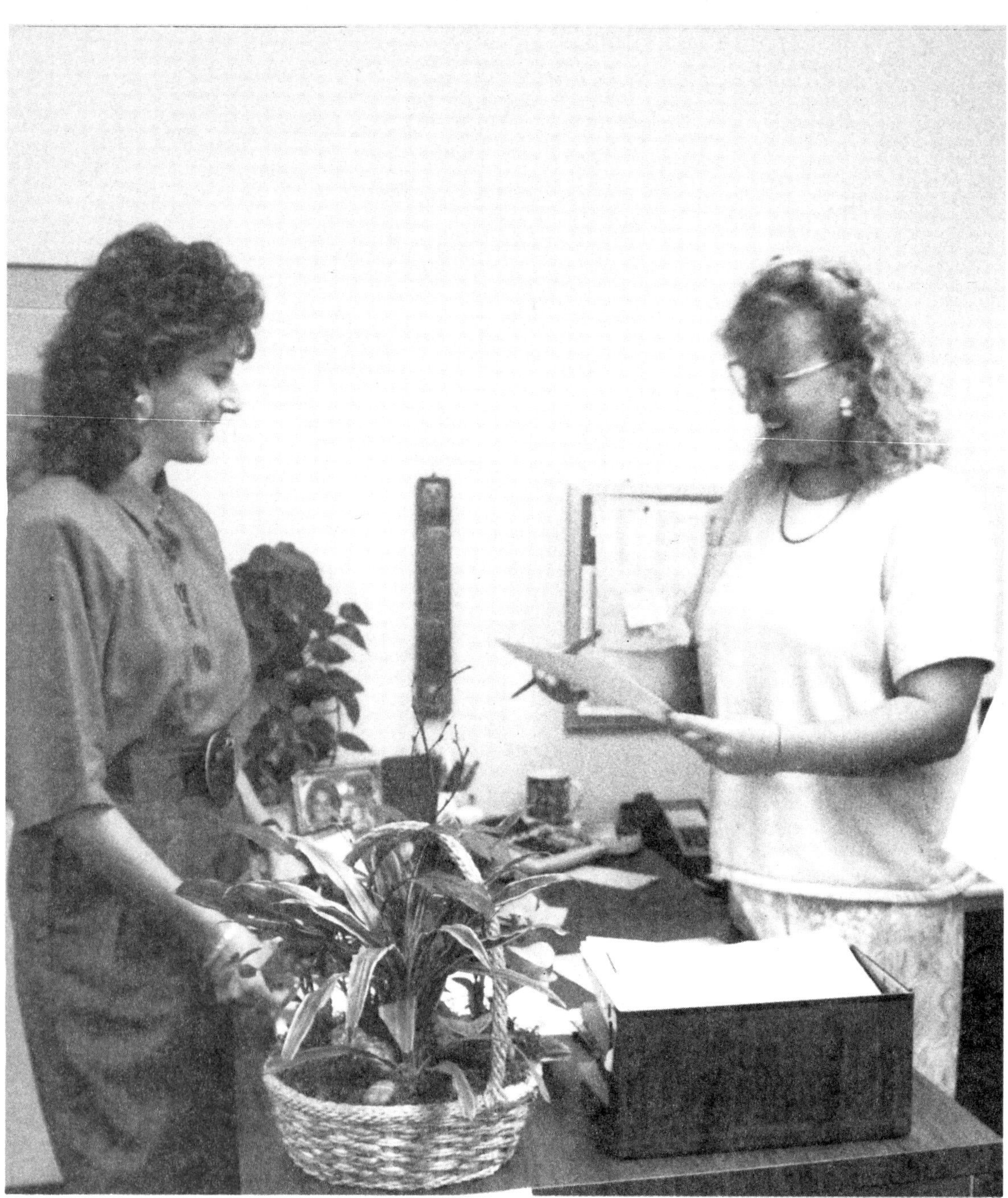

Chapter 2

Getting Started In Supervision

Since the industrial revolution, the supervisor has been a key member of the industrial organization. The supervisor is the liaison between operating personnel, about 80 percent of an organization's workforce, and the remaining 20 percent.
—William D. Clark, Educator

Learning Objectives

When you finish this chapter, you should be able to:

1. Make the transition to a supervisory position with fewer difficulties.
2. Discuss how a new supervisor can acquire the necessary skills to perform his or her job more effectively.
3. Review the functional areas of management.
4. Trace the historical evolution of managerial attitudes.

Imagine this scenario, if you will: This afternoon, as usual, you are toiling diligently at your work station. Your boss suddenly approaches you and says:

> *We feel that you've done a fine job ever since the first day you started with us. You've been consistently reliable and the quality of your work has always been up to our standards. You have a fantastic grasp of the technical aspects of your job. I guess you know that Johnson suddenly decided to leave our organization. Her supervisory position, therefore, is going to be opening up in two weeks. We'd really like* ***you*** *to consider filling Johnson's position. What do you say? Interested?*

There is a good chance one day that, if you're not already in a supervisory position, you'll experience something similar to the above announcement. What will be your reaction? Will you be ready to assume a supervisory position when the opportunity arrives? Are you ready now? If not, why not?

How Can You Get Off to a Good Start in Supervision?

New supervisors often feel a tremendous amount of stress and anxiety during their initial weeks in their new positions. As an activity, supervision doesn't come naturally to most people. Effective supervision can be considered an art that requires the development of a certain type of attitude, along with some specific skills and knowledge that can be acquired only through practice and training.

Why Is the Transition a Challenging Period?

Supervisors often attain their managerial positions by rising up through the ranks of operating employees. However, many *new* supervisors never evolve into *old* supervisors. Instead, they unfortunately fail and then return to the operative level, sometimes in disgust, sometimes at the personal behest of their bosses. Of course, many supervisors do succeed. Initially, however, making the transition from operating employee to first-line manager is quite challenging. Let's now look at some additional ideas that can make your own personal transition into management go a lot more smoothly.

How Can the Transition Period Be Eased?

Management writer Richard Gordon suggests that inexperienced supervisors follow six rules that will help them make the transition to a managerial position more comfortable.[1] Following these rules can't guarantee managerial success, of course. Doing so is likely to ease the typical transitional difficulties experienced by many new supervisors. The rules are:

1. Think like a manager.
2. Know your responsibilities.
3. Know your subordinates.
4. Minimize changes in assignments.
5. Delegate.
6. Cultivate a situational leadership perspective.

We'll briefly examine each rule.

Rule 1: Think Like a Manager. Let's assume that you achieved your supervisory position by coming up through the ranks. Of course, you should never lose your concern for operating employees, but you should recognize that, as a supervisor, there has to be a significant shift in your attitude from what it may have been when you were an operating employee. To be an effective manager, you must learn to think and feel like one. You should try to develop a **management attitude,** that is, to identify in a positive manner with the goals and objectives of your organization and willingly follow its policies and procedures.

Management attitude: *A belief in and a willingness to carry out the goals and objectives of an organization.*

Becoming a manager requires assuming new job responsibilities. Developing a management attitude makes the transition easier.

Recognize, too, that you no longer are competing with your former peers for raises and promotions. Instead, you are now expected to be a team builder. Accomplishing such attitudinal changes isn't necessarily an easy task for the person whose previous allegiance and competition were principally with fellow workers. Thinking like a manager should be far easier for you if you were promoted in an organization where you were expected to be regularly involved in decision making and problem solving.

How can you develop a *management attitude*? One way is to *learn as much as you can about the principles and concepts that apply to management,* as you currently are doing by studying this text. In addition, try to *familiarize yourself as early as possible with your own job description and understand how it relates to the overall mission of your organization.*

Another method for developing a management attitude is to *learn as much as possible about the organization for which you work.* Supervisors who acquire such knowledge more readily *develop greater self-confidence and enthusiasm* in their daily activities. Employees are more likely to have confidence in you when you radiate confidence and enthusiasm. There is a strong tendency for employees to follow as they are led, so therefore you should lead by example. And the supervisor who displays a strong ***esprit de corps*** is likely to have employees who are also proud of their organization.

Esprit de corps: An attitude of enthusiasm, support, and loyalty that members of a group have toward the workgroup.

Furthermore, supervisors who are familiar with their organizations and its goals tend to be *more loyal employees.* They are able to talk intelligently about their organizations with people on the outside. In effect, they serve in a *part-time public relations function.* Informed supervisors are generally concerned about their own self-development, an especially important factor for those who want to advance up the organizational ladder.

Table 2–1 lists much of the essential information you should learn about your enterprise. This type of knowledge will give you a greater feeling of identification with your organization, thus assisting you in developing that all-important management attitude.

Rule 2: Know Your Responsibilities. A job description seldom tells the complete story about your job responsibilities, yet you should be fully aware of them to avoid many of the pitfalls associated with being a new supervisor. "Other duties as assigned" is a common statement in many job descriptions. What are these "other duties?" Some of these unstated responsibilities tend to be extremely time consuming. You should become aware of what this statement actually represents so that you can plan your time and activities more effectively.

You could suggest to your boss that the two of you meet for a clarification of your job description. Keep in mind that your performance will be evaluated on the basis of, and your future career path influenced by, how well you perform the tasks outlined in your job description. Consequently, a complete understanding of

TABLE 2–1
Essential Types of Organizational Information that Assist New Supervisors in Developing a Management Attitude

- History and past performance
- Names of key managers and officers
- Policies and procedures
- Product or service line
- Principal competition
- Service facilities
- Future plans
- Activities in the realm of social responsibility

your tasks, duties, and responsibilities is essential early in your managerial career.

Rule 3: Know Your Subordinates. Try to get to know your new subordinates as soon as possible. If accessible, review each employee's personnel file. However, don't place a lot of emphasis on past performance reviews, since they could reflect the subjective judgment of previous supervisors. Meet individually with each subordinate. As a focal discussion topic, you could request each employee to prepare a list of his or her current assignments and their estimated completion dates. Try to prevent this first meeting from turning into a gripe session; attempt to keep it as positive and upbeat as possible.

Rule 4: Minimize Changes in Assignments. Unless absolutely necessary, you would be wise to keep changes in employee assignments to a minimum until your employees have developed a positive image of you. Excessive or unnecessary changes when you first assume the managerial position could upset the morale of your department. Furthermore, you may later discover that the changes you initiated were less satisfactory than were the previous methods. Reverting to original methods—another change—could result in your appearing to be indecisive, which could adversely affect your leadership image.

Rule 5: Delegate. Before your promotion, you probably were accustomed to being a hands-on task-oriented employee. Now you have numerous responsibilities, such as scheduling, that are indirectly, rather than directly, involved with production. For many managers (especially newer ones), assigning tasks to others, that is, **delegating,** is difficult. However, you must learn to delegate effectively if you are going to be able to find enough time to engage in the broader managerial functions of planning, organizing, staffing, directing, and controlling. Delegation will be discussed in greater detail in a later chapter.

Delegating:
The act of giving rights or assigning responsibilities to another person.

Rule 6: Cultivate a Situational Leadership Perspective. There are a variety of different styles of leadership. Which one is best? This is a topic that will be discussed in some depth in subsequent chapters. For now, be aware that the "best" style depends on a number of variables, not least of which is *the situation itself.*

How Can Supervisors Acquire Necessary Skills?

Although not everyone begins life with the same physical and mental capabilities, effective supervisors were no more born with leadership skills than good tennis players were born with on-court skills. There is nothing inborn in a person that predetermines absolutely whether he or she will be a worker or a manager at, say, age 31. Effective supervisory skills typically are developed, not innate.

Can Supervision Be Learned From Observation and Books?

To be an effective supervisor requires the development of a variety of skills, and *practice* is one way to learn and improve them. A tennis player, for example, can become fairly good at the game by practicing. But practice alone often results in considerable failure and mistakes along the path toward enhanced personal development. Some supervisors, as well as tennis players, have learned a lot by *observation*—that is, by watching the pros in action. You, too, can learn a great deal about supervision by observing how others supervise—not only the best supervisors, but even those who make an inordinate number of mistakes. Learning from the mistakes of others is useful, and it's far less costly than making your own.

Can you learn how to become an effective supervisor solely by reading a book, such as the one in your hands right now? Of course not. A book on supervision *alone* will not teach you how to be an outstanding supervisor any more than a book on tennis will make you ready for the grand championship matches at Wimbledon, or a book on auto racing will make you ready for the Grand Prix of Monte Carlo.

What good, then, is reading about supervision from a book? A major advantage is this: Studying about supervision is a way for you to be exposed to a large body of knowledge in a relatively short period of time. By studying supervision, you are able to acquire knowledge that can, and should, be applied to real work situations. Many individuals have discovered that formal studies, coupled with experience, can actually lessen the time it takes to become an effective supervisor.

What Are the Three Varieties of Skills Needed?

As a supervisor, there are specific skills that you must acquire to effectively perform your duties. Let's assume, for example, that you recently became a supervisor in the service department of a large auto dealership. What types of skills might you need to become

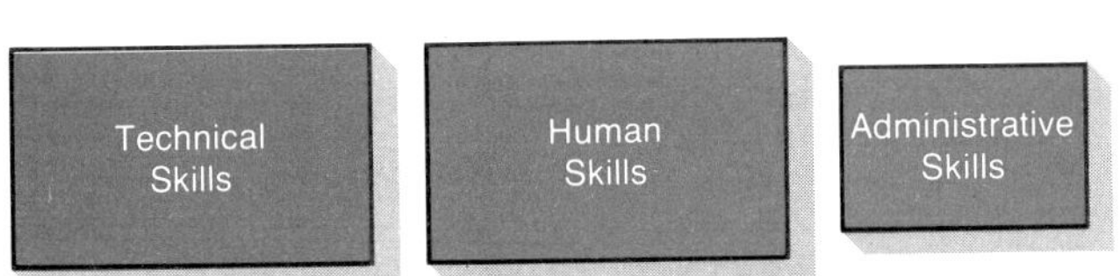

FIGURE 2–1
The Three General Types of Skills Needed by Supervisors

proficient in your newly acquired position? In general, most supervisors need to develop three broad categories of skills: *technical, human,* and *administrative* (see Figure 2–1). A discussion of the relationship of the three skills to your assumed supervisory position follows.

Do Technical Skills Remain Necessary?

The types of skills required for a supervisory position, of course, vary from organization to organization and from job to job. In some organizations, some supervisors have the responsibility for directing others, plus they are also actively involved with some of the same tasks as those who report to them. In other organizations, supervisors are primarily involved with managing other people. Regardless of which type you are, you need a certain amount of **technical skill**.

Technical skills: *The ability to apply techniques, utilize processes, and understand procedures necessary for carrying out specific tasks.*

Continuing with our auto service department illustration, could you, as a supervisor, assist a less-experienced auto mechanic in adjusting a dashboard computer, the type that calculates miles per gallon or liters per 100 kilometers, outside temperature in either Fahrenheit or Celsius, and elapsed time in either American or European (24 hour) time? Or could you assist your employees when they have problems operating certain types of highly sophisticated engine-analyzing equipment? Of course, the extent of technical knowledge necessary for a supervisor depends primarily on the nature and complexity of the specific supervisory position.

Why Are Human Skills Important?

Let's continue our automobile dealership example. When you were an operative employee, such as an auto repairperson with the service department, technical skills were highly essential. For supervisors, however, technical skills assume less importance than **human skills,** that is, *the ability to work effectively with and through people.* This includes interacting smoothly with both your workgroup, your boss, other departments, and customers. Unfortunately, the ability to manage and to work effectively with subordinates, other managers, and customers is a skill many supervisors lack.

Human skills: *The ability to motivate, communicate, and influence others in a positive way.*

Managers need a combination of technical, human and administrative skills. Technical skills usually continue to be quite important for first-line managers.

What, then, are some of the human skills that you should develop to improve your supervisory capabilities and effectiveness? Table 2–2 lists and describes some of the more important ones.

Do Supervisors Need Administrative Skills?

Administrative skills: *The ability to see the whole picture, conceptualize, and think in the abstract.*

Most supervisors have the need for **administrative skills,** an attribute that becomes increasingly important as a person ascends the organizational ladder. Administrative skills require the ability to *conceptualize,* that is, to think in the abstract. Activities that require such ability are summarized in Table 2–3. Each will be discussed in subsequent chapters.

Once again, referring to our auto service department example, can you plan purchases of supplies, equipment, and other material requirements so that you will have them available as needed? Do you understand the best procedures for organizing work flow in your department? Are you familiar with how personnel data, such as absenteeism and turnover ratios, are interpreted? Do you know methods for controlling costs? Can you develop an orientation and training program that relates to the needs of your employees? Have you developed a system of job performance standards along with the means for monitoring them?

TABLE 2–2
Useful Human Skills That Aid in Improving Supervisory Capabilities and Effectiveness

- *Empathy*—The ability to put yourself into the shoes of others and feel as they do; an awareness of the impact of your actions on the feelings, sentiments, and needs of others.
- *Communication skills*—The ability to convey an understood message both orally and in writing. Also the ability to listen actively, interview, provide performance feedback, and negotiate.
- *Motivational skills*—Learning what is effective in getting others to want to fulfill their responsibilities (recognizing, of course, that each person has different needs and desires).
- *Tolerance and understanding*—Of differences in others, especially variations in ethnic backgrounds and ability levels.
- *Training, coaching, and developing skills*—The ability to teach others how to perform tasks and to foster their growth and development.

As we've already stated, effective managers usually develop the ability to see the organization as a whole. They can visualize how one organizational activity relates to and depends on others. They also are able to see how their own organization relates to outside forces, such as to other firms and to society in general. Administrative skills are necessary for all levels of management. The extent of skill necessary depends primarily on the nature of the managerial position.

Are Supervisory Skills Transferable?

Supervisory skills can be applied to a variety of situations. For example, nonprofit organizations, such as the Red Cross or Disabled American Veterans, also need people with leadership abilities. Su-

TABLE 2–3
Types of Administrative Skills that Enhance Managerial Success

- *Planning skills*—The ability to determine and anticipate future needs and activities.
- *Coordinating, scheduling, and controlling skills*—The ability to ensure that tasks are performed as expected with the proper mix of personnel, materials, and machines.
- *Time management skills*—The ability to ensure that effective utilization of available time occurs.
- *Perceptual skills*—The ability to perceive situations as they really are, rather than as we want them to be. (Especially helpful for preventing and resolving problems and in decision-making activities.)

pervisory skills can likewise be applied to social organizations, fund-raising groups, athletic clubs, and even family situations. In fact, you could even apply leadership concepts like direction and control to your relationship with your pet German shepherd, Wolfgang! However, directing and controlling your Siamese cat, Fifi, is probably out of the question!

Supervisors in all organizations engage in a similar set of managerial activities termed *managerial functions.* The following section explores the principal functions.

What Do Supervisors Do? A Functional Approach

As early as 1916, Henri Fayol, a French writer, classified the field of management as consisting of various functional areas. His works were not translated into English until 1930, and did not become widely known until the second translation appeared in 1949. Most management writers today, however, borrow heavily from his ideas on management.

What Is the Universality of Management?

Managerial functions: *Activities, such as planning, organizing, staffing, directing, and controlling, that aid in achieving organizational goals.*

Universality of management: *The concept that all managers engage in a similar set of functions.*

Let's also do a bit of borrowing from Fayol and relate his concepts to our discussion of management. Every manager, regardless of title, position, or hierarchical level, engages in five **managerial functions:** *planning, organizing, staffing, directing* and *controlling.* This concept is termed the **universality of management.** Although each level of manager performs identical functions, the mix of each varies. As you can see from Figure 2–2, senior managers spend a larger proportion of their time in the planning function. First-line managers spend much of their time involved in organizing and directing others. Middle managers, too, spend a great deal of time organizing and directing. All three levels spend a fairly large proportion of their time controlling.

Do the Functions Overlap?

In reality, these functions merge and overlap. It's not a matter of saying "I'm going to plan this morning, direct before lunch, organize between 1:00 and 2:30 P.M., then staff and control from 2:30 until the end of the workday." You, as a supervisor, can do several of these things concurrently. Plans can't be carried out without also organizing people and resources; controls are required to assess a plan's progress while directing subordinates on how to carry it out. In other words, the management functions can be distinguished from each other for discussion purposes, but are inseparable in actual practice. Theirs is a dynamic, complementary, and mutually supportive relationship. Table 2–4 summarizes the major managerial functions and briefly describes their activities.

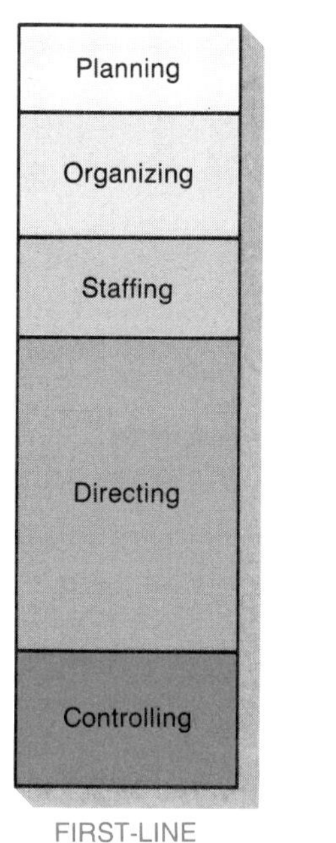

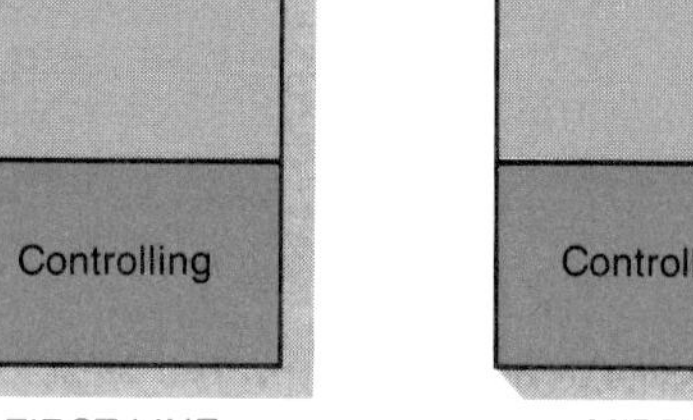

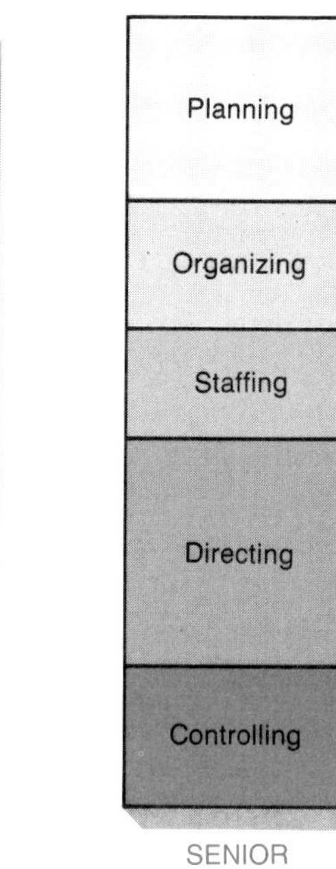

Planning
Organizing
Staffing
Directing
Controlling
SENIOR MANAGEMENT

FIGURE 2–2
Management Functions and Their Relative Significance to Each Level of Management

How Have Managerial Attitudes Evolved?

Organizational conditions are ever changing, and managerial attitudes and philosophy tend to change along with them. The following section provides a brief historical overview of the evolution of the principal managerial attitudes (also see Figure 2–3).

What Was the Scientific Management Approach?

Prior to the 1920s, managers were concerned primarily with ***technical efficiency and productivity***—an attitude and behavior known as the **scientific management approach.** Supervisors of this period were primarily responsible for closely monitoring and controlling employee output. An excessively high concern for ***tasks*** (i.e., production at the expense of the human side of organizations) tended to cause substantial organizational disharmony over time.

Fredrick Taylor - Founder

Scientific management approach:
An approach to management in which technical efficiency and productivity are all-important.

What Was the Human Relations Approach?

Various studies made during the 1920s and 1930s focused attention on the behavioral side of organizations, out of which developed

Scientific Management Approach	Human Relations Approach		Quantitative Approach	Human Resource Approach	Quality of Work Life Approach	Hard-line Restructuring Downsizing Approach
1920	1930	1940	1950	1960	1970	1980

FIGURE 2–3
An Historical Synopsis of Management Approaches

TABLE 2–4
Major Managerial Functions and Their Activities

Planning (deciding what to do and how to do it)
- Forecasting
- Setting objectives
- Deciding among alternatives
- Establishing policies, rules, and procedures
- Scheduling
- Budgeting

Organizing (blending resources to achieve plans)
- Blending human, technical, and financial resources
- Delegating
- Developing teams
- Improving quality of work life

Staffing (attracting and maintaining qualified employees)
- Determining human resource requirements
- Recruiting and selecting employees
- Training employees
- Coaching and counseling employees
- Developing employees

Directing (communicating objectives and plans to employees for carrying out)
- Leading
- Communicating
- Delegating
- Motivating
- Coordinating

Controlling (steering performance toward desired results)
- Establishing standards
- Documenting
- Appraising/reviewing
- Correcting

Human relations approach: *An approach to management that stresses that employees desire to participate in decision making and be treated with dignity and respect.*

an attitude known as the **human relations approach.** One of the most significant studies was undertaken at the Hawthorne works of the Western Electric Company in Chicago, by the late Elton Mayo, F. J. Roethlisberger, and their associates at Harvard University.

The studies, coupled with the emerging union movement (especially in the 1930s), influenced managers into recognizing that people worked for more than money alone; that employees, in general, wanted to participate in decision making and be treated with dignity and respect. Tasks, of course, continued to be important, but the human being was considered to be of comparable importance. The human relations approach was based on the belief that morale and productivity tend to rise when workers are treated as human beings rather than as robots, and when they develop feelings of pride and personal worth on their jobs as well as the opportunity to get things off their chests. The human relations movement peaked during the 1960s, as newer concepts of organizational behavior developed.

What Was the Quantitative Approach?

Influenced by the military during World War II, a trend toward management science and operations research developed and was applied to the business setting in the late 1940s and the 1950s. It augmented, rather than replaced, the human relations approach. Highly immersed in the use of mathematics for organizational decision making, this approach became known as the quantitative approach.

What Was the Quality of Work Life/ Human Resource Approach?

Higher educational levels created a new breed of worker during the 1960s and 1970s, and resulted in a greater concern for what is referred to as the **quality of work life (QWL)** and the **human resource approach.** *QWL* refers to how effectively the job environment meets the needs and expectations of employees. The key elements and assumptions of QWL are summarized in Table 2–5. As you can observe from the table, the QWL/human resource approach emphasizes individual involvement in organizational decision making.

Quality of work life (QWL)/ human resource approach: *A concern for how effectively the job environment meets the needs and expectations of employees.*

What Are the Current Trends?

The concern for QWL peaked during the early 1980s. The firing of 11,500 striking air-traffic controllers by the Reagan administration, combined with depressed economic conditions in 1981 and 1982, seemed to usher in a *hard-line attitude* toward employees in general. The 1980s wave of *hostile (unfriendly) takeovers* and **leveraged buyouts (LBOs)** (where firms were unwillingly absorbed by other firms), plus the need to meet foreign competition, often resulted in the **restructuring** of many firms. *Downsizing,* that is, reducing the size of the organization, became the omnipresent buzzword of the late 1980s. Heavy layoffs of employees at all levels, the closing of less-efficient plants, and a "lean, mean approach to bottom-line profits were commonplace."[3]

Leveraged buyout (LBO): *When one firm borrows heavily for the purpose of acquiring the assets of another.*

Restructuring: *Reorganizing an acquired firm for the alleged purpose of more efficient operation; occurs especially after hostile takeovers.*

In recent years, many managers and employees alike have believed, often correctly, that their jobs were in jeopardy. Individuals assigned the responsibility for restructuring are often derogatorily referred to as the "green-shade folks," which conjures up an image of penny-pinching, Scrooge-like characters.[4] Many employees are finding their benefits reduced or even eliminated. Reductions in pay or less-frequent pay raises, accompanied by increased workloads, have become the sign of the times in many firms. New employees sometimes receive wages on a lower scale than existing employees receive for the same work, a scheme known as the *two-tiered wage system.* **Profit-sharing,** rather than general pay increases, has become common among larger corporations as a means

Profit sharing: *An incentive-type of compensation that relates solely to the profitability of the firm and distributes a certain percentage of annual profits to employees.*

TABLE 2–5
Key Elements and Assumptions of the Quality of Work Life (QWL) Concept[2]

- *Rewards* should be:
  - –Sufficient to meet basic needs and provide security
  - –Equitable relative to the amount and quality of work and the type of work
  - –Flexible enough to meet differing needs
  - –Desirable to the people receiving them
  - –Intrinsic and extrinsic
- *Job design* should offer opportunities for meeting differing needs for:
  - –Challenges, variety, and interests
  - –Task identity
  - –Responsibility
  - –Learning
  - –Social contact
  - –Work schedule
  - –Goal setting and feedback
- The *influence* of employees should include:
  - –The opportunity to influence decisions on how the work is done
  - –The opportunity to make suggestions or inquiries and receive a reply
- *Interpersonal relations* for supervisors and coworkers should include:
  - –Concern for the welfare of others
  - –Clear communication
  - –Fairness
  - –Cooperation
  - –Friendliness and courtesy
- The *physical environment* should be:
  - –Safe
  - –Clean
  - –Comfortable
  - –A esthetically attractive
  - –Functional
- *Job facilitation* is an important philosophy entailing:
  - –Supervision that is knowledgeable about the work
  - –Adequate tools and equipment
  - –Sufficient information
  - –Enough delegation of authority so that employees can do their work without extensive red tape
  - –Training
  - –Leadership
  - –Planning and scheduling
  - –Building of teamwork

of reducing upward pressure on wages and salaries. These events, coupled with the pessimism brought on by "Black Monday" (the severe stock market crash of October 19, 1987), have had a pronounced effect on the managerial philosophy of the early 1990s.

However, the concern for QWL is far from dead. Most managers continue to recognize that people tend to perform better when their needs are recognized. Anticipated shortages of skilled labor by the year 2000 will enhance the need for effective leadership to attract workers.[5] So, in spite of some of the recent trends, there is likely to continue to be a significant need for qualified supervisors long into the future.

Summary

Individuals who previously were operating employees may find themselves unprepared for the new tasks and responsibilities that they acquire after being promoted to first-line supervisory positions. The transition from operating employee to supervisor is typically a challenging experience.

Newly appointed supervisors should attempt to get off to a good start by attempting to *think like managers, know their responsibilities, know their subordinates, minimize changes in assignments, delegate tasks,* and *cultivate a situational leadership perspective.*

Supervision is an acquired skill. Studying, observing, and practicing sound leadership techniques can aid substantially in the development of the new supervisor. Three major types of skills that most management positions require (although in different proportions) are *technical, human,* and *administrative.* Supervisory skills generally can be applied to a variety of situations where leadership abilities are necessary.

As with any manager, supervisors typically must perform the major functions of management: planning, organizing, staffing, directing, and controlling. These activities are referred to as the *universality of management.*

Managerial attitudes and philosophy have evolved through various phases, which include the scientific management, human relations, quantitative, and quality of work life/human resource approaches. In the early 1990s, approaches have been mixed. The concern for QWL still exists. Although the trend toward *leveraged buyouts (LBOs)* has subsided somewhat, the activities of *restructuring* and *downsizing* continue to be prevalent.

In spite of recent trends toward slimming down management ranks, the need for qualified supervisors will continue in the future.

Questions for Discussion

1. Evaluate the following statement: "Supervisors should never forget where they came from. Most came up through the ranks of workers. Those who identify with management instead of the workers have sold out and aren't really fit to be supervisors."
2. Why is it so essential for a supervisor to develop a *management attitude*? How can it be developed?
3. What is meant by the phrase "other duties as assigned," which is frequently found on job descriptions?
4. Should the new supervisor place any credence in past performance reviews of their subordinates?
5. Evaluate the following statement: "The new supervisor would be wise to make as many changes as possible as soon as possible after assuming the new position."
6. Is it accurate to say that some people are "born managers"? Explain.
7. Can supervisory skills be acquired as a result of studying managerial concepts? Explain.
8. What are the three broad categories of skills required of most managers?
9. Do supervisors need technical skills? Explain.
10. What are human skills? Why are they so essential for supervisors to develop?
11. Look up the words *empathy* and *sympathy* in a dictionary. How do their meanings differ? Which trait is more important for a supervisor to employ? Why?
12. Describe *administrative skills.*
13. What is meant by the term *universality of management*?
14. Describe the five major functions of a manager.
15. Do all levels of management engage in the management functions in about the same proportion? Explain.
16. What is the principal difference between the *scientific management approach* and the *human relations approach*?
17. What is the primary concern of the *QWL/human resource approach*?
18. How might current trends affect supervisory positions?

Can You Define These Terms?

Instructions: Write a definition for each of the following terms. You may check your definitions with those provided in the end-of-text glossary.

management attitude
esprit de corps
delegating
technical skills
human skills
administrative skills
managerial functions
universality of management
scientific management approach
human relations approach
quantitative approach
quality of work life (QWL)/human resource approach
hostile (unfriendly) takeovers
leveraged buyouts (LBOs)
restructuring
downsizing
two-tiered wage system
profit sharing

Supervision In Action

2–1 Can Martin Manage it?

Martin Mullberry, a good friend of yours, seems troubled lately. You ask him what is bothering him, and he responds, "You know that I'm a case worker at a governmental agency downtown. Well, recently I was asked to consider taking a job as a supervisor. I think I would really enjoy the extra responsibility, and I certainly can use the additional salary that comes with a supervisory position. But there's one thing that really concerns me, and that's my age. I'm only 23 years old. Nearly everybody I would be supervising at the agency is older than I am. Frankly, I'm somewhat afraid that they wouldn't respect me because of my youth or be willing to take orders from a young person like me."

Questions

1. What advice would you give Martin?
2. What skills should Martin try to develop that would tend to outweigh any disadvantages of his youth?
3. How might Martin acquire the skills and knowledge necessary to become an effective manager?

2–2 Well, What Do You Know About That?

Assume that during a holiday dinner at a relative's house your uncle approaches you and says, "I'm really quite impressed with some of the things I've been reading about the company you work for. As a matter of fact, I've been seriously considering the purchase of some stock in the firm. I thought that I'd like to talk with you before I contacted my securities broker about investing. What can you tell me about your company?"

Questions and Activities

1. If you are currently employed, answer the following questions in relation to your organization:

a. When and by whom was your company founded?

b. What has been its past performance from the standpoint of earnings and growth?

c. What is its rank and reputation in the industry?

d. What are the names of key company personnel?

e. What are some significant future plans of your company?

f. What has your company done in the area of social responsibility?

g. What are its principal products or services?

h. What is the extent of its service facilities?

i. How do your firm's products compare with those of its competitors?

2. If you are not currently employed, contact the public relations manager of a well-known firm located in your community and request answers to the questions asked in *a* through *i* above.

3. Besides appearing informed to relatives during holiday dinners, of what practical use to a supervisor, or any employee for that matter, is knowing the information asked for in *a* through *i* above?

Endnotes

1. Adapted from Richard Gordon, "Six Rules for Getting Started in Management," *Supervisory Management,* AMACOM Periodicals Division, American Management Associations, December 1984, pp. 24–27.
2. Jim M. Graber, "Let's Get a Handle on QWL," *Supervisory Management,* AMACOM Periodicals Division, American Management Associations, June 1983, pp. 30, 31.
3. Thomas Moore, "Goodbye Corporate Staff," *Fortune* (International Edition), December 21, 1987, pp. 43–46; and "Delegates Ask Strong Curbs on Takeovers," *AFL–CIO News*, November 2, 1987, p. 18.
4. Walter Kiechel III, "How Was Your Christmas Party?" *Fortune* (International Edition), January 18, 1988, pp. 95, 96.
5. "Needed: Human Capital," *Business Week* (International Edition), September 19, 1988, pp. 100–41; and Peter Petre, "Lifting American Competitiveness," *Fortune* (International Edition), April 23, 1990, pp. 46–51.

Chapter 3

Problem Solving and Making the Right Decisions

Many people believe that problem solving is the work of the day, and they see most of the problems as adventures for which a strategy must be developed in order to resolve the issue favorably.

—Henry Schott, Professor

The importance of a decision is not the money involved but, rather, how fast the decision can be reversed if it is wrong.

—Peter Drucker, Management Philosopher

Learning Objectives

When you finish this chapter, you should be able to:

1. Distinguish the various ways in which problems can be classified.
2. Employ some of the more common methods for making decisions.
3. Illustrate how computers are used to aid in decision making.
4. Apply group problem-solving and decision-making techniques.
5. Avoid some of the more common mistakes of decision making.

"Sure, all that theoretical scientific management stuff sounds nice when you read or hear about it, but when's a person supposed to find the time to apply it? If I tried to use all those fancy problem-solving and decision-making techniques you hear about in seminars and school, I'd never have time to do what I'm paid for!"

"Fools rush in where the wise fear to tread" is an adaptation of an old maxim, one that could be applied to supervisors who feel like the person quoted above. The saying has special meaning for supervisors who desire to avoid approaching problems and arriving at decisions in a counterproductive manner. Supervisors are loaded with a variety of responsibilities. For example, they must be concerned with both *production* and *people*. They also have to ***plan*** work activities for others. They have to ***organize*** and ***coordinate*** people and resources for the purpose of achieving organizational goals. They must be able to ***train, motivate,*** and ***direct*** workers. They must maintain ***control*** over the activities of employees and the workplace. And they must be able to ***get along with their own bosses.*** In short, many supervisors feel that there just isn't enough time to bother with so-called scientific methods for problem solving and decision making.

Unfortunately, some supervisors in their haste to solve problems waste more time than they save by employing a helter-skelter approach to problem solving. The activities of problem solving and decision making need not be negative experiences. Your attitude is a key determiner of how you feel about having to face problems. Professor Henry Schott (quoted at the opening of this chapter) has also stated, "The results of problem solving are rewarding and produce feelings of success. One can recognize an element of existentialism involved in the process of problem solving."[1] With a positive attitude, therefore, problem solving and decision making can provide you with a variety of highly satisfying experiences.

This chapter will expose you to a wide variety of problem-solving and decision-making techniques. The prudent application of these approaches to your own activities can save you considerable time in your job as a supervisor.

How Important Are Problem-Solving and Decision-Making Activities?

Roger Smith, former chairman of General Motors, once stated, "Our managers make decisions every minute of every day."[2] Don't you, too, have to solve problems and make decisions in your daily activities? Some decisions may be relatively routine and inconsequential, while others may be highly significant and affect numerous employees.

How Are Poor Decisions Costly?

Any bad decisions you make can be costly to both you and your organization. Production foul-ups, for example, can create unnecessary delays in product scheduling and in meeting the demands of customers. Poor decisions affecting employees can influence morale, increase turnover, raise training costs, and adversely affect the profits or surplus of an enterprise. Faulty decisions can damage the reputation of a company, as well as tarnish the image of the manager who made them. Your entire career could be significantly influenced by the quality of your decisions. Learning how to make workable decisions, therefore, is one of the most important responsibilities you have as a supervisor.

Does It Really Matter How You Decide?

How should you go about solving problems and making decisions? Does it really matter in which way you solve a problem? Unfortunately, because of time and job pressures (or just plain lethargy), we often are much too hasty in making critical decisions, sometimes doing so on the basis of false generalizations, insufficient information, biased opinions, snap judgments, or simply hearsay. Far too frequently we treat symptoms rather than solve problems.

The combined efforts of employees at problem solving often result in better solutions than can be achieved alone.

There are, however, more reasonable approaches to decision making that can and should be followed. Nonetheless, even the supervisor who strains to use rational decision-making techniques can't hit the target dead center all the time. Sometimes it seems as though Edsel Murphy was the only person who really understood management. He's the notorious creator of Murphy's Law, which is "Anything that can go wrong will go wrong." It is rumored that Murphy's mother Azula, also a cynic at heart, once exclaimed, "Edsel is far too optimistic!"

There are certain skills, however, that can aid you in breaking Murphy's Law with impunity. This chapter should guide you in that direction by providing suggestions for more logical approaches to problem solving and decision making.

Problems—What Are They?

Wouldn't it be delightful if events always went according to plan? In reality, many supervisors would probably become bored if they did. Most supervisors, however, don't get that opportunity. Events don't always transpire as one hopes. Problems seem to abound plentifully in most organizations.

What Is a Problem?

Problem: *A deviation from a preestablished standard.*

What actually is a problem? In simple terms, **problems result from change, and organizational life is forever changing.** A **problem** can be defined as *a deviation from a preestablished standard.* It generally occurs when *actual* events or results vary from *intended* events or results. A problem normally requires some sort of decision making. It also requires a solution that should be implemented and followed up.

A Sample Problem

Quality control specialist: *One who checks output to verify that product quality meets standards.*

To illustrate, let's assume that the goal or standard in your department is to maintain a rejection rate of no more than 3 percent of the total output of circuit boards. Let's also assume that the actual rate of rejection during the month of March, as determined by a **quality control specialist,** was 8 percent. Your actual results, therefore, deviated from your predetermined standard by 5 percent (see Figure 3–1). You now have a problem that requires a decision on your part. The basic way to solve problems is to remove their causes, which sounds simple enough. The techniques for solving problems, however, are not always so easy to successfully apply.

How Can Problems Be Classified?

There are a number of ways in which problems faced by supervisors can be classified. Three common methods of classification are:

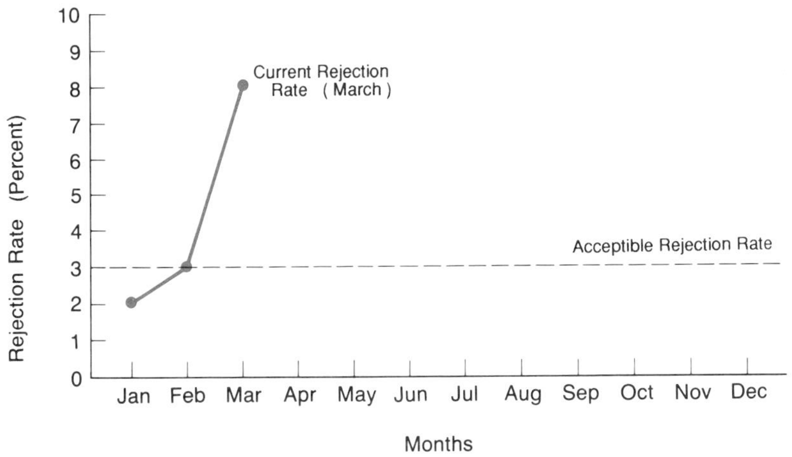

FIGURE 3–1
Rejection Rate as Compared to Predetermined Standard

1. Resource-oriented problems
2. Impact-oriented problems
3. Time-oriented problems

A brief discussion of each classification follows.

What Are Resource-Oriented Problems?

As a supervisor, you are responsible for applying the managerial functions already discussed to the resources at your disposal. In general, there are two categories of resources with which you are involved: ***human*** and ***material***. Each of those typically provide you with numerous problem-solving and decision-making challenges.

Human Resource-Oriented Problems. Vic has been late three times this month. Vivian has not yet turned in her expense account summary, which was due last Friday. Eugene and Robert had a fistfight in the men's room this morning. Herman told you that he saw Lillian departing from the premises yesterday afternoon with company property. Herb seems to be depressed most of the time lately and the quality of his work is suffering. Helen has requested to leave early this Friday afternoon. Horace is typically five minutes late returning from his rest break. Jasper was observed surreptitiously popping a pill in his mouth yesterday afternoon. All of these are considered **human resource-oriented problems,** a type of problem that can absorb a considerable amount of a supervisor's time. A later section provides methods for resolving problems and making effective decisions.

Human resource-oriented problems:
Deviations from standards involving employees and requiring decisions.

Material Resource-Oriented Problems. Equipment critical to the production process breaks down, the reject rate has begun to rise, on-the-job accident frequency has increased, bottlenecks exist on Line 3, and the supplier is late in delivering parts. These are all examples of **material resource-oriented problems.** This category of problem relates more to the *technical,* rather than the

Material resource-oriented problems:
Deviations from standards involving things rather than people and requiring decisions.

human, side of organizations. Many of these problems can be anticipated and prevented in advance with effective planning. When they do occur, however, they require problem solving and decision making on the part of the supervisor.

What Are Impact-Oriented Problems?

Another way of classifying problems is by their impact on the organization. Although there are various degrees of severity between the two extremes, for our purposes this type of problem is divided into two subcategories: *low-impact* and *high-impact problems.*

Low-impact problem: *A problem that tends to have minor consequences to the organization.*

Low-Impact Problems. A **low-impact problem** is one that tends to have few consequences for the affected department or organization. An example could be an employee's request for a window cover to block sun glare on her work station. Decisions related to this problem are relatively simple, probably have low impact, and should not take an inordinate amount of your time.

High-impact problem: *A problem that, if remaining unsolved, tends to have severe consequences on the organization.*

High-Impact Problems. A **high-impact problem,** of course, would tend to have more severe consequences to the organization if left unsolved. Decisions related to these problems should be made carefully and thoughtfully, drawing on the participative input of your employees where possible. You should carefully weigh in advance the implications that your decisions have for the future. Any specific human or material resource-oriented problems may have either a high or low impact on the organization.

What Are Time-Oriented Problems?

Time-oriented problems: *Deviations from standards that relate to present and future time frames.*

Our final classification of problems is related to time. **Time-oriented problems** that typically require action are either *current or potential.*

Current problem: *A time-oriented problem that already exists.*

Current Problems. A **current problem** is one that already exists; for example, an employee has been injured, a file is missing, a key employee is sick and absent, the budget has been drastically reduced, or the work flow is behind schedule.

Potential problem: *A time-oriented problem that is likely to occur in the future.*

Potential Problems. A **potential problem** is one that is likely to occur in the future if something is not done to prevent it from happening. For example, one of your employees has submitted a two-week notice of resignation, a machine is nearly worn out and will require replacement, a shortage of necessary raw materials is predicted to occur within two months, or the workload has increased in your department and thus necessitates a second shift.

The "When" Factor. Also related to time is *when* decisions must be acted upon. In some instances, decisions are urgent and must be made immediately to prevent high-impact consequences on the organization. On the other hand, some problems do not require immediate action, and putting off their resolution would tend to

Supervisors should attempt to avoid crisis management by using such techniques as the seven-step system for logically solving problems.

have little impact on the organization. Some of the less-urgent problems may fade away and never require direct action.

The previous section examined the typical *classes* of problems and decisions with which managers are regularly involved. The section that follows discusses the *ways* in which decisions related to problem solving are made by managers.

How Are Decisions Made?

"Decisions, decisions! All I seem to do around here is make decisions and solve problems!" If, as a supervisor, you have felt this way, then you already have a fairly good awareness of one of the major responsibilities of managers—the need to make effective decisions.

Problems occur and decisions must be made all day long in the lives of typical supervisors. Fran wants to leave work early because her husband is sick. George "needs" the same vacation period that Bill already selected. Gerty was late again this morning because her car broke down for the third time this month. Mr. Bailey, a customer, telephoned this morning complaining that his recently purchased unit would not function. And so it goes on and on like this day in and day out.

There are numerous ways to arrive at decisions, some more effective than others. Before we explore these techniques, however, we should be clear on what decision making really is. It relates closely to the planning function, an activity that we'll explore in more depth in the following chapter. Basically, a **decision** is that part of a manager's activities in which he or she chooses one course of action from two or more alternatives. Without effective decision making, managers would be unable to perform their managerial functions, accomplish organizational goals, or prevent and solve organizational problems.

Decision: *That part of a manager's activities requiring a choice to be made between two or more alternatives.*

The following are some of the more common methods for making decisions:

1. Decision making by hunch—intuition
2. Decision making by doing nothing
3. Decision making by crisis
4. Decision making with the seven-step system
5. Decision making with computers
6. Decision making with groups

Numbers 5 and 6, decision making with computers and decision making with groups, will be discussed separately in a later section of this chapter.

What Is Decision Making by Intuition?

Many decisions have been made on the basis of **intuition,** which is the process of arriving at conclusions on the basis of feelings rather than logic and facts. Intuition has also been described as immediately knowing something without the conscious use of reasoning. Numerous decisions are made this way.

Intuition: *Arriving at conclusions on the basis of feelings and hunches, rather than on the basis of logic or available facts.*

How good is intuition in decision making? A surprisingly large number of "gut-level" decisions are successful. Psychologist Judith Farina contends that a reason for their success is not solely chance, but that intuitive feelings are based on past experiences we cannot immediately recall.[3] Consequently, many managers whose decisions seemed to have been made solely on the basis of hunches may in reality have drawn subconsciously on past experiences and knowledge. Past experiences, whether they were positive or resulted in mistakes, can aid current decision making. For example, Lee Iacocca, head of the Chrysler Corporation, is noted for his extensive use of intuitive decision making.

However, defending hunch decisions that don't work to your peers is much harder. There are also numerous dangers inherent in pursuing such a gut-level, "seat-of-the-pants" approach to decision making. Far too frequently, the person making judgments based on intuition is excessively influenced by established habits, personal bias, and even present moods and sentiments, rather than current realities and logic. Intuitive decision making is subjective and frequently involves a person's emotions. We've all seen organizational managers make mistakes. Far too many of such *faux pas* are the result of decision making by hunches rather than by logic.

What Is Decision Making by Doing Nothing?

Some managers contend that in some circumstances the best decision is the decision to *do nothing* about a problem. This attitude is based on the philosophy that a trivial problem will fade away with neglect and that a serious problem will have more time in which to become better defined. In some instances, you might successfully solve problems with the **do-nothing approach,** but it must be used with extreme caution. Ignoring a problem that requires attention could cause irrevocable damage to both the organization and the manager who chooses that technique. A serious problem could worsen to the point of becoming unsolvable.

Do-nothing approach: *A decision, made either consciously or unconsciously, to let a problem work itself out.*

What Is Decision Making by Crisis?

"I'm sorry boss, but I just haven't had the time yet to finish that report you wanted. I've been too darned busy lately trying to work out some serious morale problems that exist in my department. But I'll get it to you as soon as possible. Yes, I know this is your second request. I'm sorry, boss, but I'm doing the best I can."

Does the above example sound familiar? Unfortunately, poorly organized supervisors are a lot like a firefighter during the dry season—busily scurrying from fire to fire. Although supervisors are responsible for resolving difficult problems and can't foresee and avoid every problem in advance, they shouldn't be spending their time submerged in a sea of crises. Supervisors who haven't learned to plan adequately, who don't establish realistic objectives and develop reasonable means to accomplish them, seldom have ample time to do a satisfactory job of managing. They are often engaged in what has been termed **crisis management.** Track records can usually be improved when supervisors employ more logical approaches, such as the *seven-step system*, the discussion of which follows.

Crisis management: *Decisions made after critical problems develop; often a result of poor planning.*

What Is the Seven-Step System for Solving Problems?

A more logical approach to problem solving than crisis management is the **seven-step system** listed in Table 3–1. Following is an explanation of each step.

Seven-step system: *A logical procedure for more effective decision making and problem solving.*

Step 1. Carefully Define the Problem. Have you ever seen some people leap aggressively into their problems like a savage tiger pursuing a fleeing lunch? A more effective approach to problem solving is first to *carefully define the problem.* As one maxim advises, "A problem well defined is a problem half solved." This step requires objectivity—the ability to cast emotions aside and to see the situation as it ***really*** is, not as we ***think*** it is. Before you can develop a definition of a problem, however, you have to gather as much useful information as possible within the limits of available time. You should also apply **situational thinking** to your analysis, that is, look to similar past experiences, but recognize that each situation is unique and may require a unique solution. Try not to

Situational thinking: *Drawing on similar past experiences when analyzing present problems, but recognizing that each situation is unique and may require a unique solution.*

TABLE 3–1
The Seven-Step System for Problem Solving

- Carefully define the problem.
- Gather and analyze pertinent data to verify the definition.
- Develop alternative solutions to the problem.
- Evaluate implications of each alternative.
- Choose and carry out your "best" alternative.
- Follow up (to see if your objectives are being accomplished).
- Modify when necessary.

be overeager in defining the problem. Doing so might result in developing a great solution for the wrong situation! Far too many employees have been disciplined wrongly because their supervisors hastily and incorrectly defined a human resource-oriented problem.

Step 2. Gather and Analyze Pertinent Data to Verify the Definition. Rather than going off the deep end, try to uncover information that relates to the actual definition of the problem. For example, you've noticed that the quality of Mary's work has deteriorated in recent weeks. Her entire manner seems to have changed. You might define her problem as one of a bad attitude. But is that really the *problem*, or merely a *symptom*? If you interview Mary, or even keep tuned into the **grapevine,** you may discover that her behavior on the job relates to personal problems at home. So look for factual information that relates to and verifies the *real* problem, and not to what could be false assumptions. Verification is a necessary and critical part of this step. Another old maxim warns, "That which can be asserted without proof can also be denied without proof."

Grapevine: *The network of informal relationships through which facts, half-truths, and rumors are transmitted.*

Step 3. Develop Alternative Solutions to the Problem. Now comes the step that involves choosing *alternative courses of action* to solve the problem. But note the plural form of "alternative courses." There's seldom only one solution to a problem. Continuing with our maxims, someone once said, "If you have only one alternative to a problem, you have not determined that there is a real problem." You sometimes discover after developing what you feel to be realistic and reasonable alternatives that your second or third solution seems even more realistic and reasonable than the first. Also, by developing more than one alternative, you have something in reserve in case your first attempt fails. As already indicated, in some instances you may even decide that the best alternative is to take no immediate action at all.

Step 4. Evaluate Implications of Each Alternative. This is a highly important step, far more important than it might appear at first glance. Some supervisors carry out a particular alternative without first carefully analyzing its implications and impact on the organization. You should try, however, to anticipate the probable effects—both positive and negative—that each alternative will have on the situation to avoid creating more problems by making a bad choice.

Step 5. Choose and Carry Out Your "Best" Alternative. Now comes your real challenge. You've evaluated all of your alternatives, so it's time to choose and implement the alternative that you feel will accomplish your desired objectives. Remember the concept of situational thinking, however. You might have to alter your decision if things don't turn out exactly as expected. Haven't you noticed how often the *unexpected* does turn up? Someone once said, "The only thing that continues to surprise me are people who are surprised by surprise factors!"

Step 6. Follow Up. You're not yet finished with the problem-solving process. You should establish some sort of control procedures, a system for following up to make sure that your actions accomplish your planned objectives. Before too much time elapses, then, carefully examine the situation to see if your prior actions have accomplished their intended goals.

Step 7. Modify When Necessary. Unfortunately, things don't always turn out the way supervisors hope. If during your follow-up you find that your goals weren't achieved, you may have to restudy the problem and apply other alternatives to it—or even begin the entire process over again.

You might feel a bit overwhelmed by the seven-step process at first, especially if it's a new concept to you. However, those who have learned to use and apply it have found that this more logical approach to decision making has aided them tremendously in reducing the number of failures and ineffective efforts. Using the seven-step system will actually save you time in the long run.

How Are Decisions Made with Computers?

Since the advent of the so-called computer revolution of the early 1960s, managers have increasingly discovered another useful tool for solving problems and making decisions: the computer. In conjunction with computers, many organizations have established *management information systems (MIS)* and *CAD/CAM processes,* both of which are discussed in the sections that follow.

What Is a Management Information System (MIS)?

A modern **management information system (MIS)** is typically a computer-based collection of data organized in a way that allows relatively easy access for use in planning, organizing, and controlling operations. MIS is a management tool that can provide useful information for making decisions in less time than with traditional methods.

Management information system (MIS): *Typically, a computer-based information system useful for making management decisions.*

Data:
Facts and figures that by themselves have little to do with managerial decisions.

Information:
Data that have been processed to aid in decision making.

"What if" analysis:
Decision-making technique enabling the comparison of alternative outcomes by applying various inputs.

Data versus Information. A distinction is usually made between the terms *data* and *information.* **Data** are merely facts and figures, such as the number of times an employee has been absent or the quantity of a particular part in stock. Much more useful is the information a MIS system can provide. A MIS system is frequently used to convert data into information. **Information** is data that have been processed in a manner that facilitates decision making. For example, information could reveal how profitable establishing a second shift might be. Production scheduling, materials planning, purchasing, and inventory control are additional areas where both MIS data and information could be utilized.

"What If" Analysis. Many supervisors have developed the ability to retrieve data from MIS systems and apply **"what if" analyses** to them. For example, assume that the workload in your department has increased by 15 percent during the past three weeks. Should you hire additional full-time employees, take on temporary workers, or continue to work your existing employees overtime? With adequate information from a MIS system, you could ask the computer a series of "what ifs." Here are some examples:

1. *What* would be the additional cost per unit of production per week in your department *if* you hired two additional employees for:
   a. 2 weeks
   b. 4 weeks
   c. 8 weeks
2. *What if* you had your existing 4 employees work overtime for:
   a. 2 weeks
   b. 4 weeks
   c. 8 weeks
3. *What if* you hired temporary workers from an outside agency for:
   a. 2 weeks
   b. 4 weeks
   c. 6 weeks

You could then compare the costs of the three sets of variables, thus more readily observing which one provided your organization with the optimum results.

Programmed decisions:
Computer-generated decisions made automatically after the occurrence of certain variables.

GIGO:
In computer jargon, symbolizes "garbage in, garbage out" (i.e., inadequate input results in inadequate output).

Programmed Decisions. Many decisions made by managers are relatively routine and repetitive. A MIS system can be utilized to make **programmed decisions,** which are made automatically after certain variables have occurred. For example, a computer can be programmed so that when inventories decline below certain levels the computer automatically makes a decision to reorder.

However, whenever you utilize computer-generated data and information to make decisions, continually keep in mind that old truism, *"Garbage in, garbage out."* Popularly known as **GIGO,** the acronym infers that data and information produced by a computer are only as good as the data and information fed into it. In effect, the inputting of bad data results in the outputting of bad information. Try to make certain that your MIS information is not, in reality, *mis*information!

Nonprogrammed Decisions. Many decisions resulting from computer use are nonprogrammable (termed **nonprogrammed decisions**) and thus not easily automated. In most instances, managers must actively interpret computer-based information and then make their own judgments and decisions as to its utility. Utilizing MIS for nonprogrammed decisions has been termed **decision-assisting MIS.**[4] The information developed is often in the form of reports that must be interpreted by the manager before actual decisions can be made.

Nonprogrammed decisions: *Nonroutine decisions that are a result of analyzing computer-generated data and information; also termed* decision-assisting MIS.

Decision-assisting MIS: *Nonprogrammed decisions arrived at through the utilization of MIS systems.*

Why Are Managerial Understanding and Support Necessary?

Many organizations have been unsuccessful in their use of MIS systems for two major reasons:

1. Managers did not understand how to utilize MIS systems.
2. Managers did not participate in developing the systems.

There are some managers who do not understand "computerese" and who feel somewhat intimidated by such high-tech equipment. Some people also harbor feelings of animosity toward computers on the basis of their being machines rather than humans. A computer, however, is merely a tool. As with many properly used tools, computers can make your activities a lot easier and more effective. Computers can also be misused and overused. As a supervisor, you should seek out training in the proper application of MIS systems so that you will feel comfortable and confident when using them. In addition, MIS systems have generally been far more successful when managers themselves, rather than solely computer experts, have participated in the design of their own MIS systems.

What Is the CAD/CAM Process?

Another relatively new innovation that has been referred to as "causing a new Industrial Revolution," is termed the **CAD/CAM process.**[5] This computer system assists those responsible for product design and manufacturing in making decisions. As you'll see shortly, two important links in an organization are formed through the use of CAD/CAM.

CAD/CAM process: *Symbolizes the terms* computer-aided design *and* computer-aided *manufacturing.*

Computer-Aided Design. The CAD part of CAD/CAM represents the words **computer-*a*ided *d*esign.** The CAD process utilizes computers in designing parts and products so that objects can be easily visualized and manipulated in a three-dimensional form on a video screen. CAD has resulted in the reduction of time necessary to make decisions related to product design, in some

Computer-aided design: *The use of computers in designing parts and products.*

instances from several weeks to only a matter of days or even hours. The computer can also aid substantially in determining durability and performance of parts by simulating the effects of pressure, heat, and stress on them.

Computer-aided manufacturing:
The use of computers in linking design computers with manufacturing computers.

Computer-Aided Manufacturing. CAM refers to ***computer-aided manufacturing***, which is a system linking design computuers with other computers that control various machines or robots involved in manufacturing. The design computer actually instructs the CAM computer what to do, based on the original specifications developed by the CAD system. Adjustments to the CAD system can be made with relative ease if a modification of the finished product is desired. As a result, significant product design and manufacturing decisions can be made with far greater ease and efficiency than in the past.

How Are Groups Involved in the Decision-Making Process?

When problems develop, an effective method for developing workable solutions, if time permits, is to involve the participation of your employees. Most workers like to feel that their ideas are of value and worthy of consideration. Workers who participate in decision making, especially when outcomes directly affect them, generally experience greater feelings of self-worth and ***esprit de corps.*** They are also more likely to be committed to action plans that they themselves helped to develop. Chapter 12 will discuss the significance of participation on the part of individual employees. This section is devoted to the group decision-making process.

Synergism:
The interaction of two or more independent parts resulting in an effect of which each is individually incapable.

The concept of *synergism* relates directly to group decision making. **Synergism** is formally defined as "the action of two or more substances, organs, or organisms to achieve an effect of which each is individually incapable."[6] Frequently, the combined efforts of your employees result in better problem solving and decision making than you as a supervisor might be able to perform on your own. Some of the well-known methods for group decision making include:

1. Force-field analysis
2. Brainstorming
3. Committees
4. Delphi method

What Is Force-Field Analysis (FFA)?

Force-field analysis (FFA):
A problem-solving technique useful for identifying forces that impede and foster goal achievement.

A highly useful and systematic approach to problem solving is termed **force-field analysis (FFA).** FFA is a problem-solving technique for identifying factors that could both impede and foster the achievement of goals and standards. FFA is a practical tool for involving a group in analyzing a situation that needs to be changed.

Think about one of your current problems. Why does it exist? Force-field analysis assumes that a problem exists because of *two types of forces: restraining* and *driving forces* (see Figure 3–2). The **restraining** (or limiting) **forces** are those factors in a problem situation that work in disharmony against a desired result. In effect, restraining forces are what caused the problem to exist. Of course, if restraining forces were reduced or, better yet, eliminated, the severity of the problem could be lessened or removed altogether.

Restraining forces: *Factors that cause a problem to exist.*

Driving forces are those factors in a problem situation that work in harmony with a given situation. Driving forces are positive in nature, and they aid in preventing the problem from being worse than it already is. Of course, if a driving force could be strengthened or new driving forces brought into the picture, the severity of the problem would be reduced.

Driving forces: *Factors that prevent a problem from being worse.*

The problem itself in force-field analysis is termed **equilibrium.** The equilibrium level is not where you want to be; it is the current state of the problem as a result of the two sets of forces affecting it.

Equilibrium: *In force-field analysis, the location of the current state of the problem.*

Performing the Analysis. Although FFA can be utilized individually in problem solving, it is especially useful in obtaining the participation and commitment of the group. When working with groups, be certain to utilize visual aids, such as a chalkboard or flipchart, so that group members can easily follow the analysis.

The first important step in FFA is to develop a clear *definition of the problem* (equilibrium condition). You may already have the problem defined, or you may merely know the symptoms of the problem and want group members to help you to develop a definition. Defining the problem accurately is essential for developing useful solutions. The problem should be stated as an undesirable situation, one that needs to be changed.

A simple format for presenting the analysis is the use of a "T account" (see Figure 3–3). This approach enables you to list the forces in columns.

Your next step is to involve group members in listing the forces. Restraining forces should be listed first, since they are the easiest to think of. You can also label each force as *high, medium,* or *low (H-M-L)* to indicate the strength of each force. There is sometimes the tendency for group members to present driving forces in the form of solutions to the problem. However, no solutions should be suggested at this stage. If necessary, remind the members of the

FIGURE 3–2
A Simplified Illustration of Force-Field Analysis

FIGURE 3–3
"T Account" Format for Presenting Force-Field Analysis.

Reject Ratio in Excess of Standard *(Statement of the Problem)*	
Restraining Forces	**Driving Forces**
• Inexperienced employees • Management pressure to meet deadlines • More stringent interpretation of standards by inspectors • Poor drawings • Low morale because of pressure	• Recently installed new equipment • Employees' pride in work • Management's receptiveness to suggestions • Recent change in floor layout • Funds budgeted for training
ACTION PLAN • Recommended action: Develop and offer a training program for inexperienced employees. • Recommended action: Improve quality of drawings. • Recommended action: Evaluate current quality control standards and revise if necessary. • Recommended action: Offer incentives for meeting deadlines. • Recommended action: Involve employees in solving reject problem.	

group that driving forces are those positive conditions that *currently* exist and not those actions that *should* be taken.

A Separate Action Plan. After you and the group members have finished listing and ranking both sets of forces, you can *evaluate each force individually* to determine what actions, if any, you might take to alter its intensity. Your **action plan** should include activities that are realistic, that is, you should be concerned only with those steps that can be taken with available, or potentially available, resources. Keep in mind that you are attempting to influence two sets of forces. You desire to *eliminate* or *reduce* the effect of restraining forces, and you also want to *increase* the strength of existing driving forces and develop new ones where possible.

Action plan: *Specific recommendations for resolving a problem.*

The group's suggestions in its action plan should be listed on the flipchart or chalkboard without comment or evaluation from anyone until a sufficient number of solutions have been presented. Premature evaluation can sometimes discourage the free flow of ideas. After a sufficient quantity of suggestions have been generated, each one can be evaluated individually by the group.

Brainstorming: *A nonjudgmental group problem-solving and idea-generating activity encouraging the free flow of ideas.*

What Is Brainstorming?

A popular method for arriving at decisions with the use of groups, developed by Alex F. Osborn, is **brainstorming.**[7] A supervisor utilizing this method presents a problem or objective to group members at a meeting where the following guidelines should be followed:

1. Individual group members are allowed to express themselves freely without criticism or judgment from others.
2. **Serendipity** is encouraged; that is, ideas are allowed to build on other ideas regardless of how outlandish they may at first appear.
3. Quantity of ideas is desired. The more ideas that are developed, the more ideas that will be available to select from for the final decision.
4. The improvement of ideas already generated is encouraged. Participants suggest how the ideas of others might be improved or possibly combined to develop better ideas.

Serendipity: *Making unexpected discoveries by accident.*

Assigning to one person the responsibility of recording all presented ideas on a flipchart or chalkboard for all persons in the group to view can also be beneficial. After the group has generated a sufficient quantity of ideas, group members can begin to evaluate suggestions and participate in selecting the most useful ones. Brainstorming techniques have been used successfully by numerous firms to increase the quantity and quality of ideas that can be applied to such areas as developing new product names or creating additional uses for existing products or byproducts.

What Is a Committee?

In some organizations, difficult decisions are often referred to committee, either an **ongoing (standing) committee** (such as a *safety committee*), or one established to handle a specific situation and then disbanded (such as a *planning committee* for a particular project), termed an ***ad hoc* committee.** A **committee** (sometimes termed *task force*) can be defined as two or more persons who officially meet for the purpose of considering issues or problems related to the organization. Supervisors may be asked to serve on committees from time to time.

Ongoing committee: *A body of persons formed to handle a situation on a (standing) or long-term basis.*

Ad hoc committee: *A body of persons formed to handle a specific, temporary situation.*

Committees: *Groups formed to study, act, or report on issues related to an organization; also referred to as* task forces.

What Is the Delphi Method?

In contrast to force-field analysis, brainstorming, and committees, where decision makers are generally face-to-face with each other in the same room, the **Delphi method** avoids the potential shortcomings that exist when members of the decision-making group have contact with each other. It is frequently used in making marketing decisions and in research and development (R&D).[8] The Delphi method for solving problems and making decisions typically involves three steps:

1. Each member of the decision-making group is provided with a questionnaire or problem to work on *independently* of the other members.

Delphi method: *Group decision making in which each participant works independently of others, views the others' results, and then revises his or her original recommendations.*

2. Results and suggestions are then distributed to the other members without their knowing whose ideas they are reading.
3. Each participant then revises his or her own original decisions and resubmits them to the leader. This process is repeated until adequate solutions are developed.

As you might imagine, the Delphi method tends to take more time than the more traditional group methods for decision making. However, it does tend to avoid some of the major deficiencies inherent in group decision making, which will be discussed in the next section.

What Are the Benefits and Deficiencies in Group Decision Making?

Is group decision making useful for arriving at decisions? Some managers are highly supportive of the process, while others lack confidence in group decision making. Some of the major benefits and deficiencies of group decision making follow:

Benefits of Group Decision Making. Many managers believe that *better decisions* are made by committees—sort of an application of that old adage "two heads are better than one." It is also believed that *greater quantities of ideas* can be generated in group meetings, with ideas arising out of and building on others. Further, people with different types of knowledge, abilities, and experience might be able *to see more facets of a particular problem.* And finally, *improved morale may result.* As already mentioned, participants who believe that their ideas are valued by their leaders tend *to develop a greater sense of commitment, belonging, and loyalty* to the workgroup as well as the entire organization.

Deficiencies in Group Decision Making. Not everyone agrees that groups are effective as decision makers. Critics argue that meetings *can waste a great deal of a manager's time* by discussing trivia, topics that do little to further the organization's goals and objectives. Another danger inherent in the use of group decision making, some critics argue, is that they tend *to dilute responsibility.* Since decisions are arrived at by group consensus, no one person can be blamed for a bad decision. When Ross Perot, former board member of General Motors and an outspoken critic of committees, was asked how he would turn General Motors around, he stated:

> *Starting today, most committees will be scrapped. The old system gets so many people involved that nobody can be blamed for failure, and nobody makes a decision. That system must be junked.*[9]

Groupthink: *Deriving negative results from group decision-making efforts.*

A further hazard of committee decisions lies in what has been called **groupthink,** which has been defined as the process of deriving negative results from group decision-making efforts as a result of in-group pressures.[10] People are influenced by their peers. The influence of some group members' thinking can sway an entire group into pursuing an undesirable course of action. The German philosopher Nietzsche once suggested that madness is the exception in individuals, but the rule in groups. In far too many cases, he seems to have been right. However, the Delphi approach, as we've seen, tends to eliminate the potential groupthink deficiency in group decision making. Another method sometimes used to reduce the likelihood of group influence on decision making is to assign a ***devil's advocate*** to each meeting, whose sole responsibility is to challenge ideas that are developed.

Another deficiency often resulting from group decision making rests with the *leader* of the group. Some individuals in charge of committees have their minds made up regarding specific decisions in advance of the meeting. The remaining members merely have the opportunity "to rubber stamp predetermined decisions."

A further criticism of group decision making is that it tends *to result in costly delays.* Important members of the group may arrive

"What do you think, Al?"
"Guess I'll pass, for the moment, to Ed."
"Thanks, Al, but I'm going to withhold any comment until I've heard from Alice. Alice?"
"Well, Ed, until I know where Sid stands, I yield to Ralph. Ralph?"

Reprinted with permission from *Supervisory Management,* ©.

late or be absent altogether. Other tasks must be neglected while meetings are in session. There also seems to be an excessive *tendency for indecisiveness,* rather than the ability for candid and creative thought, among group members during their attempts at arriving at rational conclusions.

In spite of the various criticisms, group decision making will continue to play an important role in many organizations. Recognizing its limitations, we still find that good ideas can emerge from group activities if such sessions are conducted properly. Table 3–2 summarizes the potential benefits and deficiencies in group decision making.

What Are Some Common Mistakes for Decision Makers to Avoid?

"To err is human," is an oft-quoted remark. However, to be an oft-erring supervisor is akin to asking your boss for a going-away party. Although all mistakes can't be avoided in advance, being aware of the more common decision-making errors and pitfalls might save you unnecessary headaches later. Management consultants Don Caruth and Bill Middlebrook suggest that supervisors avoid these common mistakes:

1. Making the unnecessary decision
2. Fighting the recurring problem
3. Not evaluating benefits in terms of cost
4. Delaying the decision[11]

Why Make Unnecessary Decisions?

We already examined the *do-nothing approach* to decision making. Caruth and Middlebrook also point out that since most decisions entail risk, a supervisor should know when to take a risk and

TABLE 3–2
Benefits and Deficiencies in Group Decision Making

Benefits

- Better decisions made
- Greater quantity of ideas generated
- Varied backgrounds enable seeing more facets of problem
- Improved morale (feelings of participation)
- Greater feelings of commitment, belonging, and loyalty

Deficiencies

- Can waste time
- Dilutes responsibility
- Possibility of groupthink
- Ineffective leadership results in ineffective decisions
- Tendency for indecisiveness and costly delays

when to let things ride. In other words, they take the risk associated with a direct decision if doing so is really unnecessary?

Why Fight Recurring Problems?

Some supervisors repeatedly do battle with the same types of problems. Rather than wasting a lot of valuable and scarce time, you would be wise, wherever possible, to develop a set of standardized policies and procedures to deal with recurring problems (in effect, an application of *programmed decision making*). For example, when employees need time off to see a doctor, instead of having to deal with each employee individually, you could establish a standard policy and set of procedures for them to follow. Doing so could reduce your involvement in the decision-making process, thus saving you valuable time. Managers in well-organized firms are typically provided with a policies and procedures manual that can be of valuable assistance in decision making.

Why Not Evaluate Benefits in Terms of Cost?

Decision making takes time and money. A supervisor should attempt to analyze the *benefits* associated with an intended decision. Do the costs outweigh the benefits? Or are the benefits worth more than the costs? Conducting a **cost-benefit analysis** prior to making a decision can often offer a tangible clue as to whether the decision should be made at all.

Cost-benefit analysis: *Comparing costs and benefits associated with a specific decision.*

In recalling our earlier example of an increased workload in your department, you had to decide among hiring additional full-time employees, taking on temporary employees, or requesting that your existing employees work overtime. Overtime pay can be costly. Adding to your staff is also expensive, since new employees must be trained and provided with benefits (e.g., medical insurance). Which choice should you make? Can you see that you also have to analyze this decision in terms of time frames? If you could accurately determine that the increased workload was likely to be temporary—say, two to four weeks—then working your employees overtime might be less expensive. However, if the increased workload was likely to continue for a longer term, temporary workers or even additional full-time employees might be the answer. The more accurately you can determine the actual dollar costs and benefits of your decision, the easier your choice will be.

In some instances, there are *nonmonetary costs and benefits* that must be considered. For example, dumping waste material into a nearby river, rather than disposing of it properly, may be cost-effective for the firm in dollars and cents. However, the environmental costs to the community in polluted rivers and streams, destroyed fish and wildlife, loss of recreational facilities, and the cost to the firm of a damaged public image, may far outweigh any benefits.

Why Delay Decisions?

Not all decisions must be made immediately. However, procrastinating on a problem that is likely to fester with time is a gross mistake. There is a tendency for people to want to avoid the unpleasant and to get on with the easier-to-deal-with, so-called normal, activities. Unfortunately, though, your energy is often diluted when you have pressing problems, rather than the task at hand, on your mind. Taking care of a problem (which at first frequently seems far worse than it really is) may not only relieve your stressed mind, but may also provide you with feelings of accomplishment and satisfaction once the decisions are made and the problem is resolved.

Summary

As a supervisor, you are continually faced with the need to make decisions and solve problems. Poorly made decisions can be costly to you and your organization.

Problems are deviations from preestablished standards. Problems generally require decision-making activities. Three common classifications of problems are *resource-oriented, impact-oriented*, and *time-oriented.*

Decisions are made in a variety of ways: by *hunch,* by *doing nothing,* by *crisis,* with the *seven-step method,* with *computers,* and with *groups.* Decision making with computers may involve the use of *management information systems (MIS)* and *CAD/CAM processes.* Decision making with groups may involve the use of *force-field analysis, brainstorming, committees,* and the *Delphi method.* There is mixed opinion as to the value of groups in decision making.

Some of the more common mistakes decision makers should attempt to avoid are *making unnecessary decisions, fighting recurring problems, ignoring costs in relation to benefits,* and *delaying critical decisions.*

Question for Discussion

1. Evaluate the following statement: "Having to deal with problems is, without a doubt, one of the most negative activities that supervisors must engage in."
2. Briefly describe the differences among *resource-, impact-*, and *time-oriented* problems.
3. Should a manager ever make decisions on the basis of *intuition*? Explain.
4. What is your attitude toward the *do-nothing approach* to decision making?

5. Why do managers sometimes find themselves involved with *crisis management*?
6. What is the technical distinction between *data* and *information*? Which tends to be more useful? Why?
7. What is the purpose of *"what if" analysis*?
8. What are the implications of the acronym *GIGO*?
9. Explain the principal difference between *programmed* and *nonprogrammed decisions*.
10. What might have prevented some *MIS systems* from failing?
11. Explain how the *CAD/CAM process* is used in decision making.
12. How does the concept of *synergism* relate to group decision making?
13. Which is better, *individual* or *group decision making*?
14. What are some of the important ground rules associated with *brainstorming*?
15. What is the major difference between *ongoing (standing)* and *ad hoc committees*?
16. What principal advantage does the *Delphi method* have over many other forms of group decision making?
17. What are the major benefits and deficiencies that may result from group decision making?
18. Is *groupthink* a positive or negative concept? What tends to cause groupthink to exist?
19. Why is carefully defining a problem so important a step in the *seven-step system* for problem solving?
20. Why does *step 3* in the seven-step system for problem solving suggest developing more than one possible solution to a problem?
21. Why is the *follow-up step* critical in the seven-step system for problem solving?
22. What are some common mistakes that the chapter recommends decision makers attempt to avoid?

● Can You Define These Terms?

Instructions: Write a definition for each of the following terms. You may check your definitions with those provided in the end-of-text glossary.

problem
quality control specialist
human resource-oriented problems
material resource-oriented problems
low-impact problem
high-impact problem
time-oriented problems
current problems
potential problems
decision
intuition
do-nothing approach
crisis management
seven-step system
situational thinking
grapevine

management information systems (MIS)
data
information
"what if" analysis
programmed decisions
GIGO
nonprogrammed decisions
decision-assisting MIS
CAD/CAM process
computer-aided design
computer-aided manufacturing
synergism
force-field analysis
restraining forces
driving forces
equilibrium
action plan
brainstorming
serendipity
ongoing (standing) committee
ad hoc committee
committees
Delphi method
groupthink
cost-benefit analysis

Supervision In Action

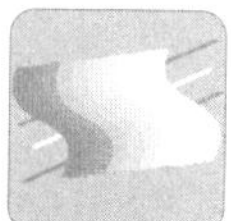

3–1 What's Your Problem?

Think about a problem that you are currently experiencing in your job. Assume that you are responsible for resolving it. Apply both the seven-step and force-field methods for solving problems to it.

3–2 Late Reports

Laura Williams was promoted about a year ago to the position of supervisor of the management information systems (MIS) department of Jaffawide Dropshippers, Inc. Peter Guest, her assistant, has consistently been late in submitting his monthly summary of field sales results. When Laura asked him to explain why, Peter said that his lateness was unavoidable because Harry Hungerford, the Pacific Northwest regional sales manager, was consistently late in submitting necessary sales information to him.

Laura contacted Harry and urged him to submit his reports to Peter on time. Unfortunately, Laura has no direct line authority over Harry, who is actually higher on the organizational hierarchy than she. Harry argued that since he was in the field two out of four weeks, he had little time to prepare his sales summaries for submission to Peter. Consequently, Laura feels frustrated and perplexed. She doesn't want to alienate Peter, but her boss has been pressuring her to make certain that Harry's reports are submitted on time.

Questions

1. What seems to be the problem in this case?
2. How would you go about attempting to resolve the problem if you were Laura?

3–3 Declining Output and Quality

Richard Fellows, an electronics engineer with the Ynos Systems Company, realized that something had to be done. Production of Ynos's major product, fire detection systems for aircraft, had declined 20 percent during the past three months. Deadlines were being missed and major customers becoming disgruntled. Quality had also declined, thus resulting in higher rejection and scrap rates.

Fellows and his two assistants are responsible for determining the work methods and production system in the plant. They are also responsible for quality control and the level of output.

Questions

1. What seems to be the principal problem in the above case incident?

2. Utilize the seven-step system for solving problems to develop a hypothetical solution to Fellows's problem. You will have to make some assumptions when involved with step 2.

3. Assume that you've decided to call a meeting of your assistants and those on the production line. You want to involve the group in force-field analysis for the purpose of developing an action plan related to the problem. Role play your problem-solving efforts with 4 or 5 other members of your class.

4. How might brainstorming be applied to solving Fellows's problem?

Endnotes

1. Henry Schott, from a staff development memorandum sent to the faculty of Merritt College, Oakland, California, May 1981.
2. "Roger Smith Replies to Ross Perot," *Fortune* (International Edition) February 15, 1988, p. 28.
3. "Psychologists Say Intuition Should no Longer Be Mistrusted," *The (Oakland) Tribune,* February 2, 1986, p. B-3. Also see Philip Goldberg, *The Intuitive Edge* (Tarcher), 1985; and Weston H. Agor, *Intuitive Management* (Englewood Cliffs, N.J.: Prentice-Hall, 1985).
4. Joel E. Ross, "Management Information Systems (MIS)," *Encyclopedia of Professional Management* (New York: McGraw-Hill, 1978), p. 516.
5. Gene Bylinsky, "A New Industrial Revolution Is on the Way," *Fortune,* October 5, 1981, p. 106; and Harry B. Thompson, "CAD/CAM and the Factory of the Future," *Management Review,* May 1983, p. 27.
6. *The American Heritage Dictionary, Second College Edition* (Boston: Houghton Mifflin, 1982), p. 1233.
7. A. F. Osborn, *Applied Imagination,* 3d edition (New York: Charles Scribner's Sons, 1963).
8. Harold A. Linstone and Murray Turoff, *The Delphi Method: Techniques and Applications* (Reading, Mass.: Addison-Wesley, 1975).
9. Ross Perot, "How I Would Turn Around GM," *Fortune* (International Edition), February 15, 1988, pp. 22–27.
10. Irving L. Janis, *Victims of Groupthink* (Boston: Houghton Mifflin, 1972), p. 9.
11. Don Caruth and Bill Middlebrook, "How to Make a Better Decision," *Supervisory Management,* American Management Associations, 1981, pp. 12–17.

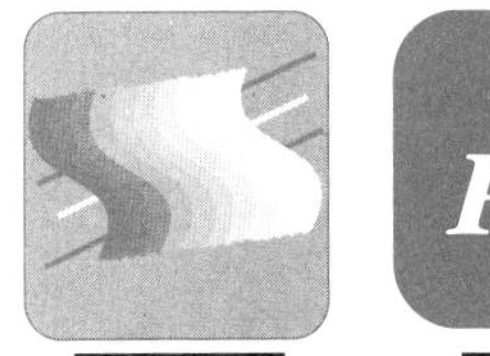

Part Two

Supervisory Roles in Planning and Controlling

DRILLING
MODEL
SHIPPING
Testing
Customer Tubs
Credit
Hold
Fiberglass
Brisa
ST1000

Chapter 4

Planning Work Activities

Management's job is to see the company not as it is, but as it can become.
—John W. Teets, Executive

Plan ahead. It wasn't raining when Noah built the ark.
—Anonymous

Learning Objectives

When you finish this chapter, you should be able to:

1. Describe the planning process.
2. Recognize the consequences of poor planning.
3. Apply logical procedures to your planning activities.
4. Prepare useful goal statements to aid you in planning effectively.
5. Explain the distinction among policies, procedures, and rules.
6. Identify five reasons why planning efforts sometimes fail.

"Plans? Of course I make them—that is, when I've got the time. But you know how it is. We supervisors are so darned busy putting out fires—you know, dealing with one crisis after another—that it's kind of hard to find the time to do much planning. But I still get by nevertheless."

". . . still get by"? Yes, many supervisors who can't "find the time" to plan (or rather, don't *take the time*) do "still get by." In the long run, however, merely getting by is usually insufficient if supervisors are to effectively achieve the overall goals and objectives of their organizations.

Planning: *A management function that establishes organizational goals and objectives and determines the means for accomplishing them.*

Planning is an essential activity. Results will be accomplished far more easily when you utilize a well-thought-out plan. To plan effectively, of course, you need a sense of direction, which evolves out of your *setting realistic goals* and then *developing an action plan designed to achieve these goals.* Planning also requires an activity termed *control,* which involves developing and utilizing systems for *steering performance toward desired objectives.* Time spent on planning, goal setting, and control, as you'll soon realize, can actually save substantial amounts of your time and significantly aid you in accomplishing far more than merely "getting by."

What is the Nature of Planning?

Although all the functions of management are important and interrelate, *planning* has often been referred to as the primary function of management—the key to sound decision making. A wise sage once warned, "Failing to plan, you are planning to fail." What is this all-important activity of planning? Simply stated, when you plan, you're deciding *now* what you want to do sometime in the *future.*

A variety of plans are utilized by managers. All of them require making decisions, but the emphasis of decision-making activities tends to differ with each kind of plan. Examples of various types of plans are listed in Table 4–1.

How Can You Reach Your Intended Destination?

Someone once said, "If you don't know where you are going, you will end up somewhere else." Many supervisors who haven't learned how to plan have found, to their dismay, that this warning is all too true.

Don't you generally like to feel that you know where you're going? If, for example, you decide to take public transportation to work this morning, is it likely that you would hop on any bus that happens to come along without first wanting to know where it is going? Furthermore, you'd be unlikely to have much confidence in the bus driver if you ask her where the bus was going and she responds, "Oh, I don't know. I just drive wherever I get the urge to drive. I'm never quite sure where I'll end up. Would you like to get on?"

Isn't it unlikely that you would get on that bus? Instead, wouldn't you want to be sure you took a bus that would enable you to get to your intended destination—your workplace? And how about after you arrive at work? Wouldn't you still need to know where you're going in relation to your job? Thoughtful planning, therefore, is the activity that can help you get to where you want to go.

TABLE 4–1
Examples of Various Types of Plans

- Missions
- Goals
- Objectives
- Strategies
- Policies
- Procedures
- Rules

What Are the Consequences of Poor Planning?

Planning involves *prediction*—forecasting the future. No supervisor has yet found a perfectly accurate crystal ball. Yet conditions not foreseen can tear apart the best-made plans.

You might, for example, plan to have a specific customer's order produced and ready for delivery by Friday. You realize that meeting the deadline will require two employees to work overtime. You've allowed for this factor in estimating the cost of the job. This afternoon, while the two workers are drawing overtime pay—at one and one-half times their normal rate—they experience an equipment malfunction. As a result, the workers must stand by idly doing nothing while waiting for the equipment to be repaired. You find your carefully designed plans rapidly swirling down the drain. Unfortunately, events like this sometimes occur regardless of careful advance planning. Every event can't be anticipated. However, even far more serious consequences are likely to occur when you haven't made a systematic attempt to plan your work unit's activities.

Some supervisors aren't very systematic in their planning. Instead, their plans are the result of gut-level feelings, which we termed *intuition* in a previous chapter. Sometimes plans made solely on the basis of intuition are successful. But there are a lot of inherent dangers associated with an intuitive approach to planning. Personal biases, emotions, and moods can easily get in the way of objective decision making. Many serious blunders made by supervisors result from decision making by hunch rather than from rational thinking.

There are a host of problems that can result from poor planning, as summarized in Table 4–2. For example, morale problems often

TABLE 4–2
Consequences of Poor Planning

- Morale problems
- A reduced sense of employee direction and commitment to organizational objectives
- Production bottlenecks
- Poor quality of work and products
- Higher frequency of accidents
- Increased operating costs
- Lower profits, salaries, bonuses, and benefits

Planning is a managerial function that enables organizations to accomplish goals with a minimum of accidents.

develop when employees feel that they don't understand where their organization is going, or what its purpose is. Employees who understand how plans, goals, objectives, and strategies relate to them as workers have a far better sense of direction and commitment to organizational objectives, especially if they've had an opportunity to participate in the formulation of the plans.

Other consequences of poor planning can include production bottlenecks, poor quality of work and products, and higher frequency of accidents among employees. Whether we're concerned with a private company or a governmental agency, poor planning tends to increase operating costs, which usually means less funds available for employee salaries, benefits, and bonuses.

What Types of Plans Can You Utilize?

Plans vary in their scope and in the time necessary to carry them out. In general, plans can be classified either as *long range* or *short range.* **Long-range plans** are typically broader and more general than short-range plans. **Short-range plans** are usually fairly detailed and designed to assist in accomplishing day-to-day objectives.

Long-range plans: *Broader, more general organizational intentions, formulated for five to twenty years or more.*

Short-range plans: *Fairly detailed organizational intentions designed to assist in accomplishing day-to-day objectives.*

Senior executives are generally more concerned with broader, longer-range plans than are first-line supervisors. Such plans, which may be formulated for five to twenty years or more in advance, might relate to long-term financing, plant location or expansion, new product development, mergers with other companies, or policy determination. As a first-line supervisor, you are typically responsible for carrying out plans formulated by top management. Your job is to translate those plans into language comprehensible to your associates. It should be mentioned that long-range plans are in a continual state of flux, since the future can seldom be predicted with complete accuracy. As a supervisor, you should be mentally prepared to modify your plans and activities based on changing long-range organizational plans.

In general, your supervisory planning activities are likely to be relatively short run and performed primarily on a daily and week-to-week basis. Your typical short-run concerns may include planning weekly work schedules and daily job assignments. However, you may at times be called on to participate in higher-level planning, especially on such matters as estimating future personnel needs, suggesting proposed changes in production processes or plant layout, developing safety programs, and other broad factors that affect your work unit over longer periods of time.

What Is the Process of Planning?

Planning is a managerial activity that should never be left to chance; it is far too important to the successful operation of any organization. Some supervisors, either by design or subconsciously, tend to shy away from planning because they feel that it takes an inordinate amount of their time. As already mentioned, however, sound planning can actually save you substantial amounts of time since it can help you to anticipate and, therefore, avoid many potentially time-consuming problems.

Planning, of course, isn't an isolated activity. Many plans that you are responsible for carrying out originate with senior executives and are then communicated to other levels of the organization, possibly in the form of *policies, procedures, rules,* and *budgets.* Likewise, plans developed in one department typically must be *coordinated* with plans developed in other departments, since production processes are often highly dependent on each other. For example, plans for producing a product would have to be coordinated with plans for purchasing materials that go into the final product. Otherwise, production bottlenecks and excessive costs might be incurred.

Furthermore, plans are unlikely to be implemented as intended if they aren't *clearly understood* by those who must work with them. Communicating the plans to affected individuals, therefore, becomes highly critical if they are to be properly carried out.

How Do You Plan For Results?

"Seat-of-the-pants" planning typically fails over time. Instead, a systematic approach to planning should be utilized. The following are some guidelines that, when followed, tend to make the achievement of planned results far more likely.

Plan to Plan. Most effective supervisors set aside a specific time each day exclusively devoted to planning activities. They ask their assistants to allow no interruptions (except for genuine emergencies) during the designated time period. Twenty minutes of uninterrupted planning time can often equal two hours of disturbed planning time.

Select a Desirable Environment for Planning. Try to select a planning site that allows for few distractions. Your planning location should also provide you with easy access to information that you need for effective planning.

Think Backwards. Ask yourself, "What is it that I am trying to accomplish?" Then think backwards from that objective. Also ask yourself, "What is it that must be done to reach the objective that I've established?"

Use Your Creative Imagination. Let your mind go off unrestricted in all sorts of directions—whether ideas generated seem logical or illogical, sane or insane, ostensibly useful or not. Often, quite practicable ideas result from thoughts that, at first glance, seem to border on uselessness.

What Is a Logical Planning Procedure?

Author Feodor Dostoevski once wrote, "Without some goal and some effort to reach it, no man can live." His words could be modified to read, "Without realistic organizational goals and planned efforts to reach them, no manager can survive." Establishing specific goals accompanied by action plans for achieving these goals are essential for the smooth functioning of any organization. Poorly developed goals and plans tend to create a sort of organizational fuzziness, resulting in an environment that often results in the ineffective use of time.

Deciding what we want to accomplish is termed **goal setting** (sometimes referred to as *establishing objectives*), and is considered the first step in the planning process. *Goals* and *objectives* are related to *results.* Of course, whether or not you establish goals, you invariably are going to achieve certain kinds of results. But will they necessarily be the results that you want to achieve? The goals you set, therefore, should be related to the specific results you desire. The achievement of your intended results develops from careful and intelligent planning followed by behavior in support of those goals.

Goal setting:
A process that aids in clarifying the activities necessary to accomplish specific tasks.

The planning process follows a logical procedure, and consists of:

1. Setting goals.
2. Deciding what action is necessary to accomplish your goals.
3. Monitoring, or controlling, activities to ensure that results are proceeding in the direction of established goals.

A Technical Detour: How Do *Missions, Goals, Objectives,* and *Strategies* Differ?

The terms *missions, goals, objectives,* and *strategies* each have similar, but distinct, meanings. A **mission** is the broadest of the four and is a type of goal that relates to the philosophical objectives of an organization. The next two—**goals** and **objectives**—are typically used interchangeably by most managers. Your text also exchanges the two terms freely. However, you should be aware that some managers prefer to make a distinction between the two words, contending that an objective is the more specific of the two and can, therefore, *fit within a goal.* Thus, a *goal* can be defined as objectives, or ends, toward which activity is directed. An *objective* is a specific statement of results that individuals or organizations want to achieve. And finally, *strategies* result from an organization's mission, goals, and objectives. **Strategies** are carefully thought-out decisions that aid in developing an action plan for achieving the end results desired by management.

Mission:
A general type of organizational goal that relates to the philosophical objectives of an organization.

Goal:
Objectives or ends toward which activity is directed.

Objective:
A specific statement of results that individuals or organizations want to achieve.

Strategies:
Carefully thought-out decisions that aid in developing an action plan for achieving end results desired by management.

Here's an example that should help clarify the distinction sometimes used among missions, goals, objectives, and strategies. Let's assume that the Flexflo Company's *mission* is that of "providing high-quality goods to the consuming public at a reasonable cost and for a reasonable profit." To achieve this mission, the sales departments in each division have established the *goal* of increasing sales by 20 percent this year. An Atlanta-based representative named Jason and his boss, Joan, have jointly established an *objective* to sell 100,000 units in Jason's territory so that he can contribute toward achieving the national sales goal. The *strategy* for attaining the sales goal is to establish an action plan for increasing the time spent looking for new customers by four hours a day. Further strategy involves mailing out prospecting letters to 50 potential accounts each week, as well as utilizing the telephone for contacting prospective customers four hours per week.

What Types of Goals Can You Set?

Goals vary in their emphasis. As you've just learned, some are quite specific and may be called *objectives.* Others are general and may even include *missions.* Some may relate to the past, while others are concerned primarily with the future. Some may attempt to maintain the *status quo,* while others are concerned with rapid change.

You are now going to learn about four general categories of goals, as illustrated in Figure 4–1. They are termed *maintenance goals, problem-solving goals, developmental goals,* and *mission goals.*

Maintenance goals: *Specific goals related to the ongoing and routine operations of an organization; goals intended to keep an organization on an even keel.*

The Nature of Maintenance Goals. Maintenance goals are related to *routine operations* in an organization. For example, a payroll supervisor has established the routine goal of regularly issuing paychecks on time. A production supervisor has established the goal of ensuring that production takes place at standard rates. In a sense, maintenance goals, although important, are considered to be at the lowest level in the hierarchy of goal-setting statements. They do little to improve the organization; that's not their purpose. Their principal function is to keep the organization on an even keel, that is, operating smoothly. However, not providing sufficient attention to maintenance (or routine) goals can lead to future problems.

Problem-solving goals: *Goals that are intended to correct deviations from previously established standards or plans.*

The Nature of Problem-Solving Goals. Problem-solving goals are slightly higher in the goal-setting hierarchy. A problem is considered to be the condition that develops when operations deviate from previously established standards or plans. In effect, the problem itself creates the need for a goal. The need to establish problem-

FIGURE 4–1
Goal-Setting Hierarchy and Principal Types of Goals

solving goals could result from any of the following: a finished product not meeting quality standards, a declining share of total sales in the marketplace, or an excessively high personnel turnover rate.

The Nature of Developmental Goals. **Developmental goals** are even higher in the hierarchy of goal categories. They are concerned with objectives related to *improving* some part of the organization and, as a result, tend to make the greatest contribution. Developmental goals often cause organizational members to stretch somewhat and, when accomplished, move an organization to new and higher levels of performance. An example of a developmental goal is to develop a new safety training program for machine operators for presentation on August 1 between 9:00 and 10:00 A.M. Another example is to complete the development of a new employee orientation procedure by September 7. A supervisor's individual desire to complete an evening college course in employee counseling by next June is a *personal* developmental goal that also fits into this category.

Developmental goals: *Specific goals intended to improve some part of the organization, such as a goal to develop personnel through training.*

The Nature of Mission Goals. **Mission goals,** frequently referred to as *mission statements,* are the loftiest in the hierarchy of goals. Although most well-written goal statements are usually specific and quantifiable, mission statements tend to be an exception and are usually more general and philosophical. Goals found on mission statements tend toward the ideal—a state not easily reached. Figure 4–2 is an example of a mission statement for Safeway Stores, Inc.[1]

Mission goals: *General goals that relate to philosophical objectives of an organization.*

Philosophical statements seldom provide supervisors with direct guidance on how to achieve maintenance, problem-solving, and developmental goals. They do, however, tend to provide a general sense of overall direction for organizational members. They are usually developed by the board of directors or a high-level planning committee.

What Are the Characteristics of Useful Goals?

Preparing useful goals isn't an easy task for the less-experienced supervisor who lacks some familiarity with the characteristics of well-stated goals. The supervisor well-versed in goal-setting techniques, however, recognizes that goals shouldn't be left to memory; they usually should be *put in writing.* Doing so not only helps you to improve your goals by enabling you to get a more objective

SAFEWAY'S MISSION

is to be a growing, profitable, world-wide retailer of groceries and related consumer goods and services.

FIGURE 4–2 Mission Statement for Safeway Stores, Incorporated look at them, but it also lessens the likelihood that they will be overlooked or even forgotten.

When preparing goals, you should also consider a strategy for dealing with ***environmental constraints,*** such as the unavailability of personnel or funds, regulations that might block your plans, and any other factor related to your desired end results. Your goals, for example, will be far more difficult to attain without qualified employees, an adequate budget, or a favorable regulatory climate.

There are a number of other characteristics inherent in well-written goal statements. By applying, whenever possible, the guidelines listed in Table 4–3, you should find that your goal statements will be far more meaningful and useful.

How Do You Develop an Action Plan?

Earlier we learned that the planning process should follow a logical procedure, one that consists of setting goals, developing an action plan designed for the attainment of these goals, and monitoring related activities to ensure that the goals are being accomplished as intended and on schedule. Let's now look briefly at the second item, deciding on the action necessary for accomplishing specific goals in an effective manner. The next chapter will deal with the activities associated with the third step, monitoring (i.e., controlling) planned activities.

TABLE 4–3
Characteristics of Well-Prepared Goal Statements

- *Realistic*—Is the goal *practical* and *feasible* rather than solely theoretical and idealistic? Will achieving your objectives make a real contribution to your organization and its personnel?
- *Precise*—Is your goal statement *definite* as to precisely what you want to accomplish? Is your goal stated in *quantitative* rather than in vague and general terms?
- *Achievable within a definite time period*—Does your goal statement include an *attainable target date?* Have you allowed for unforeseen contingencies?
- *Consistent*—Is your goal *in harmony* with those of your *peers* (e.g., other supervisors)? Do you know what your peers are currently doing or plan to do? Do you *communicate regularly* with them to avoid the possibility of overlapping, or coming into conflict with, their goals?
- *Stated in terms of end results*—Is your goal stated in terms of what you *ultimately want to accomplish* rather than in terms of ongoing processes or activities?
- *Verifiable*—Have you developed means for determining if you have reached the goal by your target date? Have you established *means of control* to compare your actual results with your planned results?

After you have *decided what you want to accomplish*—that is, developed precise, verifiable, and realistic goals—you should follow four additional steps:

1. *Gather useful information related to your goals and objectives.* Have you carefully analyzed *what* is to be done, *why* it is to be done, *how* it is to be done, *how much* it will cost, *who* is to do it, *where* it is to be done, and *when* it is to be done? (See Table 4–4.) Have you evaluated the setting, or environment, in which your objectives will be realized? What will you need from your boss to implement your plans? Have you attempted to forecast what materials and personnel will be necessary? Are they likely to be in short supply? If so, will there be substitute materials or additional funds available for overtime work? Will sufficient funds be budgeted for carrying out your action plan?
2. *Develop at least three possible courses of action for accomplishing your goals.* Do you remember Murphy's Law from the previous chapter? "Anything that can go wrong will go wrong." Have you prepared substitute plans in the event that Murphy's Law enforcement troops come after you? Do you have alternatives to which you can turn if certain objectives turn out to be unrealistic?
3. *Analyze and predict the likely results and implications of each course of action.* Have you tried to anticipate what factors might hinder the use of your action plan? Will your boss be supportive of your intentions? Are there any possible adverse consequences that would outweigh expected benefits? Is there any legislation that might prohibit carrying out your plans? Is your plan ethical? Does it go beyond the boundaries of existing company policies and rules? What are the likely effects on future employee morale and motivation?
4. *Choose and implement the "best" course of action.* Have you decided who is going to assist you in accomplishing your goals? Have you determined what will be delegated to others and what you will do yourself? Have you developed a control system to ensure that your plans will be carried out on schedule?

TABLE 4–4
Guidelines for Obtaining Significant Information Needed in the Planning Process

- What has to be done?
- Why does it have to be done?
- How is it to be done?
- How much will it cost?
- Who is going to do it?
- Where will it be done?
- When will it be done?

How Are Plans Made Understandable?

Plans are of little use to an organization if they are not *communicated to* and *understood by* its members. Many organizations have developed a highly useful communications tool called an **organization manual.** Its purpose is to provide a ready source of information for members of a particular organization. The manual usually describes, in written form, the formal authority relationships that exist within the organization. It may also spell out an organization's formal *policies, procedures,* and *rules,* all of which are necessary for supervisors and employees to understand in order to carry out their responsibilities effectively.

Organization manual: *A guidebook that provides employees with information on authority relationships; attempts to clarify formal policies, procedures, and rules.*

What Are Policies?

Supervisors should also guard against confusing the terms *policies, procedures,* and *rules,* as sometimes occurs. **Policies** are *not* hard and fast regulations to be applied inflexibly to every situation; nor are they the same as procedures. A policy is a type of plan, a *guide* to thinking and action. Policies reflect the overall goals of the organization. Policies will *not* tell you and other employees how to carry out your responsibilities. They are helpful, however, in providing you and other employees with a predictable framework within which you can make decisions.

Policies: *Guides to decision making and action for organizational employees.*

Let's look at a sample policy, one related to a work situation known as **flexible working hours.** The policy states that employees may, with prior approval of their supervisors, start working up to two hours earlier than the usual starting time in the morning and depart up to two hours earlier than usual in the afternoon. This policy is especially beneficial for the employee who wants to get an early jump on the weekend on a Friday afternoon. Working parents, too, find this policy helpful, since it enables them to be home when their children get out of school in the afternoon. As with most policies, this one has definite limits (two hours of flexibility on each side of usual working hours), but the employee is able to make decisions within the framework of the policy.

Flexible working hours: *A condition in which employees may, usually with prior approval of their supervisors, alter their usual working hours.*

What Are Procedures?

Procedures, as with policies, also serve to guide behavior, but they generally are *more specific* than policies. A procedure is a system that details *specific steps* to be followed to achieve a particular objective. Remember this point: Procedures stress *details,* whereas policies tend to be more *general* in scope.

Procedures: *A system that details specific steps to be followed to achieve a particular objective.*

For example, in a policy that permits employees to vary their working hours within a range of two hours, specific procedures for utilizing it could be included. Employees might be expected to follow the procedures described in Figure 4–3.

What Are Rules?

Rules are similar to procedures. The two terms are sometimes even used interchangeably. In reality, however, rules are perceived

Rules: *Statements of precisely what activities or conduct are (or are not) to be engaged in; generally relate to disciplinary action.*

Procedures for Flex-Time

All employees who desire to utilize flexible working hours must:

1. Notify their supervisors in writing no later than 3:00 P.M. the previous day.
2. Orally notify their own subordinates, if any, of any activities that might require special or immediate attention.

FIGURE 4–3
Example of Procedures for Utilizing Flex-Time

as being more similar to *laws.* Rules are also far more *precise* than policies and leave little room for deviation from established standards of behavior. Rules are guiding statements of what action and conduct are (or are not) to be performed. ***Discipline,*** or ***disciplinary action*** (a topic to be covered in Chapter 16), generally relates to rule enforcement. An example of a rule is "Smoking is permitted only in the employee lounge."

Rules can be stated in either a positive or negative manner. The same smoking rule just mentioned could be stated more negatively: "Smoking is prohibited except in the employee lounge." Many managers feel that rules expressed in positive statements tend to be more readily accepted by employees.

Rules should not be perceived as something fixed, like a footprint embedded in concrete. Instead, rules should be regularly reevaluated to ensure that they continue to relate to current organizational conditions. Employees typically find it more difficult to respect rules that appear illogical, out of date, or enforced inequitably or sporadically.

How Might Organizational Goals Conflict with Personal Goals?

We all have personal goals. Why, for example, are you studying a textbook on supervision? Your answer is probably related to certain goals that you previously established. Perhaps you are not yet a supervisor, but your goal is to become one someday. Your plan may include studying managerial concepts in order to help you achieve your goal. Maybe you are already a supervisor, and your objective is to improve your managerial skills and knowledge. Once again, your plan may include learning more about management techniques and concepts.

Everyone arrives at the work place with a variety of personal needs and goals. Some of the needs and goals of workgroup members may be in close harmony with those of the organization, and some may be in direct conflict. Let's assume, for example, that your organization has set goals related to current affirmative action hiring and promotion programs. Let's further assume that your organization has established a goal to reach a level of at least 45 percent minority and women supervisors within a two-year period. The personal achievement goals, therefore, of a Hispanic person or a woman about to be promoted to a first-line supervisory position would, in all likelihood, be in harmony with the organization's goals. But how about the white male worker who feels that he deserves the promotion offered to a Hispanic employee or a woman? Would he necessarily feel that his own goals and those of the organization are in harmony?

Or take the example of some managers who feel that in the interest of patriotism, the goal of acquiring new equipment should be reached through purchases made on the bases of "buy American" or "buy Canadian" policies. Other managers, however, may believe that purchases should be based on the best equipment at the most cost-effective prices, regardless of where the items were manufactured. The two conflicting sets of goals must be harmonized by the organization's managers if effective results are to be attained.

As a supervisor, one of your challenging responsibilities is that of reconciling the various goals of a complex organization with the personal needs and aspirations of your individual group members. In some instances you must convince your team of workers to sacrifice or modify their own personal goals in order to be of assistance in helping the organization achieve necessary results. For example, there were numerous examples in recent years where employees accepted pay cuts and benefits reductions to prevent their firms from going bankrupt and to preserve their own future employment.

Why Might Planning Efforts Fail?

The production and marketing of computer software programs provides us with an example of why planning efforts sometimes are unsuccessful. *Vaporware* is a term that computerphiles have kicked around regularly in recent decades. The word refers to computer software programs that are scheduled for availability to purchasers on a specific date in the near future, but end up not being ready when promised.

For example, an enhanced version of Lotus 1-2-3, previously the best-selling computer spreadsheet program, was announced for availability on several occasions in the late 1980s but consistently missed each promised date. Fed up with the repeated false availability announcements for a "new and improved" version of Lotus 1-2-3, increasingly impatient potential customers turned to competing software companies for their *realware.* Critics of the Lotus Corporation related the recurrent delays to the poor planning and unrealistic goals established by its management. In the case of Lotus, the delays proved to be costly, since the 1-2-3 spreadsheet program accounted for more than 50 percent of the company's sales and profits.

As you can realize, it's not just the *activity* of planning that aids managers in achieving organizational goals. The key factor is how *effective* the planning efforts have been in enabling their planned goals to be accomplished.

What causes planning efforts to occasionally fail? Knowing some answers to that question may assist you in developing a better track record in your own planning efforts. Let's now briefly examine five important causes of planning failure.

1. *Lack of accurate facts and information*—Accurate facts and information are essential if plans are to be useful. For example, assume that you intend to begin assembly operations of a new product in your department on December 1. Your plan is based on the assumption that all finished components necessary for the product will be available as required for assembly into finished products. You later discover, however, that the availability of one component will be delayed for three months. Your original information on availability was inaccurate and, of course, the cause of your plans going awry.
2. *Lack of clear understanding of desired end results*—Clearly communicating goals and objectives to employees is essential if plans are to be effective. Far too often the preoccupied supervisor fails to take the time to explain objectives to employees and, instead, assumes that employees already understand the plans based on "plain common sense." (Chapter 13 discusses in detail the importance of developing effective communications skills.)
3. *Lack of effective coordination among involved working units*—A common complaint among supervisors is the lack of effective communication among the various departments within an organization, which results in a lack of coordination of established plans. Departments within the same company sometimes behave as though they were directly competing, rather than cooperating, with other departments. Coordination of all involved subunits of an organization is essential, therefore, if plans are to result in goal accomplishment.
4. *Lack of learning from past experience*—Napoleon has been credited with having warned, "Those who do not learn from history must relive history." His sage words often go unheeded among some supervisors. Numerous examples exist in organizations of supervisors who ignore what they should have learned from their past experiences, especially their mistakes. In some cases, supervisors "reinvent the wheel," that is, waste considerable amounts of time merely generating ideas that were developed previously.
5. *Lack of effective monitoring and controlling of strategies and action plans*—Plans should not be formulated and carried out without continually monitoring (i.e., controlling) their progress. Conditions seldom remain static in the real world of organizations. Consequently, even well-formulated plans may have to be modified based on changing conditions. The function of control is so important that the next chapter is devoted entirely to the subject.

Summary

Planning is one of the most important of all managerial activities. It involves deciding in the present what you want to accomplish in the future. Sound planning results from setting realistic goals and objectives and then deciding how these are to be implemented.

Poor planning can cause morale problems among employees, lessen employee sense of direction and commitment, create production bottlenecks, result in low-quality work and products, cause higher accident frequency, increase operating costs, and cause a multitude of other problems.

Plans vary in their time frame, ranging from short range to long range. Supervisors are typically more involved with short-range plans and executives with long-range plans.

Effective supervisors attempt to follow a set of logical guidelines for planning. Setting specific goals is a basic part of the planning process. Four typical categories of goals are *maintenance, problem-solving, developmental,* and *mission.*

Plans are made more understandable through the use of *policies, procedures, rules,* and *budgets,* the last of which is discussed in the next chapter. Part of a supervisor's challenge is to meld the goals of the organization with the personal goals of the employees, which sometimes conflict with each other. Five common reasons why plans sometimes fail are the lack of accurate facts and information, the lack of clear understanding of desired end results, the lack of effective coordination among involved working units, the lack of learning from past experience, and the lack of effective monitoring and controlling of strategies and action plans.

Questions for Discussion

1. What is *planning?* Why is it typically considered one of the most significant of all managerial functions?
2. Evaluate the following statement: "I formulate most of my plans primarily on the basis of hunch and intuition. I'm usually right when I get that gut-level feeling about something. So why should I confuse myself with all those high-powered facts that some of those fast-track MBAs want me to analyze?"
3. What are some of the more prevalent consequences of poor planning? Why do such consequences tend to result from unsound planning?
4. In general, how does *supervisory planning* differ from *planning formulated by senior management?*
5. What was meant by the suggestion in the chapter that you *think backwards* when involved with the planning process?
6. The planning process follows a logical, three-step procedure. Why is step three, *monitoring activities,* critical to the process?

7. Briefly explain the distinction among the *four categories of goals* discussed in the chapter.
8. Why should goals be stated in *quantitative* terms where possible?
9. Why are *developmental goals* considered to be extremely important contributors to an organization's success?
10. Describe the characteristics of meaningful and well-prepared *goal statements.*
11. What do *policies, procedures,* and *rules* have in common? In what ways are they different?
12. Illustrate how an individual's own personal goals might conflict with the goals of the organization.
13. What are four common causes of *planning failure?* How might they be avoided?

Can You Define These Terms?

Instructions: Write a definition for each of the following terms. You may check your definitions with those provided in the end-of-text glossary.

planning
long-range plans
short-range plans
goal setting
mission
goals
objectives
strategies
maintenance goals
problem-solving goals
developmental goals
mission goals
organization manual
policies
flexible working hours
procedures
rules

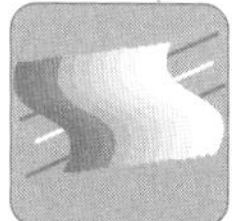

Supervision In Action

4–1 Can You See the Pattern?

The ability to develop useful goal statements is a learned art. To improve your skills in this area, respond to the following instructions.

1. Write a list of the characteristics usually included in well-written goal statements.
2. Compare your list with the characteristics cited in Table 4–3 on page 76 in this chapter. Which items did you overlook?
3. Below is a sample list of goal statements. Read each statement carefully. Which characteristics of well-written goal statements can be found in each statement?

Sample Goal Statements

- *Produce* 45,275 units of product X during final quarter of 19––.
- *Increase* the quantity of minority group employees by at least 15 percent before end of 19––.
- *Complete* training of four new salespeople by June 30.
- *Reduce* scrap rate 10 percent by December 31.
- *Reduce* by 80 percent the amount of toxic waste pollutants seeping into Columbia River from cellulose-steeping facilities by May 1.
- *Increase* productivity of milling operation by 10 percent before November 1.

4–2 Establishing Work-Related Goals—An Action Plan

Establishing work-related goals should be an ongoing activity of any supervisor. Unfortunately, many goal statements are of little value to the supervisors who prepare them. Goal setting, to be effective, requires the thoughtful and careful application of the essential characteristics of well-prepared goals discussed in the chapter. Review the characteristics and then *prepare two goal statements for each of the four general categories of goals.* Relate your goal statements to your present supervisory position with an organization. If you are not currently a supervisor, then relate your goal statements to a supervisory position with which you are familiar. (The six sample goal statements above can serve as models for your own goal statements.)

Maintenance goal 1 ______________________________

____

Completion date of maintenance goal 1 ______________

Specific requirements to achieve my goal ______________

____

Maintenance goal 2 ______________________________

____

Completion date of maintenance goal 2 ______________

Specific requirements to achieve my goal ______________

____

Problem-solving goal 1 ______________________________

____

Completion date of problem-solving goal 1 ______________

Specific requirements to achieve my goal ______________

____

Problem-solving goal 2 ______________________________

____

Completion date of problem-solving goal 2 ______________

Specific requirements to achieve my goal ______________

____

Developmental goal 1 ______________________________

____

Completion date of developmental goal 1 ______________

Specific requirements to achieve my goal ______________

____

Developmental goal 2 ______________________________

____

Completion date of developmental goal 2 ______________

Specific requirements to achieve my goal ______________

____

Mission goal 1 ______________________________

____

Completion date of mission goal 1 ______________

Specific requirements to achieve my goal ______________________

____

Mission goal 2 ______________________________________

____

Completion date of mission goal 2 ______________________

Specific requirements to achieve my goal ______________________

____

4–3 Decisions, Decisions—Even on the Moon?[2]

This is a planning and decision-making exercise for the purpose of survival. Think of yourself as a member of a space crew whose mission is to rendezvous with a mother ship on the lighted surface of the moon. Due to mechanical difficulties, your ship has crash-landed some 200 miles from the rendezvous site. All equipment, with the exception of the items listed below, was destroyed in the crash. Since survival depends upon reaching the mother ship, you and your fellow crew members must determine which among the 15 categories of equipment left intact are most crucial for survival.

The items left intact after the crash are listed below. You are asked to rank these on your own in order of their importance for ensuring survival. Place 1 by the most important item, 2 by the second most important item, and so on through number 15 by the least important item. Then get together with four or five other "crew members." Attempt to arrive at a consensus among yourselves. *Follow sound planning and problem-solving procedures.* Be certain to develop specific plans and objectives before arriving at a decision.

Items	**Individual Ranking**	**Group Ranking**
• Box of matches	_____	_____
• Food concentrate	_____	_____
• Parachute silk	_____	_____
• 50 feet of nylon rope	_____	_____
• Portable heating unit	_____	_____
• Two 45-caliber pistols	_____	_____
• One case of dehydrated milk	_____	_____
• Two 100-lb. oxygen tanks	_____	_____
• Stellar map (of the moon's constellation)	_____	_____
• Life raft	_____	_____

• Magnetic compass	_____	_____
• Five gallons of water	_____	_____
• Signal flares	_____	_____
• First-aid kit containing injection needles	_____	_____
• Solar-powered FM receiver-transmitter	_____	_____

Questions

1. What were some of the difficulties you experienced in trying to arrive at a group consensus?

2. Why did such difficulties occur?

Endnotes

1. From a pamphlet entitled "Safeway's Mission and Objectives," distributed by Safeway Stores, Incorporated, 1983.

2. Adapted from "NASA Exercise," an exercise that has appeared without credit in a variety of publications, such as J. B. Ritchie and Paul Thompson, *Organization and People: Readings, Cases, and Exercises in Organizational Behavior* (St. Paul: West Educational Publishing, 1984), pp. 262, 263.

Chapter 5

Controlling Work Activities

When employees have relatively low trust in a control system, they sometimes behave in various ways that are harmful to the organizations. They may do what is 'required' by the system.

—Waldron Berry, Educator

Learning Objectives

When you finish this chapter, you should be able to:

1. Describe the relationship between controlling and planning.
2. Restate how control standards are developed.
3. Recall which areas should be controlled in an organization.
4. Review five types of control management activities.
5. Explain why control systems sometimes fail.

"Control? What a word! Who wants to be controlled by others? Freedom is far more important than control. Nobody really wants 'big brother' to be watching over them!"

What is your reaction to the above attitude? At first glance, it may sound reasonable. Few people seem to enjoy the feeling of being controlled, especially by someone standing over them and checking their every move. The process of control, therefore, can easily be perceived by organizational members as a negative activity. Many managers feel so strongly about the word *control* that they even avoid it in ordinary conversation, preferring instead to employ the expression *monitor*. However, as we'll soon see, organizations are unlikely to attain their goals and objectives with any degree of consistency without some form of reasonable controls.

What is the Nature of Control?

Controlling is a function of management that can seldom be separated from planning. In fact, some sort of means for monitoring or ensuring that activities are moving in the desired direction should be developed during planning activities.

What Is the Controlling Function?

Controlling: *The regular and systematic comparing of actual results with planned objectives.*

Results don't always work out the way we originally planned, do they? Establishing sound control systems might help us improve our track records. **Controlling** can be defined as a set of activities involving the regular and systematic comparison of ***actual results*** with ***planned objectives*** to determine whether goals are being accomplished or if corrections must be made.

Feedforward control: *Anticipating deviations from planned objectives or standards and making modifications before a deviation takes place.*

The best types of controls are *preventive* and involve a process termed *feedforward control.* **Feedforward control** attempts to anticipate deviations from planned objectives or standards for the purpose of modifying activities and procedures *before* a deviation actually takes place. For example, assume that you are a department manager in a clothing store that is scheduled to have a gigantic three-day sale on Thursday, Friday, and Saturday of this week. You anticipate that sales in your department should reach about 145 percent of normal. As a result of looking forward to obtain the information about additional sales, you realize that you will need more money to make change for customers who make purchases. Therefore, you do not wait until you discover a shortage of change during the sale to obtain additional change; you obtain the cash in advance. You are controlling the situation before a problem occurs.

All deviations, unfortunately, can't be anticipated in advance, so another common method of controlling is *corrective* in nature.

Termed **feedback control,** it involves developing an action plan for *returning* conditions to previously established standards. For example, if you discover that a deviation from planned objectives has taken place because of a piece of equipment malfunctioning, you may have to revise your original goals.

Feedback control: *Returning conditions to previously established standards after a deviation has taken place.*

Controlling, therefore, is an activity that helps supervisors recognize when there are obstacles in the way of achieving their objectives. When you are controlling, you are attempting to make certain that activities for which you are responsible are proceeding as planned.

The control function may appear clearer by recognizing that there are three basic steps involved in the controlling function:

1. Setting standards of performance
2. Comparing actual results with preestablished control standards
3. Taking preventive or corrective action, where necessary, to ensure that actual performance meets original standards

What Is the Relationship Between Controlling and Planning?

The controlling and planning functions are closely related. Let's look at an example that can help illustrate this relationship. Assume that you are managing a bicycle sales and service shop, and that last year you established a developmental goal for increasing sales of new bicycles by 15 percent each month, a figure that becomes your *control standard.* Let's also assume that you formulated an action plan for achieving your sales objective. Periodically, perhaps weekly or monthly, you monitor your actual sales results to see if your preestablished sales objectives have been met.

By regularly comparing actual sales (a control activity) with previously established sales goals or standards (plans), you are able to realize that certain types of corrective action may have to be taken. If actual performance is below your control standard—that is, sales are below your estimates—obstacles will have to be removed in order to meet your objectives. Perhaps you will step up your advertising and sales promotion activities. You might even decide that your original objectives were unrealistic and decide to revise your sales estimates downward.

What Is the Supervisor's Role in the Controlling Process?

You, as a supervisor, play a key role in the controlling process. The failure to perform your controlling responsibilities effectively could mean that your department's (and thus your organization's) goals and objectives will not be accomplished.

Your role in the controlling process is fairly easy to verbalize, but it is not always so easily carried out. Your primary controlling responsibility is to monitor actual results and compare them with intended goals and objectives (control standards). You must then correct deviations, if any, from the standards.

Supervisors play a key role in the controlling process and attempt to ensure that departmental and organizational goals are accomplished.

Supervisors, of course, have egos. Having to change plans may imply that they were not well formulated to begin with. Being pressed into admitting that mistakes were made after considerable time and company resources have been expended can be damaging to a supervisor's self-image. Some supervisors, rather than alter the direction of their activities or honestly admitting that they made an error, have forged ahead with their plans, thus causing profits and employee morale to sag.

How Are Control Standards Developed?

The Marriott Corporation has consistently operated one of the most profitable international hotel chains. Its success has been attributed to high standards of employee performance. Employees receive extensive training, and control standards are well developed. Chambermaids, for example, are given a checklist of over 70 tasks to perform in each room (even dusting the Gideon Bible located in each dresser). Marriott seems to have found that the secret of hostelry success resides in the establishment of sound control standards.

What actually are *control standards*? Who establishes them? How much tolerance, or deviation, is allowable? Where does control-standard information come from? Should employees be involved in developing control standards? The answers to these questions will be our major concern in the section that follows.

What Are Control Standards?

Supervisors are usually responsible for ensuring that control standards are met. What actually are *control standards*? **Control standards** are defined as *predetermined goals and objectives that are expected to be met.* They may be expressed in terms of employee performance, units of production, meters, inches, percentages, dollar sales volume, and virtually anything that can be readily counted.

Control standards: *Predetermined goals and objectives that are expected to be met.*

Who Establishes Control Standards?

Control standards are derived from a variety of sources. The accounting department, for example, may develop expense account standards for managers and salespeople. Quality assurance inspectors may establish standards of quality for produced goods. The personnel department may establish standards of acceptable rates of absenteeism. All levels of management—senior through first-line—may be involved in setting control standards. In many instances, employees, too, are asked to assist in developing control standards.

What Is Tolerance?

How accurate do control standards have to be? Is there any room for variation? If so, how much deviation from 100 percent adherence is allowable? These are questions that have to be answered when developing control standards.

The allowable leeway or deviation from a control standard is termed **tolerance.** In some products there is substantial leeway. In the construction of houses—installing plaster board, for example—there would typically be far greater tolerance, of course, than in the production of a space shuttle. Plaster board to be attached to vertical wooden studs may be acceptable within an inch or more tolerance, since moldings are typically attached later to cover any gaps in the plaster board. However, an inch variation in the production of a component for a space shuttle could prove disastrous. Space shuttle *Challenger,* which exploded after takeoff in January 1986, was poignant proof of the need for more stringent control standards in the aerospace industry. Producers of parts and components for the construction of precision equipment and instruments usually strive for what is referred to as **zero defects (ZD),** a result that means *without flaws or errors.*

Tolerance: *The allowable leeway or deviation from a control standard.*

Zero defects (ZD): *A production control standard concept that strives to achieve no flaws or errors (i.e., zero tolerance).*

Where Does Control Information Come From?

Control standards are developed from information that comes from a variety of sources. Some of the more common methods for developing control standards involve:

1. Utilizing past experience.
2. Analyzing production factors.
3. Wishful thinking.
4. External factors.

Let's look briefly at each factor.

Utilizing Past Experience. Experience can be a useful guide in establishing control standards. Observing how many units of an item were previously produced per employee each week might be an indication of what quantities can be produced in the future. When past experience is used to establish future standards, however, you should ascertain that the previous level of production was not unreasonably low, and that factors such as technological advances have not made earlier production levels out of date.

Analyzing Production Factors. The numerous factors that go into the production process influence the development of control standards. A careful examination of factors such as *employee skill level, working conditions,* and the *level of technology* can provide useful information for determining standards.

"Perhaps, sire, we should be seeking quality rather than quantity."

Wishful Thinking. Some supervisors set standards based on wishful thinking rather than reality. The figure 25 percent, for example, may seem ideal to Harold, a sales supervisor, so he arbitrarily establishes a standard of a 25 percent increase in sales for all territories for the forthcoming year based primarily on high hopes. Or let's assume that a .05 percent scrap rate has a magical ring to Zelda, a department manager, so she sets a standard based merely on wishes and hopes, not reality. Standards that are unrealistic and virtually impossible to attain often discourage, and even demotivate, employees who try without success to meet excessively high standards.

External Factors. A variety of external factors, such as current economic conditions, can also influence control standards. For example, standards of productive output that are higher than the market can absorb could result in unsold inventories; attempting to meet stiff production standards when the labor market cannot provide sufficient quantities of skilled employees could also frustrate the best-intentioned efforts; or a tight money market with excessively high interest rates could discourage the purchase of badly needed replacement equipment, thus adversely affecting standards. Therefore, information from relevant portions of the general economy, as well as the impact of domestic and foreign competition on operations, should also be considered when establishing standards.

Why Is Control Sharing Important?

A continual emphasis is made in this text on the importance of drawing on the input of your employees in decision making and problem solving. We've already discussed such methods as brainstorming, the Delphi method, and force-field analysis as ways of utilizing the ideas of employees. Chapter 12 also discusses various leadership styles and techniques and explains how a participative style tends to create an environment that *motivates* employees. The need for employee involvement whenever possible cannot be overstressed, especially in planning, setting goals, and establishing control standards. **Control sharing,** that is, involving employees wherever possible in the development of control standards, can make the attainment of your goals a far easier task.

Control sharing: *Involving employees wherever possible in developing control standards.*

What Are The Major Areas of Supervisory Control?

What areas should be controlled in an organization? The answer to this question varies with the organization and the industry. In general, however, there are certain critical areas that most managers are concerned with. These areas include the following:

- Inventory control
- Production control
- Cost control
- Safety control
- Human resource control
- Time control

In an upcoming chapter, Chapter 16, we'll examine the concept of discipline and how it also serves to control, or influence, employee behavior.

What Is Inventory Control?

Inventory control: *Balancing the need to have materials on hand with the costs of purchasing, handling, and storing such materials.*

Inventory control, as can be viewed in Figure 5–1, is a system of balancing the need to have materials on hand with the costs of purchasing, handling, and storing such items. In larger companies there may be a materials manager whose full-time job involves controlling inventories. In smaller firms supervisors may be responsible for ensuring that critical items are available as needed.

Inventory control involves maintaining accurate records of existing inventories of materials and stocks used in the production process or for resale to others. Controlling inventories, of course, requires a sound system for anticipating future needs. In short, the basic objectives of inventory control are:

1. To maintain sufficient quantities of materials on hand to meet production needs.
2. To avoid tying up capital in unneeded inventory.

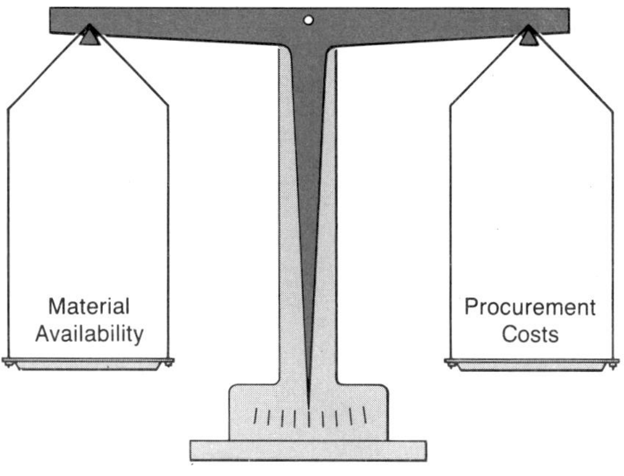

FIGURE 5–1
Inventory Control—Balancing the Need for Materials on Hand with Procurement Costs.

Automobile assembly plants, for example, occasionally have had to curtail operations because of insufficient quantities of engines available for installation in manufactured automobile chassis. Shutdowns resulting from insufficient materials or supplies can be costly for any type of organization.

Likewise, carrying unneeded inventory—that is, maintaining more parts and supplies than are necessary—is expensive and results in added expense for storage facilities, insurance, pilferage, and obsolescence. Shutdowns due to shortages or carrying excessive inventories may result from either ineffective planning or controlling.

A logical objective of inventory control, therefore, is to attempt to avoid maintaining either too much or too little inventory on hand. To combat this problem, an increasingly popular inventory control system is **JIT (just-in-time).** JIT utilizes sophisticated computer systems and effective planning and control procedures for the purpose of improving the flow of information between suppliers and the purchasers of inventory. A "hand-to-mouth" approach to inventory control, JIT involves purchasing materials from vendors under a prearranged delivery schedule so that parts or supplies arrive *just in time* to be used by the purchaser. Ideally, there will be a less than 24-hour storage period, which would result in shifting storage costs to the vendor.

JIT (just-in-time): *Purchasing materials from vendors under a prearranged delivery schedule so that parts or supplies arrive just in time to be used by the purchaser.*

What Is Production Control?

Another area of control is termed **production control.** In theory, the term means making sure that everything in the production process is done correctly. In practice, however, machines occasionally break down, workers become sick or go on strike, or critical materials become scarce. Production control is one of the most significant of all control activities, because the quantity and quality of finished products (and, therefore, the long-run success of any firm) result from how well materials, machines, and labor have been coordinated into a smooth-flowing production process.

Production control: *A set of procedures for coordinating materials, machines, and labor into a smooth-flowing production process.*

Managers generally apply five types of controls to the production process (see Figure 5–2), which are:

1. Planning
2. Routing
3. Scheduling
4. Dispatching
5. Inspection

Planning. We're back, once again, with our old friend *planning.* **Production planning** is the first significant step in production control. Assume, for example, that your firm just received a hefty order for an item that is produced in your department. Plans should be made related to materials, machines, and labor. Do you have ample materials on hand or will you have to obtain some? Can your existing employees work overtime for awhile or will you need

Production planning: *Determining future needs and activities for the purpose of making optimum use of materials, labor, and facilities.*

FIGURE 5–2
Types of Production Process Controls

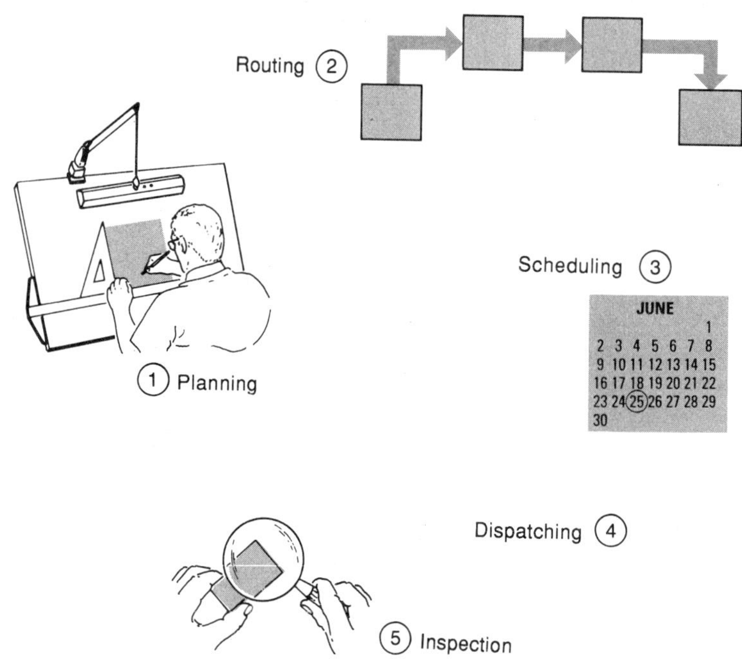

to hire additional workers? If the former, have sufficient funds been budgeted to cover overtime labor costs? Does your department have ample capacity to handle the new order, or will some tasks have to be "farmed out" to job shops or subcontractors? Will you be able to utilize the CAD/CAM process (discussed in Chapter 3) in designing and manufacturing the product? Effective planning, as you can imagine, is an essential first step as a means of making optimum use of costly and limited resources.

Routing. You've undoubtedly observed those who deliver mail and newspapers making their daily rounds. If so, you should already have a general idea of what *production routing* is in the production-control process. In manufacturing, determining the best sequence of operation is the next step after the decision has been made regarding what resources will be needed to produce a product. **Production routing** is described as the order, or sequence, in which various operations are performed throughout a department or a plant. It shows the *path* that products will take, indicating *where* each phase of the production process will occur.

Production routing: *Determining the order, or sequence, in which various operations are performed throughout a plant.*

Scheduling. When deciding which classes you are going to take at school, you are, in a sense, involved with the next step in production control—*production scheduling.* You realize, of course, that you can't sign up for two classes that both meet at 7:00 on Monday evenings. Nor would you ordinarily want to schedule a five-hour gap between two separate classes that meet on the same day. Scheduling classes has its parallel in manufacturing. **Production scheduling** involves setting up specific timetables that show *when* each operation in the manufacturing process will take place and *how long* each will take to complete.

Production scheduling: *Setting up timetables showing when and how long each operation in the production process should take.*

Accurate *timing* is critical in manufacturing. Imagine, for example, the assembly operations for a product such as refrigerators. Without sound scheduling, workers who install food racks and trays inside the units might have to stand idly by while waiting for the enamel to dry on the surfaces of the refrigerators.

Dispatching. The previous step pointed out the need for developing accurate schedules. Now comes **production dispatching,** the step that attempts to *carry out* the established schedule. The activity of dispatching involves issuing specific orders and instructions to department members regarding *when work on a job is to begin, what machines are to be used,* and *which materials and tools are to be made available for the job.*

Production dispatching: *Providing information to workers regarding when work on a job is to begin, what machines are to be used, and which materials and tools are to be made available.*

Inspection and Quality Control. The final step in production control procedures is termed **production inspection.** This activity is one of the most critical of all control activities. Good planning, routing, scheduling, and dispatching won't guarantee that the production process is trouble free. A machine may break down, a worker may become ill or have an accident, the quality of raw materials may be below par, or a job order may have been misplaced. Any number of problems may—and frequently do—creep into the production process. This is why there has to be a *follow up*—an inspection—of production sequences and operations to ensure that scheduling and quality standards have been met.

Production inspection: *Following up production sequences and operations to make certain that scheduling and quality standards have been met.*

A product may be inspected at any phase of the production cycle to determine whether or not it meets the established quality standards. This activity is termed **quality control.** If the product fails to meet standards, it may be either modified or rejected. Inspection is costly and is typically performed on a *spot* or *sample* basis. Spot inspections, of course, don't guarantee that all flaws in the production process will be discovered. Some firms stress high quality and *100 percent inspection* in the production of their products. Many managers feel that 100 percent quality is especially important in a JIT environment.

Quality control: *A part of the inspection process intended to determine if the product meets the established standards of quality; may be on a sample (spot) or a 100 percent basis.*

What Is Cost Control?

"Why should *I* worry? It's not *my* money." These words express a far too common attitude among some employees in organizations, especially those whose work environments include inadequate **cost control** plans or programs.

Cost control: *A systematic activity intended to ensure that actual financial outlays are in line with projected expenditures.*

Controlling costs ranks among the most critical supervisory responsibilities. The current and future objectives of your organization—whether it is a private firm or a government agency—will be difficult to achieve without cost consciousness coupled with a deliberate effort to keep costs within reasonable bounds. Costs affect an organization's profit, or surplus. Less surplus is enjoyed by the organization whose costs are out of line. Smaller surpluses mean less money available for distributing to owners (if a private firm) or for providing public services (if a governmental agency).

More important to employees, excessive costs likewise mean less funds available for wages and benefits, as well as for reinvestment in better tools, equipment, and facilities that can make employees' jobs easier and more productive. Furthermore, performing well in the area of cost control can enhance employees' advancement opportunities. A reduction in costs, therefore, can be as effective in increasing profits as an increase in sales, and frequently is easier to accomplish.

Cost Consciousness versus Cost Foolishness. An old cliché, "penny wise and dollar foolish," suggests that managers have not always been prudent in their efforts at reducing excessive costs. This saying can be applied to attitudes and activities that result in false economies.

For example, let's assume that a sales supervisor, Gerald, informs his outside sales staff that their expenses must be reduced. In order to comply with Gerald's directive, Courtney, a sales representative, decides to reduce parking expenses by looking for free spaces or parking meters rather than a more expensive garage. Courtney, therefore, cruises around town for up to 20 minutes searching for low-cost spots. After she finally locates one, she discovers that she has to walk an additional 10 minutes or so to get to her customer's premises. Courtney then becomes fidgety during her sales presentation, worrying about the parking meter expiring. After all this, Courtney isn't likely to be in top form when she finally meets with her prospect; she has also wasted about 25 minutes.

A Regular Part of the Goal-Setting Process. Cost awareness and cost reduction should not be activities that take place solely by chance. They should be made an integral part of the goal-setting activities discussed in the previous chapter. A major supervisory challenge is identifying those areas that need cost reduction. Typical areas that require attention are:

1. Labor costs.
2. Maintenance and repair costs.
3. Waste, rejected and defective products, scrap, and theft.
4. Supplies (rags, pencils, diskettes, photocopying, etc.).
5. Utilities (heat, light, phone, and power).

As with any plan, you should establish realistic and attainable objectives related to cost control, outline the steps or action plan necessary to achieve your objectives, and be certain to determine target dates for achieving your cost goals.

Get Employees Involved and Committed. Employees should be encouraged to realize that cost awareness is an ongoing process and not an on-again, off-again set of activities. Employees will be far more committed to a philosophy of cost awareness if they are involved in the process of developing cost standards. Inform employees of your areas of cost concern. Let them know how much your department spends each month on such items as telephone calls, photocopying, and faxing. Make certain that your employees are aware of control standards and techniques for reducing costs. Include their cost-cutting results as a part of their periodic performance and salary reviews. Make an effort to present cost awareness or reduction programs in a *positive* rather than a *punitive* or *negative* manner. In short, *make employees responsible for keeping costs in line.* Utilize the *control-sharing concept* wherever possible. For example, some companies like Xerox and Tennant have employees chart their defect rates and set goals for the workers to reduce them.[1]

Employees who aren't convinced of the need for cost consciousness may perceive cost-reduction programs as a farce, especially when such efforts have been sporadic in the past. A fairly common employee attitude in such cases is, "Here we go again for our annual cost-cutting lecture!" To overcome such preset notions, attempt to stress to employees how *they,* as well as their organization, can benefit from cost-reducing activities. We've already discussed some of the benefits to employees of realistic costs.

What Is Safety Control?

According to a report from the Congressional Office of Technology and Assessment (OTA), each year:

1. Nearly 10,000 U.S. workers are killed on the job.
2. More than 11 million occupational injuries occur that require medical attention or restrict work activity.
3. More than 2 million injuries occur that are serious enough to lead to lost work time.
4. More than 25 million workers are exposed to toxic substances on the job.[2]

The above statistics help to point out another area of concern to supervisors—**safety control,** an activity that involves establishing safety standards and then monitoring the standards as a means of preventing and reducing accident frequency and severity. Supervisors should continually attempt to instill in their employees a safety attitude.

Safety control: *Establishing and monitoring safety standards to prevent and reduce accident frequency and severity.*

Get the Message Across. Employees, in order to avoid costly and disabling accidents, need to be *safety conscious.* They should be taught to understand the nature and use of safety equipment. Rules regarding the use of safety equipment, such as face masks, goggles, and hard hats, should be consistently enforced. Unfortunately, the safety programs in some organizations involve little more than tacking up accident prevention posters throughout the work areas. Posters certainly are better than nothing, but after a while they seem to become a part of the woodwork and are hardly noticed, somewhat like the cautionary statement printed on each package of cigarettes.

How can you get the safety message across to employees? Among the more commonly used methods for raising employee safety consciousness are:

1. Providing employees with safety orientation and training programs
2. Distributing informational leaflets
3. Scheduling regular interdepartmental meetings
4. Showing accident-prevention films and videos
5. Providing recognition to individuals with good safety records
6. Encouraging employees to assist in establishing safety standards
7. Permitting employees to administer safety rules, including disciplinary action

Safety and accident prevention programs should be administered regularly. Employees need a continual reminder of the necessity for safe work habits. You can often motivate employees into following sound safety practices by setting a good example yourself.

OSHA May Be Watching. An act that became effective in early 1971, the **Occupational Safety and Health Act (OSHA),** requires organizations to provide employees with safe and healthful working conditions. As a result, you should be aware that supervisors may

Occupational Safety and Health Act (OSHA): *A 1971 act that requires organizations to provide their employees with safe and healthful working conditions.*

Employees have the legal right to know about on-the-job hazards. The OSHA Hazard Communication Standard requires employers to identify hazardous substances that they produce, distribute, or use.

be held legally responsible for their employees' infractions of safety regulations.

Workers' Compensation Laws. **Workers' compensation laws** are found nationwide in the United States and provide financial indemnification for any employee who is injured or contracts a disease (including mental illness) in a job-related activity. Benefits are also paid to a spouse or child of a worker killed on the job. Once again, you—the supervisor—have a heavy responsibility related to workers' compensation laws since workers' compensation insurance premiums, paid by your employer, are affected by three major factors:

Workers' compensation laws: *Statutes that provide financial benefits to employees unable to work because of physical injuries, disease, or mental disorders caused by job-related conditions.*

- The employer's accident claim rate
- The extent of hazard or risk inherent in the job
- The size of the employer's payroll

You, as supervisor, can especially influence the first two factors.

What Is Human Resource Control?

Employee turnover, grievances, absenteeism, tardiness, accidents, substance abuse, and theft are all examples of areas of **human resource control.** Supervisors should establish effective control standards and continually monitor employee performance related to such standards. Corrective and disciplinary action should be taken, when necessary, as a means of maintaining standards. Employees should likewise be encouraged to participate in the development and enforcement of controlling activities wherever possible.

Human resource control: *Establishing and monitoring standards related to employee performance and behavior, such as absenteeism, theft, and accidents.*

What Is Time Control?

Time control is another activity that demands the careful attention of supervisors. Time, of course, is a scarce and valuable resource. For example, customers expect to receive their orders on the date promised. Likewise, employees are expected to make effective use of their own time on the job. Supervisors, too, must manage their own time so that they are optimizing their efforts. The next chapter explores in greater depth the important topic of time and activities management for supervisors.

Time control: *Monitoring time-related activities for the purpose of improving effectiveness in the use of time.*

What Control Systems Can Be Used?

There are a host of management tools that can assist supervisors in their control management activities. Five well-known devices are discussed here. They are:

1. Budgets
2. Work distribution charts
3. Gantt charts
4. PERT
5. Project management software programs

What Are Budgets?

Budget:
Typically a financial plan that allocates operation funds for a particular period of time; serves as a control device for providing feedback.

A **budget** is typically a financial plan that allocates operation funds for a particular period of time. Budgets serve as control devices for providing feedback. Budgets also exist for other factors, such as time, material resources, and labor. They may be expressed in physical units as well as in financial terms.

Various departments in an organization are usually allocated specific amounts of funds related to their expected output or activities. Budgets may include detailed information for labor costs, materials, operating supplies, utilities, or any operating expense item. At the end of the budgetary period, actual expenses are compared with budgeted expenses. Supervisors may be expected to justify or correct any deviations from the original budget.

What Are Work Distribution Charts?

Work distribution charts:
A control device that aids the supervisor in assigning and controlling employee work assignments.

Another control tool used by many managers are **work distribution charts,** which are control devices that aid the supervisor in assigning and controlling employee work assignments. As can be observed in Figure 5–3, a supervisor is able to see at a glance what tasks have been assigned to which employees. The form does not, however, provide feedforward or feedback information related to how effectively each employee is performing.

What Are Gantt Charts?

Gantt charts:
A planning and controlling tool that utilizes a bar graph format for graphically representing the time relationships among the various tasks involved in a production plan.

A commonly used tool for planning and controlling activities are **Gantt charts,** which were developed during World War I by Henry L. Gantt. They are especially useful for charting production tasks. They utilize a bar graph format for presenting the time relationships among the various tasks involved in a production plan and can be an aid to utilizing people and equipment.

Figure 5–4 illustrates a Gantt chart. Let's assume that four separate jobs have recently been assigned to your department. Let's also assume that each job is expected to take five full working days to complete.

FIGURE 5–3
An Example of a Work Distribution Chart

Tasks	Hours/ Task	Allocation of Tasks to Each Employee (per week)					
		Olsen	Washington	Levy	Chong	Garcia	Watanabe
Switchboard	40	15			10	10	5
Word processing	40			10		15	15
Payroll	30		10		20		
Bookkeeping	50		30	5	10		5
Mail processing	45	10		25			10
Filing	35	15				15	5
Total	240	40	40	40	40	40	40

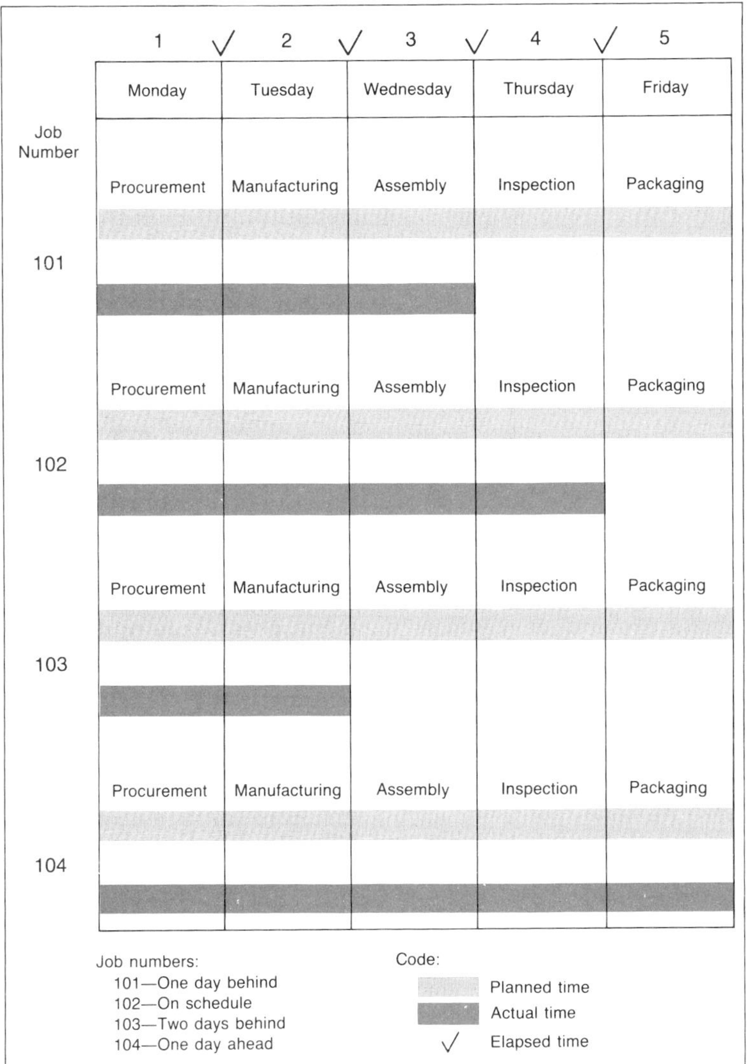

FIGURE 5–4
An Example of a Gantt Chart

The darker bar indicates the *planned* time for each job, in this case five days. The lighter bar is filled in daily and indicates the progress that has *actually* been made on each job. For example, assume that currently you are at the end of the working day on Thursday, indicated by the fourth check mark. (A check mark indicates elapsed time in days.) Note that job 101, as illustrated by the solid bar, is one day behind schedule. It should have progressed through the inspection stage, but has only reached the assembly stage. Job 102 is precisely on schedule, job 103 is two days behind schedule, and job 104 is one day ahead of schedule.

The Gantt chart is an uncomplicated way of providing feedback to the supervisor regarding the progress of each job, thus encouraging him or her to make corrective action on those jobs that are behind schedule. For example, as a means of equalizing the production flow through the department, some workers could be diverted from job 104, which is one day ahead of schedule, to jobs 101 and 103, which are each behind schedule.

What Is PERT?

PERT (program evaluation and review technique): *A planning and control technique for graphically presenting the time and paths that events take in the production process.*

PERT is another well-known management tool that assists in the planning and controlling of production operations. **PERT (program evaluation and review technique)** is a technique for graphically presenting the *amount of time* that activities are likely to take to accomplish events during the production process. PERT shows projects broken down into *planned events,* and goes beyond Gantt by showing the path that events will take during the production process and the estimated completion time that activities will take to accomplish events.

Events in a production process could occur sequentially (i.e., one event following another) or, as frequently occurs, certain events may take place simultaneously, which could save total production time. For example, visualize your morning breakfast table. Eating breakfast first and then reading the newspaper would require more time than if you simultaneously ate breakfast while reading the newspaper (assuming, of course, that your spouse didn't take your favorite section!).

A PERT flow chart should make the process clearer. Figure 5–5 illustrates a PERT network for a project that has 10 steps, or events, in its production process. Each encircled number symbolizes the

FIGURE 5–5
An Example of a PERT Network

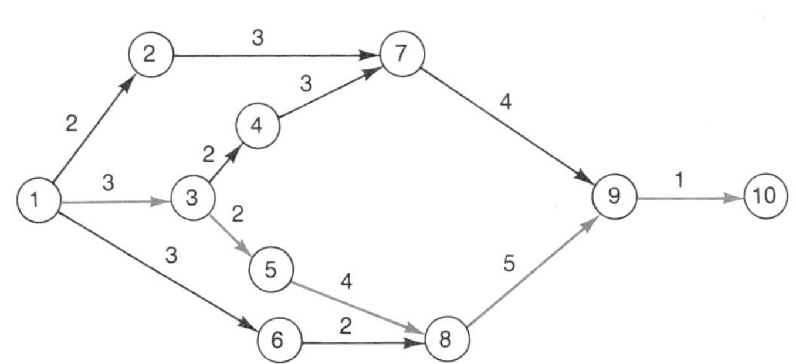

Project Path	Completion Time	Total Time
1→2→7→9→10	2+3+4+1	10 days
1→3→4→7→9→10	3+2+3+4+1	13 days
1→3→5→8→9→10	3+2+4+5+1	15 days
1→6→8→9→10	3+2+5+1	11 days

Codes
Encircled number = Events
Open number = Activity time to accomplish event
1—3—5—8—9—10 = Critical path

event that must take place. The smaller numbers between each event represent activity time, that is, the planned number of days each event will need to be completed.

The path that takes the most days in the illustration, 1–3–5–8–9–10 (15 days), is termed the *critical path.* It is the path that would have to be shortened if it were necessary to complete the project in less time than originally scheduled. A PERT network, therefore, is another useful tool that enables a supervisor to monitor the flow of production and to make corrections if an event begins to slip behind its planned schedule or an improvement in scheduled time is desired.

What Are Project Management Software Programs?

The use of computers in decision making was discussed in Chapter 3. They are also extensively used in project management. **Project management software programs** consist of computer applications that can assist managers who are responsible for projects involving planning, organizing, and controlling time, costs, and activity relationships. Some years ago, project management software was designed mostly for large computer mainframes. The popularity of PCs and workstations, however, motivated computer programmers to develop project management software.

Project management software programs: *Computer applications designed to assist management in planning and controlling activities.*

Software applications are available commercially for virtually all of the control systems discussed in this chapter. Customized software is sometimes developed for specific operations. Managers with access to either large mainframe computers or microcomputers often find it convenient to utilize various types of software for developing budgets, work distributions charts, Gantt charts, and PERT networks.

A number of factors should be considered when selecting project management software. *Need* should be your primary consideration—a lot of software gathers nothing but dust while stored indefinitely and left unused on shelves. A second factor is the *cost* of the software related to its *benefits*—some types of projects might be developed more quickly with a calculator, a pencil, and some paper. A third factor relates to whether you or your associates have, or can acquire, the necessary *training* to put it to practical use—employees with no computer background can find some software programs extremely complex and confusing. However, when put to practical use, project computer software programs can offer substantial benefits to your planning and controlling activities.

Why Do Control Systems Sometimes Fail?

A major challenge when developing control systems is deciding to what degree controls should be imposed. Monitoring activities—that is, observing operations, collecting data, and reporting on activities and things—can consume inordinate amounts of a supervisor's time. In general, more monitoring is required with tighter controls. Excessively loose controls, however, make attaining objectives less likely.

When Are Controls Too Tight or Too Loose?

Ideally, controls should only exist when they lead to improved quality, performance, and benefits that outweigh the costs of implementing the control activities. Exceedingly tight controls can lead to counterproductive results. First, they can be *costly,* because of all the time and labor spent developing and maintaining them. Second, they can lead to *poor morale,* since employees may resent what appears to be a "big brother" atmosphere and a lack of trust. And third, a tightly controlled atmosphere tends to *restrict creativity*; innovation typically thrives in relatively less-structured environments.

Excessively loose controls, on the other hand, also have their shortcomings. For example, *deadlines are more likely to be missed* and *quality to slip* if loose controls create a "what difference does it make?" atmosphere. Further, loose controls can result in *poorer coordination of the various work units and departments* in an organization, since each may be oblivious to what the other is doing.

Developing the right blend of controls, therefore, is really like performing a balancing act, as illustrated in Figure 5–6, and depends to some extent on the organizational culture that exists in the firm. In some organizations, especially where there is a climate of trust, tight controls help to create a strong *esprit de corps.* In others, the same types of controls could lead to chaos, possibly even an employee walkout.

How Much Reporting Is Necessary?

Control devices should be reevaluated regularly and simplified whenever possible. Excessive reporting requirements can demoralize the attitudes of many high-achieving employees who feel that they are wasting their time preparing seemingly redundant and useless reports. For example, this author is acquainted with a sales representative named Rick, who continually complained about the numerous reports he had to prepare and mail to his division office each evening. There was one report that particularly irritated Rick because it required the same type of information asked for on another form. I suggested to Rick that he confront his manager about the duplication. Rick did, and his manager eliminated one of the reports.

Excessive reporting requirements can also be disastrous when they obscure information that is actually needed. A handy rule of thumb is that information should be reported only when it is likely to require someone's attention.

How Do Benefits Compare with Costs?

The control function is costly in terms of activity and time. Any proposed control device should be carefully evaluated in terms of

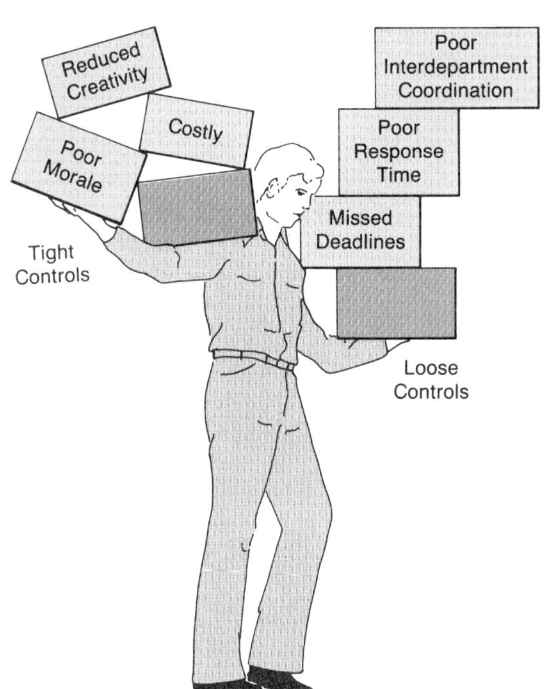

FIGURE 5–6
Effective Control Is a Balancing Act between Tight and Loose Control Activities

costs and benefits. For example, there is a real need to reevaluate a control program when service representatives must spend so much time preparing reports that they have insufficient time left to service customers adequately. Generally speaking, the tighter the controls, the costlier the control system. Modern computerized information systems, however, can reduce the cost of generating data and information.

Are Control Standards Accurate?

Control standards are more likely to be accepted by employees who have had the opportunity to participate in their development. However, one of the inherent dangers of employee-developed standards is that they sometimes are related more to hope than to reality. Employees may misinterpret the reasons for control standards. Standards may be perceived as a form of *speedup,* a management scheme for extracting more work for the same money, and perhaps with fewer employees. Supervisors who enlist the assistance of their employees in developing control standards should be certain to convince employees of their true merits. Supervisors should also attempt to ensure that any standards, whether set by employees or by management, are realistic, useful, and attainable.

Are Control Standards Up to Date?

Control systems based on out-of-date facts and information are also doomed to failure. Control systems should continually be reevaluated in light of changing conditions and new production processes to make certain that they relate directly to present realities and not primarily to past history.

Summary

Controlling is an important management function, one closely related to planning. Controlling involves systematically comparing actual results with planned objectives to determine if activities are on target or, instead, in need of modification.

Control standards are goals and objectives that are expected to be met by organizational members. Most standards allow for some *tolerance.* Standards may be developed by virtually any level of management. In larger organizations, staff specialists aid in the development of control standards. Information for control standards may be derived from *reviewing past experience, analyzing production factors,* and *engaging in wishful thinking. Sharing* the development of control standards *with employees* tends to motivate them into meeting standards.

The major areas of control activities that many supervisors are concerned with are *inventory control, production control, cost control, safety control, employee performance control,* and *time control.*

A wide variety of control systems are utilized by managers in organizations and include *budgets, work distribution charts, Gantt charts, PERT,* and *project management software programs.*

Control systems sometimes fail when they are extremely *tight* or *loose,* when they demand *excessive reporting,* when their *costs outweigh benefits,* when *standards are based on inaccurate information,* and when controls are *out of date.*

Questions for Discussion

1. What is *controlling*? Why is it typically considered inseparable from *planning?*
2. Why might some people react negatively to the word *control*? Do you agree with such feelings? Explain.
3. How do controls with *feedforward* differ from those with *feedback*?
4. What are *control standards*? How are they expressed? Who establishes them?
5. Evaluate the following statement: "As a supervisor, you play a small part in the controlling process. Almost everything that happens in controlling is actually governed by senior management."

6. What determines the amount of *tolerance* acceptable in a control standard?
7. What is the purpose of *inventory control*?
8. Describe the *five types of controls* associated with the production process.
9. Evaluate the following statement: "When we're talking about cost control, we mean you have to eliminate or reduce every expense you can."
10. Why, in addition to a humanitarian concern for the health and safety of employees, is it considered good business to *minimize accident frequency* on the job?
11. What is the major purpose of *budgets*?
12. How can *work distribution charts* aid supervisors?
13. What is the purpose of *Gantt charts*?
14. What is the purpose of *PERT*?
15. What should determine the *tightness* or *looseness* of control systems?

Can You Define These Terms?

Instructions: Write a definition for each of the following terms. You may check your definitions with those provided in the end-of-text glossary.

controlling
feedforward control
feedback control
tolerance
zero defects (ZD)
control sharing
inventory control
JIT (just-in-time)
production control
production planning
production routing
production scheduling
production dispatching
production inspection
quality control
cost control
safety control
Occupational Safety and Health Act (OSHA)
worker's compensation laws
time control
human resource control
budget
work distribution charts
Gantt charts
PERT (program evaluation and review technique)
program management software programs

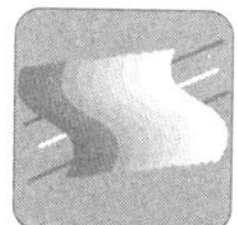

Supervision In Action

5–1 Wanted—Time Standards

Mike Marrero is a nonworking supervisor in the production department of the Equinox Company. Although they believe him to be competent, most of the personnel in his department feel that Marrero has never seemed particularly happy since he became a supervisor about two years ago. Marrero regularly takes his troubles home with him. His wife, Maria, frequently hears him complain about how poorly organized management is. On one occasion he said to her, "Maria, I'm not too sure about this supervision business. Sure, we get a little more money, but as supervisor, I get it from all sides. I'm not supposed to get too close to my workers—people I've known for years—but yet those jerks upstairs don't really accept me as one of them either. They expect me to be concerned about costs, yet they never give me any cost information. Any information I get I have to find out on my own. I don't think that management confides in any supervisors that came up through the ranks of workers."

This morning, LaVonne Lattimore, a cost accountant with Equinox, telephoned Marrero and asked him to come up to her office at 9:30 A.M. The following conversation took place during their meeting:

Lattimore: Good morning, Marrero. Please sit down. Would you like a cup of coffee or tea?

Marrero: No thanks, Ms. Lattimore. What did you want to see me about?

Lattimore: We've got a minor problem. You see, technical developments have been taking place so rapidly in our industry, especially since we began using robotics and computer-assisted manufacturing in some operations, that we're having trouble maintaining up-to-date cost information. For example, our salespeople are having a devil of a time bidding competitively for jobs, because they're not exactly sure of costs. We really need some current labor time standards to help us in estimating the cost of jobs. We haven't updated our standards for about three years, and I think we're long overdue. What I'd like you to do, Marrero, is this: Go back to your work area and establish some time standards for each of the various operations in your two departments. Can you get this information back to me by tomorrow morning at 8:30?

Marrero: *Tomorrow morning*? Well, I can try.

Marrero returned to his department and asked his senior worker, Clyde Columbo, to come to his desk.

Marrero: Well, Clyde, the people upstairs are coming down on us again. Guess what they want now? They want to know how long it takes for your group to complete each operation of work that you perform. Will you go back to your workstation and figure out some sort of standard time for performing each of the various operations you go through in the production process? Then I'll make up a nice and neat presentation to give to Lattimore. I've got to have it done and given to her by 8:30 tomorrow morning. She could have at least given us a little more time!

Columbo: What's with those white-collar clowns? I guess they think we're trying to put something over on them. All right, I'll get busy on it now.

Columbo went back to his workstation where he talked with his junior coworker, Helene Hardwicke:

Columbo: Helene, for some reason Clyde asked us to make up some time standards for the various operations we do in this department. I want you to give me some figures for how long it takes to complete each operation. But watch out. I've seen this happen before. If you set the standards too high, we'll always be expected to meet them. Frankly, I think those characters upstairs are just trying to check up on us. If we put out too much work each shift, then we're going to run out of work and be laid off. So be sure you make up some realistic standards.

Hardwicke: I got you, Clyde. I'll have them for you in a few minutes.

About 30 minutes later, Hardwicke handed the new time standards to Columbo, who immediately placed them on Marrero's desk.

Questions

1. What seems to be the problem in this incident?
2. What is your general reaction to the way Lattimore communicated the need for time standards to Marrero? How might it have been improved?
3. Evaluate Marrero's leadership techniques. Should he have established the time standards himself?
4. How would you have handled the situation if you had been Marrero?

5–2 Care to Try This Gantt On for Size?

Examine the simplified Gantt chart worksheet in Figure 5–7. Then select a typical day for planning and controlling your activities. List all your planned activities in the first column on the left. Next, to the right of the activity and under the hours, shade in one square for each 15 minutes of time that you intend to spend on that activity. For example, if you were to spend 30 minutes between 9:30 A.M. and 10:00 A.M. at a meeting, you would write "attending meeting" under the activities column. You would then shade in two squares, each symbolizing 15 minutes.

Questions

1. What is a significant benefit derived from the use of the Gantt worksheet?

2. How could you use the chart as a control device?

FIGURE 5–7
Worksheet for Gantt Analysis

Activities	7:30	8:30	9:30	10:30	11:30	12:30	1:30	2:30	3:30	4:30	5:30	6:30
1.												
2.												
3.												
4.												
5.												
6.												
7.												
8.												
9.												
10.												
11.												
12.												

Endnotes

1. "What America Makes Best," *Fortune* (International Edition), March 28, 1988, p. 52.
2. "Health and Safety," *AFL–CIO News,* July 2, 1988, p. 5; and "Job Safety and Health," *AFL–CIO News,* August 20, 1988, p. 7.

Chapter 6

Managing Time and Activities More Effectively

Time is an asset that all competitors share in common, but the management of time can be one of the decisive elements in success or failure.
—Ralph Cordiner, Executive

Those who make the worst use of their time are the first to complain of its brevity.
—Jean de la Bruyère, French Author

Learning Objectives

When you finish this chapter, you should be able to:

1. Utilize daily and weekly logs to manage time and activities more effectively.
2. Establish priorities to make more effective use of your time.
3. Employ specific planning and organizing tools for improving time management activities.
4. Avoid the typical wasters of a supervisor's time.

"If there were only more hours in the day. I don't seem to be able to get everything done that I want to get done in the time I have. What I need is a 26-hour day!"

Have you ever heard the supervisor who complains of "just not having enough hours in the day?" That's a fairly common gripe of a great number of supervisors. But let's think about it for a moment. How many hours do all of us have in each of our days? That's right, the same number—only 24. So, regardless of how you feel about the number of hours in the day, you're not going to get any more. Therefore, rather than wasting time complaining about not having enough time, what we should be concerned with is how we're going to make *more effective use* of the hours that we do have.

Arthur Brisbane seemed to be on the right track when he said, "Time is the one thing we possess. Our success depends on the use of our time, and its by-product, the odd moment." A major problem with many supervisors isn't that they don't work *hard*; in fact, they may be putting in 15-hour workdays. Their main problem is that they don't work *smart*. To work smarter, managers must learn how to make more effective use of the valuable commodity called *time*. They need to operate more by design than by instinct. The two previous chapters on the topics of planning and controlling relate closely to the subject of time and activity management.

In this chapter, you will have the opportunity to learn ways you can improve the management of your time. You'll start by learning how to analyze the way you have spent your time in the *past*. Doing so can help you improve the *future* use of it. Then you'll examine some of the *typical time stealers* and learn how to cope with them more effectively.

How Have You Been Using Your Time?

Time management: *An activity that involves analyzing activities, setting realistic goals, and coping with potential time wasters to utilize time more effectively.*

Activities management: *Virtually the same as time management.*

Time management, in reality, is **activities management.** The first step in managing your *future* activities more effectively is to analyze your *past* activities. Doing so can enable you to uncover some of your less desirable work habits and patterns. Looking to the recent past can help you decide which activities and behavior should be eliminated, modified, or delegated to others.

Many supervisors have little notion of what they do with their time and are sometimes surprised when they discover where their time actually goes. A method for analyzing your activities is to keep a *daily activities summary log* for at least two weeks and then transfer the information to a *weekly activities summary log*. You then can decide more objectively which activities can be changed or eliminated.

This process, at first glance, may seem like a time devourer in itself. However, it can be likened to investing money in more productive equipment: The benefits can far exceed the additional cost.

Why Maintain a Daily Log?

Let's start out with a method for recording your weekly activities on a daily basis. To do so requires some sort of a **daily activities summary log**—a place where you can record your principal activities each day. You might purchase a small notebook to carry with you, or develop some sort of a form similar to Figure 6–1 (on the next page) that you can keep at your desk or work place. Before you get started, however, you should decide what specific *categories* of activities you'll want to keep track of.

Daily activities summary log: *A time-management tool that can assist supervisors in keeping track of how their time has been expended on a daily basis.*

Each supervisor's position is unique to some degree, but activities common to most supervisory positions include the following:

- Planning and creative work
- Scheduling and assigning work
- Direct supervision
- Inspection
- Routine paperwork
- Using the telephone
- Counseling employees
- Attending meetings
- Unexpected tasks and projects
- Emergencies
- Taking breaks
- Miscellaneous activities

After you've determined what your own typical activities are, you can input them as headings in your own daily activities summary log.

Time can be indicated on the daily activities log in the left column in half-hour intervals. You might want to keep track of 10-minute activity segments. Each 10-minute interval can be recorded by drawing an X or check mark across from the time period and under the appropriate activity. Look again at Figure 6–1 for an illustration of this technique.

For example, let's assume that between 8:00 and 8:30 A.M. you engaged in scheduling and assigning work. You would enter three Xs or check marks on the 8:00 A.M. row under the "scheduling and assigning work" column. If from 8:30 to 8:50 A.M. you attended to an emergency, you would enter two Xs on the 8:30 A.M. row under the "emergencies" column. You still would have one more 10-minute interval within the half-hour block of time to account for, which you would enter under the miscellaneous column. Remember that in our illustration, each X represents 10 minutes. At the end of each day you should add the number of Xs in each column and multiply that number by 10 minutes.

FIGURE 6–1
Daily Activities Summary Log

MONDAY

Time	Planning and creative work	Scheduling and assigning work	Direct supervision	Inspection	Routine paperwork	Using telephone	Counseling	Meetings	Special projects	Emergencies	Taking breaks	Miscellaneous	Remarks
8:00 A.M.		√√√											
8:30 A.M.										√√		√	
9:00 A.M.						√		√√					
9:30 A.M.						√		√			√		
10:00 A.M.					√	√						√	
10:30 A.M.			√√		√								
11:00 A.M.		√				√		√					
11:30 A.M.			√			√						√	
12:00 NOON	LUNCH												
12:30 P.M.													
1:00 P.M.		√√				√							
1:30 P.M.			√	√	√								
2:00 P.M.					√	√				√			
2:30 P.M.					√	√					√		
3:00 P.M.					√			√√					
3:30 P.M.				√		√				√			
4:00 P.M.	√									√		√	
4:30 P.M.													
5:00 P.M.													
Totals	10	60	40	20	60	90		60		50	20	40	= 450 min./Mon.

$7\frac{1}{2}$ hour work day

Why Maintain a Weekly Log?

Weekly activities summary log: *A time-management tool used to summarize daily activities over a week for the purpose of analyzing how effective past utilization of time has been.*

As a supervisor, you ought to keep a daily log for at least two weeks so that you can get a fairly good idea of where your time has gone. After each week of recording your activities, you can summarize the gathered information in a **weekly activities summary log,** such as the one in Figure 6–2 (on the next page). After the two-week period of keeping careful track of your time, you are ready to analyze your past activities.

Why Analyze Past Activities?

You could begin analyzing your summary log by answering the following important questions:

1. Have my daily activities contributed directly to my planned goals and objectives? If not, why not?
2. Am I truly making effective use of my time?

FIGURE 6–2
Weekly Activities Summary Log

	Planning and creative work	Scheduling and assigning work	Direct supervision	Inspection	Routine paperwork	Using telephone	Counseling	Meetings	Special projects	Emergencies	Taking breaks	Miscellaneous	
Monday	10	60	40	20	60	90		60		50	20	40	=450 mins.
Tuesday	10	50	30	20	90	100		70		50		30	=450 mins.
Wednesday	10	60	40	20	80	100		60		60		20	=450 mins.
Thursday	10	50	30	20	90	100		70		50		30	=450 mins.
Friday	10	60	40	20	80	100		60		60		20	=450 mins.
Total mins.	50	280	180	100	400	490		320		270	20	140	=2250 mins.
Average/day	10	56	36	20	80	98		64		54	4	28	
Percentage	2%	13%	8%	4%	18%	22%		14%		12%	1%	6%	=100%

$$\frac{\text{Total minutes per activity}}{\text{Total minutes per week}} = \text{Percentage}$$

3. What activities do I seem to be spending an excessive amount of time on?
4. Am I doing important things first?
5. Am I utilizing my odd moments, or merely killing time?
6. Am I spending enough time actually planning, or am I merely running from crisis to crisis?
7. What are some activities that I could delegate, that is, what could my employees do to help me use my time more effectively?
8. Will delegating require additional training of employees?
9. Which activities might be modified to require less of my time?
10. How will I cope with my time wasters in the future?

Let's assume that after your daily and weekly analyses you discover that you typically spend 23 percent of your time on the telephone and 15 percent involved with routine paperwork. Even if you could improve your effectiveness so that you could lop off only 2 percent from your telephone time and 4 percent from your routine paperwork time, you would increase your time available for other, more important tasks by nearly one-half hour in an eight-hour day. Adding only one-half hour to your daily managerial time could provide you with an additional *120 hours* of extra managerial time per year (assuming about 240 workdays per year, after deducting holidays, Sundays, vacations, and sick leave). Can you see the importance of this process to you as a manager? You've added roughly *15 workdays* (3 five-day workweeks) to your daily activities. Imagine how this extra time can positively affect your other managerial tasks.

We've just examined the importance of *knowing where you've been.* Now let's explore the equally important topic of *knowing where you're going.*

Do You Know How You Are Going to Use Your Time?

Two friends, Winnie and Winifred, were taking a trip together. Winifred was driving. After traveling for some distance, Winnie looked at a map and told Winifred that they were lost. "What difference does it make?" said Winifred obtusely, "We're making fantastic time!"

Winifred, it appears, was a great time manager. In fact, we might even say that she was *efficient* in her use of time—she did things fast. However, she wasn't too *effective* in managing the activity of moving toward a specific goal.

Knowing where we've been, as we've seen, is important. However, it is only part of the study of time and activity management. We should try to do better than Winifred. We must also decide what our priorities are in order to achieve our goals in an *effective,* not just *efficient,* manner.

You can't do everything for which you're responsible simultaneously. You have to make some intelligent choices in managing your activities. You must decide what should be done now and what should be done later. In this section, you will learn a method for prioritizing your goals, which, as a form of planning, provides you with a greater sense of direction and feeling of organization. You will also see how breaking down large tasks or goals into smaller components can give you a greater feeling of achievement.

Why Establish Priorities?

Any type of managing requires that you make decisions among alternatives. Time and activities management is no different; it requires that you establish priorities, that is, decide *when* specific activities have to be done. It requires that you carefully distinguish what is *truly* important from what merely *appears* important.

Setting priorities requires more than just thinking about what must be done; it requires a *written plan.* A number of techniques have been developed for the purpose of deciding which tasks have to be done, and when. One well-known approach is Alan Lakein's **ABC Priority System.**[1] Lakein suggests that you first list all the tasks you have to do, long range, medium range, and short range. Then he recommends that you decide which tasks are important to do immediately, which can be done in the near future, and which can be delayed until later.

ABC Priority System: *A method for prioritizing work activities for the purpose of making more effective use of time.*

Then, you write a capital letter A to the left of those items on your list that have a high value—that is, those that must be done

Time is an important resource to managers. Supervisors should receive ample training on how to make effective use of their time in performing critical managerial functions.

immediately. Write a B for those with medium value—they should be done relatively soon, within, say, a few days to a few weeks. And write a C for those with a low value—those with no current importance or urgency. Of course, some of your ABC classifying is probably based on pure hunches or intuition. Also, tasks that were Bs or Cs may become As as their target dates draw nearer. (Table 6–1 summarizes the three categories of priorities.)

Items marked A, as we've seen, are things that have to be done now. Naturally, if you have an extensive list of As, you won't be able to do everything immediately. You can, however, further break down your As into subcategories such as A1, A2, A3, and so on.

Bs are your routine tasks, items that are relatively important but not considered urgent. You should decide specifically when Bs must be completed or they could sneak up on you and suddenly develop into urgent crises.

Cs are those tasks for which there is no particular urgency at the moment. And some may never really become necessary to do. In fact, you might even be able to eliminate them entirely from your list. Other Cs, such as reorganizing your desk drawers, might be scheduled to be done only once a week, or merely once a month.

TABLE 6–1
ABC Priority System of Time Management

- *A category:* High-priority tasks (those that must be done immediately)
- *B category:* Routine, medium-priority tasks (those that are relatively important but not urgent; to be done within a few days to a few weeks)
- *C category:* Low-priority tasks (those for which there exists no current urgency; in some instances, these may be ignored altogether)

There are some helpful questions that you might try to answer when establishing priorities. Your answers can be of tremendous assistance in deciding if your prioritizing activities are realistic. The questions are listed in Table 6–2.

How Can You Plan Activities for the Short-Term Future?

There are a number of proven tools that can help you add considerably more value to your time by improving the ways that you plan and organize your activities.

Desktop appointment calendar:
A device that serves as a written guide to, and record of, a supervisor's daily activities.

Desktop Appointment Calendar. One aid is a **desktop appointment calendar,** like those that can typically be seen on the desks of managers in many offices and plants. This device serves as a written, organized, and handy reminder and record of your daily activities. It allows you to depend far less on your memory or, even worse, illegible notes scribbled on a smattering of post-its.

TABLE 6–2
Checklist for Establishing Priorities

- *When does this task or project have to be finished?* Your answer helps you to decide when related tasks have to be done and gives you a target to shoot for.
- *How long will the task or project take to complete?* If you find that it has to be finished tomorrow but it will take three days to accomplish, then something will have to give. Perhaps you'll have to revise your deadlines.
- *How can I save time on the task?* For example, can you delegate the project to someone else? Are there better methods for doing the job that will save you time?
- *What special resources or approval will I need?* It certainly would be exasperating to work out a detailed plan only to discover that the necessary resources will not be available, or that you can't get the approval you need for a particular project.
- *Is this task or project really necessary?* Does it actually have to be done? Or can you put it aside indefinitely with little in the way of adverse consequences?

Pocket-Sized Appointment Book. A tool closely related to the desktop appointment calendar is the **pocket-sized appointment book.** This tool provides you with a ready reference to, and record of, appointments and planned activities, regardless of where you might be at the moment. Also, work-related expenses that are reimbursable or tax deductible can be recorded as they are incurred, rather than kept in your mind for a short time and possibly forgotten.

Pocket-sized appointment book:
A portable and handy reference to, and record of, appointments and planned activities.

Daily Planner. Another tool for managing time more effectively is a **daily planner.** The Gantt worksheet in Figures 5–4 and 5–7 in the previous chapter is an example of a daily planner. It is a device that is extremely helpful for your day-to-day planning. As you may recall, you list on it all of your planned daily activities and the specific times that you intend to perform them. This device gives you a graphic representation of your planned activities and helps you to see the whole picture at once. The daily planner could be modified to show how far along you are toward accomplishing your stated goals during a longer period, such as over 12 months.

Daily planner:
A form for listing all planned daily activities and the specific times they are to be performed.

Weekly Planner. A tool designed to let you know at a glance what you've planned for an entire week is a **weekly planner.** Figure 6–3 (on the next page) illustrates an example of this type of tool.

Weekly planner:
A form that provides a supervisor with an overview of planned activities for an entire week.

Electronic Assistance. A wide variety of computer software and personal electronics diaries are available now, designed to assist managers in planning their activities. However, guard against purchasing expensive computer software or electronic gadgets without carefully checking out their utility. Many managers' shelves and drawers are packed with software and electronic "toys" that have seldom or never been used.

It's Your Choice. The forms discussed above are intended merely to be illustrative of some devices that are available to assist supervisors with their activities management. There are other types of aids that can, for example, combine both daily and weekly plans. Some are mountable onto walls and are available in a magnetic board format, which permits relatively simple changing and updating. You should attempt to develop or select tools that work best for you, and then put them to use. Program into your daily schedule the time necessary for filling in your planning worksheets. One useful approach is to plan your next week's activities on a Friday afternoon, rather than to wait until Sunday evening or during the weekend when you probably would rather be devoting time to your family and friends.

Who's in Control?

Regardless of the type of time- and activities-management tools you decide to use, remember that *you*—not the tool—are in charge. *You* should control the tool, not let *it* control you. You can become imprisoned, if you're not careful, by overstructured plans and worksheets. Try, also, to allow a certain amount of time for interruptions

	Monday	Tuesday	Wednesday	Thursday	Friday
7–8 A.M.					
8–9 A.M.					
9–10 A.M.					
10–11 A.M.					
11–12 Noon					
12–1 P.M.					
1–2 P.M.					
2–3 P.M.					
3–4 P.M.					
4–5 P.M.					
5–6 P.M.					
6–7 P.M.					
7–8 P.M.					
8–9 P.M.					
9–10 P.M.					
10–11 P.M.					
11–12 Midnight					

FIGURE 6–3
An Example of a Weekly Planner

and crises that seem inevitably to crop up. Realize that the farther you plan into the future, the more likely you're going to need some flexible, shorter-range plans. Don't be excessively upset when your plans have to be revised. Flexibility is a basic part of time and activities management.

Why Not Turn Large Goals into Small Ones?

When you are assigned a project that requires many hours to complete, the time for finishing it may seem so long that you feel the project will never end. On the other hand, have you ever noticed that the act of *achieving a goal* tends to provide you with a pleasant sense of relief, satisfaction, and accomplishment? In these feelings is contained a useful idea: Larger projects should be organized in ways that offer *regular, short-term feelings of accomplishment.*

Some managers literally resign from their jobs because they perceive their activities as being greater than they can handle. Others merely procrastinate, putting off distasteful tasks. Their problem, however, may relate more to the way they organize their activities than to the size of the projects. Your own goals will seem far easier to accomplish if they are realistic and broken down into subunits.

For example, assume that you have a stack of 100 safety inspections that you must review. Rather than placing them all in one tidy stack, try crisscrossing them in batches of five inspection reports each. If you pile them all into one large stack of 100, your sense of accomplishment probably won't be felt until you finish the entire 100 reports. By staggering them in groups of five, however, you are likely to receive regular and frequent feelings of accomplishment. Your goals will be achieved more rapidly after each set of five.

What Are The Typical Time Stealers?

A key to effective time and activities management is to recognize those situations that are typical stealers of scarce and valuable time. Knowing what sort of activities tend to waste your time will enable you to do something either to prevent such activities from occurring or, at least, to reduce their adverse consequences. You should also continually ask yourself which of your time stealers could be *delegated* to your associates, thus freeing some of your own time. Some of the more common time wasters that we will now examine are:

- Lack of organization
- The telephone
- Drop-ins
- Employees' questions
- Surprise factors
- Paperwork
- Meetings
- Unnecessary reading
- Waiting
- Procrastination

Time Stealer No. 1: Lack of Organization

Some managers appear to be busy when, in reality, they are just plain disorganized. Disorganized managers tend to waste substantial amounts of time. They usually look extremely busy, often complaining about how much work they have to do, but they frequently don't realize that their main problem is *lack of organization.*

Some authorities in the field of time and activities management feel that it is extremely important to *feel* organized. They contend that an orderly workplace tends to prevent their minds from feeling cluttered and disorganized. A neat and well-organized desk, they assert, is the sign of a well-organized manager who is in control.

Not all authorities agree, however. Some argue that the really neat and well-organized desk is probably a sign of a supervisor who doesn't get much done other than incessantly straightening his or her desk. Rather than be drawn into the debate, however, let's just say that an organized work area should save you considerable time, thus increasing your productivity.

Some supervisors occasionally defend themselves by proclaiming that they know precisely where everything is under those voluminous stacks of papers—and sometimes they do! In reality, however, if they had a plan—decided in advance where things should be placed or stored—they would probably find that they saved substantial amounts of time each day. Fewer items would be misplaced. Objects, such as staplers and scissors, would be where a supervisor looked the first time rather than having to be hunted down, wasting minutes—sometimes days—until they are discovered.

Another important reason to be organized is related to the people who report to you. Your sloppiness can be an open invitation for your associates to follow your lead and likewise be sloppy.

Organizing your desk or workplace for better efficiency is practically an art. Fortunately, there are certain working tools that can be arranged in ways to enhance your efficiency. For example, the location of often-used items such as staplers, paper clips, scratch paper, and pencils can either save or waste your time. A variety of helpful devices, such as desk organizers, are available from office supply stores and can aid you in deciding where to put certain items.

Time Stealer No. 2: The Telephone

One of the principal robbers of your scarce time is the *telephone.* This omnipresent little object is one of our most useful and necessary tools. Yet it is also one of our most typical time wasters. We

"I'm sorry, but when he says he doesn't want to be disturbed, he *means* it."

Source: Reprinted from *The Wall Street Journal* by permission of Cartoon Features Syndicate, ©.

spend an estimated two years of our lives on the telephone, and they're unlikely to be among our best. This inconsiderate device can prevent you from engaging in a variety of important tasks, such as planning and creative thinking. It frequently interrupts certain blocks of time that you had reserved for other purposes.

Answering a telephone call seems to take precedence over every other activity in progress at the time. There are, however, ways to cope with this impolite plastic pest. For example, you could delegate to someone else the responsibility of screening your telephone calls, perhaps having them respond directly to routine calls (such as answering questions) that don't require your input. Or you could request an assistant to take messages during certain periods of time (such as during your planning time or when you are meeting with others) and indicate to the caller that you will return the call at a later time. You could then return calls at your convenience. Some managers set aside a certain block of time each day—say, 30 to 40 minutes—during which they return all telephone calls.

Of course, there are occasions when you cannot avoid answering the telephone yourself. Not every supervisor enjoys the luxury of having an assistant who can intercept calls. Therefore, you should also learn how to tactfully say good-bye to long-winded callers who seem to be more interested in casual conversation than conducting business. Try to develop some cutoff phrases that don't offend but do free you for more important, higher-priority tasks. You might say something like, "I know you're busy, so I'll let you go now. Goodbye," or, "I've got to go now. I'll talk to you later. Bye now."

An organized desk also relates to your telephone. Be certain to keep a pad and pencil near your telephone. Have you ever telephoned someone who wasn't in, asked the answering party to leave a message, and heard them say, "Just a minute, please. I have to find a pencil"? After you waited impatiently for a few minutes, they finally returned. Such an approach wastes both the caller's and the answerer's time and can create caller ill-will. You can also save time by having a list of often-called telephone numbers handy, perhaps inputted into an automatic telephone dialer, rather than looking them up in a directory every time you need them.

Time Stealer No. 3: Drop-Ins

Another notorious waster of supervisory time is people dropping by your work area merely to visit. As with some telephone callers, such individuals may not be interested in transacting business; they may merely require companionship or a sympathetic ear. Develop tactful ways of saying goodbye to drop-ins, as you should with telephone callers.

In order to accomplish your own planned objectives, you may have to develop a "closed-door" policy, at least on a temporary basis. However, be certain to let your associates know why you don't want to be interrupted. Otherwise, you may appear to be

Supervisors must learn how to cope with time stealers, such as people dropping by merely to visit.

trying to insulate yourself from the people whose loyalty and support you need.

Of course, you should attempt to be flexible in most any managerial activity. For example, you probably would be better off suspending your closed-door policy for the moment if the plant manager were to drop by with an urgent message for you. Remember that sound time management allows some time for interruptions. Interruptions are so omnipresent in the lives of supervisors that some observers have facetiously depicted management as *a series of interruptions interrupted by interruptions*!

Time Stealer No. 4: Employees' Questions

When an employee confronts you with questions or problems, you should listen empathetically. Listening, of course, can assist you in keeping in touch with employees attitudes and feelings. However, some supervisors spend an inordinate amount of time handling interruptions caused by *employees' questions,* which steals time away from fulfilling their supervisory responsibilities.

Employee training and direction are keys to reducing interruptions of this nature. Employees who are trained and encouraged to make decisions on their own can relieve you of many "unavoidable" interruptions. When associates do confront you with problems, encourage them to come up with their own solutions first. You might ask, "What do you think would be the best way to handle that problem?" The more your associates are encouraged to make decisions on their own, the more time you will have available to achieve the planned goals and objectives for which you are responsible.

Time Stealer No. 5: Surprise Factors

Also related to the topic of interruptions as a time stealer are the many surprises that seem to crop up in our lives. **Surprise factors** are those unexpected interruptions that continually upset the well-structured plans that you've made. However, should you really be ***surprised*** when your boss interrupts your production schedule with a rush job, or when one of your employees develops the urgent need to discuss a personal problem, or when rush-hour traffic has you filled with anxiety and stress because you didn't allow for this unexpected traffic jam when you scheduled an important meeting on the other side of town? Much frustration from surprise factors is a result of scheduling activities too tightly, not allowing a reasonable amount of slack time for such not-really-so-surprising factors. As one part-time philosopher once mused, "The only thing that continues to surprise me are people who are surprised at surprise factors."

Surprise factors: *Those unexpected, yet ever-present, interruptions that continually upset the plans made by supervisors.*

Time Stealer No. 6: Paperwork

Paperwork can be another big stealer of your time. Time management experts have been suggesting for years that a manager should try to avoid handling a paper more than once. However, a new and improved maxim has been coined by consultant Stephanie Winston: "Every time you pick up a piece of paper, make a decision about it." She suggests that you basically have *four choices* related to incoming paperwork, which can be remembered by the handy four-letter acronym, **TRAF** (*T*hrow it away, *r*efer it to someone else, *a*ct on it, or *f*ile it).[2]

TRAF: *A time and activities management acronym that represents* ***t****hrow it away,* ***r****efer it to someone else,* ***a****ct on it, or* ***f****ile it.*

A major point therefore with the paperwork challenge is to handle paper as little as necessary. Don't file everything. For example, you might receive a memo about a meeting to take place tomorrow morning. Do you really have to clutter your files with that particular memo? Why not just *act* on it—record the date and time on your appointment calendar and then *throw away* the memo?

Here's another example of acting on paperwork. Assume that you've just opened and read an incoming memo that requires you to respond. Rather than putting it aside for a second handling later, you could act on it and prepare your answer immediately, thus saving some time. You could save even more time by *using the incoming memo for your response,* rather than writing a new one. Merely jot down your response on the memo and send it back, possibly by fax machine. If you need a copy for your files, you could make a photocopy of the original.

Sometimes it's even unnecessary to write a letter of response to an incoming letter or memo. A short *telephone call* might accomplish the same thing as a letter, in less time.

Keeping letters and memos short and simple can also be a time saver. Try restricting the length of your letters or memos to *no more than one page.* In most instances you can write whatever is necessary in this space allotment.

Also, be certain to *clean out your files regularly.* Files frequently expand needlessly, becoming jam-packed with documents that will never again be used. Analyze each item and ask yourself, "Will I really need this paper anytime in the future? Has it been in my file for three or four years and never been touched? Is this item necessary, or am I merely behaving like some sort of a pack rat?"

Some time- and activities-management specialists suggest that you regularly renew new file folders. Time-management consultant Jeffrey J. Mayer warns, "As files get beat-up and dog-eared, people don't like handling their papers."[3]

Time Stealer No. 7: Meetings

Many managers rank *meetings* right up there with the telephone and drop-ins as one of the most common wasters of scarce time. Rather than from necessity, some meetings appear to be called more out of habit. ("Why did I call a meeting? Because we always have meetings on Fridays, that's why!") Some supervisors will even invent an agenda rather than cancel an unnecessary meeting.

Rather than being unnecessary time squanderers, *meetings should be called only when there's a good reason to have one.* Why call a meeting if you don't have to? When you do have to call meetings, be certain that you have a **planned agenda.** A planned agenda is useful in that it serves to guide the participants' activities toward already established goals. A planned agenda can go a long way in preventing scarce and valuable time from being eaten up needlessly.

Planned agenda: *A predetermined set of activities to be presented and discussed during a meeting.*

Try to avoid scheduling **open-ended meetings**—meetings with no definite completion time. These tend to drag on and on due to the lack of time pressures. Instead, establish precise times for meetings to begin and end. Let participants know that you expect them to arrive at meetings on time. Waiting for participants can be an additional time waster. Be sure to start meetings on time. If participants know from experience that your meetings always begin 15 minutes late, they may feel that there is no particular reason for them to be on time.

Open-ended meetings: *Meetings that do not have a definite cutoff time.*

In order to keep meetings from dragging on, some managers schedule them just before lunch—say, 11:00 A.M. to 12:00 noon, or during the hour just prior to quitting time. The theory behind this scheduling is that participants usually aren't eager to sit in a meeting during their lunch hour or on their own time. This author knows one manager who keeps his meetings short by conducting them in a room with no chairs. He feels that the less comfortable the setting of a meeting, the more quickly participants will want to take care of the business at hand. (Table 6–3 provides a checklist for conducting effective meetings.)

Time Stealer No. 8: Unnecessary Reading

Most supervisors feel the need to read in order to keep their knowledge up to date. Some supervisors, however, are what could be termed *readaholics.* They indiscriminately read everything they get their hands on. There's certainly nothing wrong with reading a variety of publications, but you probably don't have unlimited time available for reading. Furthermore, not only is some reading probably unnecessary, it can also be a tremendous consumer of your valuable time.

The person who has learned to manage time and activities effectively has also probably learned to read discriminately. Try to develop the habit of being selective in your reading. Read only those magazines and articles that are important to your work, your self-improvement, or your recreational reading activities. Don't feel that you have to read every single page of the daily newspaper or study each magazine from cover to cover. Instead, quickly browse through the publication and read only the articles that are of benefit or interest to you.

Furthermore, attempt to be selective in what you subscribe to. Guard against subscribing to every money-saving opportunity that comes in the mail. Also, don't let your reading material accumulate too long. Rather than permitting paper towers to build up, take the time to sort your unread material at least once a month. Throw out those items that you're unlikely to find time to read.

TABLE 6–3
Checklist for Conducting Effective Meetings

- Have you generally called meetings only when there is something useful to discuss?
- Have you considered a better alternative than holding a meeting?
- Have you developed and distributed a clear and useful agenda prior to the meeting?
- Do you consistently start meetings on time?
- Do you stick to your planned agenda during the meeting?
- Do you assign someone else the responsibility to record the minutes of the meeting? (This frees you to focus your attention on the meeting itself.)
- Do you keep your meetings relatively short?
- Do you end your meetings on time?
- Do you evaluate your meetings afterwards?
- Can you honestly answer "yes" to most of the questions above? If so, you are probably conducting meetings fairly effectively.

One method for preventing the accumulation of unread publications is to scan each one as it arrives, cut out anything that seems worth reading, and place it in a file folder for later perusal.

Time Stealer No. 9: Waiting

Another big waster of time is having to wait. Doesn't it seem as though nearly everyone makes you wait? Dentists and doctors make you wait, post office personnel make you wait, automobile repair firms make you wait, your manager makes you wait, and even your own employees sometimes make you wait.

Waiting can eat up a considerable amount of your limited time. If on the average you spend 45 minutes a day idly waiting, then you have allowed 270 of your productive hours a year to melt away into oblivion.

If it really frustrates you to wait, then why remain idle in such situations? You probably know by now what sort of situations are likely to require you to bide your time. Why not plan to utilize this waiting time instead of merely complaining about it?

For example, if you have a dental appointment, take along something that interests you, perhaps an article that has been among your C priorities to read. Or you could pack along your laptop computer and utilize waiting time with such activities as planning next week's work schedule or inputting a rough draft of a letter. Or you might even merely encourage your mind to wander and engage in a few minutes of creative thinking or daydreaming, a pastime that you may seldom find time for otherwise.

If the act of waiting usually bothers you (as it does many supervisors), then go to your waiting situations with activities you can work on. By being prepared to wait, you're likely to find that waiting time will pass even more rapidly than you desire.

Time Stealer No. 10: Procrastination

Procrastination: *Putting off doing something until a future time.*

"Why *do* today what you can *put off* until tomorrow?" Those are not the precise words of the original expression, yet many people behave as though they were. **Procrastination,** which can be defined as *needlessly* putting off doing something until a future time, can be a prodigious waster of your precious time.

There is a human tendency to postpone doing unpleasant tasks, such as disciplining an associate or dealing with a disgruntled customer. Unfortunately, such activities typically don't complete themselves. Instead, they tend to remain and haunt you, give you feelings of guilt, and make concentrating on other tasks more difficult. The sooner you take care of such unpleasant tasks, the sooner you feel a sense of relief and goal accomplishment.

Supervisors are often faced with large tasks that they realize cannot be completed at once. Some supervisors tend to put off working on these activities until they have a block of time sufficient to complete the entire task. Unfortunately, busy supervisors seldom

TABLE 6–4
Guidelines for Managing and Controlling Work Activities

- Do you take time out for planning?
- Do you write down your "to do's"?
- Do you establish realistic priorities and deadlines?
- Do you control time wasters?
- Do you delegate when possible?
- Do you act decisively (i.e., not put off making important decisions)?
- Do you know your energy cycles? Do you tackle difficult tasks when your energy level is high?
- Do you attempt to limit idle chatting?
- Do you utilize odd moments?
- Do you use your car as an office (utilizing a dictating machine, cellular telephone, laptop computer, fax machine, et al)?
- Do you attempt to say "no" tactfully to excessive demands on your time?
- Do you complete tasks that you've started?
- Do you attempt to work smarter, not just harder?
- Do you avoid procrastinating?

feel that they have large enough blocks of free time. As a result, the completion of such tasks is often delayed.

A better approach than postponing large tasks is to engage in what is sometimes called the **Swiss-cheese method** of activities management. Just as the Swiss cheese available in North America has holes in it, this approach involves "poking holes," *poco a poco,* in your work. Doing something on a project regularly, regardless of how little you do, is usually far more effective than procrastinating and doing nothing for an extended period of time.

Swiss-cheese method: *A time- and activities-management technique that involves working regularly on a project, regardless of how little is done.*

Do You Do These "Do You's"?

Look carefully at Table 6–4, which provides a useful checklist for more effectively managing and controlling your work activities.

Summary

Managing time and activities is another extremely important supervisory task. Many supervisors look busy when, in reality, they're merely poor managers of their time and activities.

A number of tools have been developed to assist you in managing your own time more effectively. These include a *daily activities summary log, weekly activities summary log,* and various other forms and devices for *short-term planning purposes.*

Establishing priorities is a useful way of deciding when tasks must be done. *Desktop appointment calendars, pocket-sized ap-*

pointment books, daily and weekly planners, and *electronic devices* can all assist supervisors in the management of their time and activities. To manage time effectively, you should try to organize your work activities in *segments,* which should provide you with greater feelings of achievement and satisfaction.

The workplace is loaded with potential stealers of your scarce time. In this chapter, we examined some of the more typical *time stealers—lack of organization,* the *telephone, drop-ins, employees' questions, surprise factors, paperwork, meetings, unnecessary reading, waiting,* and *procrastination.* Learning how to cope with such time wasters can assist you in stretching each of your daily working hours.

Questions for Discussion

1. Explain the difference between *working hard* and *working smart.*
2. Why is *analyzing your past activities* an essential first step in improving your future effectiveness in managing your time and activities?
3. What is the purpose of a *daily activities summary log*? How does it relate to a *weekly activities summary log*?
4. Describe the *ABC Priority System* of time management.
5. How can you save time by utilizing some of the *short-term planning tools* mentioned in the chapter?
6. Think of one of your tasks or projects that is relatively long or monotonous. How might you organize your activities in a manner that provides you with *greater immediate feelings of accomplishment and satisfaction*?
7. How can an *organized work area* save you time?
8. Evaluate the following statement: "Other than yanking the cord completely out of the wall, there's not much a manager can do about the *telephone* as a time waster."
9. How might you reduce the time wasted by people *dropping* by your workplace merely to engage in idle conversation?
10. What risk is associated with simply *ignoring employees' questions*? What might be a better technique?
11. What can be done to aid you in coping with so-called *surprise factors*?
12. Explain the significance of the acronym *TRAF* to time and activities management.
13. Why is it generally worthwhile to have a *planned agenda* before calling a meeting?
14. Evaluate the following statement: "Managers must be voracious readers. In fact, they should read everything they can get their hands on."
15. What can you do to reduce the time-wasting effects of having to *wait* to see other people?

Can You Define These Terms?

Instructions: Write a definition for each of the following terms. You may check your definitions with those provided in the end-of-text glossary.

time management
activities management
daily activities summary log
weekly activities summary log
ABC Priority System
desktop appointment calendar
pocket-sized appointment book
daily planner
weekly planner
surprise factors
TRAF
planned agenda
open-ended meetings
procrastination
Swiss-cheese method

Supervision In Action

6–1 Where Do Your Days Go?

Look at Figure 6–4. Either using the existing headings or modifying them to suit your tasks, keep track of your daily activities for one week. (See Figure 6–1 and 6–2 to refresh your memory on how to maintain the record.) Then, in Figure 6–5, summarize the information. Figure the average percentage of time that you spend on each task per week. Which items might you be able to reduce time on? Which should be receiving greater attention? What will be your action plan to make more effective use of your available time?

FIGURE 6–4
Daily Activities Summary Log

Time	Planning and creative work	Scheduling and assigning work	Direct supervision	Inspection	Routine paperwork	Using telephone	Counseling	Meetings	Special projects	Emergencies	Taking breaks	Miscellaneous	Remarks
8:00 A.M.													
8:30 A.M.													
9:00 A.M.													
9:30 A.M.													
10:00 A.M.													
10:30 A.M.													
11:00 A.M.													
11:30 A.M.													
12:00 NOON													
12:30 P.M.													
1:00 P.M.													
1:30 P.M.													
2:00 P.M.													
2:30 P.M.													
3:00 P.M.													
3:30 P.M.													
4:00 P.M.													
4:30 P.M.													
5:00 P.M.													
Totals													

	Planning and creative work	Scheduling and assigning work	Direct supervision	Inspection	Routine paperwork	Using telephone	Counseling	Meetings	Special projects	Emergencies	Taking breaks	Miscellaneous
Monday												
Tuesday												
Wednesday												
Thursday												
Friday												
Total mins.												
Average/day												
Percentage												

FIGURE 6–5
Weekly Activities Summary Log

6–2 If Only There Were More Hours in the Day

At precisely 7:30 A.M. on a damp and dreary Monday morning in February, Keith Johnson, oper ations chief of the Montclair City Fire Department, drove his pickup truck out of the garage of his comfortable lakefront home. The automatic garage door opener swung shut and Keith headed toward the administrative offices of the Montclair City Fire Department Administrative Headquarters. The trip to the office took about 30 minutes and gave Keith the opportunity to mentally map out his daily activities with few interruptions.

Keith felt good on this morning. He reflected on the attaché case full of paperwork he had completed last night at home and thought, "Today is going to be the day I get a lot of things done that I've been wanting to do for a long time." His mind began to sort out the day's work, attempting to establish priorities and goals.

"Oh, oh," he groaned out loud to himself. He had suddenly remembered that he hadn't yet worked out a specific plan for developing a first-line management program for fire station captains and lieutenants. Keith's boss, Chief Ledwith, had asked him last Wednesday afternoon if anything specific had been developed yet. The training program for first-line supervisors was one that Keith himself, while battalion chief in the training division, had proposed to the former operations chief, Franklin King, who had retired before anything was done with the recommendation. Keith's manager, Chief Ledwith, agreed that the concept and implementation of management training was long overdue, but a year had already slipped by and Keith had still done little in the way of formulating specific plans. Keith realized that this was one of the projects he should work on today.

A traffic light suddenly changed from green to red, and Keith's thoughts momentarily left his work. After the light turned green again, his mind and vehicle shifted back into gear, and he thought about another project that he had not started yet—the development of an improved appraisal system for probationary employees. Changes in firefighting equipment and methods, along with public relations demands, had rendered the old system obsolete. His thoughts focused on a few more projects that required planning, and he felt that "Today's going to be the day for sure that I get those projects out of the way."

Suddenly Keith realized that he was approaching the parking garage below the building in which he worked. As he left the elevator and walked toward his office, he met Jennifer Green, battalion chief of the training division, and sensed something was wrong.

"What's wrong, Jennifer?" asked Keith. "You look like something's bothering you."

"It is," responded Jennifer. "Heather, my new typist, hasn't come in, and she didn't show up Friday either."

"Did she notify you?" asked Keith.

"I haven't heard a thing from her," answered Jennifer.

Keith was visibly concerned and said, "Those young people fresh out of school these days just aren't dependable. Well, why don't you have Maria in personnel give Heather a call?"

"Okay," replied Jennifer, "but could you possibly get me a typist for today? I have three reports that have to be submitted to Chief Ledwith by tomorrow morning."

"I'll get back to you within the hour," responded Keith.

As Keith continued toward his desk, he saw his assistant, Bob Bruner. "Good morning, Bob," greeted Keith.

"Oh—hi, chief," answered Bob. "I'm glad to see you. I have those budgetary reports ready to be sent to the battalion chiefs and engine company captains. I checked them twice on the spreadsheet program for accuracy. Should I mail them out now?"

"Not yet," advised Keith. "I want to check the entries once more myself just to make sure there are no mistakes. I'd be embarrassed if they went out of here with any errors."

Keith left Bob and called the personnel department to see if they could find a typist for Jennifer. He then began his usual morning routine. He telephoned each battalion chief to see if they had any personnel, equipment, or budgetary problems. Then he began his morning inspection of the office. He helped a clerk find a storage place for an old typewriter, detailed two computer operators who had run out of work, helped another computer operator move the position of her desk because of the glare from a nearby window, cleared away several boxes of office forms from an aisle, and answered a telephone that was ringing on an unattended desk.

Keith then returned to his own desk and started approving vacation schedules that had been submitted by all firehouse captains for the firehouse personnel. Keith always made the final decision in the event of conflict.

The phone rang. Keith answered it and talked with Captain Franks from Engine Company 6, who wanted permission to switch shifts with one of his lieutenants. Keith agreed to the change, and then realized that he was five minutes late for a staff meeting that he himself had arranged for this morning.

After the meeting, Keith returned to his desk, looked at his watch, and realized that it was lunchtime. "Where did the morning go?" he asked himself.

After lunch, Keith began again. His afternoon went something like this:

1. Two more tours through the office
2. A telephone call from his son, who wanted to know if he could rent a video movie that evening
3. A telephone call from a firefighter who had been injured in an automobile accident and required hospitalization
4. Reviewing copies of talks given by members of the Fire Service Speakers' Bureau
5. Two meetings with battalion chiefs regarding personnel problems
6. Approving requisitions for supplies from the various fire stations

It was now late in the afternoon and Keith was exhausted. It was time to head for home again. After two interruptions on the way to the building garage, Keith entered his pickup and pulled out into the rush hour traffic. As he drove home, he asked himself, "Where did my day go? I didn't do anything on the projects I thought about this morning on the way to work. Am I really a manager, or merely a messenger? If only there were more hours in the day, I know that I could accomplish some of the longer-range goals that I've been thinking about for some time. If I only had the time. . . ."

Questions

1. Keith seems to feel that he doesn't have enough time to accomplish his goals. Do you agree? Explain.
2. If you were Keith, what might you do to accomplish more of your longer-range managerial goals and objectives?

6–3 Do You Know Your ABCs?

Here's a chance for you to apply the ABC Priority System discussed in the chapter. In the spaces provided below, list all of your ***high-value, medium-value,*** and *low-value priorities.* Evaluate each item carefully before you categorize it. Make them job-related, if possible.

A's High-Value Priorities	B's Medium-Value Priorities	C's Low-Value Priorities
1. ______	1. ______	1. ______
2. ______	2. ______	2. ______
3. ______	3. ______	3. ______
4. ______	4. ______	4. ______
5. ______	5. ______	5. ______
6. ______	6. ______	6. ______
7. ______	7. ______	7. ______
8. ______	8. ______	8. ______
9. ______	9. ______	9. ______
10. ______	10. ______	10. ______

Questions

1. Can any of your B or C tasks be weeded out entirely? Which ones?
2. When might some of your B or C activities become A priorities?
3. What is your plan for taking care of C items that must ultimately be completed?
4. How did you decide to place an item in the A category? B category? C category?

6–4 Coping with Interruptions

Interruptions seem to be an inevitable part of any work environment. In some cases, however, their negative effects can be eliminated, or at least reduced. In the spaces provided below and on any additional sheets of paper necessary, keep track of all your interruptions for at least a week. (A two-week period is even better.)

Type of Interruption	Source of Interruption	Activity in Progress during Interruption	Recommendations for Coping with Interruption
1.			
2.			
3.			
4.			
5.			
6.			
7.			

6–5 Step-by-Step Satisfaction Goal Setting

In the space provided below, list at least five of your goals, either work related or personal. Each goal is to have a different time frame for completion, as indicated below. After you've developed your list of goals, then determine some ways in which you might organize the asks associated with your goals in a manner that enables you to obtain more immediate feelings of achievement and satisfaction.

Goal	**Recommendations for Achieving Feelings of Accomplishment**
1. (requiring less than 1 day to accomplish)	
2. (requiring 1–2 weeks to accomplish)	
3. (requiring 6–12 months to accomplish	
4. (requiring 1–2 years to accomplish)	
5. (requiring 2–5 years to accomplish)	

Endnotes

1. Alan Lakein, *How to Get Control of Your Time and Your Life* (New York: Signet, 1973), pp. 28–29.
2. Walter Kiechel III, "Getting Organized," *The Wall Street Journal*, March 3, 1986, pp. 123–124.
3. "Consultant Sweeps Away Office Clutter," *USA Today* (International Edition), January 19, 1989, p. 15.

NERVOUS
BREAKDOWN
AS SOON AS THE RUSH IS OVER,
I'M GOING TO HAVE A NERVOUS
BREAKDOWN.
I WORKED FOR IT; I OWE IT TO
MYSELF; AND NOBODY IS GOING
TO DEPRIVE ME OF IT.

Chapter 7

Managing Everyday Stressors

To be alive is to be under a certain amount of stress.
—Norman L. Shoaf, Educator

It's not so much stress, within reason, but how you meet the stress, that counts in life.
—Lawrence Lamb, M.D.

Learning Objectives

When you finish this chapter, you should be able to:

1. Recognize the distinction between *eustress* and *distress*.
2. Describe three general causes of stress.
3. Employ specific remedies for reducing or eliminating stress in yourself and your associates.

"Everyone occasionally experiences feelings of stress, tension, and anxiety. These feelings, in acceptable doses, are normal. As you rise up an organizational hierarchy, you could find that you become even more prone to such feelings. To function as an effective manager, therefore, it is important that you understand the nature of stress and adopt methods for coping with the everyday stresses that, if not controlled, can wreak havoc on both your career and personal life."

The above words could be those of an employee counselor to a supervisor who had been struggling to meet deadlines for an extended period of time. Because managers tend to work in a high-stress environment, the topic of stress management has become extremely popular in recent years. This chapter should assist you in understanding the nature of stress, and, especially important, provide you with some suggestions for reducing your own stress level.

What Is the Nature of Stress?

Stress: *Pressures and demands from one's environment that, when not controlled, can cause physical and psychological disorders.*

Stress, tension, anxiety—these are words reflecting emotional reactions that we all tend to experience as a result of the daily pressures that typically accompany living and working. **Stress** is a feeling of pressure that can be caused by either unpleasant or pleasant events, such as being laid off from your job or winning big in the lottery. A certain amount of stress is both normal and beneficial. Stress is difficult to avoid in many situations, such as when you are about to be presented a plaque at an awards banquet for outstanding past performance or after you have accepted a promotion that was very important to you. So whether an event is positive or negative, it still can be the cause of stress and anxiety.

What Are Two Major Types of Stress?

Without stress, you couldn't hold your head erect. Without stress, you wouldn't be able to stay awake in a lecture hall or a movie theater. Without stress, you wouldn't be able to meet your deadlines or accomplish your goals. On the other hand, without stress you would be less likely to experience a cardiac arrest. Without stress, you would be less likely to suffer an asthmatic attack. Without stress, you would be less likely to develop ulcers, hypertension, arthritis, headaches, neckaches, backaches, and mental illness.

Stress, therefore, is not a simple black and white situation. Whether stress is good or bad depends on the nature of the stress and on your own methods for coping with it. Some people *thrive,* others *dive,* under stress. There are actually two different types of stress: *eustress* and *distress.* **Eustress** is a positive and necessary type of stress that enables you to function and accomplish your goals. Without it, you could hardly rise from bed each morning. **Distress,** on the other hand, is a negative type of stress that, if not managed properly, can cause a variety of diseases and mental depression. It can also lead to alcohol and drug abuse, family problems, and even spouse and child abuse. In short, it can cause excessive wear and tear on your mind and body.

Eustress:
A positive and necessary type of stress that enables one to function and accomplish goals.

Distress:
A negative type of stress that, if not managed properly, can lead to a variety of diseases and mental depression.

What Are the Principal Causes of Stress?

A first step in attempting to cope with stress is to recognize its causes. Some stress inducers are ***job related,*** while others occur *off the job.* Tables 7–1 and 7–2 indicate both ***on- and off-the-job*** causes of stress and frustration.

Professors Johanna and Phillip Hunsaker suggest that most types of stress relate to three general categories:[1]

1. Uncertainty
2. Lack of control
3. Pressure

Let's look briefly at each category.

TABLE 7–1
On-the-Job Causes of Stress

- Performance anxiety (e.g., caused by new job or promotion)
- Poor planning and goal setting
- Unclear job requirements
- Little recognition of performance
- Insufficient authority to make decisions
- Peer pressure
- Conflict with others
- Excessive work demands
- Underuse of skills
- Work overload or underload
- Low morale
- Insecurity (regarding job responsibilities, future, etc.)
- Lack of needs satisfaction
- Misunderstandings and ineffective communication
- Formal performance appraisals
- Working conditions
- Equipment
- Organizational politics
- Inconsistent managerial behavior
- Unsupportive manager
- Criticism received in front of others
- Rapid change

TABLE 7–2
Off-the-Job Causes of Stress

- Family problems
- Financial difficulties
- Poor health
- Substance abuse (alcohol, drugs, or cigarettes)
- Traffic violations
- Automobile problems
- Neighbors
- Current events
- Insomnia (can also be a result of stress)
- Home-maintenance problems

Uncertainty. Life is filled with uncertainties. Insurance companies, for example, thrive on society's insecurities by substituting the uncertainty of loss of property, life, or income for the certainty of a fixed annual insurance premium. Many events in your life can create uncertainty, such as how you'll perform in a new supervisory position, how an employee will react to being fired, or how you will determine your job responsibilities when they haven't been clearly spelled out. Even a messy, disorganized work area can create uncertainty.

Lack of Control. Even if a high degree of certainty exists in work situations or personal lives, some people feel stressed when there is the feeling of little or no control over events and activities. For example, you may know precisely what your job responsibilities are—your role is clearly defined in a job description—but you may lack ample *authority* to carry out those responsibilities effectively, a condition that can also lead to distress. The feelings of insufficient control can also exist in work environments that lack privacy or are excessively noisy.

Pressure. Such factors as deadlines, autocratic managers, work overloads, and last-minute changes in your work schedule can create feelings of pressure in work situations. Pressure, like uncertainty and lack of control, is a significant stress inducer. Pressure is often felt in such situations as when the demands of a job exceed a person's current skills and capability, or when there is the need to learn new processes and develop new skills. Competitive work environments also tend to create pressure.

How Can You Cause Your Associates to Become Stressed?

Our examination of stress has been primarily through the point of view of you, the supervisor. But how about your associates—the employees accountable to you? They, too, experience stresses, strains, and anxieties. Many of the types of stressors discussed so far also relate to your associates. Be on the lookout for employees who complain about constant headaches or who appear to have other symptoms of stress. It is possible that you are unwittingly assuming the role of stress inducer and causing your associates to develop stress disorders.

F. J. McGuigan, director of the Institute for Stress Management at United States International University, suggests six supervisory behaviors that can cause employee tension and stress:[2]

1. Calling frequent, lengthy meetings and then criticizing employees for not spending enough time at their desks actively producing work.
2. Setting impossibly high goals in the mistaken belief that it will make employees try harder.
3. Putting employees on the spot, especially in front of others, rather than giving them time to research answers to your questions.
4. Repeatedly taking employees off one project to work on others, requiring them to juggle many projects at the same time. Often it is better to allow them to concentrate on and finish one project at a time.
5. Involving the entire staff in every problem or crisis, even though some of the individuals can do nothing to help alleviate the difficulty.
6. Bringing up employees' past mistakes when you are correcting them for current errors.

Supervisors are sometimes unaware that they are significant causes of stress in their associates.

Supervisors who want to minimize employee stress should attempt to set a good example. Supervisors who appear harried, disorganized, and short tempered are likely to find similar behavior mirrored by their employees. Carefully reread McGuigan's employee stressors cited above. Avoiding such behavior will aid substantially in reducing the chances of your inducing stress in employees.

What Can You Do About Stress?

For many years it was believed that stress came with the territory, so to speak, when a person assumed a managerial job. Numerous managers assumed that long hours, short deadlines, pressure, pressure, and more pressure couldn't be avoided. One either accepted the inherent pressures, it was believed, or resigned. A common expression, made popular by former President Harry S. Truman, was "If you can't stand the heat, get out of the kitchen!"

Stress management: *The ability to influence, control, and adapt to the forces that create pressure in one's life.*

Stressors: *Events or factors that cause stress.*

However, during the past two decades much attention has been given to the topic of *stress management.* **Stress management** can be defined as the ability to influence, control, and adapt to the forces that create pressure in one's life. Most people have far more influence and control over **stressors**—those factors that cause stress—than they realize. Some of the more common areas that influence a person's stress level and ability to adapt to stress are:

1. Exercise (both body and mind)
2. Proper nutrition
3. Positive attitude
4. Relaxation
5. Ethical values

How Does Exercise Reduce Stress?

"Health Craze Linked to Drop in Heart Attacks"[3]
"Heart Disease Rate Falling among Men, Du Pont Study Says"[4]
"Employees Who Stay Fit Are Happier, Work Harder"[5]

The above appeared as newspaper headlines in recent years. They seem to indicate that some Americans have discovered means for gaining control over the negative effects of stress. Some persons seem to have finally developed the awareness that taking care of both their minds and bodies is important.

The mind and the body could be likened to muscles that should receive regular exercise to keep them in good condition. Busy supervisors sometimes forget, or may be unaware, that physical exercise can do wonders for the mind, especially as a stress reducer. Unfortunately, people in responsible positions seem to have less time and more excuses for not exercising: "I'm too tired," "I'm too busy," It's too early," "It's too late," "I really should start exercising—maybe next week, *if* it's not raining or snowing."

You've already learned from Chapter 6 about the importance of time and activities management for supervisors. You should include stress-reducing activities as a part of your time- and activities-management programs. You can more readily develop the habit of exercising if you assign a specific time each day for the activity (establish a goal, in effect) and then follow through with actually doing it.

Make Time for Exercise. If you're a skeptic, check with your doctor; then find out what sort of program of *regular* exercise will benefit you personally. Physical activity can benefit practically every part of your body and make a big difference in whether you feel distressful or comfortable, sluggish or energetic, optimistic or pessimistic. It can actually make you feel better than taking a 30-minute nap. One of its greatest benefits, however, is to the *mind*. Exercise, such as a daily routine of cycling, running, walking, skating, or swimming, can be a form of relief for the person beset with anger, pressures, worries, or frustrations. *A word of caution:* Before beginning any strenous exercise program, you should see your doctor to make certain that there are no reasons why you shouldn't exercise. Then start out gradually at first, especially if you're out of

Supervisors should make time in their busy schedules for exercise breaks, which can be highly effective as a reducer of stress.

physical condition. As you build up your strength and endurance, you may even find that you are developing an addiction and will miss exercising if, for some reason, you must skip the activity for two or three days.

Let's assume, however, that you believe you are truly deskbound, currently working on a project that requires your attention "26 hours" per day. "I really want to exercise," you try to convince yourself, "but there just aren't enough hours in the day." If such is your attitude, consider the guidelines in Table 7–3, as suggested by Herrick Hospital and Health Center.[6]

Try Some Mental Gymnastics. As previously mentioned, the mind, too, needs exercise. There are endless ways of stimulating your mind. You might take college courses at night, some related to your occupation and some solely for life enrichment purposes. For example, why not take that evening course in classical guitar that you've been contemplating for so long? Or do you ever fit some pleasure or escape reading into your busy schedule? Not only can such an activity be useful as a tension reducer, but it also can serve to broaden your vocabulary and improve your writing style.

Have you ever thought about taking a ***thinking break***? Some supervisors are so preoccupied with their day-to-day activities that they never take the opportunity to really get acquainted with themselves. Try a 15-minute thinking break sometime. Find a quiet room (not always an easy task in itself!), sit down, and let your mind go wherever it wants for the entire 15 minutes. You may be amazed at some of the thoughts and ideas that cross your mind. Creative solutions to problems that you've been wrestling with for weeks may suddenly pop into your mind. And especially important, the experience of meditating can be an excellent way of just winding down after a hard day at the office or plant.

Because of the proven positive effects of maintaining the body and the mind, some organizations now sponsor physical and mental

TABLE 7–3
Exercise Guidelines for the Deskbound

- Instead of using the company lot, park one block away from your office and walk briskly to work. As you get used to walking one block, start parking two blocks from your office. (One man who did this eventually felt so good that he ended up leaving his car at home and walking the entire way to work.)
- Don't take the elevator during the day; use the stairs. The aerobic stimulation of climbing and descending stairs is good conditioning, especially for your heart.
- During the workday, give yourself a quiet, relaxing moment and take time for a stretch. This can give you renewed energy for the rest of the day.

fitness through **wellness programs** designed to aid in maintaining and improving employees' physical health, sense of well-being, and productivity.[7]

Wellness programs: *Programs sponsored by employers for the purpose of maintaining and improving employees' physical health, sense of well-being, and productivity.*

How Does Proper Nutrition Relate to Stress?

Many people today have jobs that are less physically demanding than their forbears had years ago. Higher incomes and standards of living have made junk food-eating "couch potatoes" out of many Americans. As a result, close to one-third of all Americans are said to be seriously overweight. Much of their obesity is a result of improper diet. Extra pounds create stress on the circulatory system and put a strain on the heart, frequently leading to cardiovascular disease. As with exercise, a body that receives a proper diet provides that person with a better mental outlook and a greater ability to cope with stress.

Although not all experts agree on what constitutes a proper diet, Table 7–4 provides a set of eating habit guidelines developed by the U.S. Department of Health and Human Services. Many nutritional experts suggest that a daily diet should include foods from each of the following categories: (1) vegetables, (2) fruits, (3) whole-grain and enriched breads, cereals, and related products, (4) milk, cheese, and yogurt, (5) poultry, fish, lean meats, and eggs, and (6) legumes (dried peas and beans).[8]

Coffee is another stress inducer. More than two cups of coffee can provide the drinker with negative health-related side effects. And how about salt? Some people pour salt onto their food before even tasting it. Since most of our food inherently contains sodium, salt shakers could be left off the dining table with no loss and much gain. Excessive salt consumption tends to increase blood pressure and cause fluid retention.

Nor is sugar as sweet to us as it tastes. Many individuals eat cookies, candies, and other sweets when they're nervous. However, their stress levels are likely to rise over time, since refined sugar and honey increase blood cholesterol levels and thus blood pressure. Excessive quantities of certain cholesterols in our diet can cause heart disease. Eggs, shellfish (such as lobster and crab), and animal meat all tend to be high in cholesterol. Generally speaking, you're safer if you avoid foods that don't swim, fly, or grow in the ground! (One food-loving cynic, upon reading this restricted list of food sources, sardonically suggested, "How about just a toothpick and a glass of unpolluted water?")

Much has been reported in recent years about the links between cigarette smoking and fatal diseases, such as cancer. For example, the U.S. Surgeon General has estimated that people who smoke two or more packs of cigarettes a day have lung cancer death rates of 15 to 25 percent higher than nonsmokers.[9] Americans, however, seem to have heeded the warning of the hazards of cigarette smoking, since the percentage of adults who smoke has dropped from 43 percent in 1964 to about 25 percent currently.[10] Some individ-

TABLE 7–4
Guidelines for Proper Eating Habits

- Does your daily diet include fruit and vegetables, whole-grain breads and cereals, lean meats, and dairy products?
- Do you limit your consumption of fatty meats, eggs, butter, cheese, cream, shortenings, and organ meats (e.g., liver)?
- Do you cook with only small amounts of salt, not add salt at the table, and avoid salty snacks?
- Do you avoid sugar by restricting your intake of candy and nondiet soft drinks?

uals smoke because they believe doing so reduces stress. However, the many side effects brought about by smoking tends to increase their stress level in the long run. Those who don't smoke tend to be able to adapt even better to stress because of their improved physical and mental condition.

How Does a Positive Attitude Relate to Stress?

Professor Steward Wolf, M.D., has written:

> *"The ability to hope, to trust in those about one, the ability to have faith in one's destiny and to realize one's personal identity are the elements of emotional security that can sustain an individual through all manner of hazards and hardships."*[11]

Do you read the daily newspaper, watch the evening news, or read a weekly news magazine? If so, the world may seem to you each day to be crumbling a bit more beneath your shoes. Following Dr. Wolf's advice and maintaining a positive attitude toward living isn't an easy task with incessant images of physical violence, international crises, acid rain, depletion of the ozone layer, the greenhouse effect, and the AIDS epidemic.

For some persons, negative attitudes seem to be a natural means for releasing pent-up tensions. Life, however, is a relatively short experience. Many individuals don't realize how quickly time has passed until they reach their middle years and reflect back on their lives. The late Lord John Maynard Keynes, the famed British economist, once said, "In the long run, we'll all be dead." Since his assertion is difficult to dispute, we might as well try to enjoy and appreciate as much of our remaining life as possible, which is far better than being resigned to a life of pessimism and negativism. We do have a choice—if we want to make it. Someone once said that a pessimist is a person who looks at the holes and not the cheese. For the sake of our own mental health we must look at the cheese!

A Positive Self-Concept. How you perceive yourself or your status—your **self-concept**—is a part of your attitude and relates significantly to your ability to adapt to stressors. Many people have the natural but unfortunate tendency to be excessively self-critical. Perhaps a difficult task has been assigned to you recently, one with which you have little familiarity. You may develop feelings of anxiety and tension, which could cause you to doubt your ability to perform up to the level that you think is expected of you.

Self-concept: *How one perceives one's self or status.*

Try not to let such anxious feelings lead you astray. We know that stress, improperly harnessed, can be your mortal enemy. But in another sense, stress can be your best friend. Physiologically, stress is your body's way of reacting to danger. It causes changes in your blood, hormones, breathing, and muscles, which make you stronger, faster, more alert, and better able to protect yourself. For example, athletes win games, artists paint masterpieces, authors write best sellers, and workers become managers because stress serves to motivate them to stretch their abilities and achieve. Therefore, you're likely to cope more effectively with the sources of stress by convincing yourself in as many instances as possible that it is useful and necessary.

To channel stress into positive directions, however, requires that you accept yourself for what you are. Take a periodic inventory of your skills. Are you technically proficient in your job? Are your human relations and communications skills up to the level you want? Are you able to plan and manage your activities effectively? And especially important, are you doing something to try to improve your skills and overcome your weaknesses? The self-awareness that you are doing the best you can with your existing skills and continually trying to improve them is one method for developing self-respect and self-acceptance.

Positive Expectations. You probably have heard the expression, "Don't burn your bridges before you've crossed them." Some individuals, unfortunately, seem to engage daily in such bridge-burning activities. They assume, based on past bad luck or misfortune, that opportunities don't exist for them. One problem with such an attitude is that it creates stress and can cloud a person's ability to perceive real opportunities when they do come along. Try to avoid approaching situations with a preset, pessimistic, defeated-before-you-start attitude. Having such an attitude can become self-fulfilling. Don't be like the little girl whose attitude sold few raffle tickets. Her point of view is reflected in the following story:

> *"Want to buy a chance on a turkey, mister?" asked the cute little six-year-old girl.*
>
> *"I'm sorry, honey," said the friendly old gentleman, "but I live in one room and I don't have a stove. I couldn't cook a turkey even if I won it."*
>
> *"Take a chance, anyway," replied the little girl reassuringly. "You probably won't win."*

Realistic Expectations. How do you react to events that have not gone the way you feel they should? For example, do you get upset when people don't replace things exactly as you left them? Are you excessively critical of people who don't live up to your standards and expectations? Do tasks have to be done precisely the way you would do them? Do you feel that everything must be useful and efficient? If you answer these questions affirmatively, then you could have what is termed an **obsessive-compulsive personality.** Your expectations may not quite be in tune with reality—and you may be creating unnecessary tensions for yourself and others in the process.

Obsessive-compulsive personality: *Anxiety coupled with persisting, unwanted thoughts (obsessions) and/or the need to repeat certain acts over and over (compulsions).*

An improved understanding of yourself can help you in establishing realistic goals and expectations. Most people don't want to be stressed, yet many people expect everything accomplished by others to be useful, efficient, and done precisely their way. But must *everything* have utilitarian value? Should we necessarily expect sunsets and symphonies to be useful? Some things that we really care for are good in and of themselves.

How Does the Ability to Relax Relate to Stress?

The person who is in love with his or her work derives considerable satisfaction from life. There are some persons, however, who love *nothing* but their work. In fact, they are unable to relax, even when they have some spare time. They tend to fill up every available moment of their waking hours with work activities. They are suffering from an affliction that may be worse in some respects than excessive drinking—**workaholism,** sometimes referred to as a **Type A personality.**[12] Some persons apparently overwork for the same reason that alcoholics overdrink—to escape from frustration, they hope. In addition, the workaholic, or work addict, tends to feel guilty when not working.

Workaholism: *Behavior inherent in persons who experience withdrawal or guilt feelings when they are not working; also termed* work addiction.

Type A personality: *A tendency toward work addiction and an obsession with time and achievement.*

Work addiction may be a useful trait for rising in an organizational hierarchy. However, if you ever find that you have become a work addict and are not deriving genuine satisfaction from living, you should try to learn how to slip into what has been referred to as a **Type B personality,** and "decompress" from time to time. For example, some people have turned to various relaxation techniques, such as Transcendental Meditation (TM), Yoga, Zen, deep breathing, and biofeedback. These techniques are believed by their proponents to create what has been referred to as the "relaxation response."

Type B personality: *A characteristic of individuals who tend not to become addicted to work.*

TM, for example, focuses on four simple steps: Assume a comfortable position; close your eyes; concentrate on a single word, sound, or phrase; and cast off all other thoughts.[13] The *deep breathing technique* recommends taking a deep breath, holding it for a second or two, exhaling, and thinking consciously about relaxing. For some persons, merely taking a short nap or sitting quietly with their eyes closed can release tension.

Many relaxation fads have come and gone, and techniques that work "miraculously" on one person may have little effect on another. Dr. Daniel Goleman, a psychologist, points out that not everyone finds "relaxing" relaxing; instead, some people get even more tense when they try it.[14] Therefore, finding the relaxation technique that best suits you is important.

Some obsessive-compulsive people never realize that something is amiss until they develop health problems. One person began to suspect that she had caught the workaholic "disease" when her five-year-old son asked for an appointment to see her. Wouldn't you prefer to try to recognize the warning signs of work addiction and cope with them before it's too late?

How Do Ethical Values Relate to Stress?

Discussed in an earlier section was the need for a positive self-concept. Your self-concept is influenced by the degree of faith and trust you have in yourself and others. One way to maintain greater trust is to be trustworthy yourself. Supervisors are constantly faced with difficult choices. Your self-concept also influences the way you react and adapt to stress.

Unfortunately, any discussion of this nature runs the risk of sounding prudish and even naïve, but think seriously about the following: If you continually engage in unethical practices with others, say, your customers, your associates, or your own company, two principal types of problems might confront you. The first relates to *living with your own conscience,* and the second to the tendency of *assuming that others are as unethical in their activities as you.*

"Of course I don't think of business all the time. I love you. I adore you. I worship the ground you stand on. Read that back to me."

Source: Reprinted from *The Wall Street Journal,* permission of Cartoon Features Syndicate, ©

Ethics:
Established standards of conduct or morals.

What does the word **ethics** mean? Ethics is a term that is probably easier to define than to illustrate. Basically, ethics deals with standards of conduct or morals established by the current and past attitudes and moods of a particular society. Business ethics, in simple terms, relate to standards of "right" and "wrong" conduct in business relationships. A factor complicating the concept of ethics is that what is considered wrong by one person, firm, industry, or country may be considered right or even desirable by another.

There may be situations that could strain your ethical values and create distress for you, such as if your manager were to direct you to do something that you believe is either unethical or illegal. Say that you're an office manager and your boss, Ms. Nomore Upwright, asks you to keep a separate set of records—with padded deductible expense figures—for income tax purposes.

In a figurative sense, your manager has placed you in a stressful position between the Scylla of willful disobedience and the Charybdis of facing the ethical or legal consequences of your act.[15] If you do as Ms. Upwright directed, you may be as legally responsible (or as criminally negligent) as she is. If you don't do as directed, you may run employment risks, since Ms. Upwright determines your pay raises, assignments, and promotions. What do you do? How might your personal financial responsibilities influence or change your decision? What about the long-run effects on your own conscience and stress level? If you are caught, and the chances are fairly good that you will be, how might your future career and self-image be affected?

When confronted with certain temptations, you should continually remind yourself that ethical practices are not necessarily obsolete. Acting ethically is not always easy when reading articles about scandals throughout the world; nonetheless, many firms today are concerned about the ethical behavior of their employees and have developed formal policy statements on ethical procedures. You will probably discover that you can live a far more confident and distress-free existence if your activities do not border on the unethical or illegal.

Summary

Stress and *tension* are experienced by most people. Not everyone, however, has developed the ability to cope effectively with such feelings. In this chapter we learned the nature of stress and some specific methods for coping with some of its major forms.

Two principal classifications of stress are *eustress* and *distress.* We would not be able to function or to accomplish our goals without some degree of stress; but supervisors should attempt to avoid behaviors that tend to cause their associates to become too tense and stressed.

Some of the major ways one can manage stress are *exercising, eating a proper diet, having a positive attitude, utilizing relaxation techniques,* and *maintaining ethical values.*

Questions for Discussion

1. Evaluate the following statement: "We will find our lives to be far more satisfying and enjoyable once we learn to avoid all forms of stress."
2. What are the *two principal forms* of stress? How do they differ?
3. Explain why *uncertainty, lack of control,* and *pressure* tend to cause stress.
4. What are some situations you have experienced in which the feeling of lack of control brought on stress and anxiety? What might you have done to combat those feelings?
5. What are some of the activities that you, as a supervisor, may engage in that create *stressful situations for your associates*? How might you reduce such stress?
6. What can a person who is experiencing an excessive amount of stress do to *reduce* its effects?
7. In what ways can a regular program of *physical fitness* improve your present state of health and prolong your active years?
8. In your opinion, with all the unfavorable publicity that has been given to *unhealthful foods,* why do many people continue to eat them in excessive quantities?
9. How does maintaining a relatively *positive attitude* about life relate to stress?
10. What does the term *ethics* mean to you? What complicates your developing a catchall definition that relates to everyone?
11. In what ways is *workaholism* similar to *alcoholism*?
12. What do you believe the American philosopher William James meant when he said: "You don't sing because you're happy. You're happy because you sing"?
13. How might the following words of American author Ralph Waldo Emerson relate to you: "Do the thing you fear and the death of fear is certain"?

Can You Define These Terms?

Instructions: Write a definition for each of the following terms. You may check your definitions with those provided in the end-of-text glossary.

stress
eustress
distress
stress management
stressors
wellness programs

self-concept	Type A personality
obsessive-compulsive personality	Type B personality
workaholism	ethics

Supervision In Action

7–1 What I Am to Be I Am Now Becoming

Uncertainty creates stress. Therefore, one way to reduce this form of stress is to reduce uncertainty. A better understanding of yourself—your weaknesses and strengths, especially those related to your current job—as well as your future aspirations, can give you improved feelings of direction and self-worth. Here's an opportunity for you to think about your present self and make some specific plans for the future.

Using the following five-year plan as a guide, take a separate sheet of paper and indicate in the first column where you would like to be five years from now. Indicate in the second column any obstacles currently blocking the achievement of your five-year objectives. In the third column, make general statements regarding how you intend to overcome such obstacles. In the last column, make specific statements regarding how you will overcome your obstacles. Be certain to recognize both your strengths and weaknesses in establishing your goals and determining your plans.

Self-Description

Instructions: Using the columns below as a guide, take a separate sheet of paper and indicate in the spaces the adjectives that best describe your *weaknesses* and *strengths*.

Weaknesses	Strengths
1. ______	1. ______
2. ______	2. ______
3. ______	3. ______
4. ______	4. ______
5. ______	5. ______
6. ______	6. ______
7. ______	7. ______
8. ______	8. ______
9. ______	9. ______
10. ______	10. ______
11. ______	11. ______
12. ______	12. ______
13. ______	13. ______
14. ______	14. ______
15. ______	15. ______

My Five-Year Plan

Where I Want to Be Five Years from Now	Obstacles to Achieving My Objectives	General Plans for Overcoming My Obstacles	Specific Plans for Overcoming My Obstacles
1. Type of job I want to hold: ______	1. ______	1. ______	1. ______
2. Type of industry I want to work in: ______	2. ______	2. ______	2. ______
3. Geographical location where I prefer to work: ______	3. ______	3. ______	3. ______
4. Types of job-related responsibilities I want: ______	4. ______	4. ______	4. ______
5. Types of personal and family responsibilities I want: ______	5. ______	5. ______	5. ______
6. Material possessions I desire: ______	6. ______	6. ______	6. ______

7–2 How Do You Measure Up?

A short test developed by the U.S. Department of Health is helpful in enabling you to identify which aspects of your current lifestyle may pose threats to your health. The test has six sections. Complete one section at a time by circling the numbers in each section that best describe your behavior. The highest possible score in each section is 10. An interpretation of your scores follows the test.

There is no total score for this test. Each section should be considered separately.

	Almost Always	Sometimes	Almost Never
Cigarette Smoking			
If you *never smoke,* circle a score of 10 for this section and go to the next section on *Alcohol and Drugs.*	10		
1. I avoid smoking cigarettes.	2	1	0
2. I smoke only low tar and nicotine cigarettes *or* I smoke a pipe or cigars.	2	1	0
Smoking Score: (continued)			
Alcohol and Drugs			
1. I avoid drinking alcoholic beverages *or* I drink no more than 1 or 2 drinks a day.	4	1	0
2. I avoid using alcohol or other drugs (especially illegal drugs) as a way of handling stressful situations or the problems in my life.	2	1	0
3. I am careful not to drink alcohol when taking certain medicines (for example, medicine for sleeping, pain, colds, and allergies), *or* when pregnant.	2	1	0
4. I read and follow the label directions when using prescribed and over-the-counter drugs.	2	1	0
Alcohol and Drugs Score:			
Eating Habits			
1. I eat a variety of foods each day, such as fruits and vegetables, whole grain breads and cereals, lean meats, dairy products, dry peas and beans, and nuts and seeds.	4	1	0
2. I limit the amount of fat, saturated fat, and cholesterol I eat (including fat in meats, eggs, butter, cream, shortenings, and organ meats such as liver).	2	1	0
3. I limit the amount of salt I eat by cooking with only small amounts, not adding salt at the table, and avoiding salty snacks.	2	1	0
4. I avoid eating too much sugar (especially frequent snacks of sticky candy or soft drinks).	2	1	0
Eating Habits Score:			

	Almost Always	Sometimes	Almost Never
Exercise/Fitness			
1. I maintain a desired weight, avoiding becoming overweight and underweight.	3	1	0
2. I do vigorous exercises for 15–30 minutes at least 3 times a week (examples include running, swimming, brisk walking).	3	1	0
3. I do exercises that enhance my muscle tone for 15–30 minutes at least 3 times a week (examples include yoga and calisthenics).	2	1	0
4. I use part of my leisure time participating in individual, family, or team activities that increase my level of fitness (such as gardening, bowling, golf, and baseball).	2	1	0
Exercise/Fitness Score:			
Stress Control			
1. I have a job or do other work that I enjoy.	2	1	0
2. I find it easy to relax and express my feelings freely.	2	1	0
3. I recognize early, and prepare for, events or situations likely to be stressful for me.	2	1	0
4. I have close friends, relatives, or others whom I can talk to about personal matters and call on for help when needed.	2	1	0
5. I participate in group activities (such as church and community organizations) or hobbies that I enjoy.	2	1	0
Stress Control Score:			
Safety			
1. I wear a seat belt while riding in a car.	2	1	0
2. I avoid driving while under the influence of alcohol and other drugs.	2	1	0
3. I obey traffic rules and the speed limit when driving.	2	1	0
4. I am careful when using potentially harmful products or substances (such as household cleaners, poisons, and electrical devices).	2	1	0
5. I avoid smoking in bed.	2	1	0
Safety Score:			

How were your scores? Here's what they mean. The highest possible score for each section is 10. A score of 9 or 10 is one that you can boast about! You are apparently practicing good health habits in that aspect of your life. Continuing the same habits should reduce the possibility of serious health problems in the areas where you attained high scores.

Scores of 6 to 8 aren't bad, but you do have room for improvement. What changes might you be able to make in the items where you answered "sometimes" or "almost never"? Beware, however, if your scores were below 6 in any category—they could mean that you are taking unnecessary chances with your health.

Endnotes

1. Johanna and Phillip Hunsaker, *Strategies and Skills for Managerial Women* (Cincinnati, Ohio: South-Western Publishing Company, 1986), pp. 86–87.
2. "Inefficient Bosses May Contribute to Employee Stress Disorders," *Contra Costa Times/Business,* February 10, 1986, p. 12.
3. "Health Craze Linked to Drop in Heart Attacks," *Contra Costa Times,* April 18, 1985, p. 17C.
4. "Heart Disease Rate Falling among Men, Du Pont Study Says" *The Wall Street Journal,* April 18, 1985, p. 20.
5. "Employees Who Stay Fit Are Happier, Work Harder" *Contra Costa Times,* May 27, 1985, p. 22.
6. "Exercise for the Deskbound," *Herrick Hospital and Health Center Life,* Fall 1981, p. 3.
7. Brenda C. Coleman, "Workplace Fitness Programs Found to Be Effective," *Contra Costa Times,* February 23, 1986, p. 18D.
8. From an advertising brochure, "Good Health Pays Off," published by Time Incorporated, 1984.
9. Steward Wolf, M.D., "Protective Social Forces that Counterbalance Stress," *Heart Briefs,* Winter 1977, p. 5.
10. Walter H. Gmelch, "A Regimen for Stress Reduction," *Supervisory Management,* December 1982, pp. 16–24.
11. "Stress: Can We Cope?" *Time,* June 6, 1983, p. 50.
12. Meyer Friedman and Ray H. Rosenman, *Type A Behavior and Your Heart* (Greenwich, Conn.: Fawcett Publications, 1974).
13. David Stansbury, "The Art of Stress Gliding," *Campus Voice,* December 1984, p. 66.
14. Daniel Goleman, "Body Paradox: A Handful of People Get More Tense when They Try Relaxation Techniques," *American Health,* April 1986, p. 44.

The Management of Human Resources

Chapter 8

Organizing For Effectiveness

Letting loose of fear of mistakes is at the base of letting loose of employees. And letting loose of employees is good for both you and your organization.
—***Bruce D. Sanders, Consulting Psychologist***

A company in which anything goes will ultimately be a company in which nothing goes.
—***Anonymous***

Learning Objectives

When you finish this chapter, you should be able to:

1. Summarize the nature of organizations and organizing.
2. Recognize how authority, responsibility, and accountability differ.
3. Restate the typical types of formal organizational authority relationships.
4. Explain the various forms of departmentation.
5. Apply some established principles of organization.
6. Utilize the advantages of effective delegation.

" 'Next week, we've got to get organized!' That's what everyone around here keeps saying. This place is unbelievable—no job descriptions, no rules, no nuthin'. We stand around for a half-hour each morning waiting to be told what we're going to do. We're all going to be out on the street pronto if this company ever gets any real competition for its products."

How would you like to go to work each morning and have no idea of what is expected of you? Such a situation would be a bit confusing, wouldn't it? Or what if you had a job in which employees did whatever they felt like doing, since they weren't really clear on the nature of their responsibilities? Let's assume employees arrive at work anytime they want, take coffee breaks and vacations whenever they desire, and, in short, wander aimlessly around their work areas wondering what to do—or not to do—next.

As you might imagine, such unorganized situations would probably result in a high degree of chaos with little in the way of personal job satisfaction for involved employees. People would feel confused and uncertain regarding their relationships to others. They would not even know to whom they were accountable. Tasks would probably be performed in a haphazard fashion, and, in all likelihood, few of the organization's objectives—if it actually had any to begin with—would be accomplished in a sound and reasonable manner.

Work groups have to be organized into effective teams if desired results are to be achieved. Supervisors like you play a highly critical role in the organizing function. Consequently, you need to develop a sound understanding of the organizing concepts discussed in this chapter to carry out your supervisory responsibilities in an effective fashion.

What Is the Nature of Organizations?

Organizations consist of both people and things. Your family and its household make up an organization. Likewise, students in a classroom are an organization. Social and service clubs are also considered organizations. In effect, an organization could be said to exist wherever there are two or more persons joined for the purpose of achieving specific goals. All organizations are unique, but they have similar types of problems. Our concern in this text is with the sort of work organization in which you might find yourself as a supervisor.

Organization: *A group of individuals structured by specialized activities and levels of authority for the purpose of effectively accomplishing a firm's goals.*

What Is an Organization?

Organizations tend naturally to grow out of any group activities. An **organization**, for our purposes, is defined as *a group of in-*

dividuals structured by specialized activities and levels of authority for the purpose of effectively accomplishing a firm's goals. The organization for which you work is, in effect, a group of people with a common purpose.

What Is Organizing?

Related to organizations, of course, is the managerial function called **organizing,** which is the activity of ***coordinating human, material, and financial resources for the purpose of achieving preestablished standards and goals.*** The function of organizing is a broad activity, one that fits in between two other management functions—***planning*** and ***controlling.*** On a senior management level, organizing involves establishing and maintaining an overall organizational structure, or framework, with clearcut lines of authority and working relationships among its members. It further involves establishing policies, procedures, and regulations to guide personnel in their day-to-day activities.

Organizing: *Coordinating human, material, and financial resources to achieve preestablished standards and goals.*

Supervisors, too, engage regularly in the organizing function. Organizing is the activity that allows plans to be carried out more effectively. Supervisors must coordinate people with material and financial resources. Organizing also involves delegating (assigning) tasks and authority to others. In effect, when supervisors are organizing, they are concerned with making certain that the correct proportions of human and other resources are in the right place at the right time so that organizational goals can be accomplished as originally intended. Organizing, therefore, is what helps you and others in your organization put your preestablished plans into action.

How Does the Formal Differ from the Informal Organization?

Every organization has two general sides: the *formal* and the *informal.* The formal side of an organization is its ***planned*** or ***required*** part. The **formal organization** results from the deliberate planning and coordinating of people and activities for the purpose of achieving organizational goals. The formal part of an organization aids in establishing logical relationships between people and positions in a company. It allows managers to apply concepts of **specialization and division of labor;** that is, to divide up tasks and responsibilities among individuals, departments, divisions, or regions for the purpose of increasing organizational effectiveness and productivity.

Formal organization: *The planned structure; relates to the official lines of authority, responsibility, and accountability.*

Specialization and division of labor: *Dividing tasks and responsibilities among individuals, departments, divisions, or regions to increase organizational effectiveness.*

Your organization must have some sort of formal structure in order to achieve its goals. The formal system, therefore, provides some degree of *order and predictability.* For example, you assume, based on your prior planning, that your associates will be on the job at a predetermined time, say, 9:00 each morning. Functioning effectively would be difficult if you didn't have some sort of a formal (i.e., required and planned) system.

"This is what is loosely known as a 'workplace.' "

Source: Reprinted from *The Wall Street Journal* p. 31, by permission of Cartoon Features Syndicate, ©

Informal organization: *The natural self-grouping of individuals according to their personalities and needs rather than to any formal plan.*

Organization chart: *A formal document that shows the chain of command and titles officially assigned to managers.*

Chain of command: *The route or channel in the formal organization through which authority is passed and policies are transmitted to lower levels for implementation.*

Formal organizations, therefore, are created by management; the **informal organization,** however, is not. Instead, it is created naturally when individuals get together as a means of satisfying their *personal psychological and social needs.* Although informal relationships can be influenced by management, they do not show up on any formal organization documents, such as *organization charts.* (Chapter 13 discusses how communication activities are influenced by the informal organization.)

Informal groups can work either to the detriment or advantage of the formal organization. As a supervisor, you'll experience little success attempting to eliminate the informal organization, but you can exert significant influence over it. Later chapters will discuss further aspects of informal groups and their influence on the formal organization.

What Is the Purpose of Organization Charts?

Famed explorers of the past, like Ferdinand Magellan, couldn't have accomplished their navigational feats very well without something called a *chart.* Managers, too, require an aid for helping them chart their courses. A common tool for this purpose is an **organization chart,** which is a diagram illustrating the formal *chain of command* and showing the *titles* that have been officially assigned to managers. The term **chain of command** is defined as the route, or channel, in the formal organization through which authority is passed and policies are transmitted to lower levels for implementation.

An organization chart is helpful because it gives you a visual description of the *authority relationships* in an organization. As a firm grows and adds layers of managers, an organization chart helps to clarify communication networks and to show who is officially accountable to whom. Realize, however, that a formal organization chart is merely a *guide* to authority relationships; it *symbolizes* what management *believes* to be an ideal organizational structure. Some organizations are so dynamic and changing, however, that an organization chart may be obsolete before its ink has dried.

Nonetheless, charts can help to avoid the chaos and confusion that tend to exist in organizations where authority relationships among employees are not clearly spelled out. Employees are generally more effective when they know how they fit into the total scheme of an organization. *Organization manuals,* as discussed in Chapter 4, are also helpful to supervisors as a source of information on their organization's formal authority relationships, along with its policies, procedures, and rules.

How Do Authority, Responsibility, and Accountability Differ?

Three words that you're likely to hear around work organizations are *authority, responsibility* and *accountability.* Each term relates to the formal organization, but they differ in meaning.

Authority can be defined as the *right* of people in an organization to make decisions, act, and direct others to act. It is a type of *power.* For example, as a supervisor you might have the authority to schedule the work of others, determine who works overtime, approve vacation schedules, and authorize certain purchases. Authority is generally something that has been passed down—that is, assigned—to you by your manager.

Authority: *The* right *(or power) of people in an organization to make decisions, act, and direct others to act; flows down the organizational hierarchy.*

Responsibility, on the other hand, is *not* a right; it is a *duty.* It can be defined as the *obligation* you have to perform assigned work or to make certain that someone else performs it in a prescribed way. The plural term **responsibilities** usually refers to the specific *tasks* or *duties* that you have been assigned to perform.

Responsibility: *The* obligation *that organizational members have to perform assigned work or to make certain that someone else performs it in a prescribed way.*

Responsibilities: *Specific* tasks *or* duties *that have been assigned to an organizational member.*

Accountability is sometimes used interchangeably with *responsibility.* However, management purists consider accountability to be the *answerability* you have to your boss based on the responsibilities assigned to you. This concept also applies to your associates, who are answerable to you for their actions.

Accountability: *The* answerability *that organizational members have to their bosses; sometimes used interchangeably with responsibility.*

Visualize the directions that authority and accountability travel in the formal organization. Authority flows *downward.* For example, your manager delegates to you the authority to write checks up to a maximum limit for specified purchases. Accountability, on the other hand, flows *upward.* You are accountable to your manager for the ways in which you carry out your responsibilities (see Figure 8–1).

FIGURE 8–1
Authority Flows Down and Accountability Flows Up the Organization

What Are the Typical Types of Formal Organizational Authority Relationships?

Each part of an organization is important and relates, in some way, to the entire organization. As a supervisor, you should have an understanding of four widely used forms of organizational authority relationships:

1. Line
2. Staff
3. Functional
4. Matrix

Line authority: *The right of individuals who generally are* directly *engaged in achieving the primary goals of the organization.*

What Is the Difference between Line and Staff Authority Relationships?

Most organizations utilize a combination of *line* and *staff* authority relationships. Supervisors with **line authority** are said to have *direct authority* over their own employees. Further, line supervisors are directly accountable to the managers to whom they report. Typically, line personnel are those *directly engaged in achieving* *the primary goals of the organization.* Production and sales managers are common examples of managers with line authority.

Managers with **staff authority,** on the other hand, do not have direct authority over line members of an organization. Their principal responsibility is to provide assistance, advice, services, or to solve specialized problems for line personnel. Examples of individuals with staff authority are personnel or human resource managers, community relations managers, and lawyers in a legal department. However, staff managers do have direct line authority over the individuals who are directly accountable to them. For example, employees in the employee records department of a firm could be directly accountable to a personnel manager, who serves as a staff advisor to line managers. Can you see how a personnel department could be considered staff within an production-oriented organization, but would be considered line when a part of an employment agency?

Staff authority: *Individuals whose main responsibility is to provide assistance, advice, services, or to solve specialized problems for line personnel.*

By performing a variety of support activities, staff specialists contribute toward line department managers, the latter having direct responsibility for attaining organizational goals and objectives. Those in staff positions generally have specialized and technical knowledge. Staff activities are intended to free line managers from involvement with tasks that can be handled more effectively by those with such specialized knowledge. For example, a personnel specialist can save supervisors substantial amounts of time when new employees are needed. Those assigned to a personnel department (referred to as the *human resources department* in some organizations) can do the preliminary recruiting and screening so that supervisors don't have to spend time interviewing applicants who are obviously unsuited for job openings.

Many organizations start out small, sometimes in a garage of one of the founders (as was the case with the Hewlitt-Packard Company, now one of the world's largest electronics firms). As such firms grow, however, they discover the need for specialized personnel to provide input and advice to line operations. Staff activities are sometimes indicated on organization charts by dotted lines (see Figure 8–2).

What Is a Functional Authority Relationship?

As we'll see shortly when we examine some important organizational principles, it is generally preferable for each employee to be accountable to only one manager. In many organizations, however, this concept is not followed. Instead, a structure exists known as a **functional authority relationship.** It exists in organizations where staff specialists have been assigned direct authority over certain line activities. Quality assurance specialists, for example, typically have functional authority over line personnel. They generally have the authority to accept or reject the line department's output based on predetermined quality standards. They are usually directly accountable to someone other than the manager whose

Functional authority relationship: *An authority structure that allows for specialists to exert direct authority over certain line activities.*

FIGURE 8–2
A Simplified Illustration of Line and Staff Authority Relationships

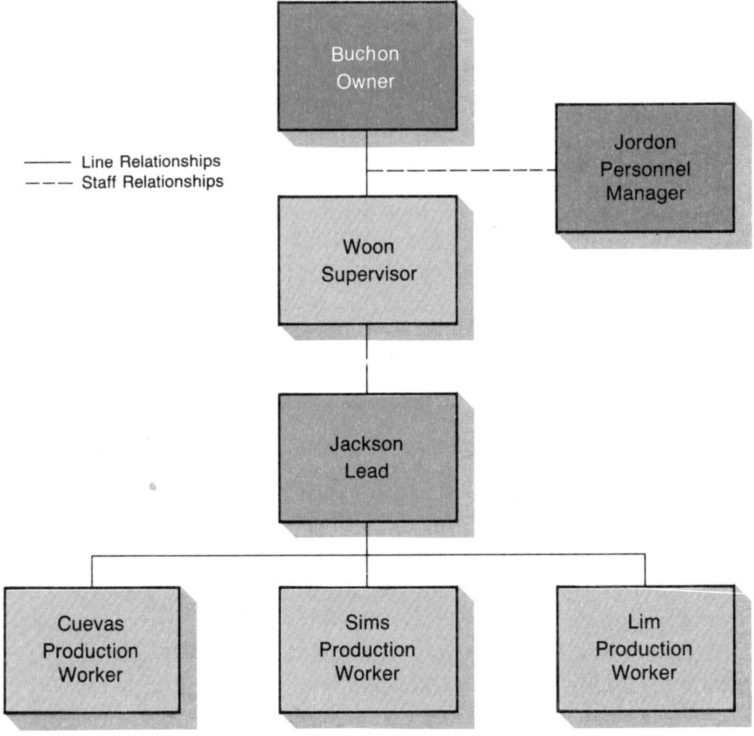

department's output they are inspecting (to be accountable to a line manager could put the quality assurance specialist in an awkward position).

What Is a Matrix Authority Relationship?

Matrix authority relationship: *An authority structure organized around specific projects, programs, or products, rather than along traditional lines.*

Another fairly common form of authority relationship is the *matrix system.* The **matrix authority relationship,** sometimes referred to as *project, program,* or *product management,* has often been used as a temporary organizational arrangement, lasting from only a few weeks to several years.

A major purpose of the matrix form is to be able to utilize key managers or other personnel where they are needed for as long as they are needed. For example, a physicist may be considered a permanent member of a research laboratory, but be *temporarily* assigned to manage or work on a specific project where his or her talents are required. After the project is completed, the physicist will either return to his or her home base or be assigned to another project. Some individuals find themselves on permanent "temporary assignments," since their talents may be needed on one project after another.

As you can see in Figure 8–3, the matrix system, in effect, overlays the established, ongoing formal authority relationships.

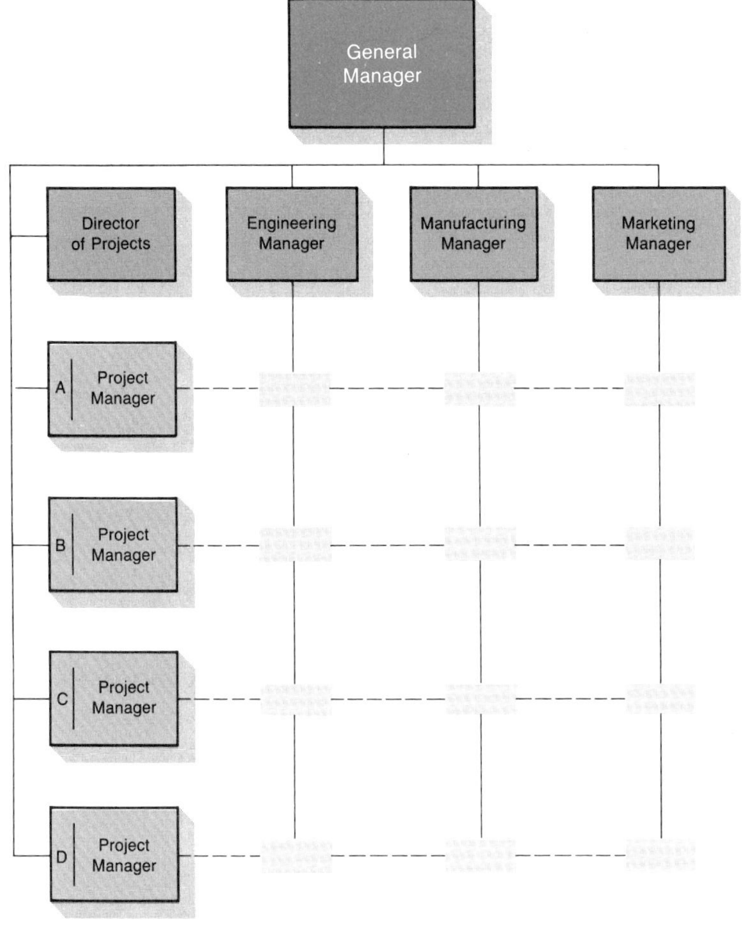

FIGURE 8–3
An Example of a Matrix Organizational Structure Designed for Temporary Projects

Matrix systems vary in their degree of complexity from one organization to another. Although used by a variety of organizations, a matrix system also poses the serious problem where individuals must "serve two masters," which is a violation of an established management principle, the *unity of command* (to be discussed shortly). *Coordination, cooperation,* and *effective communication* become especially important in order to avoid conflict and misunderstanding. A matrix system does have the benefit of utilizing people with specialized skills for particulars projects. It also tends to push decision making down to more people, thus creating greater flexibility and responsiveness for the larger company. Professor C. Edward Kur warns, however, that because such decision making occurs at a lower level in the organization than is common, the matrix system requires an above-average level of interpersonal and political skill.[1]

What Is Organizing by Departments?

Departmentation: *Organizing jobs, tasks, responsibilities, and activities into subunits or departments to improve efficiency of operations.*

Department: *The specific location or set of activities for which managers are responsible; can include activities called* sections, divisions, *and* branches.

Supervisors should attempt to become familiar with the language of management. You've already learned some terms related to organizing. Another term that you should become familiar with is **departmentation,** which in simple terms means putting things together in ways that get positive results. A more formal definition of departmentation is the organization of jobs, tasks, responsibilities, and activities into *subunits,* or departments, for the purpose of improving effectiveness of operations. A **department** is the specific location or set of activities for which a manager is responsible. The term *department* is used in a generic sense to include activities called *sections, divisions,* or *branches.*

The organizing function is relatively simple for small firms. As any work group grows, however, its managers have to make significant organizing decisions related to departmentation, especially regarding the concepts of division of labor and specialization. Departmentation, therefore, involves *grouping together similar types of activities and responsibilities into departments.* The organizational structure of work groups by departments is frequently determined by senior management. Sometimes, however, supervisors will be called on to assist in organizing or reorganizing a firm. Consequently, you should be aware of the principal types of departmentation, which are:

1. By function
2. By territory
3. By product
4. By customer
5. By time

A specific firm may be organized by any one of the above five types or may be organized as a hybrid, or combination, of them (see Figure 8–4). Each type will be examined separately below.

What Is Departmentation by Function?

Functional departmentation: *Organizing departments around major activities (functions), such as finance, marketing, personnel, and manufacturing.*

One of the most common methods for organizing departments is by *function.* **Functional departmentation** results when a firm organizes around major activities or functions. For example, manufacturing is considered an important organizational function and might be viewed as a separate department or division. Other major functions could include marketing, human resources management, corporate communications, and finance. Functions vary with the company and industry.

Figure 8–4 shows functional departmentation at the top of the organizational hierarchy, but it needn't stop there. Many firms, especially larger ones, have additional functional departments at various levels of the organization. For example, accountable to a manufacturing department could be three additional departments, such as engineering services, corporate maintenance, and environmental affairs. Engineering services might be broken down even

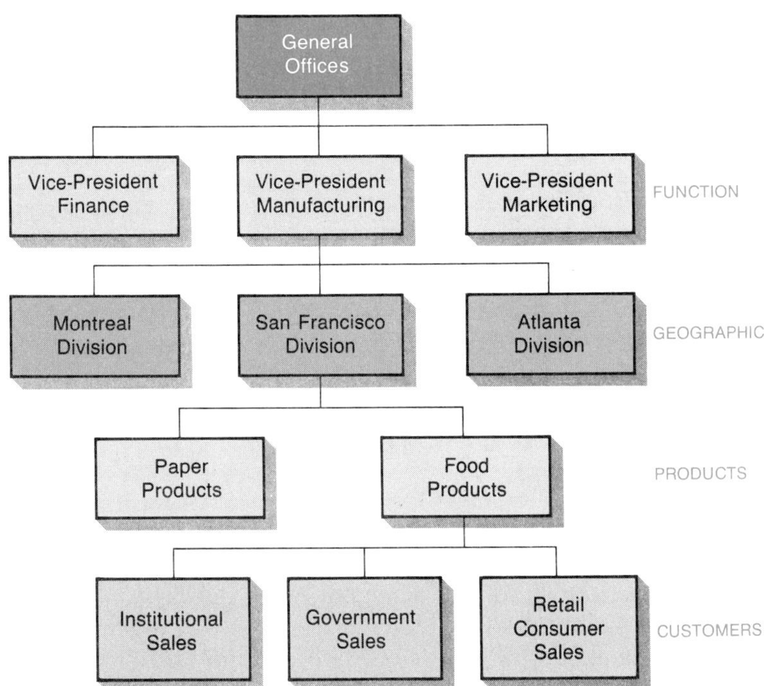

FIGURE 8–4
Examples of Departmentation on More than One Level

further into two additional departments: process technology and industrial engineering (see Figure 8–5). A disadvantage of this type of departmentation is that functional specialists tend to be *excessively narrow* in the scope of their activities and sometimes relate too exclusively to their *own interests*. Functional organization is also considered to be less suited to firms operating in a *dynamic or unstable setting* where the need exists for flexibility and innovative planning. Where unstable conditions exist, less traditional organizational forms may be more suitable, such as the matrix- or project-type organization already discussed.

What Is Departmentation by Territory?

Many firms organize along *territorial* lines. Expanding companies especially may find economic advantages in locating plants or service facilities in various parts of the country, and even in various parts of the world. **Territorial** or **geographic departmentation** is sometimes made because of favorable cost factors related to labor and materials, better access to transportation facilities, more favorable tax treatment, a need to bypass foreign trade barriers, or simply geographical preferences.

Territorial (geographic) departmentation: *Organizing departments by geographic location; locating plants or service facilities in various parts of the country or world.*

Levi Strauss & Company and Safeway Stores, Incorporated, are excellent examples of territorial departmentation. Levi's, for example, has garment manufacturing and distributing divisions throughout the world, including Europe, Canada, Latin America, and the Far East, as well as the United States. Safeway, a retailer of

FIGURE 8–5
Examples of Functional Departmentation on More than One Level

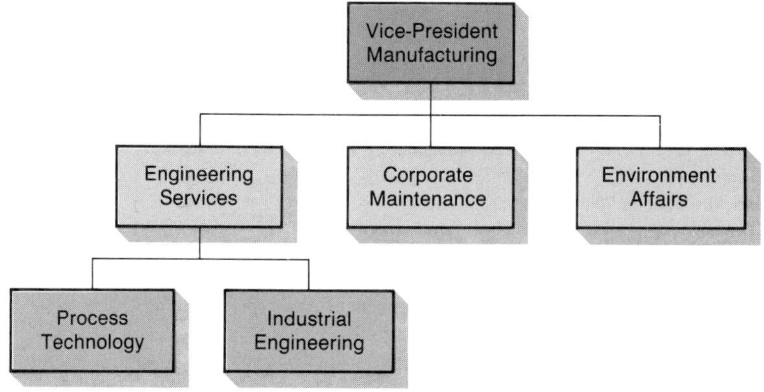

groceries and related consumer goods and services, has 23 territorial divisions located throughout the United States, and 6 others situated in Canada, the United Kingdom, West Germany, Australia, Mexico, and the Middle East.

While chief executive officer of Apple Computer, John Sculley reorganized Apple along the lines of one functional (product development) and three territorial departments (or divisions). He believed that the company could not continue its experienced rate of growth operating out of a single geographic division.[2]

Figure 8–4 illustrates geographic departmentation based on divisions located in Montreal, San Francisco, and Atlanta.

What Is Departmentation by Product?

Product departmentation: *Organizing departments along product lines.*

Quite frequently, firms that were founded on a functional basis start to feel growing pains and the need to reorganize along product lines. There may also exist the desire to make greater utilization of various employees' specialized skills and product knowledge. Under **product departmentation,** all of the various activities related to a particular product are assigned to one department or division. Although this form of organization can provide greater responsiveness to customer needs, there is the potential disadvantage of increased costs resulting from duplicated facilities. Referring again to Figure 8–4, you can see an example of product departmentation based on two classes of products: paper products and food products.

General Electric Company, a giant organization with sales around $40 billion per year, departmentalizes around 14 separate products lines, four of which are aircraft engines, lighting, locomotives, and medical diagnostic imaging.[3]

What Is Departmentation by Customer?

Customer departmentation: *Organizing departments according to type of purchaser.*

You might find yourself working for a company that departmentizes on the basis of *type of customer.* The purpose of **customer de-**

partmentation is to provide better service or to attract specific types of customers.

Commercial banks are an example of customer departmentation. They typically have various loan departments for different classes of customers. Some firms have separate marketing operations and sales forces for selling to government agencies, institutions, and merchants, as illustrated in Figure 8–4.

What Is Departmentation by Time?

Another typical and long-established form of departmentation is on the basis of *time.* **Time departmentation** may be based on around-the-clock operations, and utilize shifts (e.g., day; second, or swing; and third, or graveyard).

Time departmentation: *Organizing departments on the basis of time, such as day, second and third shifts.*

Possible problems arising from time departmentation relate to determining *who has responsibility* for the overall operations of a specific department operating on more than one shift. Also, *conflict among the various shift supervisors* sometimes develops when their standards or expectations are different from their employees'. *Morale problems* can develop in situations where employees on one shift feel that they are not given the same privileges as workers on another shift.

What Are Some Established Principles of Organization?

Supervisors have a primary responsibility to make certain that things get done. They accomplish things with and through people on a day-to-day basis. As a result, supervisors tend to be a bit suspicious of any kind of knowledge that doesn't lean toward the practical. To the hands-on type of supervisor, principles and theories may seem excessively scholarly and "ivory towerish."

But guard against an unreasonably cynical attitude toward established principles. They have generally been developed from extensive research and observation of real happenings. Employed wisely, principles can actually enable you to be even more practical in your job. Of course, with experience as a supervisor you might eventually reach the same conclusions that are embodied in principles. But why reinvent the wheel? Many principles have proven helpful to managers and have enabled them to avoid the more common types of managerial pitfalls. Of course, as with any rule or guideline, there may be exceptions that require you to adapt your approach to the situation—no theory should be blindly applied without analyzing the specific circumstances at hand.

In the next section of the chapter, we explore some of the more common principles that should prove useful to you in your managerial activities. In a later section of the chapter, we will examine other significant organizational principles.

What Is the Scalar Principle?

We've seen how a formal organization has a *chain of command*—a structural hierarchy—with each person directly accountable to

Although time can sometimes be saved, there are hazards associated with bypassing the formally established chain of command.

Scalar principle: *Assertion that authority and accountability in an organization should flow in a clear unbroken line between the ultimate authority (the manager at the top) and the workers at the bottom.*

a person at the next level. Management theorists have concluded that communication should generally follow the official chain of command. Out of this thinking has evolved the **scalar principle,** which suggests that authority and accountability in an organization should flow in a clear, unbroken line (down the *scale,* so to speak) between the point of ultimate authority (the senior manager) and the workers at the bottom of the hierarchy. According to this principle, communication should not bypass the chain of command. The scalar principle, when followed, helps to make the transmission of communication more orderly and predictable.

Ideally, the principle should be applied both up and down the organization. Here's an example of an abuse of the scalar principle. Assume that one of your associates, Marc Stevens, is upset about the behavior of coworker Sandra Sarnoff, but he doesn't mention anything to you about the problem. Instead, Marc leapfrogs—that is, bypasses—the formal chain of authority and complains directly to your manager. Can you visualize the problems that could develop if your manager also played leapfrog, bypassed you, and took direct action with Sandra? Such action would tend to *undermine your authority* and could *reduce your effectiveness* with employees in the future. Authority relationships, therefore, should usually follow formal channels; otherwise, complications related to our next principle, the *unity of command,* are likely to develop.

What Is the Unity of Command Principle?

Have you ever been in the position where you've had to "serve two masters," that is, been accountable to two managers? Even if both managers agree on goals, objectives, and methods for achieving them, such arrangements tend to place employees in unnecessarily uncomfortable positions. The situation becomes especially difficult when one manager gives an employee orders to perform specific tasks and another manager gives the same employee conflicting orders.

The **unity of command** principle recognizes this situation. The principle means that since instructions or orders from two or more bosses may conflict, no employee should take them from or be accountable to more than one manager. Where possible, try to avoid placing your associates in the position where they are accountable to more than one manager, since doing so tends to place them in difficult and awkward situations.

Unity of command: *Assertion that no employee should be accountable to more than one manager to avoid conflicting instructions or orders from two or more managers.*

Dual command is the term often used to denote such a situation where one employee is accountable to more than one boss (i.e., a situation that abuses the unity of command principle). If you can't avoid the situation in which your associates have more than one manager, as in the cases of matrix and functional authority relationships, you should try to make it clear to them whose orders take precedence under which situations. An employee could be advised to tell the second manager who gives instructions something like this: "I think you should know that your request differs from what Robin told me to do. I want to do what's right, so do you think you and Robin could work this out?"

Dual command: *The situation in which one subordinate is accountable to more than one manager; an abuse of the unity of command principle.*

What Is the Unity of Direction Principle?

Another principle related to the unity of command is the **unity of direction** principle, which suggests that each group of activities with the same goal should have only one head and one set of plans. It focuses on *process* rather than *personnel.* The unity of direction principle relates to the old adage, "Too many cooks spoil the broth." Conflict and confusion often result when more than one leader is involved in a project, each having separate and distinct methods for achieving a particular goal. Once again, however, we must recognize that in reality this principle is ignored in the case of matrix or project authority relationships.

Unity of direction: *Assertion that each group of activities with the same goal should have only one head and one set of plans; focuses on process rather than personnel.*

What Are the Realities of the Chain of Command?

We've already learned that the scalar, unity of command, and unity of direction principles are not followed when functional and matrix authority relationships are utilized. In addition, some organizations engage in an "all one family" syndrome, in which managers and employees interact on an informal, first-name basis. Further, some senior managers regularly bypass channels to deal directly with crises. These activities, coupled with the changing nature of organizations, have caused some observers to question the validity of religiously practicing principles related to the chain of command. Professor David S. Brown, for example, has written:

> *The growing complexity of today's work assignments, the interrelatedness of people at all organizational levels, the development of matrix management and the use of task forces and other work teams, and the increasing contact of those at lower levels with clients and the public, have made management conscious of the fact that the guidelines developed for other times and places may not be appropriate for today.*[4]

Consequently, since exceptions to following the chain of command tend to be relatively prevalent today, managers should recognize that some of the communication problems and departmental conflicts that arise are a result of not applying principles that have proven to be quite sound over the years.

What Is the Span of Supervision?

Let's assume that you love children and have decided to take a job at a childcare center. Let's also assume that a shortage of childcare facilities exists in the district where you work. As a result, you've been assigned to a room containing 28 energetic young children aged three to five. You have no one to assist you in supervising the children. At the end of the first day you feel like marshmallow syrup strained through a wet dish towel. Attempting to keep track of and work effectively with 28 children, you've concluded, is a virtual impossibility. To meet parents' expectations of a nursery school program, you believe there shouldn't be more than seven to ten children assigned to each teacher—and even that number could be a migraine inducer!

Span of supervision: *Depending on various factors, there is a limit to the number of employees a supervisor can effectively direct.*

This incident relates to a management concept termed **span of supervision,** which refers to the number of employees one manager can supervise directly. (This concept is also known as the *span of control* and the *span of management.*) The principle asserts that the number of individuals reporting to a supervisor should not exceed nor be fewer than can be effectively directed. In general, the larger the number of employees reporting to one manager, the harder it is for him or her to supervise effectively, since each employee requires a certain amount of the supervisor's limited time.

What, then, determines the optimum (best) span of supervision? How many people can you effectively supervise? There's no simple and definitive answer to these questions. Instead, the optimum number usually depends on five major factors:

1. The supervisor's skill
2. The nature of the work performed by employees

3. The competence of employees
4. The extent of staff assistance
5. The nature of the supervisor's job

Supervisor's Skill. Regarding the first factor, the more you've developed your *managerial skills,* such as planning, coordinating, training, and especially your ability to delegate, the greater the number of employees you should be able to work with and through.

Nature of the Work Performed by Associates. The second factor has a significant influence over your span of supervision. Are your employees' activities of a nature that require *continual interaction* with you? If so, your span would be more limited than in cases where employees' jobs are relatively routine and require little of your input. For example, the supervisor of a typing pool, assuming employees are reasonably well trained, could probably handle more employees since all are performing essentially similar tasks.

Competence of Associates. The third factor, competence of associates, is equally important. You should be able to supervise more employees as your current employees acquire greater skills and ability. Well-trained and experienced employees who are allowed to participate in the decision-making process generally require less supervision than do employees with little training and experience.

Extent of Staff Assistance. Does your organization have a human resource department that relieves you of many hiring and training responsibilities? If so, you should have a broader span of supervision. The less staff assistance you receive, the more time you must spend on nonmanagerial activities. Staff assistance can free you to engage in greater amounts of direct supervision.

Nature of the Supervisor's Job. Finally, the nature of your job influences your span of supervision. Are you a working supervisor, that is, do you operate equipment in addition to supervising personnel? How many different activities do you have to perform? Do you have to prepare a substantial number of reports? Do you have numerous meetings to attend away from your department? How much geographic territory does your job require you to cover? Are you called on to assist in other projects? Are your employees widely dispersed, or are they situated in a relatively concentrated location? Does your supervisory job require an extensive amount of time spent on "putting out fires"? These and other factors related to your job exert a significant influence over how many employees you can effectively supervise.

● Why Is Delegation so Important?

Unless you're a firefighter by trade, chances are that your job description doesn't list putting out fires as one of your typical responsibilities. Unfortunately, if you don't learn one of the most important managerial tools available—*delegation*—you're likely to join the ranks of "firefighter managers." Supervisors who have not developed the skill of task delegation often find themselves too busy to plan activities adequately. As a result, they run from one crisis to another, because they weren't able to find or take the time to plan in advance.

Delegation: *Giving rights or assigning responsibilities to others.*

The process of **delegation,** that is, the act of *giving rights* or *assigning responsibilities and tasks* to another person, is a significant challenge for many managers. As a supervisor, your job responsibilities, tasks, and duties have been assigned, or delegated, to you by your manager, as has the authority, or right, that you have to make independent supervisory decisions. In smaller organizations, delegation is less essential (and sometimes not even possible), but in larger organizations delegation is necessary if managers are to perform their assigned responsibilities effectively.

What Are the Advantages of Delegation?

Delegation offers many advantages, both to you, the supervisor, and to your employees. For example, delegation relieves you of certain time-consuming duties and activities and thus *frees you for*

Delegating various tasks to associates frees the supervisor for other managerial activities, such as planning and control.

broader responsibilities and functions, such as planning, controlling, and improving working conditions. Delegating certain tasks tends to *enrich* (make more challenging and satisfying) your employees' jobs. For employees who desire to rise in an organization, shared responsibilities provide opportunities to *develop new skills.* Further, their chances of receiving *promotions* will be far greater as they acquire a broader understanding of work activities.

What Is Delegation by Exception?

A few management principles were saved until this section, since they relate so closely to the concept of delegation. One of these principles is referred to as the *exception principle,* a concept that is often abused by "firefighter" or "crisis" managers. The **exception principle** asserts that regular, recurring activities and decisions should routinely be delegated to and handled by associates, and that unusual, nonrecurring decisions (exceptions) should be referred to a higher-level manager.

Exception principle: *Assertion that regular and recurring decisions should be delegated to employees, and nonroutine decisions be handled at a higher level.*

Some managers, although they would agree with the need to delegate, might take exception with the exception principle. They believe that employees should not only receive an ample share of routine or "grunt" work, but they should also be given the opportunity to stretch from time to time by being assigned tasks that challenge them. Many employees receive satisfaction from and are motivated by challenging work.

How Does Authority Relate to Delegation?

"I'm responsible for results in my department, but I'm not given enough authority to carry out my responsibilities!" Have you ever heard a comment like that? It's not uncommon in organizations and relates to another delegation-related principle, the **adequacy of authority principle,** which asserts that any authority assigned to managers should be sufficient enough to allow them to achieve expected results. Problems frequently develop when individuals are held accountable for specific types of results but aren't given ample authority to carry out their assigned tasks as planned.

Adequacy of authority principle: *Assertion that authority assigned to managers should be sufficient to enable them to achieve expected results.*

Do All Employees Want to Be "Delegatees"?

Knowing your employees is important. Motivated, high-achieving employees will generally accept delegated tasks willingly. However, employees who may perceive their positions as merely means to another end—that is, a temporary stop in their journey to another job or organization—may not be so gracious in accepting assigned tasks. It isn't safe, therefore, to assume that all employees desire to be "delegatees" without additional encouragement, guidance, or direction from you, their supervisor.

Understanding employees' reasons for not wanting to be delegatees can help provide you with a better understanding of how you can motivate them into accepting assigned tasks more willingly.

TABLE 8–1
Why Some Employees Resist Delegation

- Employees find it easier to let the supervisor make all the decisions.
- Employees may not be sure of their own level of authority and even who their supervisor is (a situation involving dual command).
- Employees double check with the supervisor every decision they make before implementing it (this situation exists where the supervisor is excessively critical of mistakes).
- Employees feel that they haven't received the proper information to handle the work.
- Some employees are not prepared to accept responsibility.
- Employees may not be convinced that they can gain anything by accepting responsibility.

Professors A. T. Hollingsworth and Abdul Rahman A. Al-Jafary suggest six reasons why employees resist delegation, as described in Table 8–1.[5]

Why Do Many Supervisors Have Difficulty in Delegating?

If the act of delegating offers so many advantages, why do numerous supervisors fail to delegate as frequently as they should? In some instances, supervisors don't delegate because they *lack confidence in their employees* to carry out tasks as expected. These are the managers who feel that "if you want something done right, you've got to do it yourself." However, as a believer in the value of delegating once asked, "If you don't trust them, then why did you hire them?"

In some cases, of course, employees may not be able to perform certain duties that you would like to delegate, or may complain unjustly each time you assign them a different task. With adequate training, experience, and motivation, however, many employees could do a satisfactory job.

Sometimes supervisors who can't delegate may actually *lack confidence in themselves,* fearing that they are giving something away that rightfully belongs to them. Often these are the managers who spend their last two hours in the office every day trying to determine what work they are going to take home that evening.

In some instances, persons who are afraid to delegate *fear that their employees will "show them up"* by doing even better jobs than they themselves could do. Or sometimes supervisors don't delegate because they simply *like performing certain tasks* that they feel comfortable with and do well. It should be stressed, however, that delegation is essential for supervisors who want to be free for other important managerial activities. Besides, a super-

TABLE 8–2
Guidelines for Delegating Tasks to Employees

- *Decide which tasks can be delegated.* Many tasks can be delegated. Some are minor or regularly recurring decisions or tasks. However, difficult and challenging assignments may often be assigned to your employees, aiding substantially in their development.
- *Decide who should get the assignment.* Who has ample time? Is special job competence necessary? Who will find the tasks a useful developmental experience? These are questions that should be answered when deciding who should get the assignment.
- *Delegate the assignment.* Provide the delegatee with necessary information to perform the task. Where possible, delegate by results expected, not techniques or methods to be used. Cultivate an atmosphere of free and open communication between you and the delegatee.
- *Establish a feedback system.* Provide for a system of checkpoints and/or feedback so that you will be aware of progress. Your feedback system should be carefully selected, however, since the tighter your controls, the less actual delegation will take place.

visor's own reputation is enhanced when his or her associates excel and move up the organizational hierarchy. Table 8–2 suggests some guidelines to follow when delegating tasks to employees.

Who Is Accountable for Results?

Delegation, you have learned, provides you—the supervisor—with numerous benefits. You can share your responsibilities and accountabilities, in a sense, with your employees. Who, then, is accountable for the final results after you've delegated tasks for others?

The answer to this question can be found in another principle that relates closely to delegation concepts—the **accountability for results principle**—which asserts that the obligations assigned to individuals by their managers are absolute and cannot be totally passed on to others. Therefore, when you have been assigned the obligation to perform a particular task, *you are ultimately accountable and responsible for the results,* even if you shared your accountability and responsibility with an employee. Your manager, too, is ultimately accountable for those tasks that were delegated to you, as is the chief executive officer of a corporation ultimately accountable for the overall results of the organization.

Accountability for results principle:
Assertion that managers are still held answerable for results, even when authority to achieve objectives has been assigned to their subordinates.

Why Is Delegation a Matter of Degree?

Delegation isn't an all or nothing matter. In reality there are a variety of degrees of delegation ranging from absolute to very slight.

TABLE 8–3
Degrees of Delegation that Can Be Used by Supervisors (from highest to lowest)

- *Take action*—No further contact with me is needed.
- *Take action*—Let me know what you did.
- *Look into this problem*—Let me know what you intend to do; do it unless I say not to.
- *Look into this problem*—Let me know what you intend to do; delay action until I give approval.
- *Look into this problem*—Let me know alternative actions available, list their pros and cons, and recommend an action for my approval.
- *Look into this problem*—Give me all the facts; I will decide what to do.

While director of organizational planning with the Westinghouse Electric Corporation, W. J. Nesbitt developed six typical degrees of delegation that could be used by a supervisor, as described in Table 8–3.[6]

Summary

All supervisors are members of organizations. As managers, they also are responsible for carrying out the significant managerial function of *organizing.* Organizations and organizing are essential for the accomplishment of goals in an orderly and predictable fashion.

Organizations consist of *formal* and *informal* sides. The formal side can be viewed on organization charts; the informal side arises out of the personal psychological and social needs of organizational members. Organizations can also be viewed by the manner in which their authority structures are established. Most organizations utilize one or a modification of one of the following forms: *line, staff, functional,* and *matrix.*

Authority, responsibility, and *accountability* are three important concepts related to organizational members. Authority is a *right,* responsibility is a *duty,* and accountability is *answerability.*

Organizations can also be examined from the perspective of *departmentation,* the major types of which include: *by function, by territory, by product, by customer,* and *by time.*

Although many supervisors tend to shy away from theory, the awareness of certain *principles* can help them avoid falling into certain organizational traps. Principles discussed in the chapter were the *scalar, unity of command, unity of direction,* and *span of supervision.* We also learned the importance of *delegating* tasks for the purpose of developing subordinates and freeing the supervisor for other important managerial tasks. Three additional delegation-related principles discussed were the *exception, adequacy of authority,* and *accountability for results principles.*

Questions for Discussion

1. Why do organizations exist? What is the purpose of the managerial function termed *organizing*?
2. Why does the *informal organization* exist side by side with the *formal*? Are informal organizations good or bad? Explain.
3. What is the purpose of an *organization chart?* What doesn't it reveal?
4. Explain how the terms *authority, responsibility* and *accountability* differ in meaning.
5. How do *line* and *staff* authority relationships differ?
6. Should a *functional authority relationship* be allowed to exist in organizations? Explain.
7. What sort of authority—*line, staff,* or *functional*—would an instructor be likely to have over new production employees assigned to the training department for two weeks of orientation and training?
8. Why is the *matrix* form of organization sometimes used? What inherent shortcoming does it have?
9. List and describe five forms of *departmentation.* Under what circumstances might each be utilized?
10. Should there ever be exceptions to the *scalar principle*? Explain.
11. Why should anyone ever object to being held *accountable* to more than one manager?
12. What are the differences among the terms *dual command, unity of command,* and *unity of direction*?
13. What influences how many employees you can effectively supervise? How might you expand your *span of supervision*?
14. What types of tasks should you *delegate* to employees? Explain.
15. Evaluate the following statement: "It's not the way in which a delegated task is performed; it's the results that count."
16. Describe the advantages that can be derived from *delegation activities.*
17. Why do some supervisors find delegating to be a difficult activity?
18. Describe *three principles* that relate directly to delegation concepts.

Can You Define These Terms?

Instructions: Write a definition for each of the following terms. You may check your definitions with those provided in the end-of-text glossary.

organization
organizing
formal organization
specialization and division of labor
informal organization
organization chart
chain of command
authority
responsibility

responsibilities
accountability
line authority
staff authority
functional authority relationship
matrix authority relationship
departmentation
department
functional departmentation
territorial (geographic) departmentation
product departmentation
customer departmentation
time departmentation
scalar principle
unity of command
dual command
unity of direction
span of supervision (span of control; span of management)
delegation
exception principle
adequacy of authority principle
accountability for results principle

Supervision In Action

8–1 Delegation, or Merely Passing the Buck?

Zoda Klontz supervises office workers in the payroll section of the Whetside Whistle Company, a medium-sized organization located in the suburbs of Houston, Texas. Zoda recently attended a three-day supervisory management workshop for first-line supervisors with less than two years of managerial experience.

One of the topics covered during the workshop was the importance of delegation. Although Zoda had heretofore been remiss in this area, she was now firmly convinced that she should attempt to delegate far more tasks to her employees. Zoda could readily see the advantages to both herself and to her employees.

"If I delegated more frequently," Zoda realized, "I could free some of my time to do a better job of scheduling regular work assignments to my office staff. I would also have time to plan some improvements in work methods, something that I've been wanting to do for some time. Especially important, delegating tasks to my employees should really make them feel good. They will know that I'm sincerely interested in their welfare, since the new tasks that I assign to them will give them the opportunity to develop into more rounded and skillful employees. This will enhance their chances for promotion. It will also add more variety to their jobs and improve their morale. They should love me for it!"

Zoda has decided to try out her newly acquired philosophy. It is Friday morning, and Zoda is approaching one of her employees, Steve Stevens.

Zoda: Steve, you know those transmittal reports that I have to prepare to submit to my boss each Friday? Well, from now on you're going to be responsible for doing them. What do you think of that?

Steve: Ms. Klontz, when do you expect me to find time to work on that stuff? I'm already up to my ears in my own work, and now you're going to dump your work on me? I can't believe that when I've got tons of my own work that I'm trying to get out on time, you expect me to do yours too!

Questions

1. Was Zoda's desire to delegate certain tasks to Steve a mistake? Explain.

2. What might have been a more effective approach for Zoda to have taken with Steve that would have made him more receptive to taking on new tasks?

3. If you were Zoda and had received Steve's negative response, what would you say next?

8–2 Don't Judge an Organization by Its Chart

"My name is Brian James. I'm a management professor at a community college and have an interesting story about an organization that I'd like to relate to you.

"When I lived in England, I worked for a small company where the *formal* organization looked like Exhibit 1. In actual fact, however, the *informal* organization (and the *de facto* running of the company) looked like Exhibit 2, with the size of the squares indicating a person's influence in the company's everyday operations.

"The president's secretary was an older unmarried woman, who had started with the boss's father (as his secretary) when the company was first founded. She had trained the founder's son from his first day on the job. When the father retired from the firm and the son took his place as president, Ms. Wilson (the secretary) still retained the same position. To this day, the existing president continually looks to her for guidance in running the company.

"Ms. Wilson's power is and was incredible. She had tremendous influence, and decided who would or would not get to see the president. She even gave orders to the department managers—even though on the firm's organization chart she had no link to them.

"What used to really make me smile was that some of the salespeople who called on the firm gave her a bad time (she was a very quiet and dignified woman) and they never did realize that she was the power behind the throne. Consequently, they never even got to meet the president to give him their sales presentations. She really knew how to fix them!"

Exhibit 1

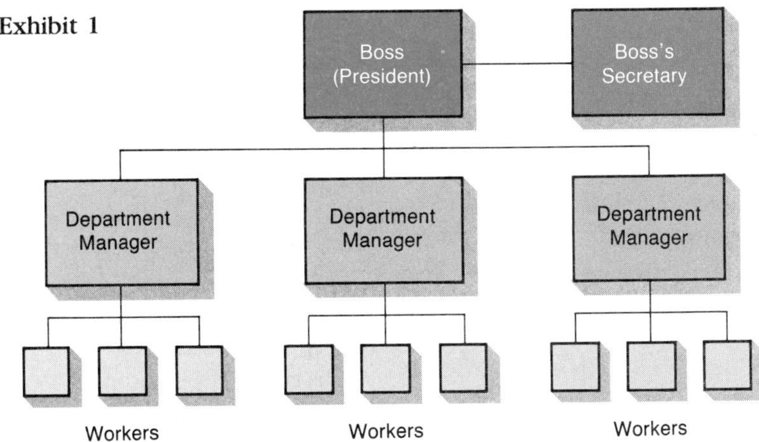

Questions

1. Why does Ms. Wilson, the president's secretary, seem to have more actual authority than is apparent on the formal organization chart?

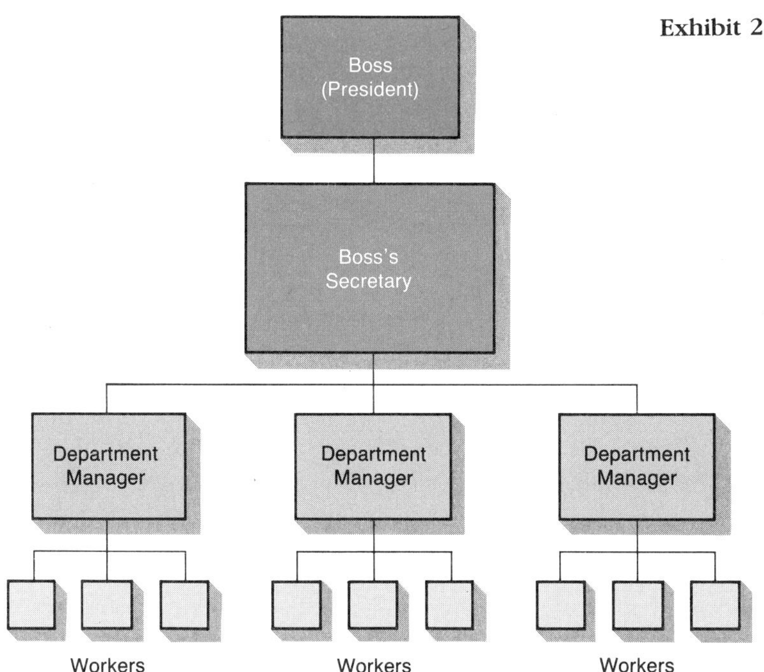

Exhibit 2

2. What conditions or factors tend to alter the planned structure of the formal organization as indicated on a firm's chart? Can such factors be eliminated? Explain.

3. What effect might Ms. Wilson's informal power have on the attitudes and motivation of the department managers?

8–3 Not Too Sharp an Organization

These are the words that shout from the lighted plastic sign located above the entrance of the small compact disc and tape store on Mimosa Street in the town of Imbad, Arkansas. The present time is 3:30 P.M., and the store if filled with noisy high-school students anxious to buy their favorite top-40 discs and tapes.

"Excuse me, lady," interrupts an eager 12-year-old girl forcing her way to the front of the counter. Jaws energetically

RAZOR'S COMPACT DISCS
AND TAPES

SHARPEST MUSIC IN TOWN!

chewing two pieces of sugarless bubble gum, she impatiently asks, "Do you have Peace Missle's latest hit *Free the Fleas,* and Kidder Pea Buddy's new disc, *Won't Worry, Be Sappy?*"

"If you'll just be patient, I'll be with you in a moment," pleaded Ernestine, who had recently taken a part-time job as a salesclerk at Razor's Compact Discs and Tapes Store.

Ernestine has been working only three weeks in her job, but she's already seen some of the types of problems that typically exist in work organizations. Everything seems to be in a state of chaos at Razor's. Tapes and discs are continually missing or filed in the wrong sections. Frequently Mr. Razor doesn't keep enough change on hand to handle the volume of transactions. Customers who placed special orders often become disgruntled and disgusted, since Mr. Razor seems to have no organized system for following up. Thefts are commonplace, probably because of a store layout that seems to encourage pilferage. There are four employees, none of whom has been assigned clearcut responsibilities or given any training for the job. In fact, Mr. Razor permits no one but himself to go into the cash drawer to make change. As a result, there often are bottlenecks and time-consuming delays when Mr. Razor is away from the front counter.

Before coming to work at Razor's, Ernestine sometimes wondered if organizations were a good thing, or whether they weren't instead merely bodies that got in the way of creative and ambitious people. After only three weeks at Razor's, Ernestine has begun to realize that virtually any firm has to be well-organized if goals and objectives of groups of people are going to be accomplished in an effective manner.

"Don't real-world businesses ever follow the management practices that we study in our college courses?" Ernestine recently asked herself. "I'm sure they can't all be run like Razor's Discs. Many of the concepts studied in my management courses could really be well applied to Razor's operations. Oh well, I'd better be cautious or Mr. Razor will think I'm one of those pushy college types who feel that they know it all after only a few days on the job."

Questions

1. Ernestine seems to have become increasingly frustrated in her new job. What specifically seems to be bothering her?
2. If you were Ernestine, what specifically would you do to improve the state of organization at Razor's?
3. What are some of the inherent dangers if Ernestine attempts to take it upon herself to reorganize operations at Razor's Records?
4. If you were an outside consultant asked by Mr. Razor to recommend methods for improving operations at the store, what would you suggest?

8–4 Reading a Chart

This exercise is designed to reinforce your understanding of organization charts. Examine the chart illustrated in Exhibit 3 and then answer the following questions (assume that each box represents one person).

Exhibit 3

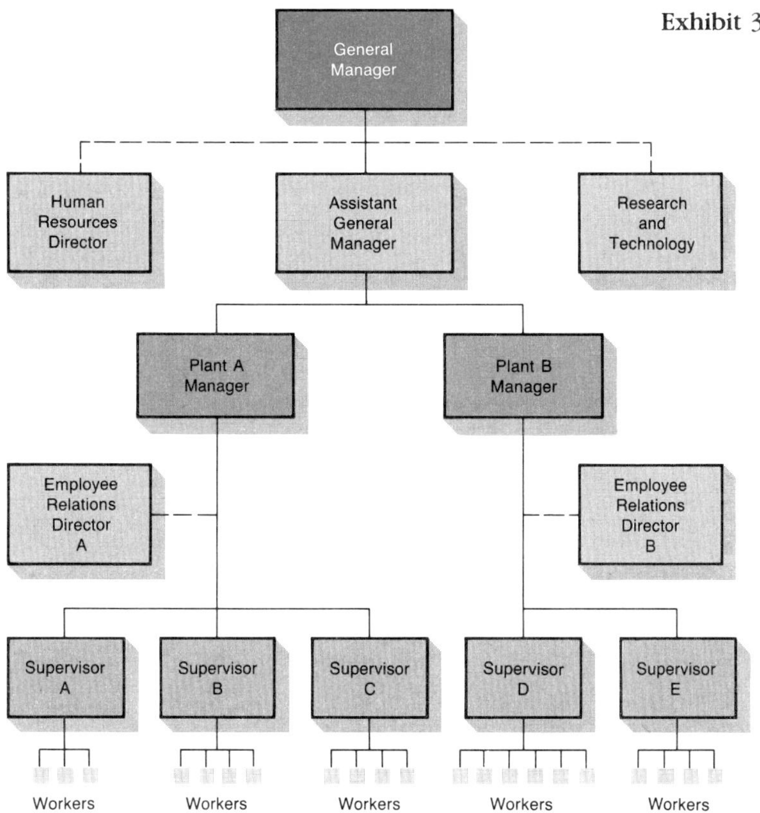

Questions

1. How many persons have staff authority relationships? What are their titles?
2. How many line managers exist in Plant A? Plant B? What are their titles?
3. Which supervisor in Plant A has the broadest span of management? How many workers are accountable to him or her?
4. Which manager in the organization has the broadest span of management? How many people report to him or her?
5. According to the chart, which type of authority, if any, does the Plant B manager have over supervisor B? Explain.

8–5 What Can You Delegate?

Instructions: The following exercise is intended to make you think in *practical* terms. Assuming that you are a supervisor where you currently work, determine three activities that you might delegate to your associates. Then complete the form. How might the time spent on this exercise actually save you time?

	An Activity I Can Delegate	Person to Whom I Can Delegate	Training Necessary before Delegation	Length of Training	Date of Delegation	Estimation of Time Saved
1.						
2.						
3.						

Endnotes

1. C. Edward Kur, "Making Matrix Management Work," *Supervisory Management,* March 1982, p. 40.
2. "John Sculley on Sabbatical," *Fortune?* (International Edition), March 27, 1989, pp. 63, 64.
3. Stratford P. Sherman, "The Mind of Jack Welch," *Fortune* (International Edition), March 27, 1989, pp. 37–44.
4. David S. Brown, "How Breakable Is the Chain of Command?" *Supervisory Management,* January 1981, pp. 2–7.
5. A. T. Hollingsworth and Abdul Rahman A. Al-Jafary, "Why Supervisors Don't Delegate and Employees Won't Accept Responsibility," *Supervisory Management,* April 1983, pp. 12–17.
6. Categories developed by W. H. Nesbitt, while director of organizational planning, Westinghouse Electric Corporation, as reported in Harvey Sherman, *It All Depends: A Pragmatic Approach to Organization* (University, Alabama: University of Alabama Press, 1975) pp. 83–84.

White Sox
PERSONNEL

Chapter 9

Selecting, Orienting, and Compensating Employees

A person is never more perfect than when filling out a job application.

—Stanley J. Randal

Learning Objectives

When you finish this chapter, you should be able to:

1. Describe the employment process.
2. Explain how human resource requirements are determined.
3. Summarize the activities associated with obtaining job candidates.
4. Screen candidates for job openings more effectively.
5. Provide employees with proper job orientation.
6. Detail the various types of employee compensation.

"Boss, some of us have been talking and we're really upset about the new employee you recently selected for the department. That person doesn't seem to fit in at all. We've had a really cohesive team until now, and the new guy doesn't seem to be the least interested in being a team member. We think we ought to be able to have some input in selecting people for the department in the future. Okay?"

As a supervisor, you expect to get things done—that is, to achieve organizational goals—with and through human resources. To accomplish this critical responsibility, however, you must select and maintain the right people for positions available within your work unit. As implied in the opening words, newly selected employees should fit into the existing departmental culture. Selecting the *right* employee is not a simple task; the activity requires a variety of finely honed supervisory skills. The hiring decisions you make can have a lasting effect not only on your organization, but also on the lives and careers of every person considered.

Your organization's reputation in the job market is partially influenced by how well it is perceived by the public in the area of providing equal employment opportunities for women, minorities, older workers, and those with physical limitations. A favorable reputation in hiring tends to attract qualified applicants; a poor reputation because of discrimination in hiring may cause some highly qualified persons to seek employment elsewhere.

Employment process: *The various staffing activities necessary to recruit and select qualified individuals for employment.*

Our focus in this chapter is on two important topics—the *employment process* and *compensation*. The purpose of the **employment process,** also referred to as the *staffing function of management,* is to recruit and select qualified employees from candidates for employment. The employment process is costly. Hiring unqualified individuals for open positions can be disastrous for your department or organization. The second critical topic is that of providing employees with fair and adequate *compensation,* including *employee benefits,* the application of which has a profound effect on employee satisfaction, motivation, and turnover.

What Is the Employment Process?

The *employment process* involves a wide variety of activities that managers engage in to select suitable applicants for available positions. Figure 9–1 summarizes a fairly typical approach to the process. Who is responsible in organizations to ensure that staffing needs are met? To what extent are you—the supervisor—involved with the employment process?

FIGURE 9–1
A Fairly Typical Example of the Employment Process

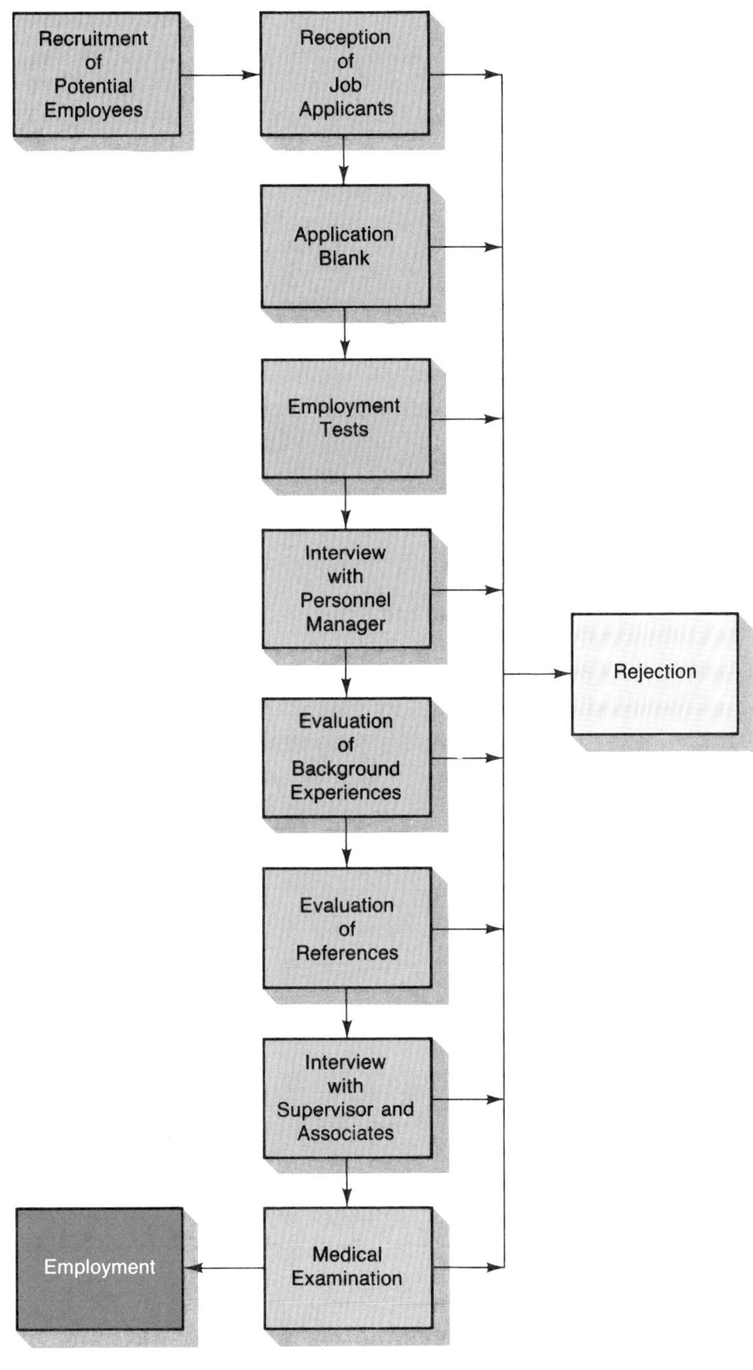

Who Is Involved in the Employment Process?

Human resource director (personnel manager): *A manager and staff specialist who generally has the major personnel responsibility to assist the organization with personnel needs, such as recruiting.*

In smaller firms, virtually any manager could be involved with the employment process. In larger firms, however, because of more diverse and complex requirements, a staff specialist, typically known as a **human resource director** or **personnel manager,** generally has the major responsibility of assisting the various departments of an organization with staffing needs.

In some organizations, your involvement with staffing activities might be slight, consisting of little more than receiving notification from the human resource department that a new person has been assigned to your unit. In others, you might have final and total authority for hiring and discharging employees. Many modern supervisors involve members of their departments (sometimes referred to as *associates*) in assisting with the selection process. Whether your own recruitment and selection responsibilities are limited or quite extensive, a knowledge of the employment process can provide you with a better appreciation of the staffing activities that exist in your particular organization.

Why Is the Employment Process So Costly?

Because of the numerous costs associated with recruiting and hiring new employees, careful consideration should be made as to whether such costs will be greater or less than the expected gain to the organization. One of the major costs that should be carefully weighed is the job candidate's probable wage or salary; but that's only a part of the total employee cost picture. Take a look at Table 9–1 for a summary of the major costs associated with recruiting, selecting, and maintaining new employees. Keep in mind that some of these costs will be wasted if the wrong selection is made and the employee must be discharged or quits.

Employee benefits, such as insurance programs, paid vacations, and sick leaves, have grown from only 3 percent of total payrolls in 1929 to current rates of between 20 and 35 percent. Do you feel that the typical employee is aware of the monetary value of these benefits?[1] Even the cost of discharging employees can be substantial, especially when employees are fired under circumstances that enable them to take their grievances to court.[2]

How Are Human Resource Requirements Determined?

As a supervisor, one of your human resource management responsibilities is to communicate useful information to others. Staff specialists who are responsible for recruiting new employees should continually be kept up to date on any of your department's future staffing requirements. Equally important is for you to inform your manager or human resource specialist of any changes that have taken place in the positions to be filled to ensure that "square pegs" are not recruited for "round holes."

TABLE 9–1
Major Costs Associated with Recruiting, Selecting, and Maintaining Employees (may amount to 20 to 35 percent of total payrolls)

Attracting and Hiring Employees
- Public relations
- Recruiting interviews
- Employment agency fees
- Advertising
- Application processing
- Testing
- Medical examinations
- Reference checks

Time Off with Pay
- Rest periods
- Paid vacations
- Holidays
- Sick and emergency leave
- Disability leave
- Family (maternity/paternity) leave
- Jury and military reserve training duty
- Sabbaticals
- Social responsibility leave
- Severance pay

Employee Services
- Recreation programs
- Child- and elder-care services and facilities
- Car pools
- Discounts on company products or services
- Counseling services (e.g., legal, financial, personal, outplacement)
- Group insurance programs (nonlife insurance, such as automobile, and homeowners, available at a discount)

Special Compensation Programs
- Contributions required by law (social security, unemployment compensation, and workers' compensation for job-related accidents)
- Profit sharing
- Tuition refund programs
- Relocation expense reimbursement
- Attendance bonus
- Longevity bonus
- Christmas gifts
- Overtime payments
- Health care insurance
- Life insurance
- Accidental death and disability insurance
- Retirement programs
- Employee stock ownership program (ESOP)
- Miscellaneous

Human resource requirements in most business firms are closely tied to future sales and production activities. Middle and senior management should be continually attuned to potential changes in human resource needs related to changes in those factors. However, future sales and production activities aren't the only factors that affect personnel needs. There is other information that you are more likely to discover before higher level managers do, such as future retirements, resignations, separations, and requests for transfer or leave. As a result, effective coordination and communication should continually take place among all levels of management to ensure that future human resource requirements are met.

Human resource needs seldom remain static. As the demand for a firm's product or service changes, its human resource requirements generally change. Some needs for additional personnel, however, are difficult to forecast accurately. Fluctuations in general business conditions, shortages of materials, international events, or even extreme changes in the weather can affect workloads and thus the number of employees needed. In some instances, the work place itself may be restructured in a way that requires increasing or reducing the number of personnel, as in the case of a change in a production process.

What Is a Job Analysis?

Before any recruiting of new employees takes place, those responsible for hiring new workers should be clear on what the *duties* of the job are and what *personal skills* are necessary to perform them satisfactorily. Rather than maintaining a hit-or-miss hiring procedure that hires five people for every one that succeeds, it is critical that *the job be carefully defined* so that candidates with the proper qualifications can be selected. A sound approach for defining a job is to prepare a *job analysis* before recruitment begins. A **job analysis** is a systematic approach to *gathering, evaluating, and organizing information about a job.* It provides data about the duties and skill requirements of the job so that two additional recruiting tools can be prepared: the *job description* and the *person description.*

Job analysis:
A systematic approach to gathering, evaluating, and organizing information about a job.

What Is a Job Description?

Job description:
Also known as a position description, *a document that summarizes the principal duties and responsibilities inherent in a particular job.*

A **job description** (also known as a *position description*) is a highly useful tool for determining the type of person needed for an available position. This document summarizes the principal *duties and responsibilities* inherent in a particular job. Job descriptions, of course, vary from job to job and from organization to organization. A typical job description provides the official *job title,* along with a *summary of the work to be performed,* plus statements that indicate specifically *the nature of the jobholder's duties.* The formal job description should be written in clear language that avoids ambiguity, distortion, or the omission of critical factors. An example of a job description can be seen in Figure 9–2.

A good job description can be a useful tool for everyone involved. Knowing the specific requirements of a job aids human resource specialists in determining the *characteristics desired* of the individual to be recruited and selected for the job. It helps you, the supervisor, to understand *what end results are expected* from the employee. Candidates for the position, and especially the person who is ultimately selected, have the right to know what sort of performance is expected of them before they accept the position.

What Is a Person Specification?

A third tool, one that can assist you in matching the right person to the available position, is termed a **person specification,** a form that summarizes the *personal qualifications* needed in the person who is to fill the job. Also known as a *job specification,* the person specification provides the basis for selecting the individual who best fits the available position. Once again, form and content vary by job and organization.

Person specification: *Also termed a* job specification, *a form that summarizes the personal qualifications needed in the person who is to fill the job.*

Customarily, a person specification breaks the job down into specific categories that indicate how much skill, training, and education are required; what the physical and mental demands of the job are; the nature of the responsibilities inherent in the job; and the conditions under which the job is preformed. Many firms grade or rate the job by *assigning points* to each factor. See Figure 9–3 for an example of a person specification.

As a means of avoiding accusations of discrimination in hiring, it is critical that *only job-related specifications be considered* when

FIGURE 9–2
A Sample Job (Position) Description

JOB DESCRIPTION

Job Title: Assistant **Department:** Training
Date: August 1, 19––

Job Summary Reports to training director, performs a variety of clerical and stenographic work related to position.

Job Duties:
1. Takes dictation and transcribes all material dictated.
2. Answers telephone and gives applicable information.
3. Prepares correspondence, memos, and bulletins.
4. Operates miscellaneous office equipment, such as word processors, fax and photocopying machines.
5. Orders supplies.
6. Maintains filing and records of training department.
7. Prepares reports and performs miscellaneous clerical and office functions as required.
8. Other duties as required.

FIGURE 9–3
A Sample Person (Job) Specification

Job Title: Assistant		Grade 4
Factor	**Qualifications of Jobholder**	**Points**
Mentality	Understand and apply basic office methods and manufacturing procedures.	54
Training and experience	Requires two years' training and experience in secretarial work, including word processing and shorthand.	181
Analytical requirements	Analyze figures, results, complex data, or situations in adapting work and attitude to supervisor's personal preference.	95
Initiative	Execute a sequence of operations connected with a variety of work. Supervision is of a general nature as superior is often out of the office.	95
Cooperation and contact	Make frequent interdepartment and public contacts both over the telephone and as receptionist, requiring poise and tact in handling delicate matters.	95
Costs	Decide matters of a routine nature where poor decisions could result in confusion and delay.	47
Dependability and accuracy	Involves moderate responsibility in transcribing correspondence, processing reports, etc. Errors could cause delays resulting in loss of customer goodwill.	42
Mental application	Perform variable operations of taking dictation and word processing, which requires moderate mental application but seldom is sustained over long periods.	29
Physical application	Involves light physical effort.	15
Job conditions	Good office working conditions.	15
Date written	August 1, 19-- **Total points**	**668**
Date revised	July 1, 19-- **Grade**	4

evaluating a candidate for a position. For example, unlawful discrimination could be charged in cases where you might want to hire only persons with high school diplomas, but where the job tasks could be readily performed by a person who has not completed high school.

A similar legal risk exists in the case where you might, for example, prefer employees who can lift 50 pounds. The requirement could be deemed discriminatory against some small-framed people if the job never actually requires lifting items that heavy. Or assume that the person specification indicates the need for a "young" or "healthy" person. This requirement, too, could be considered unlawful discrimination. Continually keep in mind that only job-related specifications may be considered. It is the responsibility of supervisors to become familiar with the criteria that cannot legally be included in a set of person specifications. (Table 9–3 list some of the major subjects and questions to avoid in the employment interviewing process, which is discussed in an upcoming section.)

There are certain exceptional cases, however, where you can legally discriminate. Section 703(e) in **Title VII of the Civil Rights Act of 1964** states that it *is* legal for an employer to discriminate against employees in hiring practices on the basis of their religion, sex, or national origin "in those instances where religion, sex, or national origin is a **bona fide occupational qualification (BFOQ)** reasonably necessary to the normal operation of a particular enterprise." For example, it would be unreasonable to accuse you of unlawful discrimination if you interviewed only female models to show your upcoming spring line of women's dresses.

Title VII of the Civil Rights Act of 1964: *Prohibits employers, labor unions, and employment agencies from discriminating against persons on the basis of color, religion, sex, or national origin.*

Bona fide occupational qualification (BFOQ): *Legislation that permits employers to discriminate against employees in hiring practices in certain instances.*

How Are Job Candidates Obtained?

Organizations vary in their approaches to obtaining employees, some being quite simple and others rather involved. Certain organizations utilize variations of the process illustrated earlier in Figure 9–1, depending on their needs, capabilities, geographic location, or degree of sophistication. For example, human resource managers in some organizations retain the responsibility for hiring second (night) shift workers, who are sometimes selected even before they meet their supervisors. In other industries, notably construction, trucking, and waterfront dock activities, workers may be sent by a union hiring hall with neither a supervisor nor a personnel specialist having the right of rejection.

The extent to which you, as a supervisor, are involved in the employment process will depend principally on the established practices of your own organization. Since you and your department associates must function as a team, it is highly desirable, of course, for each of you to be involved with decisions to select or reject candidates for job openings.

What Is an Employment Requisition?

Employment requisition: *A formal written request for additional labor, one that initiates the recruitment process.*

In many organizations, a *purchase requisition* is usually completed and approved before materials and equipment can be bought. A similar activity exists in some organizations when new employees are needed—an **employment requisition** is completed and approved. Supervisors are frequently involved with initiating personnel requests by filling out formal employment requisitions, that is, written requests for additional workers. Recruitment activities then begin after the requisition is approved.

What Does Recruiting Involve?

Recruiting: *An activity intended to obtain qualified applicants to fill available positions.*

Where do new employees come from? Actually, the sources are varied and numerous. **Recruiting,** an activity intended to obtain qualified applicants to be considered for vacant positions, can take place almost anywhere, and sometimes occurs as a surprising casual activity, such as at social functions or conventions.

There is no single source or method for locating qualified applicants. (Table 9–2 summarizes the more typical sources of personnel.) Organizations, once again, vary widely in the approaches they prefer. The nature of available positions also influences the recruitment source. For example, a managerial post, an engineering position, and an assembly-line job would be unlikely to be recruited in the same manner.

Job opportunity announcement (JOA): *Also termed* job posting *or* bidding, *a formal announcement within the organization of open positions.*

Job Opportunity Announcement. Related to *existing employees* as a source of candidates, some organizations utilize what is referred to as a **job opportunity announcement (JOA).** Also termed *job posting,* JOA is an invitation to employees to "throw their hats into the ring," so to speak, or *bid* for the job. Both placement and promotion from within can have numerous benefits,

TABLE 9–2
Typical Sources of Potential Employees

- Existing employees (through job posting and bidding)
- Employee referrals
- Walk-in applicants
- Employment agencies (including private, state, and temporary agencies)
- Computer matching services
- Unions, hiring halls, and associations
- Schools (including trade schools, vocational schools, high schools, and colleges)
- Classified ads in newspapers, trade publications, and community shopper magazines or flyers
- Radio, TV, and outdoor poster advertising
- Present customers
- Competitors

not the least of which is the enhanced motivation of existing employees. In addition, **internal placement** can eliminate many of the recruitment expenses associated with **external placement,** thereby reducing the time that a position is vacant and its tasks not performed. The work habits of existing employees are already known. Further, training and startup time are often less for individuals promoted from within. Another potential advantage is the elimination or reduction of potential employee resentment, which is sometimes brought about by existing employees having to adapt to outsiders. And finally, JOA tends to encourage existing employees to inform their friends about available job opportunities, an effective and low-cost method for expanding the applicant pool.

Internal placement: *The selection of candidates for open positions from sources located within the hiring organization.*

External placement: *The selection of candidates for open positions from sources located outside the hiring organization.*

Employee Referral Plan. A method for recruiting that has become quite popular with some organizations is the **employee referral plan (ERP).** ERP is a system that rewards existing employees with a **finder's fee** for bringing in successful job candidates. "Bounties" range from $25 to $1,000 and above. The referral fee is typically withheld from the referring employee until the new person has been employed for at least three months.

Employee referral plan (ERP): *A system that rewards existing employees with a finder's fee for bringing in successful job candidates.*

Finder's fee: *A cash reward paid to existing employees for bringing in successful job candidates.*

How Are Job Candidates Screened?

The **screening process** begins after applicants for a particular job have been located. In general, there are four basic activities that are engaged in before a candidate is selected for the available position. These are:

1. Examining the candidate's documents (i.e., correspondence, application forms, and resumé)
2. Administering employment tests
3. Interviewing
4. Evaluating the applicant's experience, references, and (if applicable to the position) medical condition.

Screening process: *Activities intended to determine whether a candidate has the necessary qualifications for the available position.*

Why Examine the Applicant's Documents?

Application forms and **resumés** are typically screened by a human resource specialist prior to any direct involvement of a supervisor. The human resource specialist usually screens the documents to see if the applicant's background information matches the job description and person specification. Applicants with the appropriate background—that is, ***education, skills,*** and ***experience***—are invited for screening interviews with the human resource specialist.

Some applicants don't get much beyond the stage of filling out an application form, which serves to screen out the obviously unqualified applicants. Interviewing unqualified individuals generally wastes both the applicants' and the interviewer's time.

Application forms should be carefully designed and periodically reviewed to ensure that they don't conflict with employment leg-

Application forms: *Forms designed to provide the interviewer with basic information about an applicant for a position.*

Resumé: *A short account of a person's career and qualifications, typically prepared by an applicant for a position.*

The employment interview is a highly critical step in the selection process. Poor selection can prove to be costly to the organization.

islation that prohibits rejecting applicants solely because of their *race, sex, religion,* or *age.* Even such factors as *education, arrest and conviction records, marital status, childcare arrangements,* and *credit ratings* could lead to charges of unlawful discrimination. The courts have frequently ruled against traditional application questions that discriminated unfairly against women, older employees, and minorities. Any queries appearing on an application should relate only to the job's actual requirements and the applicant's potential ability to perform the job.

Should Job Candidates Be Tested?

Employment tests: *A screening device intended to measure a person's acceptability for a particular position.*

The testing of applicants has been a delicate subject for human resource managers. Many **employment tests** have been judged unlawful by the courts because they appeared to discriminate against certain cultural groups or women and, therefore, constituted illegal discrimination under Title VII of the Civil Rights Act of 1964. Others, such as polygraph (lie detector) or substance abuse tests, have been considered in some cases to be an invasion of privacy. In spite of such uncertain outcomes, the National Association of Corporate and Professional Recruiters report that the use of drug tests to screen job candidates increased from 48 percent of all applicants in 1987 to 63 percent in 1989.[3]

A well-designed test, however, can be more objective about certain areas than would some interviewers. Typical areas that an applicant might be tested on include skills, intelligence, aptitude, interests, and personality. For example, a work sample test that requires the applicant to actually perform tasks required for job success could be quite helpful in selection. A typing test illustrates a commonly used work sample. Other typical work sample tests include demonstrating truck driving skills, reading blueprints, or using a computer or word processor.

To withstand potential lawsuits, organizations have had to prove that their tests are both *reliable* and *valid*. **Reliability** is a condition that exists if the results of an employment test are the same when administered repeatedly under identical situations. **Validity** is said to exist when it can be proven that a test consistently measures what it purports to measure (i.e., the test accurately predicts potential job performance).[4]

Reliability: *A condition that exists if the results of an employment test are the same when administered repeatedly under identical situations.*

Validity: *A condition that exists if it can be proven that a test consistently measures what it purports to measure (i.e., predicts potential job performance).*

Relying solely on test results to select or reject applicants would be considered foolhardy by most modern managers. Employment tests, if used, should be only a part of the entire selection process. There are some individuals who could perform outstandingly on the job but tend to freeze up when confronted with a written examination.

What Is the Nature of Interviewing?

If the job candidate has not been screened out as a result of examining his or her documents and the testing procedures, his or her next step is that all-important **employment interview.** Up to this point in the selection process (especially in most medium to large organizations), the supervisor has probably had little or no contact with the applicant. The human resource department typically will have handled most, if not all, of the preliminary screening. Your task as supervisor may be to interview final candidates and to select one who is qualified for the position.

Employment interview: *A screening procedure intended to aid in determining the suitability of an applicant for a particular position.*

As stated earlier, in some organizations you, as supervisor, may have little input. You could be expected to accept those persons screened and already selected by the personnel department. However, this procedure is uncommon. More likely is the use of **multiple interviews,** which are sessions in which you and one or more managers have the opportunity to observe, challenge, and pool your impressions of the applicant.

Multiple interviews: *An interviewing technique in which several managers have the opportunity to observe, challenge, and pool their impressions of a job candidate.*

In some instances your associates, that is, the employees who are accountable to you, may participate in the selection process. Some managers believe that involving their associates helps to build stronger, more effective department teams, since they tend to select future coworkers who are more likely to be compatible with their workgroups. However, keep in mind that effective interviewing requires training; it is an acquired skill. Any associate who is likely to be involved in interviewing activities should receive proper training prior to the experience. For example, interviewers should be aware that there are certain questions that are considered discriminatory and, therefore, should be avoided. Table 9–3 suggests some guidelines for subjects and questions to avoid during the interview.[5]

The major purpose of an interview is to uncover information that can't be discerned from an application form. Your primary objective during an interview is to discover if the applicant is suitable for the available position. You should recognize, however, that a concerned applicant probably has the desire—and the right—

TABLE 9–3
Guidelines for Subjects and Questions to Avoid during an Interview

Subject	Cannot Do or Ask	Can Do or Ask
Applicant's sex	Make comments or notes unless being male or female is a requirement of the position.	Notice appearance.
Marital status	"Are you married? Single? Divorced? Engaged?"	Discover marital status after hiring for insurance purposes.
Children	"Do you have children at home? How old? Who cares for them? Do you plan to have more children?"	Request numbers and ages of children after hiring for insurance purposes.
Physical data	"How tall are you? How heavy?"	Explain manual labor, lifting, and/or other requirements of the job. Show how it is performed. Require physical exam.
Criminal record	"Have you ever been arrested, convicted, or spent time in jail?"	If security clearance is necessary, can be done prior to employment.
Military record	"What type of discharge do you have? What branch did you serve in?"	"Are you a veteran? Do you have any job-related experience?"
Age	"How old are you?" Estimate age.	Age after hiring. "Are you over 18?"
Housing	"Do you own your home? Do you rent? Do you live in an apartment or a house?"	"If you have no phone, how can we reach you?"

to learn from you as much as possible about the job and the organization. You should be prepared, therefore, to provide him or her with information regarding wages, hours, responsibilities, future opportunities, company history, and present activities. In some instances, the applicant who has few or no questions may be looking only for a temporary position rather than a career job.

Your questions during an interview should be *open-ended* where possible, in order to draw relevant information from the applicant. An **open-ended question** is one that can't be answered with a simple "yes" or "no" response. You could use a *closed question* if you are attempting to verify factual information about the employment application: A **closed question** is one that typically *is* answered with a simple "yes" or "no". In general, however, you should avoid such closed questions as, "Do you think you'd like to work for us?" Open questions, as indicated in the questioning section of Chapter 13, are those that begin with *who, what, when, where, why,* and *how.* Table 9–4 suggests seven open-ended questions that can often reveal quite a lot about candidates.[6]

Open-ended question: *A question that cannot be answered with a simple "yes" or "no" response; intended to elicit greater response from an interviewee.*

Closed question: *A question that typically is answered with a simple "yes" or "no."*

You should plan *in advance* the types of questions you intend to ask. You're likely to appear a bit inept to the applicant if you haven't done some preliminary homework prior to the interview. A *must* is for you to have looked over the employment application before the interview begins. It's a waste of both your time and the applicant's time to ask the same questions that were answered in the application, unless yours are merely intended to verify information.

During the interview, try to help the interviewee relax, feel comfortable, and be confident enough to communicate readily with you. Be on guard against your own biases. Your task is to determine the suitability of the applicant for a job, not to feed your own ego or lecture to the candidate. Also, try not to fight the clock. Allow enough time to conduct the interview so that the session doesn't seem tense and anxiety-filled. Selecting a suitable environment for your interview in advance will aid you in minimizing distractions and interruptions. Continue to maintain alertness, even at the end of the interview. You might be astonished by how much you can uncover about an applicant after your first "goodbye."

TABLE 9–4
Revealing Open-Ended Interviewing Questions

- What are your three greatest weaknesses?
- What do you think you'll be doing in 10 years?
- How would you evaluate your last manager?
- What are your three greatest strengths?
- Why did you sign up for this interview?
- Why don't you tell me about yourself?
- Why do you want to work for this organization?

Some interviewers prefer to avoid taking notes during the interview in the belief that it tends to distract and make the applicant feel ill at ease. If notes are not taken, you should summarize and record your impressions as soon as possible after the interview concludes. Reactions tend to fade if excessive time elapses before recording your assessment in writing.

How Useful Are References?

Letters of recommendation: *Letters solicited by job applicants from friends, acquaintances, former teachers, and past employers to aid in obtaining employment; not valued by many employers.*

We're now coming down to the wire regarding the hiring or rejecting of the candidate for the open position. Once an applicant has met all of your standards, his or her references should be verified. Few managers place much weight these days on **letters of recommendation,** since few candidates would ask someone for a letter of recommendation unless fairly certain of a complimentary response. Furthermore, an increasing number of employers (41 percent) refuse to give references at all, according to the National Association of Corporate and Professional Recruiters. The number of employers refusing to give former employees references doubled in only two years. "Companies," according to NACPR Chairman John Finnerty, are "scared of being sued for libel if a current or former worker finds out that a reference was unflattering."[7]

The applicant's *credit rating* and *work references* are usually better sources of objective information. Checking references is essential to verify that information supplied on the resumé and application form is truthful.

The human resource department may have performed preliminary verification of education and recent work experience either prior to screening interviews or before interviews with the supervisor. A key responsibility of the human resource specialist is to be certain that the selected candidate actually has the education and work experience necessary to satisfactorily perform the tasks of the job.

Some resumés show dates at a job indicating three or more years of experience as a supervisor when, in fact, the applicant was never a supervisor, and the period of actual job experience was considerably shorter than stated. An applicant who has submitted spurious documents may appear to be fit for the position when in reality he or she has few if any such qualifications.

A *personal telephone call* can be a quick and useful way to verify an applicant's work history. A revealing question to ask former employers is, "Would you be willing to rehire the applicant if the occasion ever arose?" You could then ask the former employer to explain the reasons why or why not. However, in reality, many previous employers prefer not to be too candid for fear of finding themselves assuming the role of defendant in lawsuits initiated by disgruntled former employees. Many will provide you with little more than verification of the dates of employment.

Should Preemployment Medical Examinations Be Required?

Not all organizations require a **preemployment medical examination.** When required, medical examinations are usually one of the final steps in the selection process because of their cost, which is usually paid for by your company. The major purposes of a medical examination are: (1) to determine if the applicant has the *physical capabilities* necessary to perform the required tasks of the job, (2) to protect the hiring organization against *future claims* based on a physical condition that existed prior to employment, and (3) to detect any possible substance (drug) abuse. Reliability and validity, once again become important, since medical examinations are a form of testing. Your company could be accused of discrimination in cases where an applicant was denied employment based on physical requirements that were not necessary to perform the job satisfactorily, or if the applicant was rejected because of a physical condition unrelated to the job (e.g., remission from cancer or medically controlled epilepsy).

Preemployment medical examination: *Sometimes used to determine a job applicant's physical or mental fitness for employment; may be used to detect substance abuse.*

Should Rejected Candidates Be Notified?

Applicants who have been weeded out should be told of their rejection, either by personal contact or by letter. (Figure 9–4 provides an example of a rejection letter.) Prompt, courteous notification is important to minimize disappointment and to allow unsuccessful candidates to pursue other job opportunities. Applicants who are not informed that a job has been filled may feel mistreated and file charges of illegal discrimination. The burden of proof is typically on the employer, even where no discrimination has occurred.

Any organization—public or private, large or small—develops a job market reputation. People perceive an organization to be a good place to work or perhaps not so good. A major factor in job market reputation is the past personal experience of applicants. Interviews are an emotional experience, filled with anxiety for qualified as well as unqualified applicants. Employment procedures and interviewing techniques need to consider the human needs of candidates. Keep in mind that the decision to select a person for a position is merely half the equation in a good hire. A mistreated applicant might refuse your job offer and to seek employment elsewhere. Furthermore, the person could have been a customer of your firm, at least until the interview!

Why Is the Orientation of Employees Important?

"The future has its roots in the present" is an expression that especially applies to the first-day experiences of new employees.

FIGURE 9–4
An Example of a Rejection Letter

BREAKTHROUGH TOY COMPANY
4000 Playtime Lane
Pleasant Valley, CA 94545

November 11, 19––

Mr. Karl LeBlanc
1163 Lincoln Avenue
Almond Creek, CA 94546

Dear Mr. LeBlanc:

Thank you for your interest in employment opportunities with the Breakthrough Toy Company. We appreciate the effort you've made to seek a position with our organization.

After careful consideration of your qualifications, we have determined that we do not have a position that matches your background and interests.

We appreciate your consideration of the Breakthrough Toy Company as a potential employer and wish you every success in finding a rewarding position.

Very sincerely yours,

Elvis Mueller
Director, Human Resource Department

EM/rjg

The employment process is far too costly to take new employees for granted. As a means of assisting new employees through some potentially dire straits, many organizations utilize *planned orientation* or *induction programs.* Early experiences of new employees tend to exert lasting and significant influence over their future attitudes toward the organization.

Employee orientation (induction) program: *A planned introduction of new employees to the organization and other pertinent employment information.*

What Should an Orientation Include?

Can you remember the first day you reported to your present job? Was it a good experience, or did you feel somewhat bewildered and lost? There's a tremendous amount of information for the new employee to absorb about an organization and the new position. An effective **employee orientation (induction) program** can go a long way in helping the green employee get off to a good start early in his or her career with an organization. You—the supervisor—play a critical role in determining the effectiveness of a new employee's orientation to your organization. Typical activities and topics that should be covered with new workers are listed in Table 9–5.

Orientation programs vary widely among organizations. The size of the organization usually influences the scope of the orientation activities. Unfortunately, far too many employees feel abandoned after the goodwill and attention received during their hiring interviews. In some organizations, especially smaller ones, new employees may receive little more than a round of introductions, a company booklet, a handshake, and a workspace. They might not even be sure where the restroom is! In larger organizations, orientation programs tend to be more extensive and may take anywhere from an entire day to a week or more.

How Extensive Should the Orientation Be?

Some supervisors seem to feel that the new employee must be given a complete and structured introduction to *everything* in the plant or organization, all crammed into the first day. Other supervisors have either a casual, informal procedure for orienting new employees or none at all. Somewhere between these two extremes is the kind of orientation that is likely to be most beneficial for the individual employee. Genuine concern by you—the supervisor—

"Our policy is to promote from within."

Source: Reprinted from the *The Wall Street Journal,* by permission of Cartoon Features Syndicate.

The orientation provided for new employees should be complete, but not overwhelming.

TABLE 9–5
Typical Activities and Topics to Be Covered in Employee Orientation Programs

- Organizational history, organizational structure, and principal activities
- Organizational policies, rules, regulations, and procedures
- Departmental activities, responsibilities, and relationship to other departments
- A complete tour of the department
- An introduction to department members
- Employee rights, duties, responsibilities, and relationships to other employees
- Employee compensation, services, and benefits (including their financial worth to the employee)
- Working hours and overtime policy
- Employee eating, parking, and restroom facilities
- Tuition refund policy
- Personal mail and telephone calls policies
- Employee suggestion systems
- Any additional information that can assist new employees in adjusting to their new work environment

TABLE 9–6
The Major Advantages of an Effective Orientation Program

- Lessening employee feelings of isolation, fear, and anxiety
- Feeling more rapidly like a member of an organizational team
- Providing an opportunity to learn the job more readily with less stress
- Increasing the likelihood of the employee's remaining with the organization longer than those who receive little or no orientation
- Lowering turnover rates
- Reducing the amount of supervision required

for the new employee and a planned orientation are likely to have more lasting and positive effects than a haphazard all-or-nothing first-day approach.

In some organizations, supervisors assign the new employee to a *qualified associate* or *mentor* for the orientation. An advantage to this approach is that the new employee may feel more at ease with a peer than he or she would with the manager on the first day. Other advantages include freeing you for other managerial activities and providing growth and development experiences for the subordinate who assists in the orientation.

The purpose of an orientation program shouldn't be to scattershoot every available bit of information to the employee; a major goal should be to help in reducing the new employee's anxiety level. Remember that new employees are often filled with first-day jitters. They may feel overwhelmed by the many explanations they've heard and the many new people they've met. It is especially important for you to display patience and sincere understanding as a means of helping the new employee develop self-assurance. Conscientious efforts on your part will be well worth the effort. Table 9–6 summarizes some of the major advantages of an effective orientation program.[8]

We now turn to a topic near and dear to the hearts of new employees and seasoned veterans alike—employee compensation.

What Is the Nature of Employee Compensation?

Employee compensation: *The rewards provided employees for performing their job responsibilities.*

Employee compensation is an important concern for employees because it determines their lifestyles: the homes they buy, the cars they drive, the vacations they take, and the luxuries they can afford. In general, human resource specialists are responsible for measuring the relative worth of each job and establishing compensation that is fair both in relation to comparable jobs within the organization and to equivalent jobs in the surrounding geographical region. Those who determine employee compensation also have to consider various legislation that affects their activities. In some instances, union wage contracts govern the levels and amounts of compensation. Organizations generally provide several types of compensation, each based on the character of the job itself and the effect of outside influences.

In this section we briefly explore the supervisor's role in employee compensation, examine how employee compensation is established, and look at the various forms of employee compensation.

What Is the Supervisor's Role In Employee Compensation?

Internal compensation discrepancy: *A misalignment of compensation amounts in a particular department relative to what comparable positions and individuals receive in other departments.*

External compensation discrepancy: *A misalignment of compensation relative to what similar positions are paid by other organizations in the geographical area.*

Employee compensation is an equally important concern of both employees and supervisors, since employee motivation can relate to current and potential compensation levels. Even though supervisors typically have little authority in directly determining wage levels, they do *influence* the compensation that their employees receive through *performance evaluations,* a topic to be discussed in Chapter 10. Supervisors should also be alert to any *internal* and *external compensation discrepancies* and report any perceived inequities to their managers in an effort to create greater parity. An **internal compensation discrepancy** is a misalignment of compensation amounts in a particular department relative to what comparable positions and individuals receive in other departments. An **external compensation discrepancy** is a misalignment of compensation relative to what similar positions are paid by other organizations in the geographical area.

Even though supervisors may not be directly involved in determining compensation levels in their organizations, they should be familiar with the various forms of compensation and how compensation is determined.

How Is Employee Compensation Determined?

Many factors enter into the determination of compensation. Some factors have already been mentioned, such as legislation, internal and external factors, and performance evaluations. Other determiners of compensation include *job evaluations* and *pay grades.*

Job evaluation: *A method of comparing and ranking each job in an organization as a means of determining its relative worth.*

A **job evaluation** is a method of *comparing* and *ranking* each job in an organization as a means of determining its relative worth. (Try not to confuse job evaluation with the previously used term *job analysis,* which is *not* involved with comparing jobs.) A variety of methods for evaluating jobs exist, but most compare such factors as *education, skill, responsibility, external contacts,* and *working conditions.* Information can be obtained by examining previously prepared job analyses. This information aids human resource specialists in determining where each job should be ranked in a hierarchy ranging from senior managers to operating employees.

After jobs have been evaluated and ranked in their order of importance, *pay grades* are created. Referring again to Figure 9–3, a sample of a person specification, you can observe a pay grade in the lower portion of the far right column. **Pay grades** are compensation categories resulting from the job evaluation that express a monetary value for each position in the job hierarchy. A range of compensation often exists within each grade level so that raises can be provided without promotions.

Pay grades: *Compensation categories that express the monetary value for each position in the job hierarchy; a range of compensation often exists within each grade level so that raises can be provided without promotions.*

What Are the Forms of Employee Compensation?

A variety of forms of employee compensation exist, the more common of which will be discussed below.

Wage. A **wage** is a typical type of compensation paid to nonmanagement personnel. Employees who receive wages are paid according to the number of hours they work during a given time period. *Overtime pay* at the rate of 1½ to 2 times the normal hourly rate is typically given when hours worked exceed a particular number per week. The quantity of units produced by the wage earners does not enter directly into the amount of earnings they receive. Blue-collar workers typically receive wages rather than salaries. Some organizations maintain controversial *two-tiered wage* systems, in which new hires are paid on a lower scale than existing employees.

Wage: *A type of compensation in which employees receive wages according to the number of hours they work during a given time period.*

Salary. A **salary** is compensation paid to employees based on employment for a specific period of time, such as a month or year, rather than payment on an hourly basis. Quantity of units produced or sold do not directly determine the remuneration received each month. Managers and professionals typically receive salaries.

Salary: *Compensation paid to employees based on a specific period of time, such as a month or year, rather than on an hourly basis.*

Piecework Rate. A variation of wages is a **piecework rate,** which pays employees according to the number of units they produce. In the agricultural industry, for example, farm workers may be paid according to the number of bags or boxes of produce they picked.

Piecework rate: *A compensation system that pays employees according to the number of units they produce.*

Commission. Salespeople are often paid on the basis of **commission,** which is a percentage of the purchase price of each unit sold by the salesperson. Of course, the more units sold, the greater the total sales compensation received by the salesperson.

Commission: *Compensation, generally paid to salespeople, on the basis of a percentage of the purchase price of each unit sold.*

Bonuses. Additional money paid to employees as an incentive for performing more effectively is termed a **bonus.** Bonuses typically relate to improved results in the areas of production, sales, or cost reduction.

Bonus: *Additional money paid to employees as an incentive for performing more effectively.*

Profit Sharing. Another incentive-type compensation, one that relates solely to the profitability of the firm, is termed **profit sharing.** Some firms allocate a certain percentage of each year's profits for distribution to employees in addition to their regular wages and salaries.

Profit sharing: *An incentive-type compensation that relates solely to the profitability of the firm and distributes a certain percentage of annual profits to employees.*

Employee Stock Ownership Programs. An increasingly popular method for financially rewarding employees is **employee stock ownership programs (ESOPs),** which grant employees shares of

Employee stock ownership programs (ESOPs): *Programs that grant employees stock at little or no cost.*

stock (ownership in the company, in effect) at little or no cost. Some firms offer ESOPs instead of bonuses, because they are less expensive to fund and also help to stem hostile takeover bids by other companies. In a recent year, for example, the Lockheed Corporation created an ESOP allowing its employees to own 17 percent of total outstanding stock shares.[9]

Pension plan: *A fund set aside by the employer for distribution to employees after they retire.*

Vested: *A provision in some pension plans that allows employees who resign or are terminated prior to their retirement to receive a lump-sum settlement.*

Contributory pension plan: *A program in which both the employee and the employer contribute to a retirement fund that is placed in reserve for later distribution to employees.*

Pension Plans. Numerous organizations also provide a *pension plan* for their employees. With a **pension plan,** the organization sets aside a portion of its income for distribution to employees after they retire. Many plans are **vested** after a certain number of years, which means that employees who resign or are terminated prior to their retirement can receive a lump-sum settlement. Some plans are **contributory,** that is, both the employee and the employer contribute to a fund that is placed in reserve for later distribution to employees.

Employee benefits: *Also termed* fringe benefits, *considered to be nonfinancial rewards provided to employees beyond their regular compensation.*

Nonfinancial Compensation—Employee Benefits. Employee benefits, also termed *fringe benefits,* are considered to be nonfinancial rewards provided to employees beyond their regular compensation. Calling employee benefits "nonfinancial" is a bit misleading in some respects, since they typically cost employers between 20 and 35 percent of their payrolls. Many employees are not aware of the monetary value of the benefits they are receiving unless their supervisors provide them with such information. A wide variety of employee benefits exist, most of which fit into the categories listed earlier in Table 9–1.

Cafeteria-styled benefit programs: *Plans in which employees can choose a combination of insurance and other options based on their personal desires rather than on a predefined basis.*

A rapidly growing trend in recent years has been the conversion from defined, or fixed, benefit programs to so-called **cafeteria-styled benefit programs,** in which employees can choose a combination of insurance and other options best suited to their personal desires and family situations. Many firms have switched to flexible benefit programs because costs tend to be less than with fixed programs.

Summary

In this chapter, we examined the critical area known as the *employment process.* We learned the importance of making sound staffing choices, that is, selecting employees who are best suited for unfilled positions.

Supervisors often play key roles in the employment process. They are generally among the first to *recognize future personnel needs.* Supervisors are sometimes involved with staffing activities and, therefore, should be familiar with the use of *selection tools* and *interviewing techniques.* It is important for anyone involved in the employment process to be aware of the *discriminatory questions and topics* that should be avoided.

Supervisors can assist considerably in ensuring that new employees get off to a good start by providing them with a *thorough orientation.*

Employee compensation is another important area in organizations. Although supervisors generally have little direct authority for determining wage levels, they do influence employee compensation through *performance evaluations.* Many factors determine compensation rates and levels. Many organizations engage in *job evaluations* and determine *pay grades* for the various positions that exist. Employees may receive compensation in a variety of forms, such as *wages, salaries, piecework rates, commissions, bonuses, profit sharing, ESOPs, pension plans,* and through *employee benefit programs.*

Questions for Discussion

1. Evaluate the following statement: "The selection process is not so critical during economic periods when surpluses of skilled labor exist. If a bad choice is made, it's simply a matter of getting rid of the person and recruiting a better replacement."
2. What information related to future labor needs can a supervisor provide that a human resource or personnel director may be unaware of?
3. Many observers of human resource management contend that the average employee has little or no awareness of the value of his or her employee (fringe) benefits. What can an employer do to try to enhance employee awareness of the worth of employee benefits?
4. How does a job (position) description assist the selection process? How does it differ from a person (job) specification?
5. While head of the Sony Corporation, Chairman Akio Morita once stated, "I want to be able to utilize each person's unique abilities to the utmost. So we have to find the right position for each person. In the U.S.A., you write a job specification for every position, and if a person does not fit the specification, you get rid of him and hire another one. Our way [Japan's] of doing things is different."[10] What is your reaction to Chairman Morita's comments?
6. Which do you believe is a better policy for an employer to follow: internal or external placement policy? Why?
7. What is your opinion of employee referral plans? When used, how much do you feel is a reasonable finder's fee?
8. What are some of the major subjects that should be avoided on an application form or during an interview? Why?
9. Explain in your own words the following statement: "When employment tests are used as a part of the selection process, it is essential that they measure factors related to the job itself."

10. What is the purpose of multiple interviews in the selection process?
11. How valuable are letters of recommendation in the selection process?
12. Why do some firms go to the expense of providing medical examinations for applicants for job openings?
13. What can a supervisor do to assist a new employee in overcoming the "first-day jitters"?
14. What is typically a supervisor's role in the area of employee compensation?
15. What are the purposes of job evaluations and pay grading?
16. What is your reaction to the two-tiered wage system?
17. Should a bonus ever be given to employees in lieu of pay raises? Explain your position.
18. What is your opinion of flexible benefit programs?

Can You Define These Terms?

Instructions: Write a definition for each of the following terms. You may check your definitions with those provided in the end-of-text glossary.

employment process
human resource director
job analysis
job (position) description
person (job) specification
recruiting
employment requisition
Title VII of the Civil Rights Act of 1964
bona fide occupational qualification (BFOQ)
job opportunity announcement (JOA)
internal placement
external placement
employee referral plan (ERP)
finder's fee
screening process
application forms
resumé
employment tests
reliability
validity
employment interview
multiple interviews
open-ended question
closed question
letters of recommendation
preemployment medical examination
employee orientation (induction) program
employee compensation
internal compensation discrepancy
external compensation discrepancy
job evaluation
pay grades
wage
two-tiered wage system
salary
piecework rate
commission
bonus
profit sharing
employee stock ownership program (ESOP)
pension plan
vested pension plans
contributory pension plan
employee (fringe) benefits
cafeteria-styled benefit programs

Supervision In Action

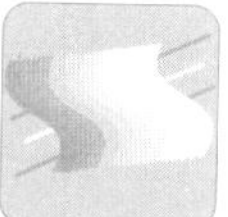

9–1 A Person Specification—What's Your Opinion?

PERSON SPECIFICATION

Job Title: Bank teller **Grade:** 1

Duties: Accepts deposits
Cashes checks
Sells money orders, cashier's checks, traveler's checks
Performs other related teller duties

Abilities: Six months' general teller experience preferred

Project

Evaluate the person specification above.

9–2 "I'd Rather Be Shiftless"

The CtrlF-10 Instruments Company is a medium-sized electronics firm situated in San Leandro, California. The firm's growth record has been phenomenal since it was founded only five years ago in the garage of one of the owners. It continues to enjoy a monopoly on a product that its competitors have not yet been able to emulate.

CtrlF-10 has had difficulty acquiring skilled employees. As with many small- to medium-sized hi-tech firms, CtrlF-10 has not yet created a human resource department and consequently has not developed systematic procedures for recruiting, selecting, orienting, and training employees. Recently, a person named Estrella Star was hired to work on an assembly line. At the time Estrella was hired, the production supervisor, Xavier Millcrest, casually told her that she would be required to work on the second shift (4:00 P.M. to 12:00 midnight) for the first six months of her employment—her probationary period. To familiarize her with job requirements, however, Estrella was assigned to a day-shift lead person on the line, Per Aghasti, for a two-week period.

At the beginning of third week, Estrella showed up for the day shift as usual. When Xavier saw her, the following conversation ensued:

Xavier: What in the world are you doing here at this time of day, Estrella? You're supposed to work on the second shift starting this evening. What happened? Did you forget what I told you when you were hired?

Estrella: Forget? What are you talking about? I was hired for the day shift, and that's where I've been working for the past two weeks.

Xavier: You must have misunderstood me, Estrella. I told you explicitly at the time you were hired that you would be assigned to the second shift during your probationary period. Don't you remember?

Estrella: No, I don't remember because you never told me that in the first place! I would never have taken the job if I thought I'd have to work until midnight every evening. I have a family, and that's the only time during the workweek that I can be with them. I'm working day shift or no shift at all!

Xavier: I guess it's going to be no shift at all then. Everyone we hire has to do their probationary stint on the second shift, and you're not going to be treated any differently than everyone else.

Questions

1. What appears to be the main problem in the above case?
2. How might problems like those illustrated in the case be prevented?
3. What are some of the principal advantages of a planned and structured employee orientation program? List some of the important topics that should be covered.

9–3 Not Able to Sell Himself

Flint Westwood recently was discharged from the Marine Corps and learned from a friend of his employed at the Micro Corporation that there was an opening in the sales department. Although Flint had no previous experience in sales, he had heard that the sales field was an area where earnings were virtually unlimited and that salespeople enjoyed a high degree of freedom because of a lack of close supervision. Flint decided to apply for the position.

Flint had a neat appearance and a "gift for gab." Charlene Ditch, sales supervisor with Micro, was favorably impressed with Flint during the job interview, and decided to hire him.

Micro had a policy of orienting new sales representatives to the company by having them spend two weeks apiece working in each of the six departments within the company. For example, new salespeople would be assigned for two weeks to the accounting department, where they would meet the staff and be assigned relatively simple, routine types of jobs that helped them become familiar with the department's operations. After the 12 weeks of in-house orientation, the new salesperson would then be assigned to an experienced salesperson for one month before being given his or her own territory.

By the end of the fifth week, Charlene received complaints from each of the three supervisors to whom Flint had been assigned thus far. Each department head indicated that Flint had been abrasive and discourteous with those around him during his two weeks in their departments. Each also said that Flint seemed to be dependable and a hard, efficient worker while in their departments, but that he was likely to damage Micro's public image if he had face-to-face contact with customers.

Questions

1. Should Flint's abrasive personality traits have been detected during the job interview? Explain your response.
2. If you were Charlene, what would you do about Flint at this time? Should he be fired? Explain.

9–4 Never Enough Staff!

Doris Booker is a supervisor in the chemical-processing department of the Papel Paperboard Company. During the 1970s, about 45 percent of Papel's production was exported overseas. As the U.S. dollar strengthened against foreign currencies during the early 1980s (thus making American products more expensive for foreign purchasers), there was a substantial decline in demand for Papel's products. As a result, one-half of Doris' 22 associates had to be laid off.

Doris was able to meet production deadlines reasonably well during this period, but she never felt that 11 employees were enough to sufficiently meet deadlines without having to drive her employees fairly hard from time to time.

During the late 1980s and early 1990s, U.S. economic policy drove the dollar down substantially, thus making U.S. products more easily affordable for foreign buyers. As a result, the workload in Doris' department rose dramatically. Unfortunately, however, Doris was unable to obtain approval from her boss to hire more than three new associates. Doris felt that she must have at least another four employees to be able to meet the production deadlines she was facing. In fact, each day during the past month, she was gradually falling behind in her schedule. She was uncertain how she should handle her problem.

Questions

1. Why do many managers attempt to discourage supervisors from requisitioning new employees after there has been a sudden upturn in the volume of orders?
2. If you were Doris, how would you handle your staffing challenge?

9–5 When Coming in First Can Mean Coming in Last

A survey of job placements shows that the first applicant was hired for open positions only 17.6 percent of the time. The number of persons interviewed for each job ranged from two to six, and the last candidate was hired 55.8 percent of the time, the survey found.[11]

Question

What, in your opinion, are the implications of the survey from the standpoint of your selection practices?

Endnotes

1. John Douglas, Stuart Klein, and David Hunt, *The Strategic Managing of Human Resources* (New York: John Wiley & Sons, 1985), p. 423.
2. "The Growing Costs of Firing Nonunion Workers," *Business Week,* April 6, 1981, pp. 95–98.
3. From a study by the National Association of Corporate and Professional Recruiters, as reported in "Drug Tests for Job Candidates," *USA Today* (International Edition), January 4, 1990, p. 8-B.
4. Robert L. Mathis and John H. Jackson, *Personnel—Human Resource Management,* 4th ed. (St. Paul, Minn.: West Publishing Co., 1985), pp. 100–104; and Randall S. Schuler and Stuart A. Youngblood, *Effective Personnel Management* (St. Paul, Minn.: West Publishing Co., 1986), pp. 204–210.
5. Adapted from "How to Keep Bias out of Job Interviews," *Business Week,* May 26, 1975, p. 77.
6. Adapted from John LaFevre, "Seven Tricky Job Interview Questions," *Moving Up Magazine,* September/October 1987, p. 26.
7. From a study by the National Association of Corporate and Professional Recruiters, as reported in an article by Mark Memmott, "More Firms Stop Giving References," *USA Today* (International Edition), December 5, 1989, p. 16.
8. William B. Werther, Jr., and Keith Davis, *Personal Management and Human Resources* (New York: McGraw-Hill Book Company, 1981), pp. 176–177; and Richard M. Hodgetts, *Effective Supervision* (New York: McGraw-Hill Book Company, 1987), p. 157.
9. Daniel Kadlec, "More Firms Are Turning to ESOPs," *USA Today* (International Edition), April 13, 1989, p. 20.
10. "Sony: A Diversification Plan Tuned to the People Factor," *Business Week,* February 9, 1981, pp. 88, 89.
11. "First Place Can Be Worst Place for Job Interviews," *The Wall Street Journal,* September 9, 1980, p. 1.

Chapter 10

Training and Evaluating Employees

No matter how badly employees want to improve their job performance, they won't be successful unless there is direction from their supervisor.

—Marcia Ann Pulich, Professor of Management

There are few things more difficult than the art of making advice agreeable.

—Bit and Pieces

Learning Objectives

When you finish this chapter, you should be able to:

1. Name the benefits associated with an effective employee training program.
2. Describe the employee training process.
3. Present an overview of the major types of training methods and techniques.
4. Explain employee performance evaluation systems.
5. Influence employee performance through the use of management by objectives (MBO).

"What kind of an organization is this, anyway? I've been working here two weeks so far, and all I've received is criticism on the way I'm doing things. But it's not my fault; I haven't received a minute of training related to my job. How can they expect me to do things their way if they don't even show me what their way is?"

Most employees, and especially new ones, usually require some sort of training. Every person, of course, is unique. As a result, each associate who reports to you, the supervisor, differs somewhat in his or her level and type of education, skill, and abilities. Some may have attended trade school or college before reporting to the job for the first time; others may be fresh out of high school. So it's probably safe to assume that many new employees have not yet developed all the skills and knowledge necessary to perform their jobs in your organization at the expected level. As supervisor, one of your major responsibilities is to help your associates acquire and develop the specific job skills needed, an activity termed *employee training and development.*

A related supervisory responsibility is that of *evaluating employee performance.* Periodic reviews of employee performance help point out deficiencies in behavior and provide useful clues about where training programs should be focused. Both of these topics—*training* and *appraising employee performance*—will be our concern in this chapter.

Who Is Responsible for Training in Organizations?

Many authorities make a technical distinction between the terms *training* and *development.* Training is commonly referred to as the teaching of specific skills and behavior, such as how to operate a film developing machine in a one-hour film processing shop. Development, on the other hand, is typically more general than training, leans more toward individual needs in addition to organizational needs, and is more often provided for management personnel.[1] An example of development would be providing an employee with a *temporary promotion* while the actual manager is attending a conference or on vacation.

Training:
Activities intended to enable employees to acquire skills, understand rules and concepts, and modify attitudes to improve job performance.

In this section, we will focus on the function of **training**, and define it as providing an instructional opportunity intended to systematically enable employees to acquire skills, understand rules and concepts, and modify attitudes for the purpose of improving job performance. The basic purpose of training is to directly improve the competency of employees in specific areas. As implied by our definition above, there are three general areas that influence how employees perform their jobs: ***knowledge, skill,*** and ***attitude.***

The previous chapter stressed the importance of an effective orientation program for new employees. In a sense, orientation is where a new employee's training actually begins. Training in well-managed organizations typically continues to be an ongoing process thereafter. Companies well known for their successful training programs include the Hallmark Corporation, 3M Company, and IBM Corporation.

Who Conducts Employee Training Activities?

Organizations differ extensively regarding who is assigned the responsibility for planning, organizing, and carrying out training activities. Sometimes they utilize internal training sources; at other times, they employ external training sources. Some organizations assign the total responsibility for the training function to only one individual, who may also continue to be responsible for other nontraining activities. Larger organizations may have up to 150 or more persons assigned to a training department. Such training specialists work closely with all levels of line managers to assist them in determining training needs and in designing and presenting various instructional programs.

There are yet other organizations in which the training director's main responsibility is to obtain *outside consultants,* who do the planning, designing, and presenting of training programs. Additionally, in some organizations the members of a training department act primarily as *in-house consultants,* who develop custom-made programs principally for internal use.

Your involvement in training activities, therefore, depends primarily on how the function has been established in your organization. As a supervisor, however, you cannot expect another department to anticipate and handle all of the training needs in your department. Supervisors in virtually all organizations have the basic, ongoing responsibility to ensure that their associates or work teams have obtained the necessary skills, knowledge, and attitudes to effectively carry out their job responsibilities. The concept of *delegation* should also be applied to training; supervisors who have learned the art of effective delegation involve their associates both in helping to determine training needs and in training coworkers. *A cautionary note:* As we shall see shortly, training is a developed skill. Therefore, anyone about to be involved with training activities should first receive the training necessary to be able to train others effectively.

Why Should Trainers Be Trained?

Training is not a simple activity. In larger organizations, a training department may train you and your associates on the techniques of effectively training others. Where such staff assistance doesn't

Training is an ongoing process in most modern organizations. Highly essential is that trainers be knowledgable on all training techniques.

exist, however, it is your responsibility to ensure that you and your associates develop the requisite training skills. Wexley and Latham suggest seven common activities that all trainers should practice:

1. Establish specific training objectives and share these objectives with trainees.
2. Be familiar with the basic principles concerning how adults learn.
3. Communicate more effectively with trainees, both orally and through audio/visual means.
4. Plan each training session so that the material is presented clearly.
5. Choose the most effective method of instruction.
6. Work with trainees individually; draw them out and deal with their anxieties.
7. Avoid improper or unethical types of behavior, such as violation of confidences, copyright violations, abuse of trainees, and giving trainees what they *want* instead of what they *need.*[2]

What Are the Benefits of Effective Training Activities?

Most organizations, whether private or public enterprises, have specific goals. These goals are difficult to attain without trained personnel. Some managers have found that the educational backgrounds of applicants have declined over the years, a condition that has created added training challenges. Recognizing the need for trained personnel, many organizations provide their employees with formal training. A recent study by the Rand Corporation for the Department of Labor revealed that nearly 40 percent of U.S. workers have taken part in training programs while on their current jobs.[3] For example, in a recent year the Motorola Corporation spent $50 million, or 2.9 percent of its annual payroll budget, on employee training and education, including teaching basic English and mathematics skills.[4]

You, as a supervisor, are often extensively involved with the training process. For example, employees newly assigned to you must be taught how to run specific equipment with which they are unfamiliar. In addition, you may periodically develop new work procedures or obtain new types of equipment that require employees to learn the proper methods for working with such changes.

There are numerous benefits that result from having trained employees. Some of the key advantages include:

1. Higher productivity
2. Lower accident frequency
3. Better morale and pride toward jobs and work groups
4. Improved advancement opportunities
5. Decreased need for close supervision, thus freeing supervisors to attend to other important tasks
6. Greater ease in upgrading employee skills when changes in technology occur

We will now examine each of these areas in the sections that follow.

Why Should Employee Productivity Improve?

A major purpose of training is to improve employee skills. Athletes spend hour after hour training, to improve their skills and enhance their performance. As with athlete training, employee training tends to strengthen worker skills and performance, which ordinarily leads to improved productivity.

Why Should Employee Accident Frequency Decrease?

Employees who have an improved understanding of their jobs as a result of solid training tend also to have a greater recognition of the hazards associated with their jobs. For example, workers who have been shown the potential risks inherent in their jobs and are trained to utilize safety equipment usually have a lower incidence of job-related accidents.

Why Do Employee Morale and Pride Tend to Improve?

Have you ever noticed how you usually feel about yourself when you've completed a task? You may feel a sense of pride and accomplishment. Training helps to supply employees with the same types of feelings. The added job familiarity resulting from training enables employees to perform their assigned duties more effectively, thus providing them with an enriched sense of self-worth. Workers who perform their tasks well, who have the belief that they are doing a decent job, tend likewise to take greater pride in their work and workgroups. Morale, therefore, tends to be higher among employees who feel that they do their jobs satisfactorily.

How Are Employee Advancement Opportunities Enhanced?

Employees who have received adequate training tend, of course, to be better qualified than those who have not. The greater the proficiency level that employees have attained, the greater the likelihood that they will be prepared for promotional opportunities as they arise.

Why Is There a Decreased Need for Close Supervision?

Employees who have received effective job training can typically work out problems more effectively without continually asking their bosses for information or clarification. As a result, a diminished need for close supervision often results, thus enabling the supervisor to focus on other important managerial concerns.

How Is the Upgrading of Employee Skills Facilitated?

Employees should be prepared for new activities as technology improves and becomes increasingly more complex. Well-trained employees tend to be able to transfer their acquired skills to new situations and to learn new techniques as the need arises. For example, a person who has learned the basics of using a computer program can more easily be trained to utilize new programs. The upgrading of skills tends to be easier for employees who have already been reasonably well trained.

What Is the Nature of the Training Process?

Transfer of training: *A condition that exists when what is learned can be transferred from the training site to the job itself.*

Training has its greatest value when what is learned can be *transferred* to the job itself. **Transfer of training** is considered *positive* when an employee's job performance has been enhanced as a result of the training. In some cases, though, transfer could actually be *negative,* because of ineffectively administered training, employee resistance to the program or trainer, or a negative response from peers or the supervisor after the trainee returns to the actual work environment. In some instances, transfer could be considered *neutral* when the training program has had no direct result on job performance.

Formal training programs should start at the top of organizational hierarchy and work down. There is little point in training workers

in philosophies, techniques, methods, skills, and approaches that are not espoused by their supervisors. This suggestion is even more valid for training received by supervisors, who are unlikely to be able to put their training to practical application without the support of senior and middle management.

Training methods and techniques vary widely among organizations and departments. Much of the training conducted by supervisors, however, is on a relatively informal, day-to-day basis. As a result, supervisors should become familiar with some of the basic concepts associated with training activities. In a very real sense, you, as a supervisor, are a lot like a coach or teacher when you are involved with the training process. Of course, some coaches and teachers are quite effective, while others seldom accomplish their training objectives. An understanding of some basic training concepts, as summarized in Table 10–1, can assist you in achieving your training objectives. The following section examines these useful training guidelines. (Training methods and techniques are given special treatment in a later section.)

How Are Departmental Training Needs Determined?

A logical first step in the training process is to ***determine the training needs*** of your department. How is this done? If up-to-date job specifications exist for your firm, you should analyze them to see what skills are required for each job in your department. Then, as discussed in the following section, you can evaluate the skills of your existing employees related to job specifications. If, for example, a job specification indicates that the jobholder must be proficient in the utilization of a computer spreadsheet software program, you should evaluate if the employee in that particular job has adequate skill in this area. If not, additional training will be necessary.

TABLE 10–1
Guidelines for Effective Training of Employees

- Determine organizational training needs.
- Know your trainees.
- Design the program around analyzed training needs and established objectives.
- Determine training methods and techniques.
- Pace and allot adequate time for training activities.
- Motivate your trainees.
- Encourage and praise trainees.
- Make certain trainees have actually learned (show, tell, and ask).
- Follow up and evaluate results.

A variety of additional factors should be analyzed to determine departmental training needs. Some of the principal reasons why you may have to provide training for your associates include:

1. *New or inexperienced employees*—Even if new employees have had training elsewhere, they still usually require additional training related to your organization's or department's standards and procedures.
2. *Introduction of new equipment, procedures, and processes*—Even seasoned veterans may require updating of their skills when new equipment and procedures are introduced.
3. *New job assignments*—A person placed on a new job typically requires training related to the new assignment.
4. *Not meeting deadlines*—Consistently failing to meet deadlines in your department could be an indication of a need for additional training.
5. *Excessive scrap and wasted materials*—High scrap and waste rates are often the result of poor training.
6. *Production costs out of line with industry averages*—High costs of production could also be the result of poor training.
7. *Rising turnover and absenteeism*—High turnover and absenteeism could be an indication of poor morale resulting from inadequate training.

What Should You Know about Your Trainees?

Are you familiar with and have you made an inventory of your employees' *existing knowledge, experience,* and *skills*? Have you carefully analyzed where your training efforts are most likely to pay off? There is little reason to provide training in areas where employees are already proficient. Instead, the payoff is greater when you build on the existing strengths of your trainees.

Therefore, prior to beginning training activities you should determine what each employee already knows and decide *who* is going to receive *what* training. Analyzing recent employee performance reviews will enable you to uncover clues as to where your training efforts need to be focused with specific employees. Some supervisors design questionnaires for the purpose of drawing on employees' opinions regarding personal training needs.

Why Should You Design Your Program Around Training Needs and Objectives?

Before you leap blindly into a training situation, you should first decide what specifically *your employees need* and what *you want to accomplish* from your efforts by answering the following three questions:

- Is your goal solely to help employees *improve their skills*?
- Is part of your goal to assist employees in *gaining general knowledge* that may not be directly related to skills?

- Is your objective to get employees to *change* or *improve their attitudes*?

Perhaps all three areas may demand your attention. To design an effective training program, you should attempt to know in advance specifically what you want to train each person for and what training techniques you intend to use. Otherwise, your program design may appear disjointed, confusing, and possibly provide the employee with a negative transfer of training. Where possible, gain the assistance of your personnel department in designing training programs.

How Do You Motivate Employees to Learn?

People tend to learn far more readily when they want to learn and when they see a good reason for learning. One of your major challenges, therefore, is to assist employees in recognizing the need for training. When employees see how they may personally benefit from training—how it may affect their careers, for example—they are far more inclined to be motivated to expend the time and effort required for developing new skills.

A related observation was made by this author while conducting supervisory management training workshops for industry. While informally talking with participants prior to the beginning of the workshops, I regularly discovered that some of them hadn't the slightest notion as to *why* they had been sent to the training programs. Several participants even felt insulted by their manager's having sent them to the workshop, assuming that such an action was a negative reflection on their past performance, which was typically not the case. Always communicate as clearly as possible the real reasons why your associates are to receive additional training.

It is essential, therefore, that you work closely with employees and *draw on their ideas* before unveiling a new training program. It is wise to work with each of your employees to *uncover their training needs,* which, of course, will vary with each individual. Many of your associates are interested in promotion, pay raises, and recognition. Show them how training can help accomplish their aspirations and how having been selected for training is, in a sense, an honor. Furthermore, training sessions will tend to have greater impact on employees if you communicate to them the training objectives and benefits prior to actual training sessions, and then reinforce the objectives and benefits during the sessions.

How Should You Pace the Training?

We've already stressed the likelihood of individual differences in the skills and knowledge attained by your subordinates. As a result of these differences, guard against presenting your material at *too fast a pace* or *in excessively large doses.* What may be a perfect bite-sized quantity of information for one trainee might be a whopping overdose for another. Professional trainers usually advise *breaking down the subject or skill into small parts,* proceeding to the next step *only after the trainee has grasped previously presented information.*

Material should be presented in a *logical sequence* and proceed from the *simple* to *complex.* Further, try to *know your trainees' abilities and limitations* so that you don't create a discouraging climate by making the training appear too complicated and confusing or the trainees appear stupid.

Spaced repetition: *Training materials presented with time intervals between each repetition rather than in uninterrupted doses.*

Trainees tend to retain information and skills more readily when they experience **spaced repetition**—presenting material with time intervals between each repetition, rather than in uninterrupted doses.

Supervisors are sometimes too eager to get the new employee actually producing. Recognize that effective training takes time. Jobs that are relatively complex may require training for longer periods of time, ranging from a few weeks to six or more months. Of course, individual learning ability should be taken into account. Where possible, the pace of the training should be varied according to the trainee's ability to learn.

Why Should Trainees Be Encouraged and Praised?

As with any human being, trainees need some sort of *positive reinforcement,* or *praise,* related to their efforts. Encourage trainees by praising their performance regularly throughout a training program. The absence of any feedback, either praise or constructive criticism, is often interpreted by trainees as an indication of a supervisor's displeasure, regardless of your true feelings. Sincere recognition of trainees' performance goes a long way in creating a favorable and motivating learning climate.

Here's an example of positive reinforcement:

Employee: Oh, darn it! I hit the wrong button again. I don't think I'm ever going to get this right.

Supervisor: No, John, that's not so. You actually are progressing quite well. Little difficulties like the one you're having are quite normal. Don't worry. You're coming along just fine. Really.

Be patient if the trainee doesn't seem to grasp all of the presented material at once. In some instances, your method of communicating might not have been clear. Or perhaps the trainee was presented with an excessive amount of material that was beyond his or her ability to grasp at one time.

How Can You Be Certain Trainees Have Actually Learned?

Effective trainers utilize the *show, tell, and ask approach* to training whenever possible. People typically learn through their senses of seeing, hearing, smelling, and touching. Utilize these senses whenever possible in training activities. Multisensory channels of communication increase both comprehension and retention considerably.[5]

Clearly *demonstrate* and *explain* (show and tell) the specific procedures or information that you want your trainees to learn, but don't assume that they understand everything you say merely because their heads bob up and down approvingly. Ask trainees specific *open-ended questions* that enable you to know if they really do understand. Then give them a chance to *show* you what you have taught them. Allow them to continue without criticism. Be sure to *offer reassurance* that you are there to assist with any difficulties they might encounter. Except in cases where danger of an accident exists, you might put trainees on their own and inform them that you'll be nearby in case any difficulties arise.

When Should You Follow Up to Evaluate Results?

The control function discussed in an earlier chapter comes back into play here. Trainees should be carefully *monitored,* both during and after training sessions, to ensure that the training has "taken" and to minimize the chances of accidents and product or equipment damage. Habits—whether good or bad—are difficult to break. You should, therefore, make certain that the trainee properly performs newly learned tasks and breaks any recently acquired bad habits before they become fixed. The trainee who does not meet your learning objectives should be tactfully corrected before the habits become so deeply ingrained that unlearning them becomes difficult.

How can you determine if your training was effective? There is a strong probability that your efforts were not in vain when you can answer in the affirmative to the following four questions:

1. Have the quantity and quality of the employee's work improved?
2. Has the employee's morale improved?
3. Has a positive transfer of training occurred?
4. Has team spirit improved?

A mistake that some supervisors make is to expect the new employee, even after training, to perform as well as the supervisor. As J. F. Ponthieu has advised:

> *No matter how well trained or developed their skills, many subordinates cannot perform beyond a certain level. Placing impossible goals and expectations on them will only frustrate and demotivate them. It also destroys feelings of support for the manager. The ability to assess an employee's capabilities is an important one.*[6]

Trainees should have the opportunity to evaluate the training program so that trainers can analyze what aspects of the program might be improved. Table 10–2 provides a sample evaluation form that trainees can fill out after attending a training workshop.

TABLE 10–2
Sample Evaluation Form for Trainees Who Have Attended a Training Workshop

Evaluation Form
Skill Development Workshop
Items below evaluated on a 1 to 10 scale.
Please circle number that indicates your evaluation.
(10 represents the most positive reaction; 1 the least positive)

1. How well did the training program hold your interest?	10	9	8	7	6	5	4	3	2	1
2. How would you evaluate the leader's knowledge of the topics?	10	9	8	7	6	5	4	3	2	1
3. How effective was the leader's presentation?	10	9	8	7	6	5	4	3	2	1
4. How useful were the notebook/handouts?	10	9	8	7	6	5	4	3	2	1
5. How useful was the group participation?	10	9	8	7	6	5	4	3	2	1
6. How useful were the audio/visuals?	10	9	8	7	6	5	4	3	2	1
7. What overall rating would you give the program?	10	9	8	7	6	5	4	3	2	1

8. How would you evaluate your participation in the program? (check one)

Overall workload	Too heavy ___ Just right ___ Too light ___
Classroom demands	Too heavy ___ Just right ___ Too light ___
Homework assignments	Too heavy ___ Just right ___ Too light ___

9. If asked by a coworker to describe the workshop and its value to you, what woud you say?
10. In what specific ways could this program be improved?

What Are the Principal Training Methods and Techniques?

After you have analyzed your departmental training needs and established specific training objectives, you then must decide which of the specific training methods, or combination of methods, you will use. Utilizing effective training methods and techniques tends to reduce the elapsed time it takes new employees to perform up to established standards of production efficiency. Although there are numerous training techniques, most of them fall under four general methods, which are:

- On-the-job training (OJT) (on company premises)
- Vestibule training (job simulation)
- Apprentice training (common in trades and crafts)
- Off-the-job training (off company premises)

What Is On-the-Job Training (OJT)?

On-the-job training (OJT) takes place on the premises of the organization and may be conducted by training specialists or the trainee's supervisor or coworkers. The supervisor typically bears most of the responsibility for OJT training. The new employee is partially productive during the training period. Table 10–3 sug-

On-the-job training (OJT): *Training that takes place on the premises of the organization.*

TABLE 10–3
Guidelines for Presenting OJT Activities

Preparation
- Have the training workplace in proper order.
- Attempt to create a nonthreatening atmosphere.
- Discern what the trainee already knows.
- Make certain that the trainee is in the appropriate position to learn properly and to avoid accidents.

Presentation
- Explain and demonstrate only one key point or step at a time.
- Emphasize each key point or step, stating reasons why.
- Instruct slowly, clearly, completely, and patiently.
- Use the tell, show, and explain method of instruction.
- Allow for feedback from trainee to make certain that he or she is actually learning.

Tryout
- Have the trainee explain and demonstrate key points or steps.
- Have the trainee perform the tasks; observe, and patiently correct any errors.
- Ask questions to be certain that trainee understands both *how* and *why*.
- Have the trainee continue, with guidance, until he or she fully understands.

Follow Up
- Have the trainee work on his or her own.
- Monitor the trainee regularly.
- Encourage questions from the trainee.
- Gradually reduce monitoring and assistance.

gests some specific guidelines to follow when involved with OJT activities.[7]

What Is Vestibule Training?

Vestibule training: *Training that simulates the actual work situation, utilizing sample equipment.*

Vestibule training simulates the actual work situation, utilizing sample equipment. Since new employees do not necessarily perform up to established work standards, the vestibule method provides a learning situation at relatively small risk, since the learning environment is mock rather than real. An example of vestibule training is the job simulation an airline attendant receives while working and practicing in a mock-up of an aircraft.

What Is Apprentice Training?

Apprentice training: *Training that generally involves both classroom (off the job at a trade or vocational school) and on-the-job or vestibule training.*

Apprentice training has traditionally been provided for individuals entering a trade or craft, such as the printing, plumbing, or carpentry fields, for the first time. Such training generally involves both classroom (off the job at a trade or vocational school) and on-the-job or vestibule training. Supervisors are frequently active in on-the-job training segments.

What Is Off-the-Job Training?

Off-the-job training: *Training conducted away from workplace settings.*

Tuition aid programs: *The practice of reimbursing employees for certain expenses incurred while attending classes off company premises.*

Off-the-job training takes the trainee away from the regular workplace setting. This type of training varies widely in technique. It could include evening courses at nearby colleges, programmed instruction, and correspondence courses. Some organizations provide **tuition aid programs** that reimburse employees for certain expenses incurred while attending classes off the premises, while other organizations allow college instructors to teach classes on company premises.

What Training Methods and Techniques Should You Use?

We've already learned the major training methods (on-the-job (OJT), vestibule, apprenticeship, and off-the-job). Your involvement with the trainee will depend primarily on which method(s) you choose. Table 10–4 summarizes and briefly explains the major techniques that are used in training.

What Is the Nature of Employee Performance Evaluation Systems?

Employee performance evaluation system: *Activities designed to determine how well employees are carrying out their duties, tasks, and responsibilities.*

You've trained your employees, and now comes the important part: performance. Are they performing as your training efforts intended them to? As a supervisor, you should continually strive to maintain an awareness of how well your associates are meeting your standards. Your awareness can be enhanced with the aid of a formal *employee performance evaluation system.* An **employee per-**

TABLE 10–4
Principal Training Techniques

On-the-Job (OJT) Training
- Job rotation (developing proficiency in various positions, thus providing for greater organizational flexibility)
- Coaching and understudy assignments (assigning a trainee to a skilled employee for guidance, thereby providing a one-on-one training relationship)
- Small-group discussions (useful for developing communication and team problem-solving skills)

Vestibule Training
- Simulation (reproducing the work environment without the risk of affecting the quality of actual production)
- Role-playing exercises (acting out parts in simulated problem situations)
- Behavioral role modeling (observing role models and practicing ideal behavior in vicarious training situations)
- Case studies

Apprenticeship Training
- Utilizes a variety of off-the-job and vestibule techniques

Off-the-Job Training
- Lectures (typically one-way communication and thus relatively ineffective unless heavily supplemented with other experiential techniques)
- Workshops/seminars (best when experientially oriented)
- Correspondence courses (an impersonal method of imparting knowledge, but not skills)
- Self-paced programmed learning (workbooks, manuals, teaching machines, and computers)
- Audio/visual techniques (videocassettes, movies, slides)
- Private TV networks (utilizing satellite communication systems to disseminate training programs on a wide geographical basis)
- Readings (e.g., articles; can provide useful information related to a job or industry)

formance evaluation system is a set of activities designed to determine how well employees are carrying out their duties, tasks, and responsibilities. It can be useful as a tool for guiding the direction of employee performance.

Although you personally aren't likely to be responsible for *designing* an employee performance evaluation system, you are likely to formally *appraise* the performance of the individuals who report to you. Since you, as a supervisor, interact every day with employees, you are best able to evaluate them.

For employees with less than two years service, evaluations may be made as often as every six months, occasionally even more often. Annual appraisals are more common for longer-term employees, although some managers feel that all employees should be appraised formally at least twice a year. In reality, appraisal activities, along with regular feedback, should be an ongoing process so that the formal evaluation is not a surprise to employees. The success of any appraisal program is largely dependent on the supervisor who administers it.

Why Review Employee Performance?

Employee evaluation systems vary, ranging from informal observations to highly sophisticated and complex programs. They are used for a variety of purposes, which include:

1. Determining whether new employees should be retained or dismissed.
2. Uncovering needs for additional employee training and development.
3. Providing formal recognition for satisfactory performance.
4. Determining promotions, transfers, salary increases, and other employee rewards.
5. Motivating employees.
6. Providing documentation to use in the event a disgruntled employee files a formal grievance or lawsuit.

Employee performance evaluation systems, also called *performance appraisals* and *performance reviews,* typically are concerned with either or both of two broad areas: (1) *employee performance,* that is, *results,* and (2) *employee traits,* such as enthusiasm, cooperativeness, and attitude, to the extent that these traits affect job performance. Numerous human resource managers believe that the review should focus principally on the employee's *performance,* and not on the *person* performing the duties.

What Is the Appraisal Cycle?

Appraisal cycle: *A five-step process that relates to evaluating the performance of employees*

One way of looking at performance evaluations is as an interlooping five-step process, an **appraisal cycle,** that begins, in effect, when you hire the employee. The steps are:

- Step I: You communicate the standards of performance.
- Step II: The employee performs the job.
- Step III: You compare the employee's performance against established standards.
- Step IV: You provide feedback, that is, positive reinforcement and/or constructive criticism to the employee during the formal appraisal interview.
- Step V: You and the employee *mutually agree* on plans for improvement during the appraisal interview.

The appraisal cycle is graphically illustrated in Figure 10–1.

Should the Issue of Salary Be Separated from Performance Reviews?

Some managers feel that appraisals for *salary administration* should be conducted separately, that is, on occasions other than performance reviews. The salary issue, it is felt, may cloud the overall constructive purpose—that of employee development and growth—of the appraisal system. When salary administration and performance review are combined, the employee tends to be more concerned with discussing future pay raises than hearing about past performance. Of course, paychecks should be related to how well employees perform. To gain optimum benefit from performance reviews, however, some organizations prefer to perform salary reviews about 30 days after completing performance reviews.

Why Is Establishing and Understanding Performance Standards Important?

If employees are to be held accountable for achieving specific levels of performance, they are entitled to know what is expected of them. You, as supervisor, must decide in advance what standards you intend to apply to a performance review. Far too frequently, an appraisal system is either misunderstood by the employee or improperly administered or communicated by the supervisor. When confusion of this nature occurs, the system becomes a meaningless exercise in which neither employee nor supervisor has much confidence. Supervisors should coordinate with the personnel department, where possible, in developing employee standards.

Standards for evaluation should be established well in advance of the actual evaluation procedure. Realistic and fair evaluations can take place only when supervisors are aware in advance of the actual appraisal interview of what should be evaluated and what constitutes satisfactory or unsatisfactory job performance. In some organizations, the human resource department (personnel) will

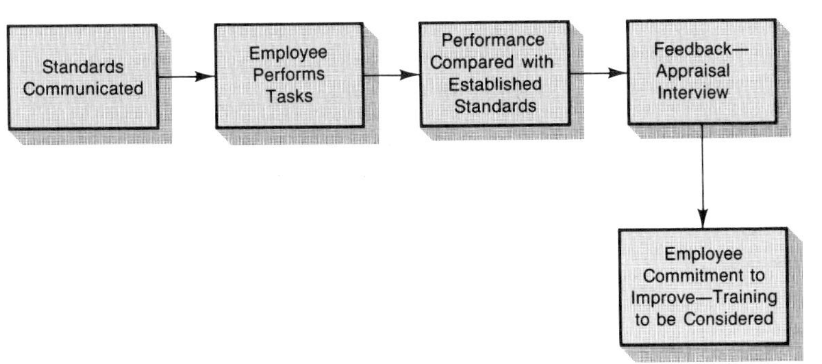

FIGURE 10–1
The Appraisal Cycle

work with you in developing evaluation criteria that relate directly to individuals in your department.

What Is the Purpose of the Appraisal Interview?

Appraisal interview: *A conference between the supervisor and an employee to discuss the employee's past performance and plans for improvement.*

Before conducting a face-to-face **appraisal interview,** you would typically complete a ***written evaluation form*** for the employee whose performance is to be reviewed. Appraisal forms vary by industry, organization, and position. An example of a form used for both reviewing employee performance and planning future personal development appears in Figure 10–2a, 10–2b, and 10–2c.

Some supervisors also have employees fill out identical forms, which are compared with the supervisor's form during the appraisal interview. The interview provides both the supervisor and the employee an opportunity to discuss the employee's past performance. The interview is an ideal time to provide the employee with positive feedback as well as to extract specific commitments on how he or she will improve performance in the future. During the interview, you ***guide*** the evaluated employee toward establishing new goals and improving or modifying future performance, such as additional employee training. The management by objectives (MBO) process, to be discussed shortly, is often tied to performance review activities.

After you've established mutual trust and respect with your associates, you might consider asking them to critique your own performance. Employees often appreciate the opportunity to express their own evaluation of their bosses. In some instances, the supervisor's performance could be the employees' biggest problem!

Why Do Some Appraisal Systems Fail?

As cited in Table 10–5, there are six principal reasons why some appraisal systems fail. Each are discussed below.

Lack of Understanding of Performance Standards. Some appraisal systems don't seem to accomplish what their users intended. Why is this? As already mentioned, ***employees may not understand what is expected of them;*** that is, they may have little awareness of what specific criteria or performance standards they will be judged on. You, as a supervisor, have the responsibility to clearly communicate to employees the nature of the evaluation process and to inform them about specific evaluation standards. In addition to orally discussing the evaluation system with each employee, you might give person a copy of the appraisal form and post a list of performance standards on the employee bulletin board for ready reference.

Lack of Objectivity. Another reason for failure of performance review systems is a ***lack of objectivity on the part of the evaluating supervisor.*** The supervisor's unconscious bias toward a particular employee may reveal itself on the evaluation form. For example,

FIGURE 10–2 An Example of a Performance Review (continued on next page)

APPLICABLE TO
Craftsmen & Operatives

This Information
is CONFIDENTIAL

Name ______________________ Date of Review ______________________

Type of Review ☐ Periodic ☐ Non-Periodic Period Covered ______________________

Rater ______________________

Job Title ______________________ Rater's Supervisor ______________________

Instructions: Evaluate the employee's performance according to the Normal Distribution rating scale shown below.

1. Place an "X" in the square which best represents performance of a factor and make appropriate comments justifying your ratings. Because of the large range of "commendable" performance, three distinctions may be made in rating commendable performance. (Comments are required for ratings of Critical, Adequate, Exceptional, or Outstanding).
2. Disregard your general impression of the employee and concentrate on one factor at a time.
3. Evaluate the employee's performance compared to other employees in the same job family and /or job grade.
4. After evaluating all factors, tabulate the Total Points and Converted Score. Then check the overall rating block corresponding to the final score.

CRITICAL	ADEQUATE	COMMENDABLE	EXCEPTIONAL	OUTSTANDING
2% - 5% of Total Appraised Group	**10% - 15% of Total Appraised Group**	**60% - 75% of Total Appraised Group**	**10% - 15% of Total Appraised Group**	**2% - 5% of Total Appraisal Group**
Performance noticeably below the commendable level. Unsatisfactory.	Results indicate performance not completely meeting all requirements.	Results indicate performance that is consistently satisfactory and sufficient in most respects.	Results indicate performance clearly exceeding the commendable level.	Results indicate performance so clearly distinguished as to be obvious to all.

1. **Job Knowledge** – Consider degree to which the employee applies fundamental knowledge and skills required to succeed at the job.

Critical	Adequate	Commendable	Exceptional	Outstanding
0	40	60 80 100	120	160
☐	☐	☐ ☐ ☐	☐	☐

Comments: ______________________

2. **Quality of Work** – Consider demonstrated ability to complete quality, finished products in a timely manner.

Critical	Adequate	Commendable	Exceptional	Outstanding
0	40	60 80 100	120	160
☐	☐	☐ ☐ ☐	☐	☐

Comments: ______________________

3. **Quantity of Work** – Consider employee's work pace, ability to meet deadlines, volume of work produced.

Critical	Adequate	Commendable	Exceptional	Outstanding
0	40	60 80 100	120	160
☐	☐	☐ ☐ ☐	☐	☐

Comments: ______________________

4. **Ability to Learn New Duties** – Consider the speed with which employee grasps instructions and masters new routines.

Critical	Adequate	Commendable	Exceptional	Outstanding
0	40	60 80 100	120	160
☐	☐	☐ ☐ ☐	☐	☐

Comments: ______________________

FIGURE 10–2 An Example of a Performance Review (continued on next page)

5. **Attendance** – Consider punctuality in reporting to work.

Critical	Adequate	Commendable	Exceptional	Outstanding
0	40	60 80 100	120	160
☐	☐	☐ ☐ ☐	☐	☐

Comments: ______

6. **Dependability** – Consider degree to which employee can be relied upon to do the job and to meet deadlines without close supervision.

Critical	Adequate	Commendable	Exceptional	Outstanding
0	40	60 80 100	120	160
☐	☐	☐ ☐ ☐	☐	☐

Comments: ______

7. **Cooperation** – Consider willingness to work harmoniously with others in getting a job done; readiness to observe and conform to the policies of management.

Critical	Adequate	Commendable	Exceptional	Outstanding
0	40	60 80 100	120	160
☐	☐	☐ ☐ ☐	☐	☐

Comments: ______

"APPRAISAL OF OVERALL PERFORMANCE"

0-25	20-55	50-75 70-95 90-115	110-145	140-160
Critical	Adequate	Commendable	Exceptional	Outstanding
☐	☐	☐ ☐ ☐	☐	☐

Total Points ______ ÷ 7 = ______ Converted Score

Strengths/Areas for Improvement:

Recommended Improvement Activities:

Employee Comments (You may attach a separate page, if needed):

Rater Signature: ______ Date: ______

Rater's Supervisor Signature: ______ Date: ______

This review has been discussed with me.

Employee Signature: ______ Date: ______

FIGURE 10–2 An Example of a Performance Review (continued)

LIST **OBJECTIVES** FOR THE PERIOD AND **RESULTS** ACHIEVED	LEVEL OF ACHIEVEMENT						
	CRITICAL	ADEQUATE	COMMENDABLE			EXCEPTIONAL	OUTSTANDING
"OVERALL LEVEL OF ACHIEVEMENT" Consider priorities and weighings of all objectives in determining this rating. Consider the rating along with **"OVERALL FACTOR RATING"** on Page 2 when calculating **"APPRAISAL OF OVERALL PERFORMANCE"**.							

ATTACH ADDITIONAL PAGES AS NEEDED

TABLE 10–5
Reasons Why Some Employee Appraisal Systems Fail

- Lack of understanding of performance standards
- Lack of objectivity
- Lack of honesty
- Employee's or supervisor's lack of understanding of the purpose of the system
- Excessive focus on negatives by the supervisor
- Faulty design of the appraisal system

some supervisors have negative reactions to beards. Let's assume that you are one of those who happen to detest beards. You're not really sure why, but you do nonetheless. One of your employees, Miguel, favors beards; in fact, he's worn a neatly trimmed Van Dyke since he was 17 years old (he's 41 now). There is a possibility that you unconsciously underrate Miguel when you formally evaluate his performance because of your deeply ingrained reaction to beards. However, isn't it Miguel's *performance,* not his beard, that you should be evaluating? With any employee, you should avoid personal comments about the individual employee that do not relate to his or her work.

Lack of Honesty. In other instances, supervisors may *fail to be entirely honest* during the interview, for fear of hurting the feelings, salary levels, or careers of employees with whom they have a close working relationship.

Lack of Understanding of the Purpose of the System. Another potential cause of appraisal failure exists when either supervisors or employees *lack an understanding of the appraisal system's real purpose.* Because of the careless way in which some appraisal systems are introduced (by insufficiently training supervisors how to employ them), the systems may be perceived merely as busy work rather than something truly worthwhile and practical. It is essential that supervisors receive adequate training in performance evaluation prior to being allowed to actually conduct such evaluations. This training will tend to reduce or eliminate many of the pitfalls involved in performance evaluation. The training should teach the supervisor the nature of performance standards and techniques of interviewing and evaluation, along with providing him or her with role-playing experiences. Supervision in Action 10–2, "Appraise This Appraisal System" (located at the end of this chapter), provides an example of a sloppily introduced appraisal system that failed to produce positive results.

An appraisal system should be "bought" by supervisors and "sold" to associates. If you, as a supervisor, are not convinced of the merits of the appraisal system, you'll probably find difficulty in administering it to others. You have the responsibility to convince employees that a performance review is a technique intended to *assist them in their development* and not one to be used to make a case against them. Employees should be informed that the evaluation procedure helps to uncover areas that may require additional training and development. You should stress to employees that you are willing to work with them in establishing useful methods for improving their skills and performance.

Excessive Focus on Negatives by the Supervisor. Counterproductive results from appraisal systems can also occur when the *supervisor focuses excessively on the negative side of the evaluation.* Doing so tends to cause employees to become defensive and less receptive to suggestions for personal growth and development. Negatively oriented interviews sometimes result in tensions and arguments between the supervisor and employees. A better approach than engaging in a no-win argument, as has already been stressed, is for you to attempt to convince employees that your intention is to assist them, not punish them. Likewise, inform employees that you and they are going to focus on the *future*, not the *past*. Since the past can't be changed, far more is to be gained when you and the employee jointly agree on methods and activities for modifying or improving future employee performance.

Faulty Design of Appraisal System. In some instances, supervisors may be unfortunate enough to be stuck with an appraisal system that is improperly designed. Anyone responsible for designing appraisal systems, however, should give adequate attention to various laws and court decisions. There have been instances in which some appraisal systems have been adjudged in violation of civil rights legislation. Keep in mind that appraisai systems are typically subject to the same standards of job relatedness as are selection techniques.

How Can You Influence Performance Through Management by Objectives?

Performance reviews, as we know, are concerned with measuring how well employees meet organizational standards. Unfortunately, some employees seldom live up to preset standards and expectations, but it's not always the employees' fault. Frequently, they aren't clear as to what their supervisors expect from them—they feel left in the dark. A major challenge that supervisors face is communicating organizational goals and standards to employees in a manner that will be easily understood and readily accepted. Although this task isn't easy, the section that follows explains a well-known technique that goes along well with performance reviews.

How Can You Share Goals with Management by Objectives (MBO)?

How can a supervisor stimulate employees in a way that will motivate them into wanting to achieve organizational goals and meet

Management by objectives: *A management activity whereby a supervisor and his or her subordinates jointly establish goals and objectives.*

standards? A fairly common technique used by many managers today is known as **management by objectives (MBO).** Also referred to as *results management,* MBO's major focus is on involving managers *jointly* with their subordinates in developing specific goals and standards of performance. Contrary to some beliefs, the act of a supervisor's sharing the goal/standard-setting activity with subordinates actually enhances, rather than reduces, the leader's control over departmental activities. As with any goals and standards, of course, mutually established ones must fit into the overall mission and goals of the organization.

What Does MBO Involve?

The MBO approach involves more than just establishing goals and standards mutually. It also entails developing specific *plans* for accomplishing established goals and standards, which are either agreed on and accepted by you, the supervisor, or modified by mutual agreement between you and your subordinates. The expected results agreed on then become a guide—control standard—for future employee performance. MBO activities are frequently tied in with formal *performance appraisals.* Figure 10–3 illustrates the sequence of MBO activities.

When Should You Provide Feedback?

The MBO process requires that you provide employees with *periodic feedback,* not only during formal annual or semiannual performance review sessions. You should have regular meetings with your subordinates to inform them if progress has been made and if objectives and standards need modifying. In reality, you should offer constructive comments to the employee whenever there is a deviation from the agreed-on objectives.

What Are the Major Advantages of MBO?

MBO provides a number of advantages, which include:

1. MBO creates a situation in which employees tend to feel *greater involvement with their work.*
2. MBO helps employees *develop more positive attitudes* toward their jobs, since they are able to participate in decision making that affects them directly and personally.
3. MBO helps to give employees a *greater sense of commitment and direction*—they have a better idea of what is expected of them.

Of course, MBO is unlikely to succeed if attempted in a climate of distrust or when a manager fails to recognize and consider subordinates' needs in relation to established objectives.

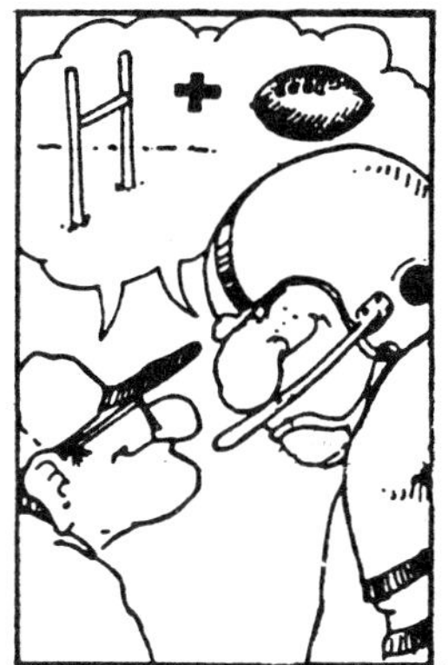

Establish objectives.

Decide on specific tasks, resources, and time frame necessary to achieve objectives.

Review and appraise actual results obtained by subordinate. Modify activities if necessary.

FIGURE 10–3
The Sequence of Events in the MBO Approach to Goal Setting

Are Goals Realistic and Attainable?

When applying the MBO process, a major difficulty you might experience is trying to make certain that your subordinates understand what constitutes realistic and attainable goals and standards. Vague statements such as, "I will perform better on my job," or "I will work harder during the next year," do not fit the guidelines of well-established objectives and standards. In our earlier discussion of goal statements we learned that to be useful, they should be measurable and expressed in quantitative terms whenever possible. Goals and control standards should also clearly state time limits for completion and be verifiable, realistic, consistent, and stated in terms of end results.

Summary

Training is an essential activity in most organizations as a means of enabling employees to maintain and acquire the skills necessary to perform their duties satisfactorily. The extent of a supervisor's involvement with training activities depends on the size and philosophy of the organization. Methods of training include on-the-job, vestibule, apprentice, and off-the-job. A host of training techniques exist. A transfer of training should result from the techniques or methods selected in any training program.

Employee performance evaluations systems are another significant part of a manager's toolkit. Supervisors have the responsibility to make certain that subordinates are aware of the standards against which their performance will be compared. Subordinates who are involved with establishing standards of performance are more likely to be motivated toward attaining those standards.

A popular technique for motivating employees to achieve and maintain organizational standards is management by objectives (MBO), in which the supervisor and employee jointly agree on goals and methods for achieving them.

Questions for Discussion

1. As implied in the chapter definition of *training*, what are the three general areas that training attempts to change?
2. Who should be assigned the responsibility for conducting training activities in organizations? Why?
3. Why is it essential for anyone involved in training others to first receive training on the use of training methods and techniques?
4. What are some significant benefits that tend to result from having a well-trained work force?
5. Describe four general methods used for training employees.
6. What is the significance of the *transfer of training* concept?
7. Assume that your boss asked you to develop a set of guidelines for conducting sessions for training your associates. List and describe some useful employee training guidelines.
8. Why is it important for you—the supervisor—to be familiar with your associates existing knowledge, experience, skills, and attitudes before actually beginning to train them?
9. Why is it advisable to draw on employee input when designing training activities?
10. How can you be certain if trainees have actually learned what your training activities intended them to learn?
11. What are the principal purposes of an employee performance evaluation system?
12. Explain the *appraisal cycle.*
13. What are some of the reasons why some employee performance evaluation systems fail? How might failure be avoided?
14. Why do some managers feel that *performance appraisal interviews* should be conducted separately from salary reviews? Do you agree?
15. Should a performance review focus on an employee's personality and other traits in addition to performance? Explain.
16. How could management by objectives (MBO) relate to *control sharing*, a concept discussed in Chapter 5?
17. What are some of the principal gains to be derived from using MBO as a tool for developing and influencing employee performance?

Can You Define These Terms?

Instructions: Write a definition for each of the following terms. You may check your definitions with those provided in the end-of-text glossary.

training
transfer of training
spaced repetition
on-the-job training (OJT)
vestibule training
apprentice training
off-the-job training
tuition aid programs
employee performance evaluation system (performance appraisal, performance reviews)
appraisal cycle
appraisal interview
management by objectives (MBO)

Supervision In Action

10–1 Maintaining Maintenance Standards

Assume that you are in charge of all maintenance activities at a manufacturing facility for a company called Servo-Technic Systems. You are currently looking over your backlog of paperwork, and you realize that annual performance review time has sneaked up on you once again.

One of your associates, Cameron Constance, has been one of your best and most dependable maintenance workers during the past five years. Cameron has consistently been able to analyze difficult mechanical problems and quickly put machinery back into smooth running condition after breakdowns.

Cameron's quality of work seems to have deteriorated, however, since his last performance review. You've intended to talk to him about the changes in his performance, but have not found time to arrange a discussion because of your heavy involvement with other problems. As a result, you've decided that the discussion of Cameron's deteriorating quality of repair work could be the main thrust of his upcoming performance review.

The problem is somewhat critical, since employees who operate the machinery are paid on a piece basis. Consequently, their income is appreciably affected during downtime of machinery. Of course, company profits are also adversely affected during such periods.

You've decided to schedule a performance review session with Cameron for next Monday morning. You feel that his performance must improve. You don't want to damage his morale, yet you know that something must be done soon. You're not quite certain how to approach the appraisal interview.

Questions

1. What types of information should you try to assemble before and during your interview with Cameron to ensure that your appraisal is fair?
2. Is there any possibility that Cameron's deteriorating results are due to causes outside of his control? Explain.
3. Develop an outline for your performance review with Cameron. Incorporate into your interview some of the MBO concepts discussed in the chapter.
4. What are some of the potential shortcomings of a once-a-year performance review? How might you supplement such a review system?
5. Role play your interview with another person who is to assume the role of Cameron.

10–2 Appraise This Appraisal System

The Oakvale Fire Department is located in a medium-sized city in the Southwestern part of the United States. It has engine and truck companies (or "fire stations," as they are typically referred to by the general public) scattered throughout the city. Firefighters at each engine or truck company are assigned a 24-hour shift once every three days. Therefore, there are three shifts of firefighters working on a rotational basis. Firefighters are free, except in extreme emergencies, during the other two days.

A supervisor, officially known as an officer, is assigned to every engine or truck company during each 24-hour shift. The responsibilities of officers are similar to supervisors working in any industrial situation: to motivate and coordinate available people and resources for the purpose of accomplishing the fire department's mission. Officers generally have very close relations with the firefighters during each 24-hour shift—they actually live, cook, and eat together.

In charge of the overall operations of the Oakvale Fire Department is Chief Rickford Gains. Recently Chief Gains attended a national conference of fire chiefs, where he participated in a number of training workshops. One of the workshops he attended stressed the importance of establishing and maintaining a sound employee performance review system as a means of motivating employees to strive for high levels of efficiency in their activities.

While flying back to Oakvale, Chief Gains thought to himself, "I've really been remiss about this evaluation stuff. Our department has grown so rapidly that it seems we've never caught our breath and taken the time to develop a formal system of performance reviews. I think it's a good idea. I'm going to talk to Captain John Entrenador, head of our human resources department, as soon as I get back to Oakvale, and have him set up a program."

Captain Entrenador agreed with Chief Gains that a performance review system should be set up. Entrenador decided to visit five other fire departments in the United States and develop a system patterned after the best of them. After Entrenador's study of the other systems, he developed a thorough 85-page manual outlining in detail the nature of the new system and the procedures associated with it. He showed the manual to Chief Gains, who thought it was outstanding in covering every facet of performance review systems. Gains officially approved the manual and told Entrenador to introduce it immediately to officers throughout the organization.

A number of personnel problems had developed in the department while Entrenador had been away doing the research for the appraisal program. One of them was the increased resistance on the part of the men in the department to hiring females for firefighting positions. Another time-consuming problem Entrenador had to face was a battle with the African-American Firefighters' Association over the validity of the examinations used to determine promotions within the department. The association had hired a consultant who advised the association members that the examination discriminated against certain ethnic groups.

These problems started taking an inordinate amount of Entrenador's time away from his intention to introduce the appraisal system. However, he realized that Chief Gains expected him to do something soon. He decided to make copies of the manual he had developed and distribute them to each officer in the department. A cover letter told the officers to study the manual and to start applying its contents to their firefighters within two weeks.

A year has passed since the distribution of the manual. Few of the officers are enthusiastic about the appraisal system. Most of them apply invectives to the system when discussing it. There is a general feeling among the officers that the appraisal system is merely a "make-work" exercise that takes a lot of time away form their other responsibilities. Few of the officers seem to take the system seriously.

Questions

1. Do you think that a performance appraisal system is really necessary in a quasi-military organization such as a fire department? Explain.
2. Why do you think the appraisal system was accepted so poorly by the officers?
3. If you had been responsible for introducing the program to the officers, what specific sort of training methods and techniques would you apply?
4. What steps could you take now to gain better acceptance and utilization of the program?

10–3 The Unfocused Performance Appraisal

Pete Hernandez, a recently appointed supervisor for Focus, Inc., has never done a performance appraisal before. He made an appointment for 2:30 P.M. this afternoon with Jane Lee, one of his associates, to go over her review with her. Ms. Lee is a divorced mother of three. Her job is very important to her, especially because of the expense of raising three children by herself with no outside support. Her eldest son wants to attend college next year, which will be an even greater expense for her. Consequently, she is quite concerned about getting a good review from Mr. Hernandez.

The time is about 2:30 P.M., and Mr. Hernandez hears a knock at the door. The following conversation takes place.

Hernandez: Come in. Oh, hello Ms. Lee. Have a seat. I'll be with you in just a moment. I'm just finishing inputting some data into my computer.

About five minutes later, Mr. Hernandez, turns off his computer.

Hernandez: Okay, I'm just about set for you now. Oh,

yes, will you excuse me for just a few minutes while I make a quick trip to the men's room? I'll be right back.

Meanwhile, Ms. Lee feels like biting her fingernails in anticipation of her review. Almost 10 minutes later, Mr. Hernandez finally returns, sits down, and his phone rings. Ms. Lee feels anxiety building up in her. After six minutes, Hernandez is finished with the phone call.

Hernandez: Ms. Lee, I don't want to beat around the bush so I'll get straight to the point. Your attitude hasn't been quite what it should these past few months, and your resourcefulness seems to have really been lacking.

Lee: I'm not sure what you're talking about, Mr. Hernandez. I am very serious about my job. I get to work early each day, and I always work a little longer than I have to.

Hernandez: Well, I don't have time to argue with you, Ms. Lee. You're just going to have to improve in those areas, that's all.

Lee: (angrily) How can I improve in something if I'm not clear on what you mean!

Hernandez: Don't take that tone with me! I told you I don't have time to argue with you. Please return to your work station.

Lee: I don't think you're being fair, Mr. Hernandez. This job is very important to me, and, as I already said, I take it very seriously. I want to do a good job.

Hernandez: That will be all, Ms. Lee. We can talk more about this later after you've cooled down, if you want.

Mr. Hernandez rises from his chair and walks to the door, opens it, and says goodbye to Ms. Lee.

Questions

1. What were the fairly obvious shortcomings in the way Mr. Hernandez handled his first review? How should he have handled it?

2. Some supervisors don't realize how anxiously and seriously employees view their upcoming periodic performance review conferences, especially since employee salaries are often related to performance. What can a supervisor do to reduce some of an employee's anxiety both before and during the conference?

Endnotes

1. John Douglas, Stuart Klein, and David Hunt, *The Strategic Managing of Human Resources* (New York: John Wiley & Sons, 1985), p. 282.
2. Kenneth N. Wexley and Gary P. Latham, *Developing and Training Human Resources in Organizations* (Glenview, Ill.: Scott, Foresman and Co., 1981), pp. 18–20.
3. Michael Brody, "Helping Workers to Work Smarter," *Fortune,* June 8, 1987, pp. 86–88.
4. Ronald Henkoff, "What Motorola Learns from Japan," *Fortune* (International Edition), April 24, 1989, p. 73.
5. Frank Watson, "Bye Bye Blackboard," *Business East Midlands* (England), October 1988, p. 21.
6. J. F. Ponthieu, "Gaining Mutual Independence through Training," *Supervisory Management,* April 1982, p. 19.
7. Adapted from materials utilized in supervisory management training workshops presented by Stan Kossen for the American Electronics Association, Palo Alto, CA.

Part Four

Providing Employees with Direction

Chapter 11

Job Satisfaction and the Motivation of Employees

You can make more friends in two months by becoming really interested in other people than you can in two years by trying to get other people interested in you.

—Dale Carnegie, Author and Educator

I don't mind being pushed as long as I can steer.

—Jerry LaRoche, Executive

Learning Objectives

When you finish this chapter, you should be able to:

1. Identify the major theories of needs and motivation.
2. Understand the factors that influence employee job satisfaction.
3. Recognize the key warning signs of job dissatisfaction.
4. Demonstrate specific techniques for improving the organizational climate.

"Jason, you lunkhead! I told you to have that job ready for me by 10:00 A.M.! What a peabrain you are! Can't you ever do anything like you're told? You're just a lazy good-for-nothing blockhead!"

"Boss, you can't talk to me like that. You have no right to call me those names and put me down in front of others."

"No right, dummy? I have every right in the world. I'm the boss around here. I can say whatever I want. Now get back to work, snail legs!"

"That's what you think, *boss, but I'm not taking any more of your hassling. You're going to have to get yourself another whipping boy. I quit!"*

"Wait a minute, Jason. Don't go off half-cocked. You can't quit. We're shorthanded around here now, and we need you. Besides, you're one of my best workers."

"So long, boss."

What do you think of the above approach to motivating employees? It certainly motivated Jason—right into quitting! The boss's approach wasn't very good for Jason's job satisfaction either, was it? Years ago, some supervisors were able to get away with using such approaches with their employees. Many employees took somewhat of a "Yes sir (ma'am), boss" stance and seemed to have a greater degree of tolerance for negative styles of leadership than do today's more independent, better-educated workers.

Job satisfaction and *motivation* are two topics of extreme concern to most supervisors. In this chapter, we carefully examine each topic. First, we focus on the twin topics of *human needs* and *motivation,* an understanding of which can help you establish a work environment that fosters the accomplishment of your departmental and organizational goals along with helping to satisfy employee needs. Next, we look at the *factors that influence employee job satisfaction* (or *morale*), that is, why some employees have positive attitudes and others negative attitudes toward their jobs and their work environment. Then, we investigate some of the major *warning signs of low employee morale.* Finally, we inspect some of the specific ways in which you as a supervisor can *design and redesign jobs* and *influence employee job satisfaction* within your own workplace.

Why Should Supervisors Understand Needs and Motivation?

Motivation: *The feelings or factors that drive a person toward achieving a particular objective.*

You, as a supervisor, get things done with and through people. To be an effective manager, you must have an understanding of *human needs and motivation.* **Motivation** can be described as the feelings or factors that drive a person toward achieving a particular objective. Stated differently, motivation is what causes people to act, perform, and want to accomplish something.

You should continually attempt to remind yourself that every employee is unique and not motivated by exactly the same incentives. To illustrate, let's take the case of Brian, one of your employees. Brian might feel motivated to work hard by an increase in pay. On the other hand, Linda, another of your employees, might be more motivated by the opportunity to be assigned more challenging responsibilities.

Traditional managers have long believed that people work mainly for money and are motivated primarily by such factors as fear of punishment and hope of financial reward. The first factor is certainly true; people *are* motivated by *fear*—in the *short run.* In the longer run, however, fear tends to motivate workers into seeking employment elsewhere! *Money,* too, *is* important to most employees. Money in the form of a bonus beyond regular income, for example, may motivate many employees. Other factors, as we'll soon explore in greater depth, are as important as money and, in some cases, even more important. A more progressive approach to supervision makes far greater use of a variety of positive factors, such as *recognition, praise, status,* and *responsibility.* All people, of course, have needs. However, professional managers recognize that not all people place the same value or priority on the objects or situations that satisfy their needs; different employees are motivated by different mixes of needs.

What Is the Nature of Needs and Motivation?

Everyone has needs of some sort. Just what are we talking about when we use the term **need**? Basically, the word refers to a condition of *deprivation*; that is, something *missing* from an individual's situation. That something might be a *physical need* (such as food requirements), a *social need* (such as the opportunity to mix with other employees), or a *psychological* or *ego need* (such as feelings of self-worth and esteem).

Need: *The feeling of deprivation; that which motivates a person into action designed to obtain relief or satisfaction.*

The absence of food, for example, would tend to stimulate activity intended to satisfy a felt hunger motive; a hungry person would try to obtain some food, either by working, seeking public entitlement assistance, growing food, or even stealing. Stated differently, if you don't have something, but you feel that you *must* have it, then you have a *recognized need.* Needs that are unsatisfied tend to cause internal feelings—tensions of sorts—that motivate individuals into acting in certain ways to satisfy their needs.

You can probably think of many things that you could survive without, such as a cellular telephone for your car, a compact disc player for your bedroom, a fax machine for your kitchen, or a portable computer for your lap. But you couldn't exist long without food, drink, sleep, air, shelter, and a tolerable climate. Such re-

Physical (primary, basic) needs:
Basic factors vital to human survival.

quirements are what psychologists refer to as **primary, physical,** or **basic, needs.**

Psychological (secondary, ego, or higher-order) needs:
Personal desires concerned with self-realization and self-esteem.

Each of us also has a variety of **secondary needs** that motivate us. These needs are known by such names as **psychological, ego,** or **higher-order needs.** Our secondary needs are sometimes *learned*; that is, we learn to need (or want) additional things that are not as basic as food and drink. Secondary needs motivate us to act in particular ways intended to satisfy those needs.

Safety and security (secondary) needs:
Personal desires concerned with feelings of safety and security.

Social (secondary) need:
Feelings that are usually learned, such as the desire to belong and to enjoy peer acceptance.

Esteem need:
The desire to be respected as a human being.

Self-realization need:
The need to feel accomplishment.

Among secondary needs are the desire to have feelings of **safety** and **security** (e.g., have safe working conditions and insurance); be **social** (e.g., be with other people); possess **esteem** (e.g., be respected as human beings); and the need for **self-realization** (e.g., accomplish a goal).

Needs create something inside of us akin to *tension*. This tension-like feeling motivates us to act in particular ways. How do we act when we feel these tensions? We behave in ways that are intended to accomplish a goal and/or relieve our tensions. If we're successful—that is, we achieve our goal—then we enjoy satisfaction, at least for awhile until new needs develop. Figure 11–1 illustrates how needs motivate. (Pause for a moment, and see if you can determine why a supervisor can be more effective with employees by understanding the nature of human needs.)

Do Needs Have to Be Felt to Motivate?

Before a need will motivate, it usually must be *recognized* as a need. To illustrate, let's assume that an employee of yours named Mary Anne never returns from breaks on time; she's always five to ten minutes late. Mary Anne doesn't seem to recognize any need for punctuality. When she was hired, she was told that breaks were 10 minutes long. Nevertheless, her breaks are typically closer to 20 minutes.

You've hesitated to say anything to Mary Anne because you feel that she should be mature enough on her own to follow company rules. Perhaps she should be, but remember that one of your primary responsibilities is to motivate employees, and perhaps Mary Anne needs to be assisted in recognizing the need to be punctual. Maybe Mary Anne doesn't realize that you believe limiting breaks to 10 minutes is important. Sometimes merely explaining to employees such as Mary Anne what your standards are and why maintaining them is important will resolve problems of this nature.

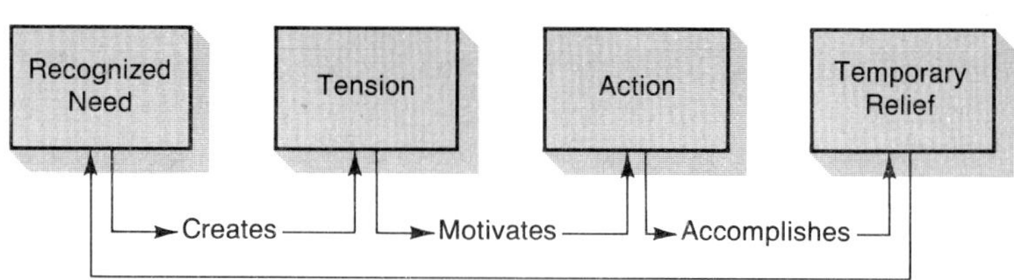

FIGURE 11–1
Recognized Needs Result in Tensions and Actions Designed to Achieve Relief

Remember, however, that *only recognized needs motivate people to action.* As a manager, you are in the position to assist employees, such as Mary Anne, in recognizing their needs.

Why Doesn't a Satisfied Need Motivate?

Another side of motivation is equally important to managers. We've learned that a need has to be recognized before it motivates. Just as important to supervisors is the realization that *a satisfied need generally ceases to motivate.* For example, if your employees receive adequate pay that enables them to maintain reasonable standards of living (i.e., they have enough food and decent housing), then other things may become more important to them. Perhaps *security* (such as a good retirement plan), *socializing opportunities* with their peers (related to the work place layout), or *status* (an impressive title or an award) may take on greater importance to them since salary no longer serves as a motivating factor.

Here's a possible exception to the concept of a satisfied need no longer motivating a person: the case of a person who has attained a standard of living that is quite satisfying. That person might fear the possible loss of this level of living if he or she doesn't *continue* working long and hard. In other words, the person was *motivated* to work hard to acquire something that *now inspires motivation* and hard work to hold on to. Generally speaking, however, as our primary (basic) needs become satisfied, secondary (higher-order) needs tend to become more important. A. H. Maslow, in his book *Motivation and Personality,*[1] is credited with having developed the concept of a *priority* or *hierarchy of needs.*

What Is the Nature of Maslow's Hierarchy-of-Needs Concept?

Maslow categorized human needs into a *hierarchy,* or *order of priority.* Maslow's **hierarchy-of-needs concept** suggests that each level of need, starting with the lowest level, must be satisfied to some extent before the next level assumes importance. Maslow's writings on human needs distinguish five levels of needs, ranging from basic, lower-order needs to social and psychological needs of a higher order (See Figure 11–2).

Hierarchy-of-needs concept: *A concept suggesting that each level of need must be satisfied to some extent before the next level assumes importance.*

Do Supervisors Have Much Control Over Employee Needs Satisfaction?

Do you, as a supervisor, really have much control over how your employees satisfy their basic physical needs? In reality, you don't have much influence. Most of your employees' basic needs are reasonably well satisfied through existing wage or salary structures. And remember: *A satisfied need usually ceases to motivate.* Employees' lower-order needs don't become unimportant, but higher-order needs take on much greater significance as basic needs are satisfied.

FIGURE 11–2
Maslow's Hierarchy of Needs Concept

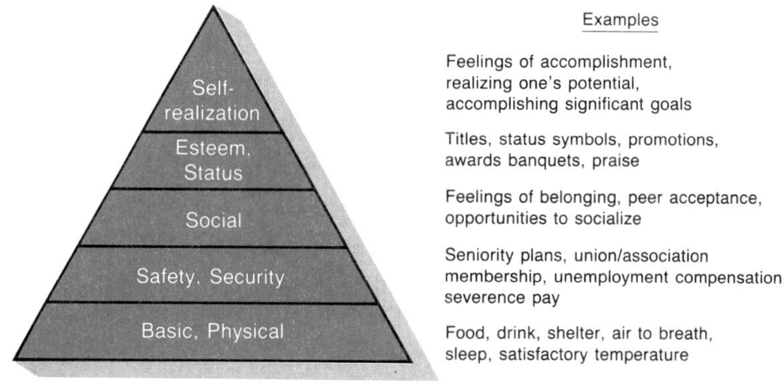

How about *higher-order needs?* Do supervisors have much influence over them? Definitely. Supervisors like you can influence the *design of jobs* and the *arrangement of work areas,* thus influencing workers' social needs. Supervisors can also significantly affect an employee's need for self-esteem through such factors as *praise, recognition, providing opportunities for achievement,* and so on. A later section of this chapter deals with a variety of methods for improving the organizational climate and thus appealing to the needs of employees.

Are Needs Mutually Exclusive?

Maslow's concepts imply that the hierarchy of needs is somewhat like a stepladder. As you lift your body past one rung on the ladder of human needs, you're all done with it. Careful analysis of needs, however, indicates otherwise. Needs aren't really mutually exclusive. For example, an employee's need for self-esteem might be stronger than his or her felt need for safety equipment, yet both might exist simultaneously. Or an employee might prefer to eat lunch with coworkers because of the need for both food and companionship.

Motivation-aintenance model: *A theory that describes two sets of factors in the work place, one set tending to motivate employees and the other tending to create dissatisfaction if withdrawn.*

Maintenance (hygiene) factors: *Factors that tend to have a neutral effect on the work environment but are likely to cause dissatisfaction if not met.*

What Is the Nature of Herzberg's Motivation-Maintenance Model?

Another well-known motivational theory, the **motivation-maintenance model,** was developed by Frederick Herzberg.[2] Herzberg's research indicates that *two sets of factors* or *conditions* influence the behavior of employees. The first set has virtually no effect on motivating employees; instead, it provides an almost *neutral* feeling among them. If withdrawn from the work place, however, these factors—called **maintenance,** or **hygiene, factors**—tend to cause *dissatisfaction.* Herzberg borrowed the term *hygiene* from the medical field where it refers to factors that help maintain, but don't necessarily improve, health. For example, hygienic activities that you may engage in regularly are brushing and flossing your teeth. Why do you do so? To *maintain* the existing condition of your teeth. Although your mouth feels a lot fresher after you've brushed your teeth, the condition of your teeth has not been improved, merely maintained.

An industrial example of the removal of a hygiene factor occurred in 1989 with an action of Eastern Airlines' senior management. Allegedly to forestall financial disaster for the company, management made the decision to reduce wages substantially. For instance, the hourly rate of a ramp services worker plunged from $13.46 to $5.00. The *hygiene factor,* existing wages and salaries, was adversely affected and dissatisfaction became so prevalent among employees that union officials called for a work stoppage (strike) against Eastern, eventually resulting in Eastern's management filing for bankruptcy.[3]

The second set of factors is termed **motivational** or **satisfiers.** These factors, when present, are said to cause *job satisfaction*—they serve as *motivators* and *satisfiers.* Absence of the satisfiers, however, will not necessarily cause dissatisfaction, but it will tend to reduce job satisfaction. Job satisfaction and job dissatisfaction, therefore, should not be considered as opposite ends of the same continuum. Instead, they should be perceived as two separate dimensions. Some additional, specific examples cited below should help to clarify Herzberg's concepts.

Motivational factors (satisfiers): *Factors that tend to motivate and cause job satisfaction.*

Maintenance (Hygiene) Factors. The following items are examples of what Herzberg has called *hygiene,* or *maintenance, factors:*

1. Company rules and policies
2. Fair supervision
3. Interpersonal relations with others in the organization
4. Working conditions and job security
5. Existing salary and certain types of employee benefits

According to Herzberg, supervisors like you would be making a mistake trying to motivate employees with any of the above five factors. These items merely keep the environment "clean," so to speak. In general, hygiene factors don't motivate, or create satisfaction. When absent, however, they can lead to dissatisfaction among employees.

What are some of the more common maintenance, or hygiene, factors? Typical examples include *sick leave, vacation, medical/dental plans,* and most other *personnel programs.* Would a good employee benefit program be likely to motivate employees? Not according to Herzberg. Instead, employees often take such programs and benefits for granted. Do you or your associates, for example, work harder all year because you know that you have dental insurance protection in case you get a cavity in one of your premolar bicuspids? Probably not. Do you or your associates necessarily work harder all week because you know that Friday you will receive your regular paychecks? Not likely. However, an important concept to remember is that if *any employee benefits are reduced or eliminated,* or if *salary is cut* (as in the case of the employees of Eastern Airlines cited above), these items quickly become grounds for dissatisfaction.

Employee benefits, such as employer-sponsored childcare facilities, do not usually motivate individuals. However, if removed or decreased, they can cause employee dissatisfaction.

Some individuals are initially surprised at Herzberg's findings that working conditions are not considered motivators. It's true that many employees, all things being equal, would tend to prefer working in a pleasant environment. But a sparkling new plant seldom substitutes for jobs that people enjoy or employee feelings of achievement and recognition. We've all probably seen organizations that function in shoddy, archaic-looking buildings, yet morale and productivity are high. Herzberg concludes that people's *attitudes* toward their jobs far outweigh the importance of working conditions or environment.

Motivational Factors (Satisfiers). Herzberg developed a second set of factors, which he referred to as *motivational factors,* or *satisfiers.* As a supervisor, you usually can exert considerable influence over these items:

1. Achievement
2. Recognition
3. The job itself
4. Growth and advancement possibilities
5. Responsibility

Factors like those listed above are said to motivate employees. Their absence, however, will not necessarily cause employee dissatisfaction. Let's briefly examine how each factor motivates.

Achievement is important to many employees. Achievement is the feeling of accomplishing a goal, that is, finishing something that has been started. Have you designed tasks so that your associates have the opportunity to develop feelings of accomplishment? Monotonous assembly-line work often makes feelings of achievement difficult to accomplish.

Recognition is appreciated by many employees. It relates to a person's feelings of self-worth and esteem. People in general like to know how and where they stand. Informing employees on how they are doing, even when the results are not completely satisfactory, at least lets them know that you care about them. There is a tendency for supervisors to overlook the need for providing employees with feedback on their performance. Some supervisors believe that it is unnecessary to say anything to an employee when a job has been done well. "Jerome knows he did a good job," is a far too typical supervisory attitude. Jerome, as with most employees, may not be certain how you—the boss—really feel about his performance without you overtly giving him some form of recognition.

The job itself is an extremely important motivating factor. Why are some employees chronically late? In many cases it's because they dread going to what they perceive as a miserable working environment. They derive little satisfaction from their monotonous jobs, and, as a result, would rather be somewhere else. People who like their jobs tend to be far more motivated, which leads to less absenteeism and tardiness.

Growth and advancement possibilities also serve to motivate. In a sense, these are like the old *carrot-on-a-stick analogy:* Employees will tend to move in directions that help them obtain the "carrot," for example, a promotion. However, supervisors must realize that if employees never get a "taste of the carrot," their interest in "carrots" will tend to diminish. Motivational tools should never be used to manipulate people; they should be used honestly and sincerely with the employee's, as well as the organization's, interests in mind. Over time, most employees can usually see through efforts at manipulation.

Responsibility is another factor that motivates many employees. The employee who has been assigned the additional responsibility to train a new employee, recognizing that time is limited, may forego taking sick leave in spite of a current illness. Even the behavior of some so-called troublemakers has been modified after they have been assigned additional responsibilities.

Supervisors should keep in mind, of course, that each employee is a unique individual. Although satisfiers cited by Herzberg tend to motivate most employees, they may not find success with all individuals. One person's motivator might be another person's hygiene factor. For example, not all individuals relish the idea of being assigned more responsibility, even though it is considered a motivator in Herzberg's theory. Understanding your employees' needs and the various factors that specifically motivate each of them will help you considerably in your motivational efforts.

As a supervisor, you don't have a lot of control over hygiene factors. You do, however, have considerable influence over motivational factors. As with Maslow's concept of the need for self-esteem, you can affect your employees' feelings of self-esteem and self-worth through your methods and actions for recognizing the value of their performance.

The diagram in Figure 11–3 illustrates the relationship between Maslow's hierarchy-of-needs concept and the two-factor motivational theory of Herzberg.

What Is the Nature of Vroom's Expectancy Theory?

Expectancy theory: *The theory that individuals will be motivated by their belief that specific behavior on their part will lead to a desired outcome.*

"People tend to be more motivated by what they are seeking than by what they have" is an expression that fairly well sums up another well-known concept of motivation, Victor Vroom's **expectancy theory.**[4] Other analysts, such as Lyman Porter, Edward Lawler, and Richard M. Steers, have built on Vroom's research.[5]

The expectancy theory contends that people behave in particular ways because of what they expect from such behavior. This theory goes beyond the needs theories of Maslow and Herzberg. Needs continue to be significant, but an employee's behavior, according to expectancy theory, results primarily from the way they perceive a situation, what they expect from it, how much they

FIGURE 11–3
The Relationship between Maslow's Hierarchy-of-Needs Concept and Herzberg's Two-Factor Theory

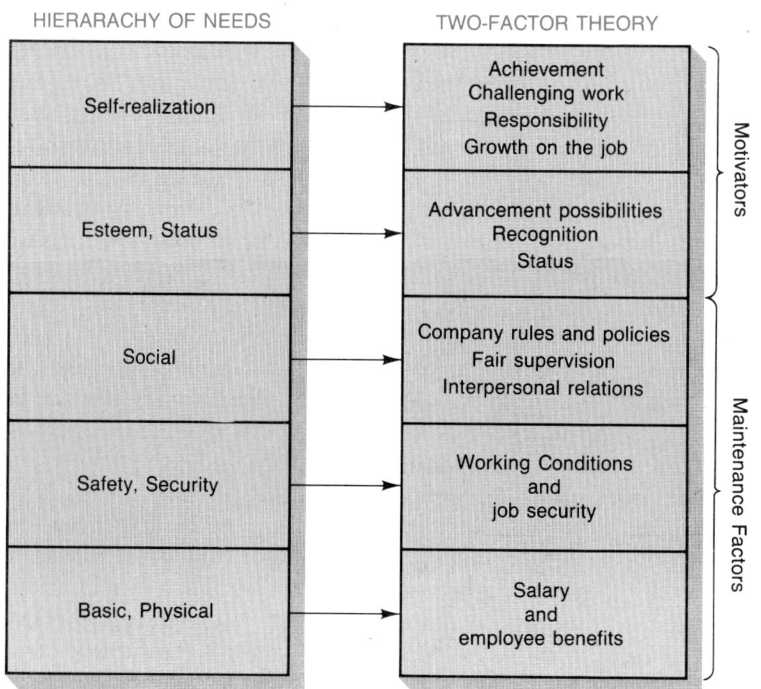

value such expectations, and what they feel will happen from certain types of behavior.

Motivation, in effect, is a function of three factors. The first is the probability that exerting effort will lead to changes in performance. The second is the probability that changes in performance will lead to a preferred outcome. The third is the value employees place on such outcomes or rewards.

As a supervisor, it is important to keep in mind that each individual's expectations vary. An employee who has had unfavorable experiences with authority may not expect hard work to result in higher pay or a promotion. Once again, understanding the values and needs of your associates (especially what they want and expect) is all important, and can aid you in creating a positive motivational climate. The following section provides additional insights into how certain aspects of these motivational theories can be applied to the real world of work.

How Does Equity Relate to Motivation?

We know that employees generally want their needs to be satisfied. However, needs satisfaction is only part of the motivational package; employees also expect *fair treatment* in the way tasks are assigned and rewards are distributed. Another well-known motivational theory—**equity theory**—concentrates on the notion of *fairness.* Developed by J. Stacy Adams, equity theory examines the tendency for employees to compare the fairness of what they are expected to do on the job (termed *inputs*) with what they receive as a result of their efforts (termed *outcomes*). As illustrated in Figure 11–4, people generally expect some sort of a balance between their personal inputs (skill, effort, performance, education, age, and seniority) and their personal outcomes (pay, benefits, privileges, recognition, job satisfaction, and opportunities). Equity theory also stresses the tendency for employees to compare ***their own personal contributions and outcomes with those of other employees.***

Equity theory: *The theory that individuals are motivated by their perception of how fairly or unfairly they are being treated compared to their efforts and to others.*

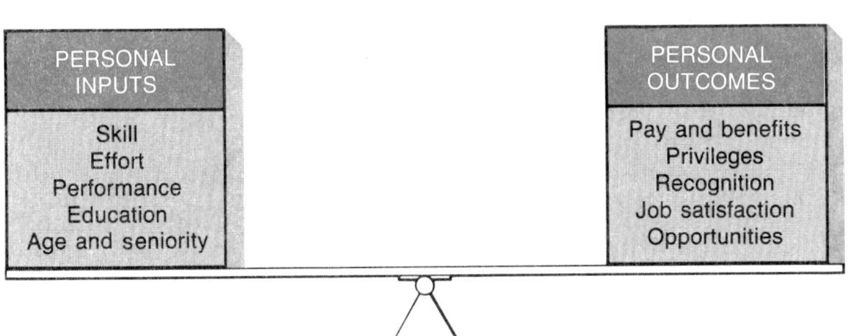

FIGURE 11–4
The Equity Theory of Motivation Focuses on a Balance between Personal Inputs and Personal Outcomes

For example, assume that you have an employee named Jerry who thinks that his expectations aren't being met. Jerry feels that his job responsibilities are excessive related to the amount of pay he receives. His expectations of fairness, therefore, are not being met, which tends to make him dissatisfied, discouraged, and less motivated. Not all employees would necessarily perceive the situation in the same way. Some employees might merely grin and bear it, assuming that there is little sense in worrying about something they can't control. Jerry, however, believes that such lack of equity is a good reason to seek employment someplace else, where he hopes to receive what he feels is more equitable treatment.

As already mentioned, many employees also feel that they should receive equity *related to the inputs and outcomes of other employees.* Let's take the case of Jane. Her motivation decreased after she learned that she was receiving less pay than Robert for doing comparable types of work. She believes that she is receiving less pay principally because of her sex. The concept of *equal pay for equal work* has been at the heart of the women's movement for many years, and numerous women have expressed their dissatisfaction with salary inequity through protests and votes.

Another example relates to Ralph, a 59-year-old employee who has been with the Pyrotech Company for 20 years. He has become increasingly dissatisfied in recent years as he has observed younger employees with little practical experience being offered salaries comparable to his. Ralph believes that his salary should be substantially more than employees with far less time on the job. However, managers with the Pyrotech Company feel that good salaries have to be offered in order to attract talented young people to the company, a situation Ralph considers less than equitable.

What happens when employees feel that they are receiving "fairer than fair" treatment, that is, outcomes *greater* than their inputs? Some employees tend to move toward an equilibrium by being more productive or by improving the quality of their work. Some employees may merely assume that they are receiving more income because they are worth more than others. You can observe from the discussion of equity theory that numerous organizational behavior problems, especially in the area of wage and salary administration and morale, can develop as a result of the way employees perceive the fairness of the outcomes they receive.

What Influences Job Satisfaction?

Job satisfaction (morale): *The atmosphere created by the attitudes of the members of an organization.*

Let's begin our discussion of job satisfaction by developing a clear understanding of its meaning. **Job satisfaction** relates to the *attitudes* employees have toward the organizations they work for or toward particular job factors. For our purposes, the terms *job satisfaction* and *morale* can be used interchangeably. Job satisfaction can relate to either the *individual* or the *group* to which an employee belongs. *Job satisfaction,* or *morale*, then, can be defined as *the atmosphere created by the attitudes of the members of an organization.* Basically, job satisfaction is influenced by *how em-*

ployees perceive the organization and its objectives in relation to their own interest and needs. These attitudes are influenced by a number of different factors, which include:

- The organization itself
- The type of work activities
- The leadership climate
- Relationships with peers
- Employee activities off the job
- The extent to which employee needs have been satisfied

How Can the Organization Affect Morale?

You may have noticed how some organizations seem to have large numbers of employees who have a high degree of organizational pride, while employees from other organizations seem to feel the opposite. Typically found in the former type of organization is a strong *esprit de corps,* a term discussed in Chapter 2 that symbolizes the good feelings employees have toward their organization. In the latter type of organization, many employees regularly and consistently criticize their workgroups and nearly everything within their working environment.

Why do some organizations experience a low degree of *esprit de corps* among their members? A host of factors can be the cause, such as *a negative opinion of the organization on the part of the general public.* Imagine, for example, working for the Exxon Corporation after the 1989 Valdez oil spill in Alaska's Prince William Sound, the worst accident of this nature ever to occur in the United States. The media heavily publicized the manner in which the cleanup efforts took place, after which the general public developed an attitude of outrage. Tens of thousands of Exxon's customers cut up their credit cards and mailed half of each card to Exxon's chairman. The public's attitude toward the handling of the spill had an adverse effect on employee morale and was expected to affect the future exploration rights of the company.[6]

Employees are also likely to lose pride in a company that develops a reputation for *putting shoddy products on the market, providing poor service, making false promises,* or *bilking the public.* Companies that have favorable public reputations tend to enjoy a positive level of morale among its employees.

How Does the Type of Work Affect Morale?

Numerous jobs today have become increasingly specialized and routinized, dull and monotonous, and require little skill. As a result, many production workers feel somewhat alienated from their jobs. Because of dissatisfaction with their work place and the nature of their work, many employees perceive their jobs solely as a means to a personal end—a higher standard of material living—and look forward only to paydays, holidays, vacations, sick leave, and retirement.

Supervisors are a critical element in determining the job satisfaction (or dissatisfaction) of their associates.

To cope with such dissatisfaction, many managers have attempted to redesign jobs and modify the work environment, topics that will be discussed in a later section of this chapter. Dissatisfaction problems highlight the need for today's supervisors to understand human needs and motivation. The aim of many contemporary managers is to introduce creativity, responsibility, and variety to manual work wherever possible, in the hope that industrial monotony and boredom will be reduced.

Volvo, the Swedish automobile manufacturer, practices this concept in its plant in Uddevalla, Sweden, where it converted operations from traditional assembly line techniques to a team system. Starting in 1989, the plant has used teams of seven to ten hourly workers. Each team works in one area and assembles four cars per shift, and each team member is trained to handle all assembly jobs. The employees are able to work an average of three hours without repeating a task. (In the typical auto plant, tasks are repeated every one or two minutes.) The Volvo teams manage themselves, handling scheduling, quality control, hiring, and other duties typically performed by supervisors.[7]

How Does the Leadership Climate Affect Morale?

Although all members of any workgroup contribute toward the attitudes and atmosphere of their organization, management sets the tone and has the primary responsibility for establishing a healthy organizational climate. When a supervisor is continually bad-mouthing the company, or is negative about things in general in the organization, there is a tendency for his or her associates to emulate such attitudes. An old but still valid cliché is, "People tend to follow as they are led." As a result, the existing leadership in an organization exerts a powerful influence over the job satisfaction of the work force. High rates of turnover, for example, often indicate ineffective leadership. Leaders who draw on their employees for input in decision making and problem solving often enjoy higher levels of worker morale and job satisfaction.

How Do Peers Affect Morale?

In an earlier section of this chapter, we learned that one of the needs inherent in most individuals is the need to *socialize*; that is, to have a feeling of belonging and conforming to group norms and expectations. Most employees want to feel accepted by their peers; conforming to group standards and attitudes makes this much easier.

Some years ago, Solomon Asch conducted an experiment that helps to illustrate the apparent need people have to conform to group standards.[8] Asch assembled several groups of eight persons to participate in the experiment. The eight persons sat around a table and were asked to judge the length of various lines. However, only one person in each cluster of eight was a true subject; the others had been told by Asch to conspire against the unknowing one. They were told to give the wrong answers in a confident manner two-thirds of the time. The guinea pig (the one innocent victim in each group) had to make the last choice. In almost 40 percent of the trials, the unaware individual went along with the incorrect decision of the group because he or she didn't want to look silly in front of the others, not because he or she truly believed the group's answers.

The **Asch conformity studies** clearly brought out the effect of group pressure on the perception and attitudes of individual members of a group. The same effect can take place in workgroups. Assume, for example, that Helmut, one of your employees, has generally had no unfavorable attitudes toward company policies in the past. As a member of a group, say, a collective bargaining unit, Helmut's attitude toward working conditions could be swayed by the collective actions of his peers. A condition that formerly did not disturb him may suddenly have adverse effects on his morale because of the group's influence and pressures.

Asch conformity studies: *A study conducted by Solomon Asch that illustrated the apparent need people have to conform to group standards.*

How Do Employees' Self-Concept Affect Morale?

How employees perceive themselves—that is, their **self-concept**—also tends to influence attitudes toward organizational environments. For example, people experiencing incessant pain from an illness or accident, or individuals who lack self-confidence, sometimes develop sagging morale.

Self-concept: *The manner in which a person perceives him- or herself.*

How Do Employee Off-the-Job Activities Affect Morale?

Both on- and off-the-job experiences influence employees' attitudes and thus their job satisfaction. For example, employees are affected by their total environments—those who are having marital or financial problems, abusing substances, or are in poor physical or mental health are likely to develop attitudes that affect their on-the-job performance. Although most managers feel that employees should have the right to their own personal lives, if off-the-job activities are affecting on-the-job performance, supervisors have to become involved to some degree. Supervisors should *not* attempt, however, to be amateur diagnosticians or psychologists, nor become involved in discussing illnesses that they aren't qualified to handle. Instead, supervisors should focus on *job deficiencies* and *corrective action,* and, if necessary, refer the employee to a professional counselor or physician. An increasing number of organizations employ trained counselors to assist employees in overcoming personal problems.

How Do Personal Needs Affect Morale?

Employees who feel that their *personal needs* have not been sufficiently satisfied may develop morale problems. Paychecks and employee benefits, although not considered to have a significant motivating effect on employees, do help to satisfy many personal needs. Morale problems may develop, for example, when an employee believes that other employees are unjustly receiving higher rewards, or when inflation erodes the purchasing power of take-home pay. Although certain factors, such as employer-provided medical insurance, have a somewhat neutral influence on morale and employee motivation, when they are reduced or eliminated employee morale tends to become depressed.

Attentive supervisors attempt to recognize symptoms of deteriorating job satisfaction. Some of the more significant warning signs of low morale are discussed in the section that follows.

● How Can Signs of Job Dissatisfaction Be Detected?

Morale is something that supervisors should never take for granted. Too frequently, however, managers seem oblivious to employee attitudes until near-chaos develops. Failure to nip morale problems in the bud can create organizational wounds so deep that they are difficult to heal. There are a number of warning signs that indicate that something may be amiss. The principal ones are:

- Absenteeism and tardiness
- Strikes, picketing, slowdowns, and sabotage
- High amounts of wasted materials and product rejects
- Low levels of production
- Missed deadlines
- High frequency of accidents

- Employees' negative attitudes toward being given directions and orders

Alert supervisors attempt to recognize symptoms of deteriorating morale before serious problems are created. To improve or maintain job satisfaction, you first must uncover what the likely causes of poor morale actually are. There are a number of ways in which morale can be measured and evaluated, such as through:

- Statistical evaluation of personnel records
- The use of employee counselors
- Attitude surveys
- Observation and listening
- Periodic feedback sessions

Let's look briefly at each of these aids.

What Can Statistical Evaluation Tell You about Morale?

Existing personnel records and production information can serve as valuable sources of statistical information that can help you in evaluating morale and employee attitudes. Records that keep track of absenteeism, turnover, number of grievances filed, deadlines missed, and accident frequency can provide useful information. You might look for trends. Numerous computer software programs are available that can assist you in plotting such data.

For example, let's assume that turnover among personnel in your department has doubled each year over the past five years. Taken alone, these figures would not be absolute proof that morale has deteriorated. But combined with other techniques of evaluation, the statistics could give you some clues as to morale trends and the potential for future problems.

How Can Employee Counselors Uncover Signs of Low Morale?

Some organizations have **employee assistance programs (EAPs)** with in-house counselors, whose principal job is to assist employees with their personal problems (including substance abuse) and complaints. Companies that use this resource hope that employees will feel free to discuss their problems and complaints with a counselor in confidence. It is essential, however, that counselors have the trust of employees. A trusted counselor is in the position to learn of potential or existing morale problems early, before any real damage is done. Any information uncovered during an interview should not be used against an individual employee. Some counselors have lost their effectiveness as a result of developing the reputation of being an "undercover" agent or management "lap-dog."

Employee assistance programs (EAPs): *Formal personnel programs designed to aid employees with personal problems.*

How Can Attitude Surveys Uncover Morale Problems?

An approach some managers employ to uncover employee attitudes and opinions is to use **attitude surveys.** (This technique is

Attitude surveys: *An approach used to uncover employee attitudes and opinions in some depth.*

also known as *climate survey, opinion survey,* and *morale survey.*) There are two typical methods used for surveying attitudes: *interviews* and *questionnaires.*

Interviews. Interviews with both current employees and those about to leave the company can uncover information related to employee attitudes. However, there are potential problems in any interviewing activity. *Currently employed workers,* for example, might fear possible reprisals and conceal their real opinions, answering questions according to what they think their manager would like to hear. Interviewing employees in the process of *leaving* the organization, termed **exit interviews,** also has its limitations. Some employees will not be candid for fear that honest opinions could cost them a favorable letter of recommendation. Interviews do, however, have the advantage of providing face-to-face interaction between the interviewer and the interviewee, something that questionnaires generally lack. Additional suggestions on conducting exit interviews will be given in Chapter 13.

Exit interviews: *Sessions with departing employees, especially those who resign, to determine reasons for leaving and to uncover possible organizational problems.*

Questionnaires. Another widely employed method of surveying attitudes is the use of *questionnaires.* There are two main types: **descriptive questionnaires,** which ask open-ended questions, and **objective questionnaires,** which ask multiple-choice questions. Objective questionnaires are more common because they are easier to respond to and less costly to administer to larger groups. Some companies prefer a combination of both types.

Descriptive questionnaires: *Surveys of employee attitudes that ask open-ended questions.*

Objective questionnaires: *Surveys of employee attitudes that ask multiple-choice, rather than descriptive, questions.*

Attitude surveys can be a useful management tool when conducted in a climate of trust. Remember, too, that since you—the supervisor—will probably be the person carrying out attitude surveys, you are in the position to significantly influence their success. When improperly administered, surveys can cause employees to feel suspicious of management's true motives and thus not answer the questions truthfully. The management of a well-known supermarket chain, for example, once found itself locking horns with union officials after distributing an attitude survey questionnaire to all of its employees. Although employees didn't have to identify themselves by name on the form, they were expected to answer information about their district, store number, race, sex, and specific position. The union officials' reaction was negative, since they feared the information on the questionnaires could be used to the detriment of individual employees, and thus they directed union members to refrain from completing and submitting the forms to their bosses.

How Can Observation and Listening Uncover Warning Signs of Low Morale?

A number of sophisticated techniques exist for evaluating morale, such as statistical analysis and attitude surveys. A relatively simple approach, one that is so obvious and common sense that it is often overlooked entirely, is *observation and listening.* As a supervisor, you're in an ideal position to *observe* when one of your employees is behaving differently. A sudden or even gradual change in an employee's mood or performance, such as continual irritability or frequent accidents, could be a clue that something significant is disturbing him or her.

You might be surprised just when or where observation can take place. We tend not to pay close attention to the response when we greet someone with, "Hi, how's it going?" Start listening more carefully in the future. You may notice subtle nuances in a person's response that could be further clues of morale problems. Frequently the tone in a person's answer of "Okay" may reveal that things aren't really going *that* okay. One of the most effective ways of uncovering what actually is bothering employees is to ***ask them*** and then ***listen carefully*** to their responses.

How Can Periodic Feedback Meetings Uncover Morale Problems?

Some managers hold weekly or semi-monthly meetings with their associates to provide an outlet for questions and to correct any misinformation. Meetings such as these can be used effectively as a method of determining what is disturbing employees. You might want to allocate a certain time each week, say, Fridays from 9:00 to 9:30 A.M., to give employees a chance to air their feelings. If you've developed a climate of mutual respect and trust, you should find such meetings to be a valuable way to learn about employee attitudes.

How Can the Organizational Culture Be Improved?

Herzberg, as we've learned, stresses that *the job itself* strongly influences an employee's attitude, job satisfaction, and motivation. Drawing on Herzberg's ideas, developing ways to make the job more satisfying to employees should help maintain an organizational culture in which job satisfaction is high. Many managers strive to increase productivity in ways that lead to *counterproductive results*—that is, productivity actually declines. Attempting to increase efficiency and productivity without considering the attitudes and needs of employees frequently results in many of the warning signs of poor morale that we've already discussed, such as higher absenteeism, tardiness, and turnover. However, there are techniques currently employed by many organizations that have resulted in modified work environments and greatly improved attitudes among employees. We will address these next.

How Can You Redesign Jobs for Greater Satisfaction?

Most supervisors are generally concerned with the *results* rather than the *methods* of performing a job. Many try to modify the design of jobs wherever possible in order to provide workers with greater job satisfaction. *Job enlargement* and *worker teams* are two currently used methods for attempting to create a better motivational working climate. Both techniques have become increasingly popular in the United States, especially since Professor William G. Ouchi brought substantial attention to **Theory Z,** a management approach that places far more emphasis on the employee in the total organizational framework than many previously espoused theories.[9]

Theory Z: *A concept that combines the ideal characteristics of Japanese and American firms and places more emphasis on employees.*

Job Enrichment. The process of **job enrichment** attempts to make direct application of Herzberg's motivators or satisfiers. Basically, job enrichment is a form of *redesigning* or *improving* a job so that a worker is likely to be more motivated. It provides the employee with the opportunity for *greater recognition, achievement, growth,* and *responsibility,* thus helping to overcome some of the principal causes of worker alienation and poor morale. For example, job enrichment might enable workers to be more directly involved in planning and controlling their own work activities. A secretary's job might be enriched by letting her or him formulate and sign outgoing correspondence, rather than only typing letters that someone else has dictated. The secretary would be responsible for the quality of the letters, thus providing greater opportunities for personal recognition.

Job enrichment: *A form of changing or improving a job to create a more motivating work environment.*

Job enrichment sometimes utilizes **job enlargement,** which is the process of *increasing the complexity of a job* in order to appeal to the higher-order needs of workers, thus reducing monotony. The philosophy behind job enlargement is that a more complex job requires employees to make greater use of their intellect and acquired skills, and, as a consequence, contributes to the satisfaction of their need for self-esteem and dignity. An example of job enlargement is when a person on an assembly line performs more than one specialized function. Be cautioned, though: Since each employee is unique, it is important to recognize that not all employees would necessarily appreciate their jobs being enlarged, nor even enriched. Some employees, for example, might perceive their jobs merely as means for satisfying off-the-job wants, such as owning a boat or paying for ski trips.

Job enlargement: *The process of increasing the complexity of a job to appeal to the higher-order needs of employees.*

Table 11–1 summarizes some important principles associated with job enrichment.[10]

Worker Teams. Another popular job redesign technique is to create **worker teams,** which, when properly administered, tend to have positive effects on morale, quality, and productivity. One type of worker team, originated in the United States but used more extensively in Japan, has been **quality circles** or **QCs** (also called **problem-solving teams**). Such groups usually consist of volunteers from different areas of a department who meet one or two hours each week to discuss and solve problems associated with their work activities.

Worker teams: *A group of employees organized to work together.*

Quality circles (QCs; problem-solving teams): *Groups used to improve the quality and quantity of output.*

A second type of worker team that became prevalent during the 1980s is the **special-purpose team.** More common in unionized

Special-purpose teams: *Groups generally consisting of both operating employees and management representatives who participate in decision making at various levels of the organization.*

TABLE 11–1
Principles Associated with Job Enrichment

- The job should be a *complete piece of work,* so the employee can perceive a series of tasks resulting in a specific product.
- The employee should have *contact with the product's user* where possible.
- The employee should have the *opportunity to plan and make choices* in how to perform the work.
- The employee should receive *regular and direct feedback* on his or her performance.
- The job should provide the employee with *opportunities for growth.*

industries, such teams may be involved with designing and introducing work reforms and new kinds of technology. Team members generally consist of both workers and management representatives who participate in decision making at all levels of the organization.

A third form of worker team that appears to be setting the trend for the 1990s is the **self-managing team.** This form of employee involvement allows team members to take over various managerial duties, including selecting compatible workmates for their group, scheduling work and vacations, and ordering materials. Team members may be authorized to set up their own job and work rotation assignments.

Self-managing teams: *Groups who are allowed to take over various managerial duties.*

Team membership should be kept relatively small as it increases *cohesion.* Teams typically consist of between 5 and 15 members. The 3M Company calls its groups *action teams,* and recruits full-time members from technical areas, manufacturing, marketing, sales, and finance. The teams design products and determine how to manufacture and market them. They also develop new uses and product line extensions. All team members receive promotions and pay raises as the team's goals are accomplished.[11]

Proponents of the team approach contend that it increases individual feelings of *responsibility* and *achievement* by eliminating single repetitive tasks. For example, an automobile factory might utilize the team approach by assigning production responsibility to each group for its own part of the automobile, such as the gear box, the brake system, or the steering mechanism.

Once again, the way in which any technique is administered and the nature of the existing organizational culture will largely influence its success. For example, benefits of such techniques will be lost if employees perceive job enlargement as a manipulative method to increase their workload with no increase in pay. Neither job enrichment programs nor worker teams can function effectively without genuine support from senior and middle management. Nor is it likely that expected results will be achieved from either approach if individuals and team members have not received adequate training in advance.

What Are Flexible Working Hours?

Flextime (flexible working hours): *A program in which employees have the freedom to choose, within certain limits, what time they begin and quit their jobs each day.*

Full flextime: *A program in which employees decide each day, without prior notice to their managers, what time they will arrive and depart.*

Modified flextime: *A program in which employees decide on an eight-hour frame of working time within predetermined hours.*

Another increasingly common approach for improving worker attitudes is **flextime,** or **flexible working hours.** This system helps to alleviate the 9-to-5 syndrome faced by many employees, and enables workers to enjoy hours that more closely match their personal lifestyles. Although workers still must work a preestablished number of hours per week, under flextime they have the freedom to choose, within certain limits, what time they begin and quit their jobs each day.

There are two common types of flextime—*full flextime* and *modified flextime.* **Full flextime** permits employees to decide each day what time they will arrive and depart without giving prior notice to their managers. Employees typically leave eight hours after they start. Some organizations allow employees to accumulate hours, thus enabling them to take time off in the future.

Modified flextime permits employees to decide on an eight-hour frame of working time falling between predetermined hours, such as 7:00 A.M. and 9:00 P.M. For example, an employee may request that his or her regular hours fall between 7:00 A.M. and 3:00 P.M., rather than 9:00 A.M. and 5:00 P.M. These will be his or her regular hours until the employee and the manager renegotiate them.

Flextime offers many advantages to workers. Individuals can take care of family and other personal affairs more easily, which tends to reduce absenteeism in organizations. Employees with children, for example, can arrange their hours to coincide with childcare or school requirements. Employees can adjust their work schedule to their energy levels, helping to increase productivity and reduce stress and burnout. Employees setting their own hours can possibly avoid the normal rush hour traffic. A number of firms, such as Hewlett-Packard, Control Data, and Metropolitan Life, have found that flextime has improved employee morale; reduced lateness, absenteeism, and turnover; and increased productivity. Such firms have also discovered that flextime has given employees a greater sense of control over their own lives.

What Is Job Sharing?

Job sharing: *An approach to job enrichment in which two employees share a full-time position; also known as* twinning.

A practice referred to as **job sharing** is an idea that can also influence job satisfaction. Under this system, two workers divide one full-time job. Not only are hours divided, but so are salary and employee benefits. Also called *twinning,* the job sharing concept is especially favored by mothers and fathers who desire income plus additional time to spend with their families or pursuing other interests. Others who lean toward job sharing include older people who want to retire gradually, those with physical or intellectual disabilities, and students.

An advantage of job sharing for employers is easier tapping of labor markets for the purpose of achieving affirmative action hiring goals. Another observed advantage is that part-time workers tend to approach their work with far more energy and enthusiasm, and, as a result, tend to put in more than a proportionate day's work. Absenteeism also tends to be cut down since one of the "twins" can cover for the other in the event of illness or other reasons for being absent.

What Is Job Rotation?

Job rotation involves moving individuals from one job to another on a regular basis and is sometimes done as a means of reducing employee boredom. Some people argue, however, that moving a person from one dull job to another does little to truly enrich jobs. Also, some employees may resist being placed in less pleasant jobs, even on a temporary basis. A significant advantage of job rotation, in addition to providing more variety for the employee, is the cross-training factor: Employees who are familiar with a variety of jobs can cover for absent workers. Well-trained employees also have greater opportunities for advancement.

Job rotation: *Shifting employees from one job to another for the purpose of reducing boredom and increasing skills.*

What Can We Conclude about Job Satisfaction?

We've covered some of the current methods being employed for improving working environments for the purpose of maintaining a favorable organizational climate and positive job satisfaction. It must also be mentioned that such programs are not introduced solely for humanitarian means; they can only exist over time if they have a positive impact on an organization's productivity, quality, and profits.

Imaginative supervisors can develop many innovations in addition to those discussed in this chapter to design jobs that are more interesting and challenging. An important factor is that supervisors determine the success of any job enrichment programs, as they do with so many other activities. To administer such programs, supervisors must learn as much as possible about work redesign techniques and procedures. Supervisors who are quality circle leaders must learn the QC technique, be thorough in training QC members, and conduct meetings in a manner that maintains employee interest in the process. Unfortunately, some supervisors feel that job enrichment and worker team programs are a threat to their own decision-making authority. Also unfortunate is that some employees view such programs as deceptive management schemes designed solely to increase their workloads. Programs are unlikely to succeed unless there exists a climate of trust and understanding, which is essential for the effective use of morale-building techniques.

Summary

In this chapter we emphasized the importance of supervisors learning the nature of *employee needs and motivation.* Needs have been categorized by Maslow as *primary* and *secondary*. Supervisors usually have more influence over the satisfaction of employees' secondary needs than they do over primary ones. Needs, if they are to motivate, must be *felt*. Satisfied needs usually cease to motivate. *Maslow* categorized human needs into a *hierarchy* or *order of priority,* suggesting that each level must be satisfied before the next level assumes importance. Needs, however, are not mutually exclusive; a person may recognize the need for more than one thing simultaneously.

Herzberg's studies indicate that there are two sets of factors—*motivational* and *maintenance*—that influence the organizational environment. In general, maintenance factors, unless withdrawn, tend to have a neutral effect on employees, while motivational factors tend to stimulate employees into attempting to achieve their potential.

Vroom's expectancy theory shows how people behave in certain ways because of what they expect such behavior to achieve.

Adams's equity theory focuses on how fairly or unfairly employees perceive themselves as being treated in relation to their inputs and to other employees.

Some of the more important concepts related to the topics of *morale* and *job satisfaction* were covered. We also examined the major *warning signs of job dissatisfaction,* along with methods for measuring and evaluating morale. Supervisors, we learned, can influence morale—that is, *employee attitudes*—in a positive manner, with such techniques as *job redesign* (*job enrichment* and *worker teams*), *flexible working hours, job sharing,* and *job rotation*.

Questions for Discussion

1. Evaluate the following statement: "People work solely for money and the fear of what will happen to them if they don't have it."
2. What is a *need*? How do needs relate to *motivation*?
3. Over which do supervisors tend to have greater influence: *primary* or *secondary* needs?
4. Why must a need be *felt* before it will motivate?
5. Are needs *mutually exclusive*? Explain.
6. Why, according to *Herzberg's motivational-maintenance model,* do maintenance factors not necessarily motivate employees?
7. What seems to be the major distinction between the *motivational theories of Maslow* and *Herzberg* on the one hand, and *Vroom* and *Adams* on the other?
8. How do the six factors discussed in the chapter influence employee *job satisfaction*?
9. Describe the nature and purpose of the *Asch conformity studies*. How do they relate to organizational situations?

10. What could cause an *employee counselor* to lose effectiveness and credibility with employees?
11. What is an *exit interview*? What are some of its possible strengths and weaknesses?
12. What largely determines the success and usefulness of *employee attitude surveys*?
13. What are some *changes in employee behavior* that could be an indication of some sort of *morale problem*?
14. Explain the meaning of the following statement in your own words: "The *results* of a job, rather than the *methods* of performing it, are generally what most supervisors are concerned with."
15. Explain the five important principles associated with a *job enrichment program.*
16. What are some of the potential benefits of the *team approach* to production?
17. What largely influences the success of *job enrichment* and *worker team* programs? Why do some of them fail?
18. What are some major advantages of *flextime* and *job sharing* to both the organization and the employee?
19. Evaluate the following statement: "Rotating a person from one dull job to another will do nothing to enrich the employee's job environment."
20. Should programs of *job enrichment* be established even when they are unlikely to be cost-effective?

Can You Define These Terms?

Instructions: Write a definition for each of the following terms. You may check your definitions with those provided in the end-of-text glossary.

motivation
primary (physical) needs
secondary (psychological or ego) needs
safety/security needs
social needs
esteem needs
self-realization
hierarchy-of-needs concept
motivation-maintenance model
maintenance (hygiene) factors
motivational (satisfiers) factors
expectancy theory
equity theory
job satisfaction (morale)
Asch conformity studies
self-concept
employee assistance programs (EAPs)
attitude surveys
exit interviews
descriptive questionnaires
objective questionnaires
Theory Z
job enrichment
job enlargement
worker teams
quality circles (problem-solving teams)
special-purpose teams
self-managing teams
flextime (flexible working hours)
job sharing (twinning)
job rotation

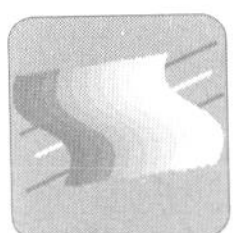

Supervision In Action

11–1 The "Dirty Job" Assignment

Emmy Wentworth, Marsh Wong, and Peppy Gonzales are three of the best workers assigned to your department. They have always been dependable employees and have seldom griped about their work assignments in the past.

Two weeks ago, you assigned all three of them to what is considered a "dirty job" due to the complexity of the project. The assignment is to be for only three months. You chose Emmy, Marsh, and Peppy because you believed that they were the best qualified to handle the job due to its critical nature.

Emmy and Marsh complained a little at the time you assigned them the new activity, but accepted it begrudgingly. Peppy said nothing at the time of assignment.

This morning, all three of them stormed into your office demanding that they either be given their old jobs back or receive a substantial raise in pay.

Questions

1. Attempt to apply relevant concepts discussed in the chapter and discuss why the three employees seem to be dissatisfied with their new assignments.
2. As supervisor, what would you do now?

11–2 A Messy Workplace

Tom Terry came to work in your department about two months ago. Tom is one of your best workers, but he tends to be careless about maintaining an orderly work environment. He continually leaves materials and tools lying around his workbench and in the aisles.

On two occasions you've talked to Tom about his messy work area. Each time he temporarily improved and then slipped back into his old ways within a few days.

After you arrive at work this morning, you discover that last night a window washer slipped and injured his right shoulder near Tom's work area. The window washer will be unable to work for about three weeks while his shoulder mends. You're quite upset and angry about this event, since you've talked to Tom twice before about the problem of his sloppiness.

Questions

1. In your opinion, why does Tom continually maintain a messy work area?
2. What might you have done previously to prevent the continual recurrence of Tom's careless habits?

3. What should you do now about the situation? If possible, role play the situation with another person who assumes the role of Tom.

11–3 A Case of Enrichment Headaches

Morale has been extremely low among employees of Systemics, Inc. since Abe O'Reilly, the firm's founder, died about three years ago. Abe knew all 300 employees by their first names and ran the organization so that most employees felt that they were part of one large, contented family.

After Abe's death, H. Wadsworth Tinkerton, a graduate of the Harvard School of Business, was recruited from the Latchkey Company, where he had been CEO for two years. While at Latchkey, Tinkerton had developed the reputation of running a tight, nonunion ship. Recognizing that his approach to management at Latchkey was not working at Systemics, and hearing through the grapevine that many employees had considered joining a union for the first time, Tinkerton decided that some significant changes had to be made. Tinkerton had recently attended a "Quality of Worklife" seminar sponsored by the American Management Associations, where he learned about such processes as job enrichment and quality circles. He also learned that such programs tended to enhance morale and productivity in many of the firms where they were introduced.

Tinkerton got together with his human resource manager, Marilena Vella, and together they devised a plan. They agreed that a job enrichment program would be an excellent way to meet one of their primary objectives—keeping the union out. They believed that if they could convince the employees that management really cared about them, the employees would abandon their interest in a union.

The following enrichment activities were initiated at Systemics:

Quality circles or teams (referred to as *excellence circles* at Systemics). One worker each from various departments was arbitrarily selected to be a member of an excellence circle that met once a week. Each week the circle was led by a different person.

Job enlargement. Each employee's job became less specialized, with certain elements added that previously were the responsibility of others. No tasks were removed from any jobs, however.

Full flextime. This system allowed employees to decide each day (without informing management) the time they would arrive and depart. Each employee was expected to work an eight-hour shift every day.

Work sharing. This program created a temporary or permanent reduction in working hours of all members of worker teams during slack periods, as a means of eliminating layoffs.

Tinkerton and Vella thought that the employees would really appreciate their efforts. Contrary to their expectations, however, morale seemed to get worse. Workers selected for the circles couldn't see what they were gaining. Suddenly they seemed to have more responsibility without more pay. They also found that their work assignments remained the same even though they had to devote time to the circles, which created more pressure for them.

Most employees felt that the job enlargement "enrichment" program was a deception intended to increase their workload and responsibilities, once again without any additional rewards.

Employees with seniority were angry about the work sharing program. They believed that they should not be subjected to a reduction in hours and net pay on the same basis as employees newer to the company.

Four months later, Tinkerton's receptionist informed him that a union official named Frank Perez wanted to talk to him about an upcoming union certification election that a number of workers had called for. Tinkerton sat for a moment in silence and then asked himself, "Where did we go wrong?"

Questions

1. How would you answer Tinkerton's question? Where did he and Vella go wrong?
2. How do you feel about Tinkerton's primary motive for inaugurating a job enrichment program to deter employees from joining a union?
3. Should participation in excellence circles be compulsory or voluntary? Explain.

Endnotes

1. Abraham H. Maslow, *Motivation and Personality* (New York: Harper & Row, 1954).
2. Frederick Herzberg, *The Managerial Choice: To Be Efficient and to Be Human* (Homewood, Ill.: Dow Jones-Irwin, 1976).
3. "Special Report: Eastern Airlines' Employees," *USA Today* (International Edition), May 9, 1989, p. 19.
4. Victor H. Vroom, *Work and Motivation* (New York: Wiley, 1964).
5. Lyman W. Porter and Edward E. Lawler, III, *Managerial Attitudes and Performance* (Homewood, Ill.: Dorsey Press and Irwin, 1968); and Richard M. Steers and Lyman W. Porter, *Motivation and Work Behavior,* 3d ed. (New York: McGraw-Hill, 1983).

6. "Keep Big Oil Honest, but Don't Halt Drilling," *USA Today* (International Edition), May 11, 1989, p. 6.
7. Jonathan Kapstein and John Hoerr, "Volvo's Radical New Plant: 'The Death of the Assembly Line'?" *Business Week* (International Edition), August 28, 1989, pp. 54–55.
8. Solomon E. Asch, in H. Guetzkow (Ed.), *Groups, Leadership, and Men* (Pittsburgh, Pa.: Carnegie Press, 1951).
9. William G. Ouchi, *Theory Z—How American Business Can Meet the Japanese Challenge* (Reading, Mass.: Addison-Wesley, 1981).
10. Lyle Yorks, *Job Enrichment Revisited,* An AMA Management Briefing (New York: American Management Associations, 1979), pp. 8–9.
11. "Masters of Innovation," *Business Week* (International Edition), April 10, 1989, p. 36.

Chapter 12

Leadership Skills and Techniques

A good supervisor is a lot like a cross-eyed javelin thrower—he doesn't win many medals, but he sure does keep the crowd alert!

—Anonymous

Learning Objectives

When you finish this chapter, you should be able to:

1. Describe the personal qualities and skills that aid a person in being an effective leader.
2. Explain how attitudes influence leadership behavior.
3. Relate how the Pygmalion effect influences people's behavior.
4. Contrast the major styles of leadership.
5. Recall the nature of the Managerial Grid.

The chairman of the board of a large corporation looked around the boardroom making her speech in favor of a particular course of action. "Now," she said, "We'll take a vote on my recommendations. All those in opposition raise your right hand and say, 'I resign.'"

Does the above incident sound a bit harsh? It should. However, in spite of the increasing proportion of current-day managers who are well educated and professionally trained, there still remain far too many bosses who believe that the "If you can't hack it, get your jacket" approach is the only sound course for leading their associates.

In the current chapter, however, we'll observe that there are more positive approaches to leadership. First we'll examine the general nature of leadership. Then we'll see how the attitudes of managers affect their leadership styles. And finally, we'll explore the various styles of leadership and evaluate whether there is any one "best" style for all situations.

What Is the General Nature of Leadership?

Managers vary in their approach to leadership. For example, some types of leaders are generally *positive* in the way they perceive their associates, while others have the *negative* attitude that "most people just don't give a darn about much of anything." Some leaders may even find that they shift back and forth between positive and negative attitudes.

Other forms of leadership also exist, such as *autocratic, participative, free-rein, results-oriented,* and *contingency.* We'll examine the differences among these forms, plus the factors that determine the "best" style of leadership.

Furthermore, some types of leadership exist by *decree*—that is, they are created by the *formal organization.* In other instances, leadership grows somewhat naturally out of the needs or atmosphere of the *informal organization.* For example, factors such as *age, seniority, knowledge, assertiveness, education, charisma,* or *popularity* enable some individuals to develop influence over other members of a workgroup.

Leadership:
The use of developed skills to influence or change the behavior of others in order to accomplish organizational, individual, or personal goals.

What Is Leadership?

What is meant by the term **leadership?** Basically, it is a set of *developed skills* that attempts to influence or change the behavior of others in order to accomplish organizational, individual, or personal goals. Note the emphasis on *developed skills.* Although some inborn traits, such as intelligence, would certainly assist a person in a leadership role, leadership skills can generally be developed with knowledge and practice. Leadership is so involved with decision making that it has also been called the *activity of deciding.*

What Personal Qualities Can Aid a Leader?

A person can be promoted or hired for a leadership position, but a management title won't guarantee that the person holding it will be an effective leader. To be effective over time, leaders must have employees who are consistently willing to follow them.

Do effective leaders have anything in common? There isn't complete agreement on the issue of whether effective leaders share a common set of traits. Critics of a "trait theory" point to the exceptions: the various examples of well-known leaders who seemed to differ in those characteristics believed to be essential for leading or influencing others in a positive fashion.

One of these exceptions is Marshall Hahn, chairman and chief executive officer of the world's largest paper maker—Georgia-Pacific—who has been described as ruthless and tough. While president of Virginia Polytechnic Institute in 1970, for example, he was faced with students protesting U.S. involvement in Vietnam. The students barricaded themselves inside a campus building. Hahn had the police come on campus, break down the doors, and haul the students off to jail. After the students were released, Hahn had them expelled from school. Hahn's "success" in squelching future protests impressed Bob Pamplin, who was then chairman of Georgia-Pacific and an alumnus of the school. Pamplin later put Hahn on his board in 1973. In seven years as chief executive of Georgia-Pacific, Hahn saw sales double and earnings soar from $20 million in 1982 to a record $661 million in 1989. Far from being considered a "Mr. Nice Guy," Hahn has been referred to as "a man with steel in his spine."[1]

Regardless of the many differences of opinion as to what constitutes an effective leader, there are certain personal qualities that would tend to enhance a person's leadership activities. Among these characteristics are:

- Well-developed communication skills
- Reasonable intelligence
- Ambition
- Varied interests and sociability
- A positive attitude toward people
- Self-confidence
- Enthusiasm
- Self-discipline
- Emotional stability
- Manners

All of these traits except intelligence are usually shaped by one's environment, which we have the power to influence. Even intel-

Since people tend to follow as they are led, supervisors should take an active role by setting a positive example for their associates.

ligence, modern psychologists point out, is influenced to some extent by environmental experiences.

How Can Leadership Skills Be Developed?

Why do some people get appointed to managerial positions while others are continually passed over for promotion? We've already stated that leadership traits are largely shaped and influenced by one's experiences and environment, but these traits are seldom developed by accident.

People who rise to leadership positions are often those who have established goals for themselves and are motivated to work toward achieving those goals. A portion of their goals involve plans for developing leadership skills.

How are leadership skills developed? One way is by *observation*. For example, you can learn techniques of leadership (both desirable and undesirable) by thoughtfully observing leadership (both yours and others') in action. You can learn much from both successes and failures.

You can also develop leadership skills through *trial and error* on the job. Learning from your mistakes is not the most efficient or cost-effective method, but can often result in a lesson you'll never forget.

A third way to develop leadership skills is by *taking advantage of training and educational opportunities.* For example, does your manager know that you are interested in attending in-house company training programs? Have you ever asked for approval to attend a public seminar on developing supervisory skills? Have you considered taking evening management courses at a nearby college? Do you have a scheduled self-improvement reading program?

An additional way to develop leadership skills is to *seek out "stretching" experiences.* Are you willing to *reach out* for responsibility? Are you willing to *risk failure* by volunteering for difficult tasks? Your *future* leadership path depends greatly on the steps you take in the *present.*

What Influence Do Attitudes Have on Leadership Behavior?

A fairly safe generalization is that all organizations have some degree of people problems. Certain organizations, however, seem continually submerged in a sea of strife and conflict, while others appear to work out their human relations difficulties with a minimum of discord. What accounts for such differences among organizations? As might be expected, the *attitudes of leaders*—positive or negative, for example—toward their personnel exert immense influence over the organizational climate and employee morale. Let's now explore such leadership influence in a little more depth.

Should the Leader Serve as a Role Model?

People, it has been aptly said, tend to follow as they are led. If true, can you imagine some of the significant implications of this statement? A leader who is dependable, punctual, well organized, and concerned with people, production, and quality will tend to serve as a role model for his or her associates. Such leaders will tend to have followers who emulate their positive behavior and attitudes. On the other hand, a leader who isn't particularly concerned about such things will tend to have similarly indifferent followers. Although everyone in an organization affects its tone and climate, the leader is the key factor in maintaining positive relationships among people.

Which Are You—X or Y?

Most management literature discusses the late Douglas McGregor's theory related to the ways managers tend to perceive employees.[2] According to McGregor, some leaders have rather positive and favorable beliefs about their workers, while other managers tend to see their employees in negative and suspicious ways. McGregor labeled these two sets of beliefs as **Theory X** and **Theory Y,** *X* having been assigned to the *negative beliefs* and *Y* to the *positive.* Take a look at the two sets of convictions listed in Table 12–1.

Theory X: *Developed by Douglas McGregor, describes a traditionally negative set of assumptions held by some managers toward employees.*

Theory Y: *Developed by Douglas McGregor, describes a positive set of assumptions held by some managers toward employees.*

TABLE 12–1
Assumptions of Douglas McGregor's Theories X and Y

Theory X Beliefs

- Typical individuals basically dislike work and will avoid it whenever they can.
- Typical workers are self-centered and have little concern for organizational goals.
- Because most people dislike work, they have to be pushed, closely supervised, and threatened with punishment to achieve the objectives of organizations.
- Most workers are not particularly creative or imaginative and need to have their work organized and directed by others.
- Most people are basically lazy, have little ambition, prefer to avoid responsibility, and desire security as a major goal.
- People are by nature resistant to change.
- Management provides wages, salaries, and numerous employee benefits that should motivate people to work harder.

Theory Y Beliefs

- Most people find work as natural as play or rest and develop attitudes toward work related to their experiences with it.
- Workers will concern themselves with company needs when they can relate them to their own needs.
- People don't have to be threatened with punishment to be motivated toward assisting an organization to accomplish its goals. They will be somewhat self-directed when they are able to relate to the objectives of the organization.
- Imagination, creativity, and ingenuity in solving problems are widely, not narrowly, distributed in the population.
- Within a favorable human relations climate, the average person learns not only to accept but also to seek responsibility.
- People have learned to appear resistant to change for reasons of self-protection.
- Existing rewards, such as wages, salaries, and employee benefits, provide satisfaction *off* the job, or sometime in the future when employees leave the job. Therefore, they do not motivate *on* the job.

If you examined the table, which of the two sets of attitudes seemed to suit your frame of reference? Leaders who agree with the X set of beliefs, as you may have already deduced, are somewhat negative or pessimistic in the ways that they view others. Theory Y leaders, on the other hand, are said to believe that workers will do far more than expected if they are treated fairly and allowed to experience pesonal satisfaction on the job.

Leaders who subscribe to Theory X sometimes accuse their Y counterparts of being back-slapping, glad-handing leaders who act

as though they are running a country club. This attitude, however, is also excessively negative, since a Y-rated leader is concerned about far more than being perceived as a nice person. The Y-type leader is not opposed to authority and structure, but he or she is concerned about achieving the organization's goals in ways that are in harmony with the needs and attitudes of employees. Theory Y-oriented leaders often experience far less employee turnover and higher levels of productivity over time. Modern leaders tend to lean toward the Theory Y set of beliefs.

What Is the Selective X-Y Theory?

Since things are seldom clear-cut in the real world, it's unlikely that all managers would be completely X or Y in the real world of organizations. Most supervisors' views of their personnel are unlikely to be so absolute and clearly defined.

Take yourself as an example. Don't you find yourself somewhat *selective* in the way you perceive others? Do you ever find yourself getting a Theory X feeling toward some types of people and a Theory Y feeling toward others?

An offshoot of McGregor's theories, **Selective X-Y Theory,** is probably natural for most leaders.[3] For example, assume that you have some associates who seem to prefer close supervision and have actually expressed the desire to avoid greater responsibility. Let's further assume some members of your staff have even told you that all they really want from their jobs is a paycheck, nothing more. As a result of these experiences, you might be selective in the way that you make assumptions about your employees.

Selective X-Y Theory: *An approach that assumes that attitudes toward employees are not fixed, but may vary with a person's past experiences and current prejudices.*

There are some dangers, however, associated with such selectivity. Leaders who are prejudiced against certain ethnic minority groups might find themselves in a Theory X position with a minority applicant—a person whom they haven't even met before—for an open position. Or they might find themselves taking a Theory Y stance that is biased in favor of an applicant who attended their alma mater. So you can see that our past experiences can condition us to be selectively X or Y and result in unfair hiring practices, improper disciplining of employees, or poor employee placement, all of which could be legally hazardous to your organization's health, as well as morally unfair. Therefore, we should attempt to avoid making unrealistically negative assumptions about others. As we shall observe in a later section, negative assumptions about subordinates may actually create the very behavior we wish to avoid.

What Is the Derived X Theory?

Most supervisors probably hope that their approach to leadership is the right one. For example, you have now learned that a Y-oriented leader is generally considered to be a more modern leader, and, of course, don't you consider yourself modern? You also have been forewarned about the dangers associated with the Selective X-Y

TABLE 12–2
Assumptions of the Derived X Theory

- I want to feel that people are conscientious and find work a natural activity, *but I've been burned too many times* by some of my associates.
- I've given my subordinates the chance to make decisions and to assume responsibility, *but I've been burned too many times;* they've simply taken advantage of me.
- I've tried to create an atmosphere of growth and development for my subordinates by giving them the freedom to make mistakes and to fail, *but I've been burned too many times.* They haven't grown and developed; they've merely made mistakes and failed.
- I've tried to get workers to participate in planning activities for achieving organizational goals, *but I've been burned too many times.* They're more interested in paydays than in accomplishing organizational goals.

Derived X (I've-been-burned) Theory: *A managerial attitude toward employees that has shifted from positive to negative.*

Theory, so you won't fall into that trap as a leader. Unfortunately, however, some of your experiences with employees may cause you to develop an attitude that has been called **Derived X Theory.**[4] Also called the *I've-been-burned theory,* it assumes that you really believe that you're positively oriented, that you know a Y-rated supervisor is supposed to get better results, but you've had too many experiences in which you've been burned, so to speak. Table 12–2 lists a set of attitudes that can be derived from negative experiences with employees.

What can you do if you start getting that Derived X feeling? As Socrates advised, begin with an examination of yourself. Could your changing feelings be caused by stereotyped attitudes you hold toward certain employees? Are you really concerned about your employees and actually *showing* them your concern, or is your concern only expressed by words, not action? Remember, *words are not substitutes for action.* Unfortunately, your negative attitudes or expectations, as we'll soon see in greater detail, may actually bring about the very conditions you want to avoid.

You do, of course, have to be realistic. Some employees may (through no fault of your own) fit the X pattern of assumptions—some workers do prefer close supervision and little responsibility. To them, their jobs may merely be the means to more satisfying ends somewhere else. Don't give up, however. Negative employees may ultimately come around to a more positive stance by your repeated positive responses to them.

What Is the Pygmalion Effect?

"The rain in Spain stays mainly in the plains," articulates a fatigued, albeit persistent, Professor Higgins in the musical play and film *My Fair Lady,* which is based on George Bernard Shaw's play *Pyg-*

malion. In the story, Professor Higgins believes that he can create a "duchess out of a flower girl," and through untiring faith, perseverance, and unrelenting training efforts, he finally motivates a poor Cockney working girl, Eliza Doolittle, to appear triumphantly in high society after acquiring a "correct" English accent and impeccable manners and bearing.

Shaw's writing alludes to Pygmalion, a figure in Greek mythology and classical literature. Ovid, in the *Metamorphoses,* wrote about the sculptor Pygmalion, who made an ivory statue representing his ideal of the perfect woman. Pygmalion was so enthralled by his work that he fell madly in love with his statue and yearned for the statue to come to life. His desire and faith in his creation were rewarded by the goddess Aphrodite, who came to the rescue and brought the statue to life, thus fulfilling Pygmalion's expectations and desire.

Do Employees Really Live Up and Down to Your Expectations?

How do the works of Ovid and Shaw relate to you as a supervisor? Well, out of these stories developed a managerial concept termed the **Pygmalion effect,** or **self-fulfilling prophecy,** which mandates that *the expectation of an event can actually cause it to occur.* Can you visualize how your expectations can influence the behavior of your subordinates?

Pygmalion effect (self-fulfilling prophecy): *The concept that the expectation of an event or certain types of behavior can actually cause the event or behavior to occur.*

For example, let's assume that you have a substantial amount of confidence in the ability of an associate, Tim. Let's also assume that you demonstrate your faith through both action *and* words; that is, Tim can easily sense your high regard for him. Your positive mental attitude toward Tim may well become self-fulfilling. Conversely, if you have negative expectations toward Tim (that is, you are X-oriented toward him), he'll probably pick up on your attitude through your words and your body language. The accompanying result could be that Tim's performance will be less than satisfactory. His performance, therefore, may be *down* to your expectations.

By understanding the Pygmalion effect, you should be able to see that some leaders actually create the conditions that cause themselves to be either X- or Y-oriented toward their associates. Say, for example, that the needs of employees in a particular organization are *not* being satisfied because of insensitivity on the part of management. Negative employee attitudes may develop and be reflected in a variety of undesirable ways, such as increased absenteeism and tardiness. Such negative behavior helps to strengthen the Theory X assumptions of management. A manager is likely to become increasingly negative if he or she focuses only on what an employee has done wrong rather than providing positive feedback to that person.

Can the Pygmalion Effect Work in Reverse?

If your positive or negative expectations as a supervisor can influence the behavior of your associates, couldn't it also be true that

Upward Pygmalion effect: *The influence that an employee's expectations have on the behavior of his or her manager.*

your associates' expectations can affect your *own* behavior? To illustrate what could be termed an **upward Pygmalion effect,** let's assume that you recently hired a young high school graduate named Lisa, who was raised in an economically disadvantaged household by an extremely autocratic stepfather. Lisa has grown up with a fairly bitter attitude toward authority in general. Her experiences with authority and rules while in high school were anything but positive. Many of her unpleasant experiences with nonsupportive teachers and family caused her to develop a chip on her shoulder toward authority.

You sensed Lisa's hostile attitude toward you shortly after she was hired. She sometimes looks at you as though she hates you, and she also thinks you hate her. Although you didn't have anything against Lisa when she was hired, you now find yourself reacting somewhat negatively toward her. Her cold and piercing glances are becoming increasingly difficult to tolerate. You've begun to distrust her and have started checking her work more closely. Even though you know it's unfair, you find yourself becoming more critical of Lisa than of your other associates. You realize that you could be misinterpreting some of her actions and words, but nonetheless you have allowed Lisa to create an *upward Pygmalion effect* on you. Her expectations toward you as an authority figure have caused you to behave as she had expected when she was hired.

It is important that you, as a supervisor, develop both a "tough hide" *and* a high degree of sensitivity (empathy) in your interpersonal relations with others. You have to be strong and confident enough to prevent your associates' negative expectations from becoming self-fulfilling. Yet, you must be sensitive enough toward your associates' needs and feelings so that you can understand *why* their expectations are what they are. Your goals, and those of the organization, are far more likely to be achieved if you can offset any employee's negative expectations toward you with constructive expectations toward him or her.

What Are the Major Styles of Leadership?

We've already learned that some leaders tend to have positive attitudes toward their employees, while others perceive employees negatively. A supervisor's *attitude* toward associates certainly influences his or her style of leadership. For example, a supervisor who doesn't trust associates would tend to supervise them more closely than would a supervisor with confidence in his or her employees.

The following are some of the major leadership styles that will be described in the following sections:

- Autocratic (authoritarian)
- Participative (democratic)
- Free rein (laissez-faire)

- Results centered
- Contingency

The Autocratic Style—Should the Supervisor Make All the Decisions?

Autocratic (authoritarian) leadership: *A style of leadership in which managers keep decisions and controls to themselves.*

One style of leadership employs a *telling* approach. Termed **autocratic** or **authoritarian,** this style of leadership is often used by supervisors who feel that they know precisely what they want. They tend to express such wants as direct orders to their employees. Autocratic leaders don't share decision making; they generally keep decisions and controls to themselves. Employees accountable to an autocratic leader do have one thing in their favor: They are protected from being held accountable for making bad decisions, since their autocratic bosses assume full responsibility for decision making.

Autocratic leaders tend to follow a Theory X pattern in the way they perceive associates. A danger that exists with autocratic leadership, therefore, is that employees may, as we've already learned, live *down* to the boss's expectations.

Is an autocratic leader doomed to failure? Not necessarily. Some managers have *a personality that seems to lend itself to an autocratic style with success.* Some bosses seem to have a facade of gruffness, yet their employees know that their bark is worse than their bite. In such situations, employees tend to perceive their bosses as sort of "benevolent autocrats." To be successful with an authoritarian style usually requires that the leader *enjoy the respect of subordinates.* Autocratic leaders must *have broad and diversified backgrounds.* In short, they'd better know their stuff, or they won't have the same followers for long!

In some of the more structured organizations where autocratic leaders are successful, a sort of Darwinian "natural selection" has taken place. Employees who *prefer their work situation to be highly structured,* who *like to be told what to do and merely follow orders,* generally remain with the organization under an autocratic manager. Those employees who need a feeling of involvement with the decision-making process tend to move on to more receptive work environments when the opportunity presents itself.

However, there may be situations in which a supervisor has little choice other than applying an autocratic approach. For example, during emergencies or crises, there may not be time for a democratic give-and-take, group problem-solving session. (However, even during emergencies you would be wise not to ignore the pleas of an employee who might see some aspect of the solution that you missed while under tension.) An autocratic approach under the "right" circumstances doesn't necessarily mean that you are a Theory X/negative Pygmalion manager. Actually, your concern for employees (Theory Y) may be the cause of a more direct supervisory approach under those circumstances.

Many employees accomplish departmental and organizational goals with a participative style of leadership. Why wouldn't this style apply to all situations?

In general, most modern managers today tend to look on an autocratic style of leadership as a negative, counterproductive way to manage. Such a style ***does little to help employees to grow and develop.*** It also tends to ***stifle creative thinking and individual initiative.*** Finally, an autocratic approach frequently ***leads to higher employee turnover and training costs.***

The Participative Style—Should Employees Share in Decision Making?

Don't you generally feel good when your manager asks for your opinion or advice on certain matters? Many employees appreciate the chance to be able to take part personally in the decision-making process. Those who are offered the chance to do so are typically far more committed to achieving the goals of the organization than those whose opinions are not consulted.

Participative (democratic) leadership:
Involving employees in decision making; results in greater employee commitment toward organizational goals.

Our concern now turns to the **participative,** or **democratic,** style of leadership. A participative leader often realizes that people tend to follow those persons in whom they see a means of achieving their own personal goals. The skilled supervisor attempts to mesh such personal employee goals with the goals of the organization. Most people are more inclined to go along with a program or project that they've helped to develop, one that relates to their own needs and interests.

A participative approach doesn't mean that you—the supervisor—make no decisions. Instead, it really means that you must know in advance what the organization's objectives are and then draw on the knowledge and input of your group as a means of deciding ways to accomplish such objectives. Try to avoid the preset notion that your associates don't have the intelligence or background to participate in decision making. Properly used, the participative approach often reveals that the combined knowledge of the group far surpasses the knowledge of one individual (the supervisor). In addition, working on problems with your work team can often result in new ideas growing and flourishing from the members interacting and building on each other's thoughts.

For a variety of reasons—*especially fear of the unknown*—many employees tend to resist change. The way in which you introduce change, as well as the timing of its introduction, will significantly influence the degree of acceptance your employees will have toward a particular change. Once again, the participative approach can effectively be used to develop support for altered conditions. Employees who have taken part in deciding how a change will come about are usually more anxious to see it succeed than when the change appears to have been forced down their throats. Supervisors should encourage their employees to express their views regarding proposed changes. Changes that can be discussed openly often seem far less threatening to employees.

Where possible, allowing employees to participate is probably the most effective style of leadership to employ. Why, then, do some managers tend to shy away from it? Certain managers fear that a participative style will cause them to lose control over their associates. The opposite, however, usually results. An open and participative climate tends to eliminate feelings of hostility and opposition and, as a result, tends to enhance a supervisor's control over employees. A participative manner *does* give up some authority, but control is actually *gained* as a result of extracting greater commitment from the group.

Unfortunately, the participative approach doesn't work in all situations; in fact, there are some situations in which it might not even be applicable. For example, perhaps certain decisions can't be made by employees because they are contrary to company policy. Or, in other cases, there may be some workers in your group who truly *want to be excluded from any decision making.* They feel far more comfortable being *told* what to do. Sometimes, however, these are workers who are not deriving much satisfaction from their jobs.

An assumption that must be made when employing the participative approach is that associates have the necessary knowledge and skill to participate in decision making. If necessary skill and knowledge are lacking, you might find yourself *stuck either with a bad decision* or having *to override the person's decision,* thus offsetting the benefits of participative management. Rejecting the ideas of employees may cause them to *feel alienated from the workplace.* A participative approach, on the other hand, might cause workers to *feel that they should be able to participate in all future decisions*—a condition that you might not be able to fulfill. Furthermore, workers with cynical attitudes *may distrust your democratic approach.* They might feel that you are trying to *manipulate them.* And finally, *participation takes time*—a resource that you may feel doesn't exist in ample enough quantities for you to be able to spend it conferring with associates.

Regardless of the possible shortcomings of the participative approach, remember a key advantage of drawing on the input of your employees: *a greater worker commitment toward fulfilling organizational goals.*

The Free-Rein Style—Should Employees Make Decisions Alone?

Free-rein (laissez-faire) leadership: *The leader serves more to facilitate rather than directly lead the group.*

A third style of leadership is termed **free rein** or **laissez-faire.** This approach *does not* mean the *total* absence of leadership; it *does* mean the absence of *direct* leadership. Ordinarily, the free-rein leader works through organizational goals. His or her subordinates, however, are free to accomplish those goals in the manner they feel is best. For example, a task may be presented to a group by the leader. The group then works out its own techniques for accomplishing the goals within the framework of organizational policy. A major function served by the leader is to make certain that necessary resources are available to the group.

Could a free-rein style of leadership fit all circumstances? Not likely. In fact, in some instances a free-rein approach might create confusion and chaos. In other cases, the absence of direct leadership would be appropriate. For example, the director of a research laboratory doesn't have to be involved in every decision made by his or her research staff. Instead, the director might present a task to a researcher who would decide how to accomplish the organizational goals.

What Is the Nature of Results-Centered Leadership?

Results-centered leadership: *Involves informing the employee of the organizational and departmental goals; the employee then works with the supervisor in deciding how those goals will be achieved.*

Many supervisors believe that *results,* rather than the *methods* for achieving them, are a highly critical part of the management process. You already learned about a form of **results-centered leadership** in Chapter 10, where you studied about MBO (management by objectives). The MBO technique is a blend of the participative and free-rein forms of leadership. The supervisor utilizing the results-centered technique of leadership generally informs the employee of the goals of the organization and department and suggests that the employee work with him or her (the supervisor) in deciding how those goals will be achieved.

A Contingency Approach—Which Style of Leadership Is "Best"?

Has our discussion of leadership implied that there is one "best" style of leadership? Not necessarily. As we've seen, in some instances employees should be encouraged to participate in making some of the decisions that affect the achievement of your organization's goals. At other times, however, you may discover that you don't have, for a variety of reasons, the time required for a participative style of leadership.

There actually is no one style of leadership that fits nicely into every conceivable situation. The so-called best style of leadership, therefore, depends on three significant factors: the *situation,* the types of *followers,* and the type of *leader.* Students of leadership, recognizing that a variety of factors influence the most desirable style of leadership at any given time or situation, have increasingly been drawn to a more modern way of categorizing leadership, referred to as **contingency leadership.**

Contingency leadership: *Applying a style of leadership that is called for by the particular situation.*

A number of contingency theories of leadership have appeared in management literature in recent years. Space limitations preclude our doing more than briefly mentioning two major contingency theories in this section.

Although many researchers agree that various contingencies influence the most desirable style of leadership for particular situations, they don't all agree on the specific contingencies. Fred Fiedler, for example, believes that each leadership situation contains a mix of three "critical dimensions" that influences a leader's most effective style: *position power, task structure,* and *leader-member relations.*[5] Paul Hersey and Kenneth Blanchard contend something different—that the *maturity level of the individual employee* is the contingency that best determines the leadership style to use with that employee.[6]

Therefore, we can conclude that there isn't one best style of leadership for all situations. In general, the most effective style of leadership not only varies with the *occasion,* but also is influenced by the types of *leaders* and *followers.* In practice, you should tailor your style of leadership to fit a specific situation. You probably wouldn't use the same style of leadership during a crisis or emergency as you would during less hectic times, nor would you be likely to use the same style of leadership with a new and inexperienced employee as you would with a seasoned veteran. A few words of warning: Leaders who appear *inconsistent* in the manner that they lead employees sometimes lose the employees' respect. Likewise, the use of an autocratic style with one employee and a free-rein or participative style toward the others could be interpreted by some employees—women or minorities, for example—as a violation of their civil rights.

What Is the Managerial Grid?

Researchers Robert Blake and Jane Mouton developed another way of looking at leadership styles. Blake and Mouton believed that managers, to be effective, should have a concern for *both* production and people. They also realized that managers vary in their attitudes toward production and people, some having a high degree of concern for production and little concern for people, others with a high degree of concern for people and little concern for production, while still others are situated between the two extremes in their concerns for production and people.

What Are the Major Positions on the Grid?

Managerial Grid: *A device for dramatizing the various concerns—either for production, people, or combinations of both—that managers have.*

Blake and Mouton developed and popularized the well-known **Managerial Grid,** which is a device for dramatizing the various concerns—either for production, people, or combinations of both—that managers have.[7] According to the two researchers, a manager's style of leadership could be placed on the grid to illustrate a production/people relationship. Questionnaires have been devised as a means of quantifying a manager's current values and positioning them on the grid. A manager's position can fall into any of 81 positions. As can be viewed in Figure 12–1 (on the next page), the grid generally shows examples of five different positions:

- *1,1: Impoverished management.* This position represents the manager who has all but given up. He or she has little concern for either production or people. This type of manager may not have yet quit the organization, but probably wouldn't be missed if he or she did.
- *9,1: Task management.* This management style symbolizes the manager who has very little concern for the people in his or her department. The major concern is for production; very little else matters.
- *1,9: Country club management.* At the opposite corner from task management we find the type of manager who has little concern for production. The major managerial concern is to keep everybody happy. People may not get much done, but they sure have fun not doing it!
- *5,5: Middle-road management.* This style is right on the fence. The manager with this position doesn't want to rock the boat too much nor appear to be excessively pushy. Medium concerns for both production and people exist; however, neither is outstanding.
- *9,9: Team management.* This is the style considered to be the ideal under most circumstances. The 9,9 manager has a high degree of concern for both production *and* people. The manager attempts to obtain employee willingness to accomplish goals in a manner that satisfies both individual and organizational needs.

Where Are Managers on the Grid? Where Should They Be?

Every manager, we have seen, has to consider two questions: How is the work going to get done, and who is going to do it? We've learned from the grid that some managers are more concerned with production than people; others put people over production. As can be seen on the grid, the 9,9 position tends toward the ideal—a high degree of concern for both production and people.

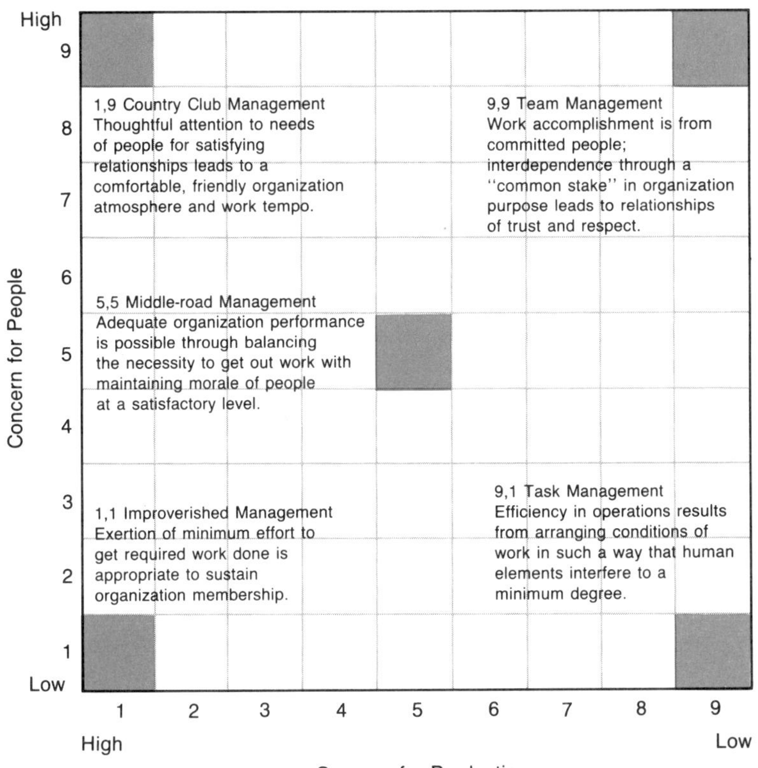

FIGURE 12–1
The Managerial Grid

According to Blake and Mouton's research, most managers prefer the middle-of-the-road, fence-riding position. Their findings were corroborated by this author's study of 185 officers and firefighters with the Oakland and Berkeley, California, fire departments: 90 percent of the individuals studied revealed leanings toward the 5,5 position. Officers (supervisors, in effect) in the fire service are quite close to their personnel, in many instances actually living with them in the same engine or truck companies (fire stations) for 24-hour shifts. This closeness seems to foster a leadership attitude of not wanting to hurt morale by displaying too much concern for production, yet being able to retain just enough control to accomplish firefighting missions. (Only a small proportion of a firefighter's job involves actual firefighting; most of it is concerned with fire prevention.)

Blake and Mouton's research further indicates that most managers use at least two styles—a *dominant* and a *backup*. Pressure, for example, can bring out a manager's backup style. A person may ordinarily assume a 5,5 position, but when under pressure suddenly shift to a 9,1 style of leading as a means of getting the production accomplished. Other managers who customarily have a 9,1 style may shift to a 1,1 backup position. Such individuals, ordinarily concerned mostly with production, may develop a defeatist attitude when discouraged or pushed and shift to a 1,1 style—little concern for either production or people. Managers who develop substance abuse problems, such as drug addiction or alcoholism, sometimes assume a 1,1 style.

What Can the Grid Be Used For?

The managerial grid is sometimes used in management training and development programs as a means of enabling managers to become more familiar with their existing styles of leadership. This awareness then becomes a basis for determining what modifications in leadership styles could be made to improve managerial effectiveness.

Summary

In the current chapter we discussed a number of important characteristics of *leadership.* We observed that some managers lean toward *positive* and others toward *negative* styles of leadership. Although not everyone agrees on a "trait theory" of leadership, there are a number of personal qualities that, when present, tend to aid leaders. Leadership skills, as with other skills, can be developed with training and practice.

We also learned something about *Douglas McGregor's X-Y Theory*—a negative-positive set of attitudes that leaders have toward employees. We also learned that these assumptions are not fixed; they may be *selective* or result in *Derived X.*

The *Pygmalion effect* is another important concept discussed in this chapter. It relates to the expectations that people have toward others and how such expectations influence events.

The *"best" style of leadership* depends on the situation, the types of employees, and the leader. Five ways of classifying leadership styles are *autocratic, participative, free rein, results centered,* and *contingency. Blake and Mouton* have further classified management styles on a *grid* in a manner that illustrates a manager's attitude toward both production and people.

Questions for Discussion

1. Evaluate the following statement: "Most good leaders are born that way. They've either got it from the start or they're never going to get it. And there's not much anyone can do about that."
2. What determines, even more so than a managerial title, whether or not a person is an *effective leader?*
3. Is leadership a *concept* or a *skill?* Explain.
4. Describe the ways cited in the text for *developing leadership skills.*

5. What, according to Douglas McGregor, is the difference between an *X* and a *Y* way of *perceiving employees?* Are these attitudes fixed in each supervisor and therefore applied in the same manner toward all employees?
6. What tends to cause a person to become *Derived X?*
7. How does the *Pygmalion effect* relate to the self-fulfilling prophecy? To Theory X? To participative management?
8. What is meant by the notion that the Pygmalion effect can work either *upward* or *downward?* Could there be a self-directed Pygmalion effect where your own expectations and self-image could influence your own behavior?
9. What determines the *"best"* style of leadership?
10. In general, what are some of the major disadvantages inherent in the *autocratic* style of leadership? Is the autocratic style of leadership always counterproductive?
11. Why do many employees tend to respond positively to the *participative* form of leadership style? What are some possible disadvantages?
12. Which of *Blake and Mouton's styles of management* typified on the *grid* tends to be considered the ideal? Which tends to be the most typical? How do you account for the difference?

Can You Define These Terms?

Instructions: Write a definition for each of the following terms. You may check your definitions with those provided in the end-of-text glossary.

leadership
Theory X
Theory Y
Selective X-Y theory
Derived X Theory
Pygmalion effect
upward Pygmalion effect
autocratic (authoritarian) leadership
participative (democratic) leadership
free-rein (laissez-faire) leadership
results-centered leadership
contingency leadership
Managerial Grid

Supervision In Action

12–1 Two Approaches to Supervision

Marc Cameron had been a department supervisor with Aztek, Inc., for about two years before leaving the company for a better-paying position with a competing firm. While at Aztek, Cameron had become notorious as a hard-nosed, no-nonsense type of manager with his people. He supervised associates closely and demanded that work be completed according to his standards. He kept close tabs on all 14 members of his crew and spent about half of each day in the work area observing and "assisting" them.

A number of employees had trouble adapting to Cameron's style of leadership when he was first promoted from another department to the supervisory position. During his first six months as supervisor, nearly 60 precent of his crew either quit or requested and received transfers to different departments in Aztek. The morale of the department seemed so bad that Jean Lambroughton, Cameron's manager, was about ready to remove him as supervisor.

Before any decision to dismiss Cameron was actually made, however, it almost seemed as though the problem took care of itself. The remaining and newer members of Cameron's department seemed to accept his style of leadership. In fact, productivity increased substantially, production costs were reduced, and requests for transfers subsided. Largely because of his success with the department after the problems diminished, he was offered the position he accepted with another company.

As a result of Cameron's sudden departure, Lambroughton had to quickly find a replacement to fill the open supervisory position. No one within the department itself was ready for promotion, so Lambroughton transferred Claudia Mullen, a production supervisor in another department, to the vacant position. For Mullen, the new position was not really a promotion, but she thought the change might offer her some fresh challenges and experiences. She was considered a competent supervisor in her prior position, and she had an outstanding technical background.

Claudia Mullen had recently attended a seminar on management by objectives and strongly subscribed to it as a management technique. Mullen determined objectives before assigning tasks to her subordinates and let the workers decide independently on the procedures and methods for achieving the objectives. Although available for input in the event of complications, Mullen usually attempted to avoid getting involved in the details of her crew's work.

After about a month and a half, it seemed fairly apparent to Lambroughton that things were not running too smoothly in Mullen's department. Recent deadlines had been missed, three jobs were currently behind schedule, and two jobs had experienced cost overruns. Lambroughton recently talked informally with two of the people in the department who expressed dissatisfaction with the way Mullen was supervising. They said that she didn't really seem to understand the work she was supervising, and wasn't really a leader. She never told them how they were to accomplish the goals, yet they were held accountable for the jobs that weren't done on time. The workers said that they weren't getting enough guidance from Mullen, and weren't really sure if she was capable of giving it in the first place.

Questions

1. Describe Marc Cameron's and Claudia Mullen's styles of leadership in terms of the chapter's discussion of principal leadership styles *and* the grid positions of Blake and Mouton.
2. Were the employee reactions to both Cameron's and Mullen's management approaches predictable? Why, or why not?
3. What should Jean Lambroughton do about the situation now? Assume that you are Lambroughton and role play your approach with another student who is to assume the role of Mullen.

12–2 Production at All Costs

Barbara Batson has been a supervisor in the stamping department for about 18 months. Prior to her promotion, she was considered one of the best workers in her department. David Newhouse, the plant manager, recently met with Barbara for her annual performance review, and the following conversation took place:

Newhouse: Barbara, I certainly can't complain about production in your department. You know our production processes well, and you've exceeded your department's quota every month but one. But there is an area that I'd like to discuss with you—your workgroup. Since you took over stamping, the turnover rate in your department has exceeded that of any other department in the plant.

Batson: I know that our turnover is high, Mr. Newhouse, but I really don't think I should be blamed for that. Most of the people I've been getting in the past year and a half act like a bunch of prima donnas. They work well for awhile and then they start complaining about everything.

Newhouse: As you probably know, Barbara, our personnel manager conducts an exit interview with each person who leaves the company, and a few of your ex-employees have complained about the breakneck speed you expect them to work. What's your reaction to that?

Batson: I think it's a lot of nonsense. As I said, those people were a bunch of loafers. I think I know the ones you mean. Heck, they were late for work half the time, and used up more than their allotted sick leave last year—and I don't think they really were sick! But I don't really see the point of all this, Mr. Newhouse. You seem to be blaming me for the high turnover. Whatever the reason for it, you've got to admit that my department has put out the work. In fact, you already did admit that. And I think you know that I've always been cost conscious. We don't have much scrap or other waste in my department.

Questions

1. What type of managerial skill does Barbara seem to be lacking? Explain.
2. What style of leadership does Barbara seem to practice? Where does she seem to be on the Blake/Mouton Managerial Grid?
3. Barbara's department has been productive, she has been cost conscious, and she has a good technical knowledge of her job. With all this going for her, why should her boss be concerned about the high turnover in her department?

12–3 Assumptions about People

The purpose of this exercise is to aid you in understanding the assumptions you make about others and their attitudes. Below are 10 pairs of statements. First, reach each pair. Then assign a weight from 0 to 10 to each statement in the pair based on the relative strength of your belief in each statement. *The points assigned for each pair must total 10.* For example, in pair No. 1, your feelings may indicate a weight of 8 in the *a* statement and a 2 in the *b,* for a total of 10.

Be as honest with yourself as you can. Resist the natural tendency to respond as you would like to *think* things are. This exercise is not a test. There are no right and wrong answers. It is designed to help you learn more about yourself and the assumptions that you make about other people.

1*a.* It's only human nature for people to do as little work as they can get away with. X ______

b. When people avoid work, it's usually because their work has lost its meaning. Y ______

2*a.* If employees have access to more information than they need to do their immediate tasks, they will usually misuse it. X ______ *b.* If employees have access to any information they want, they tend to have better attitudes and behave more responsibly. Y ______

3*a.* One problem in asking employees for ideas is that their perspective is too limited for their suggestions to be of much practical value. X ______

b. Asking employees for their ideas broadens their perspective and results in the development of useful suggestions. Y ______

4*a.* If people don't use much imagination and ingenuity on the job, it's probably because relatively few people have much of either. X ______

b. Most people are imaginative and creative but may not show it because of limitations imposed by supervision and the job. Y ______

5*a.* People tend to lower their standards if they are not punished for their misbehavior and mistakes. X ______

b. People tend to raise their standards if they are accountable for their own behavior and for correcting their own mistakes. Y ______

6*a.* It's better to withhold unfavorable news because most employees want to hear only the good news. X ______

b. It's better to give people both good and bad news because most employees want the whole story, no matter how painful. Y ______

7*a.* Because a supervisor is entitled to more respect than those below him or her in the organization, it weakens his or her prestige to admit that a subordinate was right and he or she was wrong. X ______

b. Because people at all levels are entitled to equal respect, a supervisor's prestige is increased when he or she supports this principle by admitting that a subordinate was right and he or she was wrong. Y ______

8*a.* If you give people enough money to feel secure, concern for such intangibles as responsibility and recognition will be less. X ______

b. If given interesting and challenging work, people are less likely to complain about such things as pay and supplemental benefits. Y ______

9*a.* If people are allowed to set their own goals and standards of performance, they tend to set them lower than their boss would. X ______

b. If people are allowed to set their own goals and standards of performance, they tend to set them higher than their boss would. Y ______

10*a.* The more knowledge and freedom a person has regarding the job, the fewer controls are needed to keep him or her in line. X ______ *b.* The more knowledge and freedom a person has regarding the job, the fewer controls are needed to ensure satisfactory performance. Y ______

Instructions: Subtract the smaller number in each set from the larger number. If the *net amount* relates to the X statement, indicate the value by drawing a small dot above the corresponding number on the X side of the continuum below. If the net amount relates to the Y statement, indicate the value by drawing a dot on the Y side of the continuum. For example, if in set No. 1 your X response was 8 and your Y response was 2, your net amount would be 6. You would then place a dot over the corresponding number (in this case, 6) on the X side of the continuum.

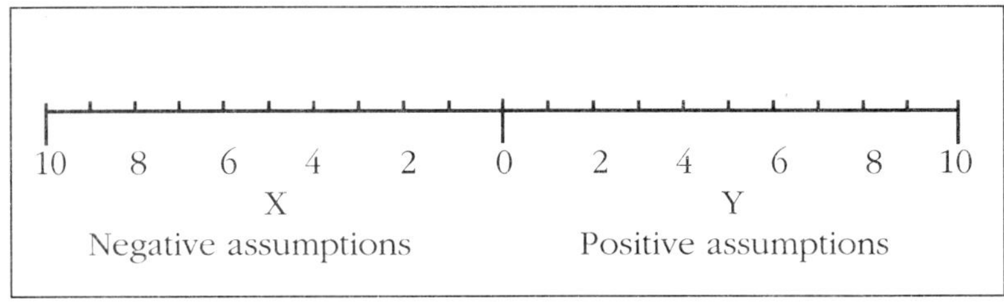

The validity of this exercise depends largely on your ability to respond accurately to the statements above. If most of your dots are clustered on the right (Y) side of the continuum, the chances are fairly good that your assumptions about other people in general lean toward the positive. If, on the other hand, most of your dots are clustered on the left (X) side of the continuum, you could probably benefit from determining ways in which you could improve your attitudes toward and assumptions about others.

12–4 Do You Understand Blake and Mouton's Managerial Grid?

Based on Blake and Mouton's Managerial Grid, match the numerical type leadership in Column 2 with the explanation in Column 1.

	Column 1	Column 2
______	1. Adequate organizational performance is possible through balancing the necessity to get work out with maintaining people's morale at a satisfactory level.	A. 1,1 management B. 9,9 management

_____ 2. Efficiency in operations results from arranging conditions of work in such a way that human elements interfere to a minimum degree.

_____ 3. Work accomplishment is from committed people; interdependence through a common stake in the organization's purpose leads to relationships of trust and respect.

_____ 4. Thoughtful attention to people's needs for satisfying relationships leads to a comfortable, friendly organization and work tempo.

_____ 5. Exertion of minimum effort to get work done is sufficient to sustain organization membership.

_____ 6. *Impoverished*—"Don't make waves; do as little as possible to keep the boss off our backs."

_____ 7. *Task*—"The objective's the thing. We'll take the hill even if all the troops are lost in the battle."

_____ 8. *Country club*—"Why should I worry about production? My boys and girls like each other and have a good time."

_____ 9. *Middle-of-the-road*—"People and production . . . they are both somewhat important."

_____ 10. *Team*—"Yes, this is the finest staff that anyone would want to work with. They really work as a team to accomplish team goals."

C. 5,5 management

D. 9,1 management

E. 1,9 management

Answers: (1) 5,5; (2) 9,1; (3) 9,9; (4) 1,9; (5) 1,1; (6) 1,1; (7) 9,1; (8) 1,9; (9) 5,5; (10) 9,9.

Endnotes

1. Erik Calonius, "America's Toughest Papermaker," *Fortune* (International Edition), February 26, 1990, pp. 48–51.
2. Douglas McGregor, *The Human Side of Enterprise* (New York: McGraw-Hill, 1960).
3. Stan Kossen, *The Human Side of Organizations,* 5th ed. (New York: Harper Collins, 1991), Ch. 8.
4. Ibid., pp. 214–216.
5. F. E. Fiedler and M. M. Chemers, *Leadership and Effective Management* (Glenview, Ill.: Scott, Foresman and Company, 1974).

6. Paul Hersey and Kenneth Blanchard, *Management of Organizational Behavior* (Englewood Cliffs, N.J.: Prentice-Hall, 1988).
7. Robert R. Blake and Jane S. Mouton, *Managerial Grid* (Houston, Tex.: Gulf Publishing Company, 1964).

Chapter 13

Communicating Directives

Communication is not simply sending a message . . . it is creating true understanding—swiftly, clearly, precisely.

—From an Hitachi advertisement

Once you start thinking about speaking and writing in terms of feedback, a great many things become startlingly clear. You realize that the effectiveness of speech and writing depends largely—maybe entirely—on whether the feedback is in good working order. Without the feedback, words may never hit the target.

—Rudolf Flesch, Author

Learning Objectives

When you finish this chapter, you should be able to:

1. Describe the communication process.
2. Apply some proven communication techniques for handling typical supervisory concerns.
3. Express the various ways in which supervisors communicate.
4. Contrast *upward, downward,* and *horizontal communication.*
5. Avoid some of the more common causes of communication breakdowns.

"What do you mean, you quit? You started working here only a week and a half ago. You can't be serious about quitting . . . can you?"

Does this example seem a bit exaggerated? It isn't. Many early terminations by employees are a result of breakdowns in a process that is the primary focus of this chapter—*communication.*

Communication is an important process that touches virtually every aspect of organizational life. It has been estimated that typical individuals spend between 70 and 80 percent of their waking days in one form of communication or another. Supervisors are no exception to this general rule. As we'll see shortly, virtually anything a supervisor does relates either directly or indirectly to the communication process. Likewise, a large proportion of the problems any organizational member experiences is caused by communication breakdowns or misunderstandings.

In addition, communication significantly relates to our earlier discussion of planning. Organizational plans can be carried out only if they are communicated effectively to employees. Morale is another factor that can be affected by the way supervisors communicate what upper management wants carried out, as we'll see shortly when we discuss the communication of policies to employees.

In this chapter we examine reasons why communication skills are so critically important to supervisors. We also look at the basic communication process along with some of the principal communication concerns of supervisors. Then we discuss the main communication methods and channels at the disposal of supervisors. And finally, we conclude with suggestions for minimizing communication breakdowns. An understanding of these concepts should lessen the frequency and severity of your own communication difficulties both on and off the job.

What Is the Nature of the Communication Process?

Some years ago, any discourse on the topic of communication generally presented the information as something akin to using a bow and arrow. For example, assume that you—the communicator—have in your possession a bow and arrow. The bow, according to classical theory, symbolizes the communication source, and the arrow is the communication medium. You forcefully pull the arrow and string back toward your body and let them snap loose. The arrow speedily soars through the air until it enters your receiver's head, so to speak, and—zaaap!—you have thereby communicated, at least according to early theory. Some deeper analytical thought on the subject, however, refutes those beliefs, as we'll now see.

Why Should Communication Be Two-Way?

Communication, of course, requires much more than a bow and arrow (although you might be "saying" something to an employee if you aimed an arrow at him or her!). Let's look now at what communicating actually is. An understanding of this information is essential if you are to minimize your own communication difficulties in your daily activities.

First of all, for effective communication to take place, there are *three essential ingredients* that must exist:

1. A sender
2. A receiver (listener)
3. An understood message (including feedback)

Communication, therefore, can be defined as a *two-way process resulting in the transmission of information and understanding between individuals.* Note the nature of **two-way communication.** It's virtually impossible to know for certain how effectively you've communicated without some sort of **feedback,** which is the process through which you learn of the response to your message. For example, have you communicated if you were to ask one of the human resource managers in your organization, "Jason, when do you think we can fill that vacancy in my department?" and Jason responds, "How did you know I went to the dentist?" Yes, you have communicated, but not quite as you intended. However, the opportunity to receive instant feedback when you heard Jason's words enables you to correct the misunderstanding. Whenever possible, try to avoid **one-way communication.**

Communication:
A two-way process resulting in the transmission of information and understanding between individuals.

Two-way communication:
A necessary ingredient of communication that helps to ensure that understanding has taken place.

Feedback:
The process through which you learn of the response to your message.

One-way communication:
A message flowing in one direction with no feedback or certainty of understanding involved.

Why Are You Both a Producer and Consumer of Communication?

In a sense, therefore, both you and Jason (or anyone else, for that matter) are simultaneously both *producers* (senders) and *consumers* (receivers) of communication. You produced and sent Jason a message, but you also consumed and received a message from Jason. Figure 13–1 illustrates the basic communication process and its two-way nature.

What Are Feedback Systems?

As we've already suggested, we find out if we've been understood by a process called *feedback.* In a later section of this chapter, we explore some of the typical ways in which managers can receive information from employees—that is, with feedback—such as *suggestion systems, open-door policies, deep-sensing meetings,* and *exit interviews.* In Chapter 10 we discussed a method in which employees receive feedback through *performance reviews.*

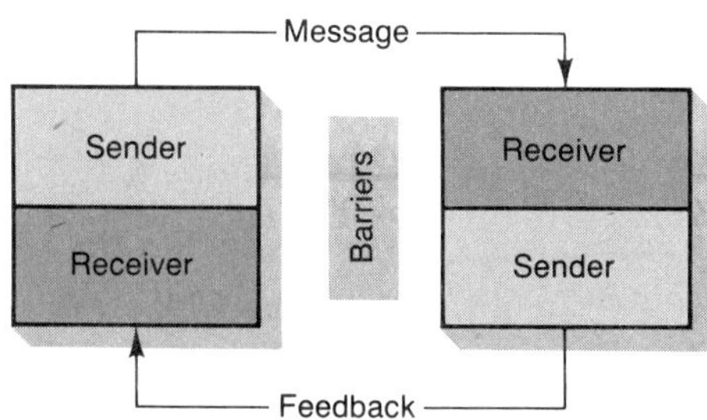

FIGURE 13–1
The Basic Two-Way Communication Process

What Are Some Special Supervisory Communication Concerns?

Most supervisory responsibilities involve communication of some sort. Let's briefly examine some of the major activities related to communication with which you, as a supervisor, could be involved.

How Do You Communicate Policies, Procedures, and Rules?

Have you ever heard any members of organizations complain about all the "red tape" they're expected to plow through? A myriad of *policies, procedures,* and *rules* exist in virtually every organization. These items are either established by government fiat or developed by senior management for the purpose of creating a more organized and predictable work environment. But such items are of no use and can create legal complications if they are not known, understood, and followed by those who are responsible for carrying them out.

You Are Responsible. As a supervisor, you have the responsibility to make certain that all affected members of your department understand and carry out established policies, procedures, and rules. Periodic meetings can be useful for imparting such information. You also may be responsible for making certain that your associates have read and understood your company's *organization manual,* which provides employees with a ready source of information related to your company. Remember that this information isn't inscribed permanently in stone. It is influenced by a variety of factors, including government regulations and executive orders, which in some cases seem to change by the minute. These changes must be communicated to and understood by employees.

Don't Pass the Buck. As we've indicated, *you* are responsible for communicating policies to your associates. When talking with employees, never "pass the buck" to higher management by saying something like, "Now those "fast-trackers" upstairs want us to accept returns from customers with no questions asked, and that's going to lower our commissions." If you show a lack of enthusiasm for organizational policies, you will probably have much more difficulty getting today's better educated and more outspoken employees to accept and carry them out. Many employees want to know *why* a policy is necessary to carry out. Also unacceptable is for you to merely say, "Do this because I told you to."

A better approach could be, "We have an improved company policy that should really enhance customer relations in the future and make us more competitive with other retailers. Starting immediately, we will accept returned merchandise from customers with no questions asked. Both sales and our commissions should increase as public awareness of our new policy spreads." Especially important is for you, as a supervisor, to learn the meaning and purpose of policies so that you can communicate them clearly to your associates. Consultant Robert W. Braid suggests that when explaining a policy or procedure you ask yourself:

- What are the people supposed to do with the information?
- How technical is it?
- How long will they have to remember it?
- Am I trying to explain too much in a short time?
- Will everyone understand the words, terms, and the like being used?
- Am I apologizing or blaming others?
- Have I provided a technique for getting feedback?[1]

How Do You Train Your Associates to Communicate Effectively?

We often equate the act of communicating with talking. However, have you ever said something to someone only to later be told, "You never told me that." Yet, you know deep in your own heart that you did tell the person something. You can even recall the precise place and moment when you said it. Unfortunately, without formal training in communications skills, most organizational members are somewhat doomed to excessive numbers of communication failures and misunderstandings.

As a manager, you can assist other organizational members in improving their communication skills. In some organizations, you personally may develop training programs related to communicating, including some to improve *listening* and *writing skills*. *Communicating effectively with customers* is another important skill for employees to develop, especially for those who frequently interact with the public. Some organizations hire outside consultants to develop in-house communication skills training programs. Others send their employees to skill development seminars presented by either private consulting firms or member-supported associations, such as the American Electronics Association and the American Management Associations.

How Do You Communicate Human Resource Needs?

Supervisors need *people* in order to carry out their responsibilities. As a result, you must anticipate your future human resource needs well in advance and be able to accurately communicate those needs to the personnel department so that current employees can be developed or new employees recruited for available positions. You should also communicate any changes that have taken place in jobs to be filled to ensure that "square pegs" are not recruited for "round holes." Furthermore, personnel requirements in most business firms are closely tied to future sales and production volume. In government agencies, political and budgetary constraints continually influence hiring practices. Managers should be tuned in to potential changes in human resource needs before a crisis develops.

Future sales, production volume, legislation, and budgets aren't the only factors that affect future personnel needs. Other considerations, such as future retirements, resignations, separations, and requests for transfer or leave, require continual coordination and communication among all levels of management to ensure that personnel needs are met.

How Do You Communicate During the Employment Selection Process?

The entire employee selection process (covered in Chapter 9), ranging from recruitment to hiring decisions, involves communication activities. Interviewing prospective employees requires effective communication skills. Knowing how to ask questions during the interview, for example, is a highly critical skill. Interpreting application forms and resumés, administering employment tests, and checking references all require finely honed communication skills. Selling qualified candidates on the job opening in your company is also necessary. Communicating your offer of salary and benefits is likewise important to avoid later misunderstandings.

How Do You Communicate to New Employees?

The *orientation* of new hires also requires skill in communication. The first impressions that new employees develop are influenced by the manner in which information about the organization is communicated to them, and these first impressions tend to persist long after the initial orientation sessions. A variety of topics, as previously discussed in Chapter 9, are typically covered during the orientation period. Employees must know what is expected of them; benefit and safety programs are only a small part of what new employees must learn. In addition, supervisors must make certain that employees receive adequate training. Training others is also a task requiring well-developed communication skills.

Management information system (MIS):
A computer-based information system that assists managers in their planning and controlling functions.

How Do You Utilize Information Systems?

A communications tool that has become a common part of the organizational environment since the advent of the computer age is the **management information system (MIS).** Basically, MIS is a computer-based information system that assists managers in their planning and controlling functions. MIS can assist substantially

Information about organizational problems can sometimes be uncovered during exit interviews with departing employees.

in the decision-making process. In order to gain from the use of your company's MIS system, you, as a supervisor, must develop and maintain the necessary computer skills.

Of course, not all organizations have highly sophisticated computer-based MIS systems. However, most well-managed organizations do maintain information and data on personnel that are essential for planning and controlling labor requirements. Any information related to human resources could be stored in a personnel information system, including budgetary information, sources of applicants, personnel data regarding promotability, accident frequency, and career movement patterns.

How Do You Handle Exit Interviews?

Exit interviews: *Sessions with departing employees, especially with those who resign, to determine reasons for leaving and to uncover possible organizational problems.*

Exit interviews are another special area of communications for supervisors. As we learned earlier, these typically are given to persons who resign from an organization. Sometimes the real reason why an individual quits a job is related to something about the position, such as poor working conditions or few opportunities for promotion. A well-administered exit interview can sometimes uncover problem areas and indicate where changes might be made to reduce turnover and enhance morale in the future. In some cases, however, it may be difficult to gain accurate information because of some employees' reluctance to jeopardize future careers. Some of the types of questions that can be asked during exit interviews are listed in Table 13–1.

How Do Supervisors Communicate?

Communication is a process that comes in a variety of shapes and sizes. As a supervisor concerned with communicating effectively, you have to choose among various alternatives every time you attempt to communicate with others. The various choices include:

- Verbal (spoken and written)
- Nonverbal (body language, symbols, use of time)
- Formal
- Informal
- Mechanical/electronic

Let's take a brief look at each of these.

How Should You Transmit Verbal Symbols?

Verbal symbols: *Words that are used in either oral conversations or written messages.*

A major way in which we communicate is through the use of **verbal symbols** that are transmitted either by *speaking* or *writing*. Which form is best for you in carrying out your supervisory management activities? As with most things, each option has its advantages and disadvantages, and both are used regularly in organizations.

TABLE 13–1
Typical Types of Questions Asked during Exit Interviews

- Why are you quitting?
- How were your relations with your supervisor?
- How do you feel about the opportunities for advancement in this organization?
- How do you feel about the training you received on your job?
- How successful are management's efforts at communicating with employees?
- How do our pay scales and employee benefits compare with other organizations?
- How do you feel about the equipment and general working conditions here?
- What would you suggest be improved for the benefit of coworkers who are staying behind?
- What could be added to our orientation program that it currently lacks?
- What did you especially dislike about the work?
- What additional comments would you care to make about your work experience here?

Spoken Communication. There are a number of *advantages* that spoken communication has over written forms. These are:

1. The opportunity for immediate feedback
2. The opportunity to observe how the receiver is emotionally and physically reacting to your message
3. The opportunity to use and listen to vocal tone and inflection
4. The opportunity to ask questions of the receiver to confirm understanding
5. The opportunity to save time

Principal *disadvantages* of spoken communication include:

1. The tendency to waste time with unrelated small talk
2. The lack of documentation of important topics
3. The lack of opportunity for the receiver to digest the message

Written Communication. In our organizational lives, we're continually bombarded from all sides with written types of communication. Some of the communications are necessary and useful; others are never read. However, written communication has some significant *advantages* over spoken forms, which are:

1. Providing a permanent record or reference
2. Providing documentation for disciplinary action and other personnel activities, such as promotion and salary changes
3. Requiring more thought and planning by the sender of what the message will contain before it is transmitted
4. Enabling the receiver to give more thought to the interpretation of the message

Key *disadvantages* of written communication include:

1. The lack of opportunity for immediate feedback
2. They are more time consuming and costly
3. The possibility that the message will be set aside and overlooked
4. The lack of opportunity for the sender to observe and interpret nonverbal forms of communication

What Are Nonverbal Forms of Communication?

Communication with spoken and written words are only a small portion of any communication transactions between people. Much of the communication process takes place through the use of **nonverbal language**, such as *vocal inflections, facial expressions,* and other forms of *body language.*

Nonverbal language: *Forms of communication other than the spoken or written word.*

For example, an associate's current mood may be reflected in the manner in which he or she *walks* through the office on a particular day. Even *inactivity* communicates—a supervisor not greeting employees in the morning or failing to praise their work might be interpreted as being displeased with their performance.

Let's look at two examples of body language. Assume, for example, that you are interviewing one of your department members, Suzy Bagg, for an upcoming promotion. The messages she conveys with her body can tell you quite a lot. For example, the way Suzy is *sitting* may tell you whether she is really interested in the promotion. If Suzy is *leaning forward intently,* the chances are good that she is interested, whereas if she is sitting and anxiously *tapping her feet or fingers,* she may be indicating that other things more important (to her) are on her mind.

Let's assume that another employee, Steve Hough, requires some disciplinary action from you. If you observe that Steve's *arms are folded,* this could be an indication of defensiveness or lack of receptiveness toward your comments. *Open, relaxed-appearing arms* may indicate a willingness to listen. The stance of *hands on hips with elbows turned outward* is said to indicate feelings of self-satisfaction. Even the way people carry themselves can indicate their feelings: *Stooped shoulders* could be an indication that a person is troubled by something, while an *erect posture* could indicate good feelings.

Nonverbal forms of communication are present in other, *symbolic* ways in organizations. For example, the way *space* and *height* are used in office situations can reveal something about the patterns

What does the employee's body language appear to convey in this scene?

What does the employee's body language appear to convey in this scene?

of authority of various employees. (A larger office, for instance, tends to symbolize greater status and authority for its occupant.) The way people regard *time* may also tell us something about them—concerned employees seldom arrive late for work, meetings, and appointments. People who are consistently late may consciously or unconsciously be saying that they wish they were working elsewhere (and some get the opportunity!).

But remember that old adage about a little knowledge being a dangerous thing. Guard against the possibility of misinterpreting nonverbal language, as we frequently do with verbal communications.

How Does Formal Differ from Informal Communication?

Another way of looking at communication is viewing both its formal and informal sides. **Formal communication** is the official communication that travels through the structured (formal) organizational network. An example of formal communication would be a request initiated by your manager and transmitted to your associates through you.

Formal communication: *Official communication that is transmitted through the structured organizational network.*

Informal communication, however, is the real workhorse of organizational message networks, one that sometimes helps and other times hinders an organization's efforts at accomplishing goals. Informal communication travels through a channel usually referred to as the **grapevine,** a network typically substantially quicker than official channels. Grapevines exist in every organization and are the primary means for transmitting **rumors,** which are statements or reports without known authority for their truth. More simply, they are the parts of the grapevine that are unverified and generally incorrect. Supervisors need to be concerned with controlling rumors, which can adversely affect the morale of organizational members in certain circumstances.

Informal communication: *Unofficial communication that supplies information to supplement information transmitted through the formal network.*

Grapevine: *The network of informal relationships through which facts, half-truths, and rumors are transmitted.*

What causes rumors to spread? Basically, rumors feed on ambiguity that develops when employees lack accurate or sufficient information. Rumors are less likely to spread if the organizational culture is one of trust and openness. Rumors tend to thrive, however, in organizations where employees want more information than is provided, and especially when crises have been prevalent. Rumors can best be prevented or squelched when you—the supervisor—supply employees with correct information, which can be done through face-to-face communication or meetings. Be certain that your "facts" are factual. For example, informing employees that rumors of a relocation of your plant from Buffalo, New York, to Tuscaloosa, North Carolina, are absolutely unfounded will create credibility gaps in the future if the move actually takes place.

Rumors: *Information transmitted through the grapevine, usually without a known authority for its validity.*

What Are Mechanical/Electronic Forms of Communication?

A wide variety of mechanical and electronic forms of communication are used in organizations. For example, a sales supervisor may send taped motivational cassettes to field salespeople. A service manager may attempt to explain something to a customer over the telephone. A training director may use various audio/visuals, such as sound movies, videocassettes, flipcharts, and transparencies, during training sessions. The list goes on and can include such sophisticated communications systems as electronic mail, voice messaging, and teleconferencing, just to name a few. The use and effectiveness of mechanical/electronic devices, of course, depends on their quality and the situation in which they are utilized.

What Directions Do Communications Take?

You should be aware of the many facets of communication that affect you, including the various twists and turns messages take in moving through your organization. As we've already learned, there are two major channels through which communications travel: *formal* and *informal.*

As a supervisor, you must function in a world of symbols. You are continually bombarded from all sides with communications. You receive directives from your bosses, memos from other department heads, and both requests and complaints from associates. In a sense, you could be considered in charge of a department called "Communications Central," with messages coming to you from all directions and radiating outward from you. The nature of communications flowing through your communication center may be *upward, downward,* or *horizontal* (see Figure 13–2). Let's now look briefly at each.

What Is Upward Communication?

Upward communication: *The type communication that flows up the organizational structure.*

Filter factor: *The straining out of ingredients that are essential to the understanding of messages as they rise up to management levels.*

As you can observe in Figure 13–2, supervisors are on the receiving end of a variety of upward types of formal communication. Examples of **upward communication** (the type that flows from the employees in an upward direction) include suggestion systems, open-door policies, employee grievances, labor news publications, attitude surveys, exit interviews, listening, and observation.

Supervisors frequently believe that they know exactly how subordinates feel about a particular situation or problem. "All of my people think this is a great place to work," some supervisors have boasted. Then—bang!—with little obvious warning, near-mutinous behavior erupts, and the stunned supervisor says, "I can't figure this out. They all seemed so contented until now. What went wrong?" Unfortunately, a phenomenon termed the **filter factor** has the habit of straining out ingredients that are essential to understanding messages as they rise up to management levels. We'll examine methods for minimizing some of these difficulties in a later section of this chapter.

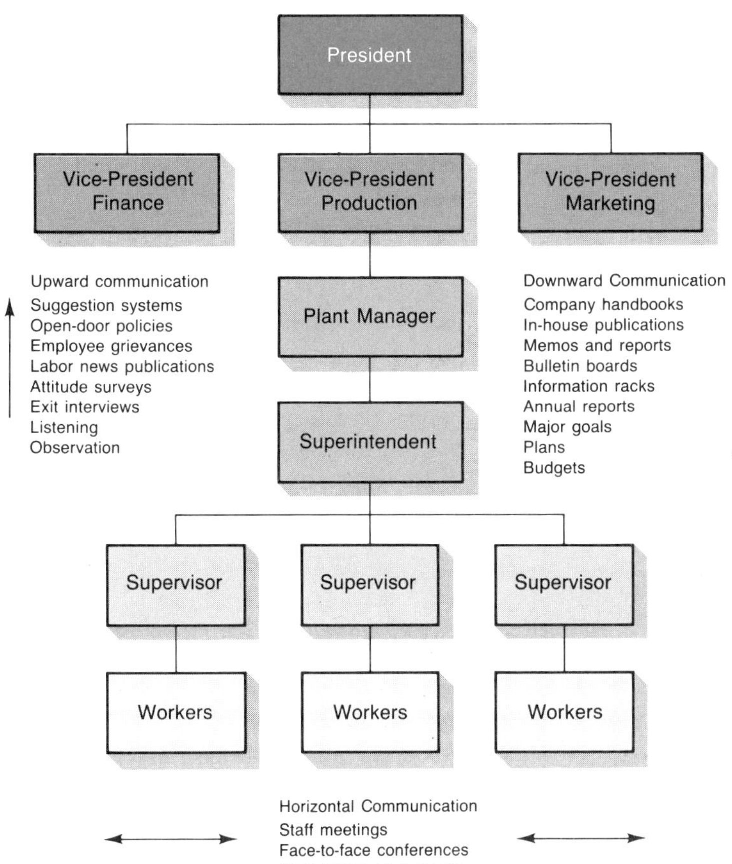

FIGURE 13–2
Formal Types and Channels of Communication

What Is Downward Communication?

Communication that conveys messages from higher to lower levels of an organization is termed **downward communication.** Filtering, unfortunately, can also take place as messages travel down the organizational hierarchy from managers to workers. Employees typically receive such tremendous volumes of downward communication that they often engage in **selective reception,** that is, they hear or see the information they are set to hear or see and tune out much of the rest. Anyone who has regularly attempted to convey information to others recognizes how difficult the process can be. With concentrated effort, however, communication breakdowns can be minimized.

Downward communication: *Communication that conveys messages from higher to lower levels of an organization.*

Selective reception: *Exists when individuals hear or see information they are set to hear or see and tune out much of the rest.*

Some of the more typical forms of downward communication include company handbooks, in-house publications, memos and reports, bulletin boards, information racks, annual reports, major goals, plans, and budgets.

What Is Horizontal Communication?

Horizontal communication: *Communication that takes place between departments or people on the same level in an organization.*

Another type of communication that allows managers on the same level in an organization to coordinate their activities more effectively is termed **horizontal communication.** The opportunity for cross-communication among department heads—either informally or through formal channels—helps to avoid problems such as duplicated efforts, ineffective use of resources, lack of coordination, and potentially destructive interdepartmental rivalry.

Horizontal communication results in time and effort being saved as departments solve problems between themselves without having to refer each matter to upper management. But watch out! Problems can result from horizontal communication when a bypassed boss feels that his or her decision-making authority has been reduced. Remember to inform your boss of any communication that might affect him or her. To do otherwise could place him or her in an uninformed and embarrassing position.

How Can You Minimize Communications Breakdowns?

Many organizations today are staffed with people from various parts of the world, thus bringing an international flavor to their workgroups. Their first languages are not necessarily English, and, as a result, periodic communication breakdowns or misunderstandings are somewhat predictable. Misunderstandings can be quite prevalent when attempting to communicate with some individuals whose native tongues are not the same as yours. There may be confusion even when you allegedly speak the same language as someone else, such as a person from Great Britain, who might suggest that you close the *bonnet* (hood) or *boot* (trunk) of your *saloon* (sedan automobile) before driving out onto the *motorway* (freeway or expressway). Basically, this lack of a totally common language contributes toward the numerous communication barriers that abound in any organization.

Supervisors, as with any manager, have considerable communicating to do with other people in their organizations. Being able to identify various stumbling blocks to effective communication and to understand some of the proven methods for coping with them can assist you in minimizing communications breakdowns in the future. Some methods for minimizing obstacles to effective communication include:

1. Perceiving things accurately
2. Obtaining feedback
3. Encouraging upward communication
4. Avoiding faulty translations
5. Controlling emotions
6. Avoiding credibility gaps

7. Listening actively
8. Asking questions effectively
9. Writing for understanding

Let's now briefly look at each barrier along with recommendations for overcoming them.

Why Is Seeing Sometimes Deceiving?

Look at the illustration in Figure 13–3. How many perfect squares do you see?

Now compare your answer with someone else's. Some people see 16, some 17, some 26, and still others different amounts. This "simple" conundrum helps to illustrate the reason why supervisors sometimes have difficulty in communicating information to others. (See endnote No. [2] for the answer.)

There's the human tendency to believe that what we see and hear is the truth. If there's a difference in opinion, it must be the other person who's out in left field. When we see or hear what we want, or are set to see or hear (regardless of reality), we are guilty of what psychologists refer to as **mental set.** It's wise to continually remind yourself that not everyone interprets your messages in the precise manner you intended, nor will you necessarily have a perfect record in "reading" others correctly. *Feedback,* that all-important ingredient of effective communication, can once again come to the rescue and assist you to avoid being misled by perceptual attitudes that were mentally set.

Mental set:
The tendency to see or hear what we want, or are set, to see, regardless of reality.

How Can Feedback Improve Understanding?

We too often assume that we've communicated when, in reality, we've merely transmitted words in the direction of another person.

FIGURE 13–3
How Many Perfect Squares Do You See?

(Remember the bow and arrow analogy?) Consequently, obtaining feedback from the receiver is essential in order for you to be relatively certain that you've been understood.

Asking your listener "Do you understand?" doesn't necessarily ensure that he or she really understands your message. There is the tendency for people on the receiving end of closed questions to respond with a "yes" because of the fear of appearing stupid to the sender of the message. A more effective feedback technique would be to say something such as, "Sean, how about running that information by me once to make sure that *I* was clear." (Note the phrase "*I* was clear" rather than "to make sure *you* understood me." Saying the latter—". . . *you* understood me"—may imply that you believe your receiver is not very bright.

Should You Encourage Upward Communication?

We've already pointed out that one of the directions organizational communication flows is upward. There are a number of methods for enabling communication to flow up the organizational hierarchy that can help to reduce communication breakdowns and misunderstandings. A formal **suggestion system** is one of the techniques used by some organizations as a means of encouraging upward communication. Such systems must be used with caution, however, or they will be looked on by employees as a farce. For example, *recognition* should always be given to a person submitting a suggestion, whether or not the idea is useful, in order to encourage the upward flow of creative ideas and employee gripes. Many managers not only provide an explanation in writing to the employees, but also give face-to-face explanations of the reasons for the acceptance or rejection of ideas. Some organizations present cash rewards or other incentives to employees who offer cost-saving ideas.

Suggestion system: *A feedback mechanism used to encourage upward communication in organizations.*

An **open-door policy** is another approach promoted by some managers as an indication of their interest in upward communication and feedback. The actual usefulness of open-door policies, however, is disputed by some students of management. Many employees hesitate to walk into their bosses's office unannounced. Often when they have attempted to drop in in the past, they were greeted by someone who said, "I'm sorry, but Mr. Blockout isn't available right now. Would you like an appointment?" An open-door policy isn't of much use if employees don't believe that the door is *truly open.* Many managers feel that the real value of an "open door" is to enable them to walk through the opening themselves in order to observe what is actually going on in the office or on the plant floor.

Open-door policy: *The practice by some managers of permitting others to drop by their offices without appointments.*

Deep sensing, another activity for encouraging upward communication, has become prevalent in many organizations. Deep sensing is the attempt by *senior managers* to find out what is on the minds of *rank and file employees.* It typically involves top executives holding regular sit-down sessions with groups of 10 to 15 employees for the purpose of sensing how employees feel about various factors that affect them and the organization's operations.

Deep sensing: *The attempt by senior managers to find out face-to-face what is on the minds of rank and file employees.*

The purpose of deep-sensing sessions varies with the organization using them. Some senior managers feel that the meetings are an effective way of communicating organizational goals and objectives to operating employees. Other managers use the meetings to provide an outlet for employee questions, concerns, and gripes as a means of preventing serious problems later. Deep sensing sessions are sometimes held as breakfast meetings, and sometimes as on-premises conferences.

Attitude surveys, discussed in Chapter 11, are another form of upward communication employed in some organizations to explore specific attitudes and opinions of employees in some depth. Such surveys may be taken of current employees' attitudes, or as we've already learned, may include *exit interviews* with departing employees—especially those who have voluntarily resigned—to determine reasons for leaving and to uncover possible organizational problems.

How Might Translations Be Faulty?

A young lady named Sandy worked in a pharmacy where she once had an embarrassing experience after a customer with a fairly heavy foreign accent walked in and requested something for "breath control" for his wife. The young clerk handed him some mouthwash and said, "Tell your wife to put two or three drops on her tongue as needed." The foreign customer looked at Sandy in utter disbelief. Red-faced, she soon discovered that the man had said "birth control," not "breath control"!

Sandy's dilemma relates to another barrier to effective communication—**faulty translations.** People frequently apply faulty translations to messages for reasons ranging, once again, from mental set to ineffective listening habits. Consequently, the sender's intended message can be easily misinterpreted when we don't find out what *he* or *she* means by a message.

Faulty translations: *The misinterpretation of communications because of ineffective listening, mental set, or other causes of misunderstanding.*

How can communications barriers of this nature be overcome? First, we should recognize that too often we assume that we've communicated when, in reality, we've merely transmitted words in the direction of another person. Consequently, *obtaining feedback from the receiver is essential* in order for you to be relatively certain that you've been understood.

How Can Emotions Affect Communications?

Emotions, either yours or your associates', can create disasters in communication efforts. When interacting with others, attempt to avoid using words, expressions, or directives that cause your listeners to feel either embarrassed or pushed. Also, try not to let others make you lose control of your own emotions. Make every effort to maintain a calm, positive, and friendly atmosphere in your interpersonal relationships, even if others come at you in an excessively hostile manner. Supervisors can lose far more than they gain when they lose their tempers with other organizational members. When you find yourself causing someone else to become highly emotional, listening actively to their messages can assist substantially as a means of enabling them to release their tensions.

How Can You Avoid Credibility Gaps?

Workers often come to a job with a distrust of management, a cynicism sometimes perpetuated as a result of poor communication and misunderstandings. To aid in reducing such employee attitudes, you should remember that *words do not substitute for action.* For example, assume that one of your associates, Seth, has asked you if he could change the starting date of his vacation, say, from June 1 to July 1. If you promise Seth that you will analyze the vacation schedule and get back to him tomorrow with the information but never follow through on your promise, you may soon discover that Seth will disbelieve many of your future promises.

Some supervisors seem to feel that a simple statement like, "Sure, I'll take care of that for you" will get people off their backs. It very well might ease your pressures temporarily. However, when dealing with employees, your manager, or anyone within or without your organization, keep in mind that they will frequently remember all those promises you made to them. Each time you make a promise and don't follow up, you widen the chasm of disbelief between you and others. As a supervisor, you need all the help you can get in maintaining the confidence and trust of your associates. So always remember to *follow up* on any promises or commitments that you make to others in order to minimize credibility gap problems.

You Hear, but Do You Listen?

Someone once said:

> *Folks are not hard of hearing; they are hard of listening.*

Why do so many people seem to be "hard of listening"? Much of their ineffective listening habits could be attributed to lack of training in listening. For example, if someone were to ask you if you had ever taken a course in writing or reading, you'd be likely to say "yes," wouldn't you? You undoubtedly had to study those subjects at some time in your educational experiences. If you were asked if you had taken a course in speaking, the chances are fair that you've had some training in that subject as well. However, if you were asked, "Have you ever had any formal training in listening?" the chances are quite remote that your response, or that of many others, would be in the affirmative.

We spend the bulk of our day communicating in one form or another. However, we spend only about *9 percent* of our communicating time in *writing* activities, about *16 percent* in *reading,* about *30 percent* in *speaking,* and the largest segment—approximately *45 percent*—in a *listening* mode. Yet, look at how little training or education we've acquired to help us develop listening skills. Some estimates suggest that we tend to operate at about a 25 percent level of efficiency when we listen to a 10-minute talk.[3]

If these figures are anything close to reality, think about their implications: We lose 75 percent of every 10-minute conversation. We think we *listen* when we *hear,* but do we really? Hearing is *not* listening. Many organizational managers today recognize that few employees are "born listeners." As a result, an increasing number of training departments have established listening workshops for the purpose of improving the listening skills of employees. See Table 13–2 for some useful guidelines for effective listening.

How Should Questions Be Phrased?

Supervisors are frequently involved in interviewing activities. Unfortunately, many interviews tend not to accomplish the interviewer's objectives because he or she has not learned to apply effective techniques of phrasing questions.

For example, assume that a supervisor named Brittany has noticed that an employee's behavior or work habits have undergone significant changes recently. Any sudden variation in an employee's performance from established standards could be a warning signal of personal problems, such as marital strife, financial difficulties, or alcohol and drug abuse. Any problem that affects a worker's on-the-job performance must be the concern of the supervisor, who may be able to offer assistance after discovering the nature of the problem. However, merely asking the employee, "Michael, is there anything wrong?" will typically elicit a negative, "No, not really" response. There are better ways of phrasing questions to obtain more complete answers. In general, questions may be phrased as **closed questions** or as **open questions.** Open questions usually generate better responses than do closed questions.

Closed questions: *Questions that typically can be answered with only a yes or no.*

Open questions: *Questions that cannot be answered with a simple yes or no response; intended to elicit greater response from an interviewee.*

TABLE 13–2
Guidelines for Effective Listening

- Give the speaker your complete attention. Display body language that shows your interest in the speaker's message.
- Withhold judgment. Listen to the speaker's entire message before forming strong opinions about its meaning.
- Ask pertinent questions to clarify vague points. Don't assume that you know the meaning of the speaker's words without asking questions to be sure.
- Be flexible. Be willing to change your interpretation of the speaker's message as the speaker supplies more information.
- Be empathetic. Attempt to put yourself in the speaker's position as a means of understanding his or her point of view.
- Listen *actively.* Recognize that listening is not a relaxed activity; it requires deliberate and conscious effort.

TABLE 13–3
A Summary of Key Words for Open and Closed Questions

Open	Closed
Who	Is
What	Do
When	Has
Where	Can
Why	Will
How	Shall

Closed Questions. A question is *closed* when it is phrased in such a way that it can typically be answered only with a simple yes or no. Here's an example: "Whitney, do you have a problem?" The typical response to a query phrased like that—whether honest or not—will be "no." Nor should you ask a question during an employee's performance review like this: "Lauren, are you going to reduce your scrap rate in the future?" A better choice would be: "Lauren, how do you plan to reduce your scrap rate in the future?"

Open Questions. A question is *open* when phrased in such a way that it typically can't be answered with a simple yes or no. Here's an example: "Whitney, I've noticed some changes in your work lately. What seems to be happening?" The questioner who asks an open question, exercises patience, and says nothing until Whitney finally responds will typically discover that Whitney will be far more likely to express her inner feelings about her personal problems.

Practice asking questions using the open-question technique. Table 13–3 lists *key words* that determine whether a question is open or closed.

Listening responses: *Various methods for showing interest in what a speaker is saying.*

Listening responses are related to questioning techniques. When interviewing, for example, there are certain things you can do that convey to the interviewee you are interested, attentive, and wish him or her to continue. Listening responses should be made *quietly* and *briefly* so as not to interfere with the interviewee's train of thought. You are likely to come across in a manipulative, artificial fashion if you are not genuinely sincere in your approach. Responses are usually made when the speaker pauses. Five types of listening responses are summarized in Table 13–4.

Do You Write for Understanding?

K.I.S.S. approach: *An acronym that symbolizes either* Keep It Simple, Stupid" *or* Keep It Short and Simple.

Writing styles have changed markedly over the years. In the past, for example, "acceptable" writing tended to be somewhat stiff and formal. Many managers have since learned that being understood should be a major goal of any written message. They now try to employ the **KISS approach,** which means "Keep It Simple, Stupid!" (or—more tactfully—"Keep It Short and Simple").

TABLE 13–4
A Summary of Listening Responses

- *The nod*—Nodding the head slightly and waiting
- *The pause*—Looking at the speaker expectantly, but without doing or saying anything
- *The casual remark*—"I see"; "Uh-huh"; "Is that so?"; "That's interesting"
- *The echo*—Repeating the last few words the speaker said
- *The mirror*—Reflecting back to the speaker your understanding of what has just been said ("You feel that . . .")

TABLE 13–5
The Four Cs of Written Communication

Complete
- Have you provided all the necessary facts?
- Have you answered all the receiver's questions?

Concise
- Have you avoided unnecessarily long and complicated words?
- Have you said what you wanted in one page or less?
- Are your paragraphs short and easy to read?
- Have you avoided "hiding" important information, such as where, when, and at what time a meeting will be held?

Correct
- Have you checked your correspondence for accuracy?
- Are your commitments in agreement with company policy?
- Have you checked your grammar, spelling, and punctuation?
- Have you eliminated sloppy corrections?

Conversational
- Have you written in a friendly, receptive manner?
- Will your writing style evoke the response you want?
- Have you avoided excessively complicated and flowery phrases?
- Have you avoided words and expressions that are likely to antagonize your readers?
- Have you put life into your writing through the use of active words?

Supervisors are frequently involved with written communications. Almost any correspondence or memo can be improved by applying what has been termed the **four Cs of written communication.**[4] The four Cs stand for *c*omplete, *c*oncise, *c*orrect, and *c*onversational. The checklist in Table 13–5 can aid you in determining if your written communications are likely to accomplish your objectives.

Four C's of written communication: *An aid for recalling the essential elements of written communication, Complete, Concise, Correct and Conversational.*

Effective communicators typically realize that **empathy**—the ability to put yourself (figuratively) into the shoes of the other person and feel as she or he does—substantially helps to open the avenues of two-way communication. Empathy can enable you to anticipate how your words will be interpreted by others and, therefore, be a guide as to the best approach to follow when attempting to communicate.

Empathy: *The attempt to feel something as another person feels it.*

Summary

In this chapter, we examined the nature of the *communication process* and its importance to supervisory management. We also explored a variety of situations that require the application of communication skills by supervisors. We stressed the *two-way nature* of the process and the need for *feedback* to ensure understanding.

The various alternatives when choosing a communication medium include *verbal (both spoken and written), mechanical/electronic, nonverbal, formal,* and *informal.*

Communication travels in various *directions* in organizations—for example, *upward, downward,* and *horizontal.* Bypassing formal channels of communication can create potential problems and conflict among organizational members.

We discussed a number of ways to minimize communication *breakdowns.* These include *perceiving accurately, obtaining feedback, encouraging upward communication, avoiding faulty translations, controlling emotions, avoiding credibility gaps, listening effectively, asking the right questions,* and *writing clearly and concisely.*

Questions for Discussion

1. Read the following statement aloud two times, first in a natural and friendly manner, and then in a pushy and demanding way: "Scott, I want you to drop by my office before you go home this evening." What does this simple exercise tell you about the meaning of words?
2. Evaluate the following statement: "Communication is simply the act of talking to someone—nothing more, nothing less."
3. Describe *seven major concerns* related to communications with which supervisors could be involved.
4. Describe the *basic communication process.* What is necessary for effective communication to occur?
5. What is meant by the statement "We are simultaneously both *producers* and *consumers* of communication?"
6. What are the major advantages of *spoken* over *written* communications? Written over spoken?
7. Many years ago there was a song with the words, "Your lips tell me 'no no,' but there's 'yes yes' in your eyes." What concepts discussed in the chapter relate to these words?
8. Describe some examples of *nonverbal language.* How do they communicate messages to others? Be specific.
9. How does *formal* differ from *informal communication*?
10. Should managers attempt to squelch the *grapevine* as a means of communication? Explain.
11. What are some problems that can develop from *upward, downward,* and *horizontal communication*?
12. What can assist you in avoiding being misled by perceptual attitudes that were *mentally set*?
13. Why might asking an employee "Did you understand?" not provide you with adequate *feedback*?
14. What is the proper way to administer *suggestion systems*? Why are some employees not inclined to submit written suggestions?

15. How might the shortcomings of an *open-door policy* be overcome?
16. Give an example of a *faulty translation* that you have recently experienced.
17. How do *emotions* affect communications? What should you do if you caused someone else to become excessively emotional and noncommunicative?
18. In your own words, explain this statement: "Words do not substitute for action."
19. Interpret this statement: "We may have *heard* a particular message, but we may not have *listened* to it."
20. Which tends to be more effective in eliciting a response: *open* or *closed questions*?
21. In what way does *empathy* assist a supervisor in communicating more effectively with associates?

Can You Define These Terms?

Instructions: Write a definition for each of the following terms. You may check your definitions with those provided in the end-of-text glossary.

communication
two-way communication
feedback
one-way communication
management information system (MIS)
verbal symbols
nonverbal language
formal communication
informal communication
grapevine
rumors
upward communication
filter factor
downward communication
selective reception
horizontal communication
mental set
suggestion system
open-door policy
deep sensing
faulty translations
closed questions
open questions
listening responses
KISS approach
Four Cs of written communication
empathy

Supervision In Action

13–1 Talking Isn't Communicating

Shayne Kirk, a young supervisor, was promoted about six months ago on the basis of his outstanding technical skill working on the production line of the Cinosanap Vapor Company. Shayne is in charge of 14 production employees.

Shayne wants to be an effective supervisor, but, unfortunately, some of his communications skills seem to be lacking. Whenever policy changes are made, Shayne communicates the new policies in a somewhat negative and unenthusiastic fashion; for example: "Those guys upstairs are never satisfied. Here's the latest garbage they expect us to comply with. We've got no choice, so be sure you do it."

When training his associates, Shayne frequently asks such questions as, "Do you understand?" and "Got it?" An amusing incident once occurred when he asked an employee to "Please *close the door,*" and the employee got a broom and started *sweeping the floor!*

Shayne is especially remiss in fulfilling commitments. He often fails to follow through on employee requests. For example, employees who request changes in their existing vacation schedules will be told something like, "Let me check on that and see if we can work it out. I'll get back to you as soon as possible with the information." Unfortunately for the employees, he seldom follows through with answers to their requests.

Once an employee complained about the difficulty of being able to see at her work station, where most afternoons the sun shone brightly through the window. The employee asked Shayne if he could possibly arrange for the purchase of some window covering so that the sun's glare would not reflect off of the work station. Shayne, in a cordial fashion stated, "Yes, I can understand your problem. I'll check to see if we have any budget for it, and we'll take care of your problem as soon as we can." Shayne discovered that there was no excess budget at this time for window covering, but he never got back to the employee.

Questions

1. Identify the principal communication weaknesses inherent in Shayne's supervisory style.

2. What would you do if you were Shayne's manager and learned of his communication shortcomings?

13–2 "They're Really Nice, but Who Needs Them?"

You are an office manager for the EasyWriter Mail Order Co., Inc. Many of EasyWriter's customers place their orders by telephone. In recent weeks there has been a marked increase in the number of complaints from customers. You discover that the main problem is that your catalog operators have been recording incorrect information on purchase orders, even though they are utilizing computers in their operations. Typical errors relate to colors, sizes, items, credit card numbers, and quantities of merchandise.

Questions

1. What seems to be the problem?
2. As office manager, what would you do to correct the problem?

13–3 Horace Bought a House[5]

Horace won the lottery and had $300,000 remaining after his tax payment. He bought a house with his net winnings and sold it for $400,000. Horace then bought the same house back again for $500,000 and sold it for $600,000. How much money did Horace make in the real estate business?

Instructions

1. On your own, solve the above problem. Record your answer in the space below.
2. Now break into groups of four or five participants. In your group, attempt to arrive at a *consensus* on the correct answer to the above problem. Record the group answer in the space provided below.

Individual Answer	**Group Answer**
_______	_______

3. How did the opportunity to obtain feedback from your partners influence your understanding of the above communication?
4. To what degree was empathy used by individual group members when trying to convince others of the correct answer?

13–4 An Open and Shut Case

A question is *open* when phrased in such a way that it *cannot* be answered with a simple yes or no. A question is *closed* when it *can* be answered yes or no. Review the key words for open and closed questions listed in Table 13–3.

Problem

Assume that you are talking to an employee whose job performance has deteriorated recently. Make up two questions: one each from the open and closed lists of key words in Table 13–3.

Endnotes

1. Robert W. Braid, "Explaining Policies to Subordinates," *Supervisory Management,* June 1985, p. 21.
2. The correct answer is 26 squares.
3. Adapted from "Your Personal Listening Profile," an undated pamphlet distributed by Sperry Corporation.
4. Stan Kossen, *The Human Side of Organizations,* 5th ed. (New York: Harper & Row, 1991), Ch. 3.
5. Adapted from Gail E. Myers and Michele Tolela Myers, "Man Bought a Horse," *The Dynamics of Human Communication* (New York: McGraw-Hill, 1976), pp. 407–408.

Chapter 14

Administering Change

Human beings are the corporation's most flexible form of capital. When change is the surest constant, it makes sense to develop a work force that can quickly adapt to unpredictable developments.

—Robert Gilbreth, Consultant

As actors and not just spectators in a dynamic economic process, managers have no choice but to operate in the uncertain realm of ceaseless change.

—John E. Flaherty, Author

Learning Objectives

When you finish this chapter, you should be able to:

1. Recognize the reasons why people tend to resist change.
2. Summarize the typical reactions people have toward change.
3. Apply some proven techniques for introducing change more effectively.
4. Explain the importance of following up and monitoring the effects of change.

"Of course I like change. Everybody does. I thrive on the new and the different. You'll never find me resisting something new when it's useful. Hey! What this? Who said we're switching over from the Word Estrella *word processing system to the* Word Modelo *system? I don't care if* Word Modelo *is supposed to be better. I just got used to* Word Estrella*!"*

Many people believe they like change. As in the example above, if you were to ask someone if they like new and different things, they'd probably say yes. But if you were to alter (change) their daily life—something that significantly affects their routine activities—you might find a far different attitude toward the new and the different.

People tend to resist change. An interesting characteristic of change is that it tends to create stress, even when the change relates to a happy event, such as receiving a promotion. We usually find greater solace and comfort when functioning within a predictable environment, one that helps us to maintain some sort of physical and mental equilibrium.

Along these lines, someone once said that people prefer *the certainty of misery over the misery of uncertainty.* Stated differently, discomfort that we can be sure of is frequently favored over potential benefits that are uncertain. Events or activities that alter stability and certainty tend to upset our equilibrium. The uncertainty that change can bring can also cause a degree of tension and anxiety, conditions that people naturally try to avoid. Change typically is accepted only when it is self-imposed to alleviate a current unpleasant situation. It tends to be rejected or resisted when people feel that it has been forced on them. The citizens of Eastern European nations, such as East Germany, Czechoslovakia, the Soviet Union, and Poland, have provided us with vivid examples of this concept in recent years.

We live in an ever-changing society. Change today is seldom the exception; it is the norm. Successful (and even unsuccessful) organizations continually experience change. A supervisor can be considered an *agent* of change.

Why Is Change Necessary?

The world is unlikely to wait for those who don't make the effort to keep up with it. Leaders, if they are to be successful, must learn how to *accept, create,* and *administer* change. They must continually remind themselves of the natural tendency many individuals have to resist change. They must also recognize the impact that changes in their own departments may have on other departments in the organization. As we explore the concepts of **change** in this chapter, we use the term to mean *any variation in conditions that previously existed.*

Change:
Any variation in conditions that previously existed.

Why Wait Until There Is a Crisis?

Unfortunately, too often change occurs only *after* supervisors recognize that conditions are in a state of crisis. Of course, a far more rational approach, and one that is far less costly, is for leaders to attempt to *anticipate* the need for change and to develop creative innovations *before* serious problems evolve.

Have You Allowed Time for Analyzing the Effects of Change?

Supervisors sometimes neglect to set aside the necessary time for analyzing changing conditions in their departments or the changing attitudes or performance of their associates. As a result, some leaders soon find themselves loaded with serious problems. As we discussed in Chapter 8, learning to delegate effectively can enable you to utilize more of your time for planning necessary changes. With proper planning, such problems as high turnover or absenteeism can often be anticipated and prevented before they occur.

Why Do People Tend to Resist Change?

None of us is likely to achieve success in preventing change from occurring. Change is one of those events as certain as death and taxes. Of course, not everyone resists change to the same degree. Some people tend to thrive on new experiences and challenges, while others see only the negative side in anything different. However, the manner in which change is introduced influences the way employees accept or reject it. Learning why people tend to resist change enables supervisors to administer change more effectively. Let's briefly examine some of the more common reasons why people tend to resist change. Principal reasons include:

- Past experiences
- Financial reasons
- Peer pressure
- Effect on personal life
- Habit
- Fear of the unknown
- Failure to recognize long-term benefits

How Do Past Experiences Affect Attitudes Toward Change?

Past experiences have a pronounced effect on how people accept or resist change. The influence of parents, for example, is considerable. Many child psychologists contend that the first six years of people's lives deeply influence the values they hold during their

Some employees naturally resisted the changeover from typewriters to computers. Many of the same employees would resist to an even greater degree their having to return to typewriters.

remaining years. The training and environment that children grow up with strongly influence the way they perceive any changes they may confront. But people are willing to modify their values *if they recognize the need or benefit* of doing so. A supervisor becomes a part of employees' adult environment and can influence attitudes and behavior by appealing to their needs and helping them recognize the benefits associated with particular changes.

How Do Financial Reasons Affect Attitudes Toward Change?

Financial reasons can also influence attitudes toward change. Work, as we know, helps individuals to earn the money necessary to satisfy their basic needs. Uncertainty about the future of their jobs can cause many employees to resist change. For example, new and more efficient processes introduced *with little employee involvement* may be perceived by some employees as threats to their jobs and thus to their primary source of income. Some employees have felt so threatened by such changes that they have attempted to sabotage a new process or product. Such feelings can often be avoided or overcome if the change is introduced by managers with greater sensitivity toward employee needs. We'll be learning about more effective ways to introduce and manage change in a later section of this chapter.

How Do Peers Affect Attitudes Toward Change?

In some workgroups, a high degree of cohesiveness exists. The behavior of individual members within the group is often intended to gain acceptance by the group as a whole. Consequently, even a change initially accepted by one group member may later be rejected because of that person's *desire to be an accepted member of the team.*

How Do Personal Lives Relate to Change?

The effect on employees' *personal lives and social patterns* will also influence their reactions to change. For example, let's take the case of Erik, a young married man with a six-year-old child, who was hired for a sales position without being told that advancement opportunities would exist only if he were willing to relocate to other parts of the country. Erik is ambitious and would like to become a manager, but he is also the type who likes to establish roots in a community. Erik's morale could be negatively affected upon learning that a promotion to a managerial position will only take place if he relocates to another region. He perceives such change as unfairly uprooting his family. His child will have to transfer to a different school, and the entire family will have to leave its friends and cultivate new acquaintances. To some employees, such prospects would be exciting and challenging. To Erik, and many others, they are threatening.

Related to effects on personal life are changes that affect employees' established patterns of job-related social interaction or conversation. For example, a change from bench-work to assembly-line production might have the effect of eliminating the informal communication system that previously existed among the employees, which some workers might resent. Similarly, a loner-type employee might resent a change to worker teams, which require more interaction with peers than he or she desires.

How Do Established Habits Affect Attitudes Toward Change?

Established habits make it difficult for many people to accept change. We all tend to be creatures of habit; it requires far less energy and thought than being a ground-breaker at every opportunity. Habits seem to make life less threatening and more comfortable.

Have you ever noticed how things always seem to have been better in the "good old days"? Sometimes, however, we become so accustomed to doing things in a particular way that we fail to recognize that there may be better ways to do them. New forms, processes, and procedures require expending energy to learn. Once again, employees are likely to resist change unless they recognize the purpose or need for it.

How Does Fear of the Unknown Affect Attitudes Toward Change?

Fear of the unknown is one of the basic reasons for resisting change. Many corporate raiders during the hostile takeover wave of the 1970s and 1980s soon learned about this phenomenon. Employees who had read about the slashing of employment rolls in other companies soon after takeovers became preoccupied about similar cutbacks occurring in their own organizations. Many employees started freshening up their resumés upon learning of a possible hostile takeover of their employer. Employees frequently fear change because they don't understand how the change might affect them; they fear, quite naturally, the unknown. What might you, as a supervisor, do to reduce the effects of such fears?

How Does Failure to Recognize Long-Term Benefits Affect Attitudes Toward Change?

In some instances, employees reject change because of their *failure to recognize its long-term benefits.* To illustrate this point with an example similar to the one used at this chapter's opening, assume that an employee named Demetria has been trained to be proficient in utilizing the *Wordpoint* system of word processing. Demetria's boss, Alice, is also familiar with *Wordpoint,* but has recently discovered a new system called *Edselscriben,* which is much more user-friendly and contains more logical commands. Two objective studies have revealed that office productivity tends to be higher in organizations that utilize *Edselscriben.* Alice has decided to convert to the new system.

Demetria had tremendous difficulties during her first week of using *Edselscriben,* since she was already accustomed to the commands of the other system. Demetria went to Alice and pleaded with her to allow her to continue using *Wordpoint.* Demetria's anxiety with the new system does not let her recognize its long-term benefits, one of which would make her more efficient in her work. Whose responsibility is it to aid her in recognizing long-term benefits? You've got it! It's the supervisor's.

What Are the Typical Reactions to Change?

The organizational life of a supervisor would be much more pleasant if all employees readily accepted change. But that is not the case with most organizations. In reality, there are four possible reactions to change that will be discussed in the section that follows. These are:

1. Refusal
2. Resistance

3. Acquiescence
4. Acceptance

Why Would a Person Refuse to Change?

Refusal exists when organizational members disapprove of a change and attempt to avoid complying with it. Outright refusal tends to result when workers perceive the change as damaging to their personal economic or psychological well being. For example, a New York-based company once decided to close its San Francisco offices as a cost-cutting measure. Key San Francisco personnel were offered comparable positions at the New York location, but many employees refused to accept the change. They were accustomed to West Coast life and did not want to uproot their lives and the lives of their families for an unfamiliar existence on the East Coast. Some of them even accepted lower-paying jobs with firms in the San Francisco area.

Refusal: *An employee reaction that exists when organization members disapprove of a change and, therefore, attempt to avoid complying with it.*

Why Would a Person Resist Change?

Resistance is another common reaction to change. It frequently takes the form of employees merely giving lip service to a particular change. These employees don't openly refuse to accept the change, nor do they necessarily quit their jobs. Instead, they may appear to accept the change but do everything within their power to sabotage its objectives.

Resistance: *Employee reaction that may appear to accept a change while engaging in activities intended to sabotage its objectives.*

For example, a situation existed some years ago in a printing plant that utilized an older form of zinc lithographic printing plates. A newer aluminum type of plate became available, one that reduced preparation time by 80 percent. Employees became highly resistant toward the new process when production managers introduced it, fearing that its use could cost them their jobs.

Platemakers "appeared" to accept the new process. However, workers allowed chemicals to remain on the surface of the plates longer than prescribed, resulting in their malfunctioning when attempts were made to run them on printing presses. A production manager, recognizing employee resistance, decided to apply a different tactic. He called a meeting of the employees and said:

> *"The new aluminum plates are currently being used successfully by our competitors. These plates have also proven to be as high in quality as the old zinc ones. We really have to utilize the new process or all our jobs will be on the line. We are going to lose our customers to our competitors if we can't compete pricewise with them.*
>
> *"The new process is* not *going to reduce the total amount of work you will have for the future. I can assure you that your jobs will not be in jeopardy as a result of this change. In fact, our improved competitive position will probably increase our workloads.*

"What I would like you to do is keep a running record of each plate that goes bad. Also, record your personal opinions as to why the plate malfunctioned. After one month, we'll analyze the results we've had with the new process, and if it appears that it just isn't going to work out, we'll abandon its use. How do you folks feel about that? Are you willing to give it a try?"

Pilot study: *A trial period intended to analyze and enhance the acceptance of a change.*

The production manager's *pilot study* approach seemed to work. A **pilot study** is a trial period intended to analyze and enhance the acceptance of a change. The manager's explanation, the feelings of comfort and security the workers developed from the manager's words, plus the opportunity to take part in an analysis of the new process seemed to melt their resistance. Within the month, employees became accustomed to the new process. They no longer resisted and complained.

Why Would a Person Acquiesce to Change?

Acquiescence: *An employee reaction that exists when an employee passively complies with a change without protest.*

Some organizations have developed a positive climate in which employees tend to maintain a high degree of confidence in managerial decisions. Management has treated workers fairly in the past, job security has generally been satisfactory, and employees have seldom felt threatened by previous changes. In such environments, a certain reaction to change, termed *acquiescence,* is fairly common. **Acquiescence** exists when employees passively comply with a change without protest. Acquiescence does not mean that employees favor the change; it means that they accept the change because they perceive no threat to their well being.

To illustrate, in 1989 employees of Hewlitt-Packard, a high-technology electronics firm situated near San Francisco, California, were called back to work the day after the second-most destructive earthquake in U.S. history had devastated portions of the Bay Area. Two thousand employees were asked for the first time to wear hardhats around their offices and work stations. Although employees were unaccustomed to working fettered by such headgear, they willingly acquiesced because they recognized that management was concerned with their safety.

Why Would a Person Accept Change?

Acceptance: *An employee reaction that exists when an employee feels virtually no threat connected with a proposed change.*

Acceptance is the dream of every change-introducing supervisor. It usually exists when employees feel virtually no threat from the change and readily see how they personally will gain from it. For example, a change in company policy that allows workers to take one-year sabbaticals with pay after they have been employed five or more years would probably not be resisted. Such a change is voluntary and could provide substantial benefit to employees themselves.

How Should Change Be Introduced?

A wise sage once said, "Time changes everything except something within us that is always surprised by change." Since most people quite naturally tend to be "surprised" by or resist change, the manner in which you, as a supervisor, introduce change largely determines how successful your efforts will be. Even changes that are useful—such as new equipment or processes that make jobs easier—tend to be resisted for reasons that we've already discussed. Your efforts in reducing resistance to change, however, should be more effective if you recognize and apply the following concepts:

1. The change should be *necessary.*
2. The supervisor should understand the *employees' feelings and needs.*
3. The change should be *clearly communicated and understood.*
4. The change should involve *employee participation* where possible.
5. The *benefits* should be emphasized.
6. The *timing* of the change should be considered.
7. The changes should take place at a *reasonable pace.*
8. The effects of change should be *followed up and monitored.*

Employee work stations have changed substantially in recent decades. Such changes are accepted more readily by employees who have been prepared for such advances in technology.

Let's now examine each of these concepts separately.

Is the Change Really Necessary?

Have you ever been on the receiving end of what appeared to be change merely for the sake of change? Unless workers are able to see a valid reason for a new situation they will tend to resist it. When introducing change, be certain that your employees understand its utility.

There is another school of thought, however, that suggests that to maintain a dynamic organizational atmosphere, regular changes (even for the sake of change) should be introduced so that employees will be accustomed to change and, as a result, offer less resistance to useful and necessary changes. What's your opinion?

Do You Understand Employees' Feelings and Needs?

You might not perceive proposed changes in the same manner in which your employees will. You should attempt to be empathetic, that is, try to understand how your employees perceive and are likely to react to any change. If the employees are members of a union, you should also consider how union officials might react. Is there any likelihood of their rejecting outright the change or calling for a strike? Attempting to anticipate employee reactions can provide you with some clues for introducing change more effectively.

A change can cause considerable stress and anxiety for affected employees. Consequently, they should have the opportunity to vent their emotions. Attempt to provide your associates with regular opportunities to express their views and to get any negative feelings off their chests. Frequently, the mere opportunity to express oneself removes the obstacle to acceptance.

Has the Change Been Clearly Communicated?

We've indicated earlier that many organizational problems result from ineffective communication. The activity of introducing change especially requires that effective communication takes place. Strong resistance to change frequently occurs in situations where employees don't understand the nature, purpose, and reasons for it. Resistance is also likely in cases where management merely announces a change and expects it immediately to become accepted and followed.

Employees typically want information about impending changes before they will accept them. For example, assume that the current and anticipated demand for your products is so great that your firm has decided to open an additional plant in another region of the country. No changes are proposed for the existing plant. However, rumors might start flying among the workers if no official explanation for opening the new plant is given. They may feel that the existing plant may be closed down and that their jobs will be in jeopardy. You should strive to recognize the need for keeping employees informed of impending changes in order to help stamp out harmful rumors and fears.

Have You Involved Employees in the Change?

We've already learned in Chapter 12 about various styles of leadership. One type discussed was the *participative* style—a leadership technique that involves employees in decision making. A key advantage of employee participation is that it has the tendency to develop greater *commitment* on the part of those involved. This concept especially holds true when introducing change. Employees tend to be more eager to see self-imposed changes succeed than those that appear to be forced on them. Supervisors should attempt to maintain a climate that encourages employees to air their complaints and feelings about proposed changes. Changes usually seem much less threatening when employees can discuss them openly.

Have You Emphasized Benefits?

Supervisors need to "sell" certain ideas to employees. A professional salesperson generally focuses on selling the *benefits* of buying his or her product. The same technique can work for a supervisor. Employees want to know how *they* are going to benefit, not just how the company is going to gain. For example, a new rule requiring employees to wear safety goggles is likely to have *less* impact if you stress that fewer accidents will result in lower insurance costs *for the company.* A more effective approach is to stress *how the employee will benefit* through reduced injuries, less work time lost, and perhaps even higher wages if insurance costs are reduced. To get people to accept change, you should try diligently to show how those affected by the change are likely to benefit.

Have You Considered the Timing of the Change?

You should attempt to choose a good time for introducing change. Doing so is not an easy task, since there may be no perfect time to introduce a modification of the work environment. In announcing upcoming layoffs, for example, would it be better to inform employees just before or after the Christmas holidays? Would it be advisable to announce a reduction in employee benefits at the same time a union is seeking certification of your employees? Are there certain problems that should be ironed out before introducing new equipment or processes to your department? Many factors should be considered in choosing the best time to introduce change. Your efforts are likely to be more effective when they have the least amount of competition from other forces.

Have Changes Been Introduced at a Reasonable Pace?

Too much change introduced at too fast a pace can be overwhelming and create tension and frustration in some employees. As a result, change should be introduced at a rate that can be comprehended and accepted by employees. Try to be patient with employees who must learn new methods. Some employees need more time than others to become accustomed to new processes. Knowing your associates well can make it easier to understand how much change they can accept and absorb in a given period of time.

Have You Followed Up and Monitored the Effects of the Change?

Chapter 4 discussed the need for planning and establishing goals. These activities are especially important when attempting to introduce change. The only way to determine if your changes are effective is to compare their outcomes with your originally established objectives.

Keep in mind that after change is introduced, circumstances sometimes get worse before they get better. People, of course, need some time to learn new ways and to adapt to new conditions. Nor should you expect results to always be achieved precisely as you planned. Allow some leeway for cost differentials and other surprise factors that might occur.

Summary

Many people react defensively to *change* because of the effect it has on their equilibrium. Among the reasons people tend to resist change are their *past experiences,* the *economic effects of the change, reaction of peers, effect on personal lives, habit, fear of the unknown,* and the *failure to recognize the long-run benefits* of change.

Typical reactions to change include *refusal, resistance, acquiescence,* and *acceptance.*

Efforts at administering change tend to be more effective when the following concepts are considered: the change is *necessary, employee feelings and needs are considered,* the change is *communicated clearly, employee participation* is encouraged, *benefits* are emphasized, *timing* and *pace* are acceptable, and *follow up* and *monitoring* occur.

Questions for Discussion

1. Evaluate the following statement: "Everybody likes change. I don't think there's anyone who doesn't look forward to the *new* and *different.*"
2. Why do employees tend to have a *natural resistance* to change?
3. Assume that a radical reorganization of your department is necessary. What are some major factors and techniques that

should be considered in administering necessary changes with a *minimum of upset to employees?*

4. Express in your own words the meaning of this statement: "The certainty of misery is better than the misery of uncertainty."
5. How do *past experiences* of individuals influence the way they respond to change?
6. Why might a group member who favors a particular change resist it because *other participants* are opposed to the change?
7. What are some of the likely consequences of a supervisor's failure to understand the *feelings and needs of employees* when attempting to introduce change?
8. What is a major benefit that results from *involving employees* in the change process?
9. Why does emphasizing how the company alone will benefit tend to have little effect on reducing employee resistance to change?
10. In what ways are *timing* and *pace* significant in introducing change?

Can You Define These Terms?

Instructions: Write a definition for each of the following terms. You may check your definitions with those provided in the end-of-text glossary.

change
refusal
resistance
pilot study
acquiescence
acceptance

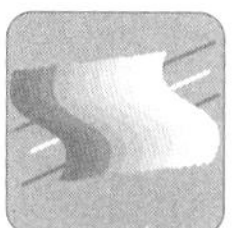

Supervision In Action

14–1 Not Ready for Change

Until about three years ago, the Exxar Company's products always enjoyed a price advantage over the products of its competitors. Unfortunately, much of Exxar's equipment was aging and no longer able to produce its product line as competitively as in the past. Obsolescent equipment, coupled with increasing competition from Asian companies, had resulted in a rapid decline in the company's share of the market until the decision was made two months ago to switch over part of its operations to a new semi-automated system that makes partial use of robots in the production system. Within six months, all of Exxar's operations will be converted to the new system. Sales volume has already increased steadily, so there seems to be little likelihood of any layoffs.

Recently, Bob Wilson, production supervisor, noticed a significant change in the behavior of Ron Cook, one of his older employees. Ron's attitude seems to have soured since the system changeover, and he has made an inordinate number of mistakes recently. During a meeting between the two this morning, Ron told Bob that the mistakes were due to shortcomings in the new system. Ron further stated that the new system will never work and should be disbanded. Bob responded to Ron's remarks by telling him that he suspects that Ron is trying to sabotage the new system. Bob added that Ron's job will be on the line if he doesn't "get his act together soon."

Questions

1. What, in your opinion, might account for the recent changes in Ron's performance?
2. What is your evaluation of Bob's supervisory approach with Ron during the meeting? What would you have done differently?
3. What might Bob have done months ago to have possibly prevented his current problem with Ron?

14–2 The Effects of Too Much Change

Change—whether perceived as good or bad—tends to produce stress in an individual, according to Thomas Holmes, Professor of Psychiatry at the University of Washington at Seattle. Holmes also contends that too many changes coming too close together may produce physical illness or mental depression.

RATING LIFE CHANGES

Life Event	Value	Mine
Death of spouse	100	_____
Divorce	73	_____
Marital separation	65	_____
Jail term	63	_____
Death of a close family member	63	_____
Personal injury or illness	53	_____
Marriage	50	_____
Fired at work	47	_____
Marital reconciliation	45	_____
Retirement	45	_____
Change in health of family member	44	_____
Pregnancy of a family member	40	_____
Sex difficulties	39	_____
Gain of a new family member	39	_____
Change in financial state	38	_____
Death of a close friend	37	_____
Change to different line of work	36	_____
Change in number of arguments with spouse	35	_____
Mortgage over $100,000	31	_____
Foreclosure of mortgage or loan	30	_____
Change in responsibilities at work	29	_____
Son or daughter leaving home	29	_____
Trouble with in-laws	29	_____
Outstanding personal achievement	28	_____
Spouse beginning or stopping work	26	_____
Beginning or ending school	26	_____
Change in living conditions	25	_____
Revision of personal habits	24	_____
Trouble with boss	23	_____
Change in work hours or conditions	20	_____
Change in residence	20	_____
Change in schools	20	_____
Change in recreation	19	_____
Change in religious activities	19	_____
Change in social activities	18	_____
Mortgage or loan of less than $100,000	17	_____
Change in sleeping habits	16	_____
Change in frequency of family get-togethers	15	_____
Change in eating habits	15	_____
Vacation	13	_____
Christmas	12	_____
Minor violations of the law	11	_____
Total		_____

Holmes developed a tool for measuring the values of changes that can affect people. If enough occur within a year, and exceed a value of 300, Holmes suggests that there could be trouble ahead. Holmes' study showed that 80 percent of the people whose value totals exceeded 300 became pathologically depressed, had heart attacks, or developed other serious problems. Of those scoring between 150 and 300, 53 percent had similar experiences, as did 33 percent of those scoring up to 150.

Look at the life events listed in the previous chart. Check the ones that relate to you and add up their total values. A word of caution, however: There is an inherent danger built in to an exercise of this nature. You may feel just great before doing it, and then become depressed solely because your score indicates that you should be depressed. Regardless, the exercise helps you to know yourself somewhat better. If your score is high, maybe your lifestyle could stand a bit of modification.

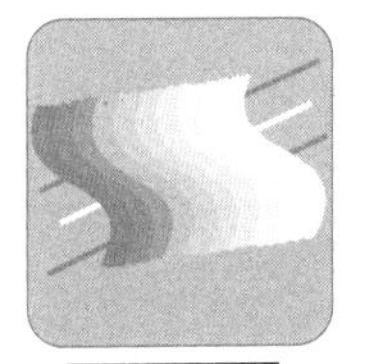

Part Five

Problems, Challenges and the Supervisor

Chapter 15

Labor Relations and the Grievance Procedure

Employees don't vote for labor unions; they vote as a protest against management.
—***Stephen J. Cabot***

Managers are often surprised to learn that the primary concern of employees—and often the major reason for unionization—is not benefits and wages but their ability to resolve problems.
—***Charles W. Eisemann***

Learning Objectives

When you finish this chapter, you should be able to:

1. Identify the major labor legislation that supervisors should understand.
2. Review the supervisor's role in the unionization process.
3. Describe how collective bargaining works.
4. Express the supervisor's role in the formal grievance procedure.
5. Explain how grievances are handled in nonunion organizations.
6. Discuss how grievances are handled in public organizations.

First person's singular attitude: *"You know what's wrong with this country? Unions! That's what. We lost our competitive edge in the world because of them. They're on their way down now, and to that I say,* good riddance*!"*

Second person's singular attitude: *"Unions aren't what's wrong with this country! It's employers who don't give a hoot about the workers. Sure! Go ahead and be happy about the declining percentage of the work force in unions, and maybe one day you, too, will get paid $10,000 a year less than a union worker!"*

Whew! Fairly strong views, aren't they? *Unions*—this a word that seems to create an immediate, and sometimes highly emotional, reaction in the minds of individuals who hear it. In general, people's opinions tend to be predisposed and polarized about unions; that is, people are usually on one or the other side of the fence when it comes to supporting or resisting unions. The battle has become increasingly heated in recent years, as evidenced by some nonunion employers sending their managers to "preventive labor relations" seminars for the purpose of learning how to discourage unions from gaining footholds in their plants and offices.

Are Unions on Their Way Out?

According to the Bureau of Labor Statistics, union membership as a percentage of the total U.S. work force has declined from 25.5 percent in 1975 to about 16 percent in 1990 (see Figure 15–1). Statistics, of course, don't always tell the entire story. Membership *in absolute terms has actually grown* in many of the larger unions. However, the trend toward increased proportions of the work force employed in service and high technology industries—both areas that have not yet become extensively unionized—has had a significant effect on the declining percentage of union membership in recent years.

"Which side are *you* on?" are some of the words found in an old labor union song. In reality, however, choosing sides is less beneficial than recognizing that unions are likely to continue to exert a significant influence over the workplace in certain industries for some time to come. For example, the National Education Association alone has about 2 million members and 12,000 affiliates. The International Brotherhood of Teamsters Union has 700 locals and about 1.6 million members. The United Food and Commercial Workers Union has 600 locals and about 1.3 million members. The six largest unions in the United States have more than 1 million members each. Twenty-seven unions have more than 200,000

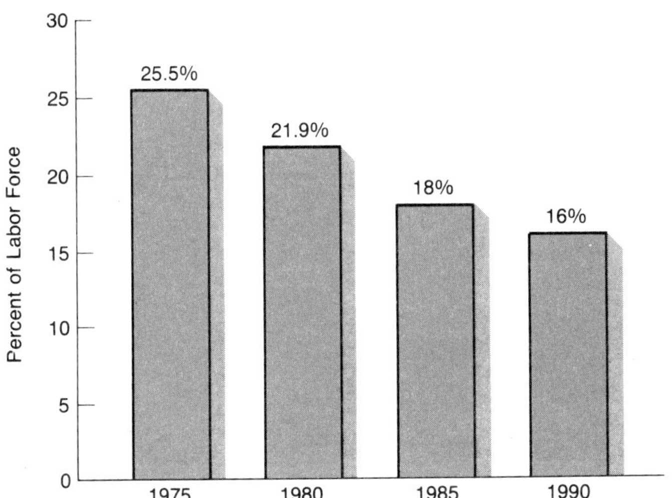

FIGURE 15–1
U.S. Union Membership, 1975–1990

Source: Bureau of Labor Statistics.

members each.[1] A Roper Poll completed in July 1988 indicated that the number of respondents who indicated "great confidence" or "fair confidence" in union leaders had risen to 59 percent, up from 50 percent in 1984 and only 48 percent in 1977.[2]

Do Supervisors Still Have to Be Concerned about Unions?

Although union influence is unquestionably down somewhat from its historical highs, unions don't seem to be out quite yet. Supervisors continue to need an understanding of the nature of unions, collective bargaining, and grievance procedures. Supervisors are a critical link between the managers who negotiate bargaining agreements and the employees who expect to be served by their elected union officials. Consequently, supervisors should attempt to understand the nature and objectives of unions. A "we versus them" attitude tends to accelerate conflict between representatives of management and labor, each side typically losing to some degree. Cooperation, understanding, and compromise, on the other hand, tend to be far less costly to both parties over time.

The purpose of the first portion of this chapter, therefore, is to assist you in acquiring the skills and knowledge necessary to work effectively with employees who are union members. The latter part of the chapter will deal with another important aspect of employee relations—the supervisor's role in the area of grievance procedures.

What Actually Is a Union?

Union:
Association of workers formed to improve conditions related to employment.

A **union** can be defined as *an association of workers whose major objective is the improvement of employment conditions.* Some groups refer to themselves as *associations* rather than unions, but their goals usually parallel those of unions.

Why Do People Join Unions?

Why have more than 20 million workers felt inclined to join unions and associations? Of course, no single reason exists. Different workers have distinct motives and needs. As we learned in Chapter 11, individuals with unsatisfied needs tend to behave in a manner that is intended to achieve satisfaction. Many employees believe their needs are more likely to be satisfied through *collective,* rather than *individual,* efforts. Table 15–1 summarizes the major reasons why workers join unions.

● What Key Labor Legislation Should Supervisors Understand?

Unions have been around the United States in one form or another for about 200 years. Their beginnings can be traced to 1792, when a local union was formed in Philadelphia by cordwainers (shoemakers). Although the Philadelphia group disbanded in less than a year, the idea caught on. Within 10 years, unions of shoemakers, carpenters, and printers sprang up in Baltimore, Boston, New York, and other cities situated mostly along the Atlantic seaboard.

Unions had anything but smooth sailing until the 1930s. The period prior to the 1930s has been called the "repressive phase" of the labor movement. Most judges came from wealthy backgrounds, and, as a result, tended to favor the establishment of the time. Union leaders argued that some of the rights of the establishment should belong to the working class. The courts, however, didn't agree and customarily ruled against labor on conspiracy grounds. Without labor legislation to aid them, union efforts aimed at acquiring the right for workers to bargain collectively with their

TABLE 15–1
Major Reasons Why Workers Join Unions

- *To secure certain types of employment.* Some industries traditionally employ only individuals willing to maintain union membership.
- *To ensure fair treatment of workers.* Working conditions, hours and duties, safety measures, and grievance procedures are usually negotiated for employees and made into a formal contractual agreement.
- *To improve economic situations.* Unions usually seek higher wages, employee benefits, and job security.
- *To gain power.* Unions typically have greater bargaining strength than do individuals.
- *To satisfy social needs.* The desire to be accepted by peers who are members of the union may encourage union membership.

employers were generally thwarted by the courts. For example, legislation originally intended to prevent excessive concentration of economic control by "big business"—the Sherman Anti-Trust Act of 1890—was used to restrict union organizing efforts. Union activity was even considered un-American by many people until the severe depression of the 1930s.

The depression, with unemployment approaching 25 percent of the labor force, caused public attitudes to shift away from business and toward labor unions. With the 1932 election of Franklin D. Roosevelt (himself a person from an enormously wealthy background), the pendulum swung quickly to a side favoring the formation of unions in the private sector of the U.S. economy. Since that period, some significant pieces of legislation affecting unions have been passed. Supervisors should be aware of their major purposes.

What Did the Norris-LaGuardia Act Do?

The **Norris-LaGuardia Act of 1932** was considered one of the outstanding legislative victories for labor. Its principal intent was to regulate court injunctions against unions. The act made it more difficult for employers to use injunctions to prevent work stoppages by employees. It also made the **yellow dog contract** illegal. Previously, the contract, which was sometimes forced on employees by management, made union membership illegal under the penalty of discharge.

Norris-LaGuardia Act of 1932: *Act outlawing yellow-dog contracts and restricting use of injunctions against unions.*

Yellow-dog contract: *Forced agreement prohibiting employees from joining a union as a condition of employment.*

What Was the Purpose of the Wagner Act (National Labor Relations Act of 1935)?

In 1935, an act sometimes referred to as the "Magna Carta of organized labor" was passed, resulting in a period that could be termed labor's "supportive phase." Popularly known as the **Wagner Act,** but officially termed the **National Labor Relations Act of 1935,** the legislation required employers to recognize and negotiate with unions chosen by a majority of their employees. Management or court interference with the efforts of unions to organize workers became illegal. Supervisors of the 1930s suddenly had to reevaluate their approach to managing human resources.

Wagner Act (National Labor Relations Act of 1935): *Act providing employees with the right to engage in collective bargaining.*

Section 7 of the Wagner Act conveys its basic philosophy:

> *Employees shall have the right to self-organization, to form, join, or assist labor organizations, to bargain collectively through representatives of their own choosing, and to engage in concerted activities for the purpose of collective bargaining or other mutual aid or protection.*

A **National Labor Relations Board (NLRB)** was established to supervise union elections and to ensure that management avoided unfair labor practices.

National Labor Relations Board (NLRB): *Government agency established to enforce the Wagner Act.*

Why Was the Taft-Hartley Act (Labor-Management Relations Act of 1947) Passed?

Public sentiment shifted dramatically away from unions during the mid-1940s as a result of the many work stoppages that occurred shortly after the end of World War II. In 1946 alone, about *113 million worker days* were lost because of the wave of strikes that plagued the United States. (By contrast, there were fewer than *4.5 million* worker days lost in 1988 from work stoppages.) Key industries, such as coal and public utilities, were paralyzed during portions of 1946.

Those who were elected to Congress in November of 1946 sensed a public attitude favoring restrictive labor legislation. As a result, on June 23, 1947 (over President Harry Truman's veto) the **Taft-Hartley Act,** or **Labor Management Relations Act of 1947,** became law. Needless to say, union supporters were upset and immediately branded Taft-Hartley the "Slave Labor Relations Act." The underlying purpose of Taft-Hartley was for employers to regain some of the power they had lost under the Wagner Act. Basically, the Taft-Hartley Act defines and prohibits certain unfair labor practices on the part of unions. It also provides a countervailing balance to the Wagner Act by requiring labor to bargain in good faith with management. (Table 15–2 summarizes the principal types of union "shops.")

Taft-Hartley Act (Labor Management Relations Act of 1947): *Legislation prohibiting unions from engaging in certain unfair labor practices.*

What Are "Right-to-Work" Laws?

Section 14b of the Taft-Hartley Act contains a controversial provision. It permits states themselves to outlaw **union shop** contracts, thus allowing states to pass **"right-to-work" laws.** The legislation is referred to as "right-to-work" because it enables employees to maintain a job without the requirement of joining a union. The laws have the effect of reducing the bargaining strength of unions, since employees cannot be required to join a union within a certain period after being employed. Union officials often angrily point out that workers earn less in states where the union shop is prohibited under "right-to-work" laws.[3]

Union shop: *Agreement requiring all employees to join the union within a specified period of time.*

"Right-to-work" laws: *State laws prohibiting the requirement that employees join a union or pay union dues to obtain a job.*

Why Was the Landrum-Griffin Act (Labor Management Reporting and Disclosure Act) Passed?

Congress became quite concerned during the 1950s with alleged union official racketeering. After a prolonged investigation of possible union corruption and misuse of funds, Congress passed another restrictive act related to unions—the **Landrum-Griffin Act (Labor Management Reporting and Disclosure Act of 1959)**— as an amendment to the Taft-Hartley Act. The Landrum-Griffin Act requires unions to provide detailed reports to the Department of Labor related to financial and nonfinancial activities. Regularly scheduled elections of officers by secret ballot are also required of unions. The law also makes it illegal for any payments to be

Landrum-Griffin Act (Labor Management Reporting and Disclosure Act of 1959): *Act restricting the use of union funds by union officials.*

TABLE 15–2
Principal Types of Union "Shops"

- *Closed shop*—Only union members may be hired. The closed shop is not permitted by either the Taft-Hartley Act or "right-to-work" laws.
- *Union shop*—All workers hired by the employer must join the union within a specified time after they are hired. The union shop is permitted by the Taft-Hartley Act, but is outlawed by the "right-to-work" laws.
- *Agency shop*—Workers may or may not join the union. If they choose not to join, they must pay the union an amount that represents expenses associated only with collective bargaining activities.
- *Maintenance of membership*—Workers who are union members when the union-management agreement is signed, and nonmembers who join the union later, must remain members of the union for the duration of the contract. Maintenance of membership agreements are permitted by the Taft-Hartley Act, but are outlawed by the "right-to-work" laws.

made to union officials other than their usual salaries. The personal use of union funds by union officials is also restricted.

What Is the Unionization Process?

Supervisors should be familiar with the **unionization process,** which basically consists of two broad areas:

Unionization process: *Activities associated with organizing nonunion employees and bargaining for union employees.*

1. Attempts at *union organizing* intended to encourage employees to join a union
2. Activities associated with *collective bargaining* related to organizations that already have union representation of employees

How Is the Supervisor Involved in the Unionization Process?

Supervisors vary in the extent of their involvement in the collective bargaining process, the second item above. They are, however, highly instrumental in the decision that employees make whether to vote for or against union representation in organizations where no union currently exists. Employees' attitudes toward their jobs are significantly influenced by how they feel toward their supervisors and toward all levels of management. Attempts at union organizing have seldom proven successful in organizations where employees felt completely satisfied with their jobs and working conditions. An important point to keep in mind is that unions have achieved their most successful results at organizing in situations where communication is poor between management and employees, where inequities exist regarding promotions, and where management seems unconcerned with employee problems and needs.

What Can a Supervisor Do and Not Do During a Union Organizing Campaign?

How do unions get started in an organization? The pressure to begin the unionization process may have built up inside and been derived from existing employee discontent. Or union representatives may have initiated contact with employees of an organization for the purpose of attempting to uncover specific areas of employee dissatisfaction.

You and other managers may learn of attempts at unionization either from the grapevine or from union literature—leaflets and brochures that are intended to promote the union's point of view. As a supervisor, you must be extremely prudent in your comments and actions during organizing campaigns.

Certain provisions of the Wagner Act prohibit unfair labor practices. For example, you cannot attempt to coerce or threaten an employee regarding his or her interest in joining a union. It is generally advisable for supervisors to carefully weigh the implications of anything they do or say during an organizing campaign. Be especially certain during a union organizing drive to avoid any activities that may be considered illegal. Table 15–3 lists certain activities that are considered illegal under the Wagner Act.

Under the "free speech" provision of the Taft-Hartley Act, managers can communicate with employees about the unionization drive provided they offer no rewards or threats to employees. You can likewise correct any false statements that might have been made by union officials. You can also require that organizing activities take place during nonworking hours if they interfere with the conduct of normal work activities. The National Association of Manufacturers has compiled a comprehensive list of things supervisors *cannot do* in situations arising before union representation takes place (See Table 15–4).

Authorization cards: *Cards that, when signed by employees, indicate their desire to vote for union representation.*

During the early stages of unionization, a union attempts to get **authorization cards** signed by at least 30 percent of the employees in the organizational unit it wants to represent. After securing the necessary number of authorization cards, the union can petition

TABLE 15–3
Activities Considered Illegal for Management to Engage in during a Union Organizing Drive

- Threats, physical interference, or violent behavior toward union organizers
- Interfering with employees involved in the organization drive
- Disciplining or discharging employees for pro-union activities
- Spying on employees' union activities

TABLE 15–4
Guidelines for Supervisors (from a leaflet prepared by the National Association of Manufacturers)
(*continued on next page*)

What You as a Supervisor *Cannot* Do

- Promise employees a pay increase, promotion, betterment, benefit, or special favor if they stay out of the union or vote against it
- Threaten loss of jobs, reduction of income, discontinuance of privileges or benefits presently enjoyed, or use intimidating language that may be designed to influence an employee in the exercise of his or her right to belong, or refrain from belonging, to a union
- Threaten or actually discharge, discipline, or lay off an employee because of his or her activities on behalf of the union
- Threaten, through a third party, any of the foregoing acts of interference
- Threaten to close or move the plant or to drastically reduce operations if a union is selected as a representative
- Spy on union meetings (Parking across the street from a union hall to watch employees entering the hall would be suspect.)
- Conduct yourself in a way that would indicate to the employees that you are watching them to determine whether or not they are participating in union activities
- Discriminate against employees actively supporting the union by intentionally assigning them undesirable work
- Transfer employees prejudicially because of union affiliation
- Engage in any partiality favoring nonunion employees over employees active on behalf of the union
- Discipline or penalize employees actively supporting a union for an infraction that nonunion employees are permitted to commit without being likewise disciplined
- Make any work assignment for the purpose of causing an employee who has been active on behalf of the union to quit his or her job
- Take any action that is intended to impair the status of or adversely affect an employee's job or pay because of his or her activity on behalf of the union
- Intentionally assign work or transfer personnel so that those active on behalf of the union are separated from those you believe are not interested in supporting a union
- Select employees to be laid off with the intention of curbing the union's strength or to discourage affiliation with it
- Ask employees to express their thoughts about a union or its officers
- Ask employees how they intend to vote
- Ask employees at time of hiring or anytime after whether they belong to a union or have signed a union application or authorization card

TABLE 15–4
(*Continued*)

- Ask employees about the internal affairs of unions such as meetings, etc. (Some employees may, of their own accord, walk up and tell of such matters. It is not an unfair labor practice to listen, but you must not ask questions to obtain additional information.)
- Make a statement that you will not deal with the union
- Make statements to the employees to the effect that they will be discharged or disciplined if they are active on behalf of the union
- Urge employees to try to persuade others to oppose the union or stay out of it
- Prevent employees from soliciting union memberships during their free time on company premises so long as such does not interfere with work being performed by others
- Give financial support or assistance to a union, its representatives, or employees
- Visit the homes of employees for the purpose of urging them to reject the union
- Make speeches to massed assemblies of employees on company time within the 24-hour period before the opening of polls for a representation election
- Speak to an employee in your office or the office of some other management official about the union campaign and urge him or her to vote against the union (Remember—the best place to talk to employees about such matters is at their work stations or in work areas where other employees are present.)
- Help employees to withdraw union memberships
- Ask employees about the identity of the instigator or leader of employees favoring the union

Certification election: *Election officially recognizing a union as the legal bargaining representative of employees.*

Decertification election: *Election resulting in the elimination of a union as the legal bargaining representative of employees.*

Collective bargaining: *Negotiation between management and labor representatives to establish a written agreement.*

the National Labor Relations Board (NLRB), or any other appropriate agency, for the right to hold a **certification election.**

If an election is held and the union receives a majority vote, the election proceedings are then reviewed by the NLRB or an appropriate agency. The union is then certified to be the official bargaining agent for the employees. A majority vote, by the way, means a majority of those *voting* in the election, not necessarily the majority of total employees in the work unit.

If a group of employees who already belong to a union feel that they no longer desire to be represented by it, they can utilize a similar election process called a **decertification election**.

How Does Collective Bargaining Work?

Another phase of the unionization process is that of **collective bargaining,** which is the process of negotiation between representatives of management and labor for the purpose of establishing a written agreement with a minimum of conflict. The negotiators attempt to reach agreement on wages, fringe benefits, working conditions, and other matters of their choosing. The written contract is legally binding on both the employer and the employees. Both sides are expected to approach the bargaining sessions in good faith after each has engaged in extensive research into the strengths and weaknesses of the other's bargaining position.

Supervisors generally are not directly involved in the bargaining process, although they should be aware of the issues to be negotiated. Supervisors may be asked by representatives of management to provide statistical or other information to assist them during negotiations.

What Topics Are Typically Covered in Collective Bargaining Negotiations?

Demands by union representatives during contract negotiations are quite diversified and sophisticated, ranging from automatic cost-of-living wage increases (*COLAs*) to prepaid group legal services and paid time off for celebrating one's own birthday.

Collective bargaining agreements vary from firm to firm and from industry to industry. Table 15–5 summarizes the provisions included in the typical labor-management collective bargaining contract.

When Is the Collective Bargaining Process Over?

Although formal negotiations usually take place only once a year, or sometimes once every two to three years, supervisors should recognize that the bargaining process is not complete merely because the formal contract has been drawn up by the lawyers and signed by the representatives of labor and management. Interpretation of the terms of the agreement takes place year-round. Keep in mind that the contract is merely a set of symbols. Although the wording should be as precise and clear as possible, the contract

TABLE 15–5
Provisions Included in the Typical Collective Bargaining Agreement

- Union recognition
- Management rights
- Grievance procedures and arbitration
- Disciplinary procedures
- Wages
- Insurance and employee benefit programs
- Hours of work and overtime
- Health and safety
- Discrimination provisions
- Employee job rights and seniority
- Contract duration

has been prepared by human beings and is interpreted by human beings. Not all human beings apply the same meaning to the same symbols.

Representatives of both management and workers have significant responsibilities. Supervisors must strive to understand the intended meaning of the contract and be able to communicate it convincingly to employees. Union representatives, too, have similar responsibilities to make certain that union members understand the terms of the contract. Conflict and strife are far more likely without effective communication and understanding. Each party has far more to gain than lose in an atmosphere of open communication and mutual trust.

Grievances, a topic covered in the following section, are often the result of different interpretations of the collective bargaining agreement. The cost of some types of conflict can be enormous. Some work stoppages, for example, have cost disputing parties millions of dollars in sales and profits and thousands of dollars in lost wages and benefits. The conflict can also hurt the public by causing garbage to pile up on the streets, transportation systems to be disrupted, burials temporarily made impossible, and fire or police protection to cease.

Collective bargaining is the process of negotiation between representatives of management and the workers. Effective negotiations tend to result in fewer employee grievances.

What Should a Supervisor Know About Grievance Procedures?

Collective bargaining agreements are legal documents and, as such, are enforceable by law. However, disputes over the interpretation of contents can erupt at any time, although carefully worded and clearly communicated agreements can lessen the frequency of such differences. Such disputes are termed **grievances,** which can be defined as a dispute over the interpretation of a collective bargaining agreement. Grievances are complaints, sometimes valid, sometimes invalid, that employees have about their employment situations.

Grievances: *Complaints by employees who feel that they have been treated unfairly.*

Most contracts include grievance procedures that cover all employees within the bargaining unit. Such procedures can substantially enhance industrial relations by providing a safety valve for tensions arising in disputes between managers and their employees. Of course, supervisors should continually strive to keep abreast of the procedures covered by the contract.

What Are the Formal Steps in the Typical Grievance Procedure?

Grievance procedures are not standardized in all collective bargaining contracts, but they do follow a similar pattern between three to five steps, as illustrated in Figure 15–2.

A concerned and sensitive supervisor is usually able to handle most grievances in a somewhat informal manner before they begin the arduous journey through the formal grievance pathway. Unfortunately, there may be instances in which you—the supervisor—and the employee just can't see eye to eye. In such instances, the first step in the formal grievance procedure typically involves a third party—the **union steward** (or **shop steward**)—who joins the aggrieved employee in discussions with you. Although the steward is also an employee of the same organization as the complaining worker, he or she is elected by union members or appointed by union officials to represent employees in their disputes with management.

Union (shop) steward: *A designated employee who assists other employees with unresolved complaints.*

During sessions with the steward, the supervisor should attempt to employ the various concepts of effective leadership that have been discussed in earlier chapters. For example, don't let the steward, who may feel the need to come on quite aggressively to impress his or her "client"—the employee—cause you to lose your temper. Also be certain that you are standing on firm ground by being familiar with contract provisions as well as company policies and rules. Be firm, but also fair, by expressing your concern and understanding of the employee's point of view. Be sure to listen, which can work wonders in helping to diffuse emotional situations. Try to settle the grievance amicably without having to involve the time and expense of proceeding to higher steps in the grievance mechanism. Also, remember to *document*—that is, maintain ac-

FIGURE 15–2
Typical Steps Followed in a Grievance Procedure

1. Steward and worker take it up with supervisor.

5. Arbitration.

2. Chief steward takes it up with department head or superintendent.

4. International union representative meets with director of human resources or corporate officer.

3. Union-management grievance committees confer.

curate records on the outcome of the grievance procedure—for future reference.

The next step in the grievance procedure usually involves a discussion between the union's *chief steward* and the supervisor's manager. Tensions may mount as a complaint rises in the grievance hierarchy. In some instances, the second stage is omitted altogether and higher-level conferences take place.

What Are the Differences between Mediation and Arbitration?

Mediation:
Use of an impartial third party who assists opposing sides in reconciling a dispute.

If representatives of management and the grievant cannot settle the dispute within a specified period of time, they may then submit the complaint to either *mediation* or *arbitration.* **Mediation** utilizes the services of a disinterested third party, called a *mediator,* who is someone not directly affiliated with the company or the union. The mediator attempts to *bring together* the two sides involved in a dispute in an effort to effect a *compromise.* The mediator has no binding authority—he or she can only *suggest* solutions for resolving the dispute. The term *mediation* is frequently used interchangeably with *conciliation.* In some instances, mediation is distinguished from conciliation, the latter being merely an *attempt to bring the two sides together,* and mediation offering specific *compromise solutions.*

In some cases, **arbitration** may take place instead of mediation. Arbitration involves a person, called an *arbitrator,* who performs a function similar to that of a mediator but acts more like a judge in the dispute. The arbitrator ***makes a binding decision*** for the disputing parties based on his or her interpretation of the facts. Both parties involved in the conflict agree in advance to accept as binding whatever decision is made. Arbitration is considered *voluntary* when both parties agree to submit disputed issues to it, and is *compulsory* if required by law.

Arbitration:
Use of an impartial third party to develop binding decisions during management-labor disputes.

How Are Grievances Handled in Nonunion Organizations?

The grievance procedures outlined above are quite typical among private firms whose employees are represented by unions. Similar formalized procedures can also be utilized by firms that are not unionized, but in many companies no such "official" procedures exist.

Employee dissatisfaction and discontent need some sort of "safety valve" for releasing pent-up tensions and frustrations. A formal grievance procedure aids substantially as a means for venting negative employee feelings and provides higher levels of management with opportunities to become better aware of employee sentiments. However, because fewer workers have union protection today against unfair management practices, more and more nonunion employees are looking to the courts for protection against arbitrary management decisions. Most states have now passed laws, comparable to those that have long existed in Western Europe, that reduce the employer's ability to fire employees for little or no reason.[4]

There are five general types of grievance systems used by nonunion organizations.[5] These are:

1. Open-door policies
2. Ombudsperson
3. Peer decisions
4. Hearing officers
5. Binding outside arbitration

How Is an Open-Door Policy Used for Grievances?

A typical grievance procedure in a nonunion organization (sometimes informally stated, rather than official policy) is an "open door" to senior management, in which disgruntled employees allegedly have open access to air their gripes to their own manager or their manager's manager.

As humanistic as it may appear, there are many dangers inherent in this system. An employee's boss who is the actual cause of the employee's grievance may find it difficult to be objective when speaking with his or her own boss about the dispute. Further, a "bypass approach" (i.e., an open door to the manager's manager) tends to abuse some of the sound principles of professional management discussed in earlier chapters, such as the scalar (chain-of-command) and exception (delegation) principles. Especially important is the negative effect on supervisors' attitudes that may develop if their bosses usurp their authority and make decisions for them. In addition, a supervisor can easily lose face with the members of his or her department under such circumstances. A major point of our discussion, therefore, is that employing an open-door policy as *the* grievance procedure must be done with caution; it generally is not as effective as the formalized types of procedures already discussed.

How Is an Ombudsperson Used for Grievances?

Employee counselors: *Staff individuals who assist employees with their problems and complaints.*

Ombudsperson: *An objective third party who assists employees with grievances.*

Some organizations use **employee counselors** for the purpose of assisting employees with their problems and complaints. For example, Xerox Corporation has employed a person with the title of Employee Relations Manager to act as a company **ombudsperson,** with whom employees have the opportunity to discuss their gripes and problems in confidence.

Counselors are in the position to discover morale problems early. A snag can develop, however, if management regards the counselor as a source of information about employees, and the word gets out that he or she is a management "lap-dog" or spy. Counselors quickly lose effectiveness when employees distrust them.

How Are Peer Decisions Used for Grievances?

Peer decisions: *Solutions to grievances recommended by a jury of employees and managers.*

In some organizations, grievances are handled by **peer decisions.** In such cases, a panel or review board is established and consists of employees and managers whose function is to recommend solutions for grievances. The peer decisions are typically not binding, and panel members often lack expertise in human resource management matters. Consequently, many of such panels' recommendations are of poor quality, and management hesitates to enforce the panel's recommendation, which causes the panel to lose credibility with employees.

How Are Hearing Officers Used for Grievances?

Hearing officers: *Human resource management specialists who listen to and rule on employee grievances.*

Larger organizations sometimes employ full-time **hearing officers,** whose function is to listen to employee grievances and make fair and impartial rulings on them. Such persons are typically experienced human resource management specialists assigned to a personnel department. To be effective, they must have the confidence of company employees.

How Is Binding Outside Arbitration Used for Grievances?

Nonunion companies can follow the same practice as union organizations and utilize the services of outside arbitrators. However, **binding outside arbitration** is not commonly used in nonunionized companies because of the expense and inconvenience. Many managers prefer to avoid this procedure because of its identification with union situations.

Binding outside arbitration: *The use of an outside party to settle disputes in nonunion organizations.*

How Are Grievances Handled in Public Organizations?

Much has changed in the area of employee relations in the public sector over the past few decades. Union membership in the public sector was quite sparse during the first half of the century. Many of the collective bargaining rights extended to employees of private firms were not provided for government employees. In fact, prior to 1970 government employees were not allowed to strike, thus preventing the use of one of the unions' most powerful weapons.

The unrest and militancy accompanying civil rights movements spread to the public sector during the 1960s. For the first time, large cities experienced strikes among teachers, sanitation workers, firefighters, and police. Air traffic controllers called in "sick." Reflecting the mood of the times, in January 1962, President John F. Kennedy issued Executive Order No. 10988, which, for the first time, extended to federal employees the right to bargain collectively. Remember that employees of private companies had been given that right about 30 years earlier. However, a different attitude had existed for government employees. The earlier philosophy, in general, was that government employees were "public servants," a concept originating from the relationships that ancient European kings had with their subjects. To allow public employees the right to bargain collectively—and especially the right to strike—was traditionally believed to be contrary to society's interest and security.

But change continued to take place. On October 29, 1969, President Richard M. Nixon issued Executive Order No. 11491, which established a **Federal Labor Relations Council (FLRC),** comparable to the NLRB, to coordinate federal policy in labor relations.

Federal Labor Relations Council (FLRC): *Federal agency that coordinates federal policy in labor relations.*

Collective bargaining agreements are now commonplace among agencies at all levels of government—federal, state, and local. Currently, more than 40 percent of all public employees belong to unions. The National Education Association has about 2 million members; the American Federation of State, County, and Municipal Employees, about 1.2 million members; and the American Federation of Teachers, approximately 700,000.

As in the private sector, most public sector contracts include grievance procedures that, over the years, have become increasingly similar to those used in private industry. Several states have

TABLE 15–6
An Example of Grievance Procedures Utilized by Firefighters

- The aggrieved firefighter discusses the problem with an immediate supervisor.
- If the problem is not settled at that point, the firefighter discusses the problem with a union representative, who then submits the grievance in writing either to the same immediate supervisor or to the officer at the next higher level.
- If the grievance is not settled, the union can appeal to the chief, the fire commissioner, or the governing body.
- If the grievance is not answered or resolved to the satisfaction of the employee or the union, it can be submitted to an arbitrator or a panel of arbitrators. Arbitrators usually are agreed on by both parties or, depending on the stipulations of the contract, may be appointed by an impartial group such as the American Arbitration Association or the Federal Mediation and Conciliation Service.

given public employees a limited right to strike. Although the individual collective bargaining contracts vary in content, Table 15–6 provides a fairly typical example of grievance procedures utilized by firefighters (who are usually considered public employees).[6]

Summary

Unions are associations of workers and have as their major objective the improvement of conditions related to employment. Although union membership consists of only about 16 percent of the work force, union presence is still felt in many fields.

Workers *join unions* for a variety of reasons. Sometimes joining a union is the only way *to obtain specific types of employment.* Other reasons include *to ensure fair treatment, to improve economic situations, to gain power,* and *to satisfy social needs.*

Various *legislation* has affected management-labor relations throughout the years. Key legislation includes the *Norris-LaGuardia, Wagner, Taft-Hartley, Landrum-Griffin,* and *"right-to-work" Acts.*

Regardless of a supervisor's position toward unions, he or she should be familiar with the *unionization process.* Supervisors need to be especially cautious during union-organizing campaigns and avoid engaging in activities that could be considered unfair and illegal practices. In general, supervisors should carefully evaluate the implications of all that they say and do during an organizing campaign.

Collective bargaining agreements generally contain provisions for *grievance procedures.* Supervisors should strive to anticipate and resolve conflicts and complaints before they become a costly, time-consuming part of the grievance mechanism.

Grievances in nonunion organizations are typically handled through *open-door policies, an ombudsperson, peer decisions, hearing officers,* or *binding outside arbitration.* Grievances in public organizations have become increasingly similar to those used in private industry in recent decades.

Although you—the supervisor—may have a limited role in the negotiation aspects of collective bargaining process itself, this does not mean that you are unable to play an important role in handling grievances in nonunion as well as union situations. In fact, your role is vital. Establishing an *open and trusting relationship* in which employees feel free to discuss their grievances with you can frequently turn potentially serious complaints into solutions. Be certain to act promptly and fairly on all reasonable complaints. Listening actively to all grievances—that is, giving employees the chance to air gripes—often eliminates the complaint itself.

Questions for Discussion

1. Can *unions* truly be considered a significant force in the U.S. economy when their membership constitutes less than 16 percent of the work force?
2. Why do most employees individually have little in the way of *bargaining power* with their employers? Can you think of any exceptions to this general rule?
3. What motivates some employees to *join unions*?
4. What legislation outlawed *yellow-dog contracts*? Why?
5. What was the major purpose of the *Wagner Act*?
6. What influenced the social climate that resulted in the passage of the *Taft-Hartley Act*?
7. About 40 percent of the states have passed *"right-to-work" legislation.* Do you feel that there should be a comparable national law? Why or why not?
8. What is the difference between a *union shop* and an *agency shop*?
9. What was the purpose of the *Landrum-Griffin Act*?
10. In what ways do supervisors have to be careful in relation to employees during a *union organizing campaign?*
11. What is the distinction between *certification* and *decertification* elections?
12. What are some of the typical topics covered in a *collective bargaining contract*?
13. What responsibility does the supervisor have in relation to a *collective bargaining agreement*?
14. What role does the *union steward* have in grievance procedures?
15. What is the principal distinction between *arbitration* and *mediation*?

16. What are some shortcomings of the use of an *open-door policy* as a grievance procedure? Do these shortcomings suggest that open-door policies should not be used?
17. How do you feel about the use of a company *ombudsperson* to handle employee grievances in nonunion organizations?
18. Should *peer decisions* be used to handle nonunion grievances? Explain.
19. Why do nonunion companies tend to shy away from the use of *binding outside arbitration*?
20. Why have public employees traditionally not been permitted to strike, as are employees in the private sector? Do you feel that public employees should have the *right to strike*? Why or why not?

Can You Define These Terms?

Instructions: Write a definition for each of the following terms. You may check your definitions with those provided in the end-of-text Glossary.

union
Norris-LaGuardia Act of 1932
yellow-dog contracts
Wagner Act (National Labor Relations Act of 1935)
National Labor Relations Board (NLRB)
Taft-Hartley Act (Labor Management Relations Act of 1947)
union shop
"right-to-work" laws
Landrum-Griffin Act (Labor Management Reporting and Disclosure Act of 1959)
unionization process
authorization cards
certification election
decertification election
collective bargaining
grievances
union (shop) steward
mediation
arbitration
employee counselors
ombudsperson
peer decisions
hearing officers
binding outside arbitration
Federal Labor Relations Council (FLRC)

Supervision In Action

15–1 Discord on the Docks

Hench Fitchbar is a dockworker for the Fresh-Fast Freight Company of Denver, Colorado. He has worked for Fresh-Fast for about 10 years, and his job classification is checker/loader. You are a new dock supervisor responsible for the unloading section of Fresh-Fast's 28-worker dock.

You were assigned to your current supervisory position only two weeks ago. You have learned through the grapevine which workers are considered "machos." Further, you have been told that Fitchbar is one of the most difficult workers to supervise. You've heard that your predecessor even wanted to get rid of him. In fact, Fitchbar was fired on three different occasions, but each time was reinstated with full back pay. You noticed through personal observation that he becomes extremely belligerent when given a directive and seldom seems to put in a good day's work.

On August 9, Fitchbar reported to work, punched in, and went on the dock before you saw him. About a half-hour after the shift began, you noticed that he was wearing running shoes, which is contrary to company safety rules.

You decided to approach Fitchbar and suggest that he correct the situation, since it constitutes a serious safety hazard. Fitchbar seemed resentful of your comments but went to the locker room, where he changed into acceptable footwear.

About an hour later, Fitchbar was again seen wearing running shoes. You approached him and asked why he had put his running shoes back on again. At this point he became highly irate and started shouting at you to "Get off my case!" You then asked him to come with you to the office to talk with the dock superintendent, Dunfey Dohrlock.

After several refusals and more shouting Fitchbar went with you, but not before insisting that the shop steward, Per Larson, be present. By this time you were beginning to feel frustrated, and knew that it wouldn't take much more for you to lose your temper.

As you were in the process of getting Fitchbar to the office you noticed an odor of alcohol on his breath. Based on the odor and his obnoxious behavior, you decided to discharge Fitchbar for drunkenness on the job.

Questions

1. In your opinion, what seems to be the problem in this case?
2. Role play your role as supervisor with three other persons assuming the roles of Fitchbar, Larson, and Dohrlock.
3. What can you, as a supervisor, do to ensure that justifiable dismissals of employees "stick"?

15–2 One-Shot Bonuses versus General Increases in Base Pay

A trend in recent years has been employers writing into collective bargaining contracts single-payment bonuses to employees rather than the usual increases in the base wage. The lump-sum approach appeals to employers since it is not so costly as general wage increases. The one-shot payments do not raise the base pay of employees nor affect the costs of other contract provisions such as holiday pay and overtime, which typically are related to base pay.

Union leaders generally oppose the bonus payment approach. William W. Winpisinger, president of the International Association of Machinists Union, said he has long opposed lump-sum arrangements because "it's nothing but standing still—it's just as though nothing happens in the contract settlement. But at times management's been in a position to force it down our throat."[7]

Questions

Which approach to wage administration do you feel is fairer—an increase as a percentage of a previous year's wage or a lump-sum bonus that may be more directly dependent on the profitability of the company? Fairer to whom? Why?

Endnotes

1. *The World Almanac and Book of Facts 1990* (New York: Pharos Books, 1990), pp. 107, 108.
2. "Roper Poll Finds Public Confidence in Labor Growing," *AFL–CIO News,* August 19, 1989, p. 3.
3. "Average Income Lowest in 'Right-to-Work States'." *AFL–CIO News*, December 8, 1984, p. 10.
4. John Hoerr, "Needed: A Replacement for the Bargaining Table," *Business Week* (International Edition), January 9, 1989, p. 24.
5. A. Balfour, "Five Types of Non-Union Grievance Systems," *Personnel,* March–April 1984, pp. 67–76.
6. Didactic Systems, *Management in the Fire Service* (Boston: National Fire Protection Association, 1977), pp. 334–335.
7. Kenneth B. Noble, "Employers Favor Bonus Payments Over Wage Increases, Study Says," *Contra Costa Times/ Business,* April 28, 1986, p. 5; Vivian Brownstein, "Here Comes the Pay Packet Price Push," *Fortune* (International Edition), March 14, 1988, pp. 34, 35.

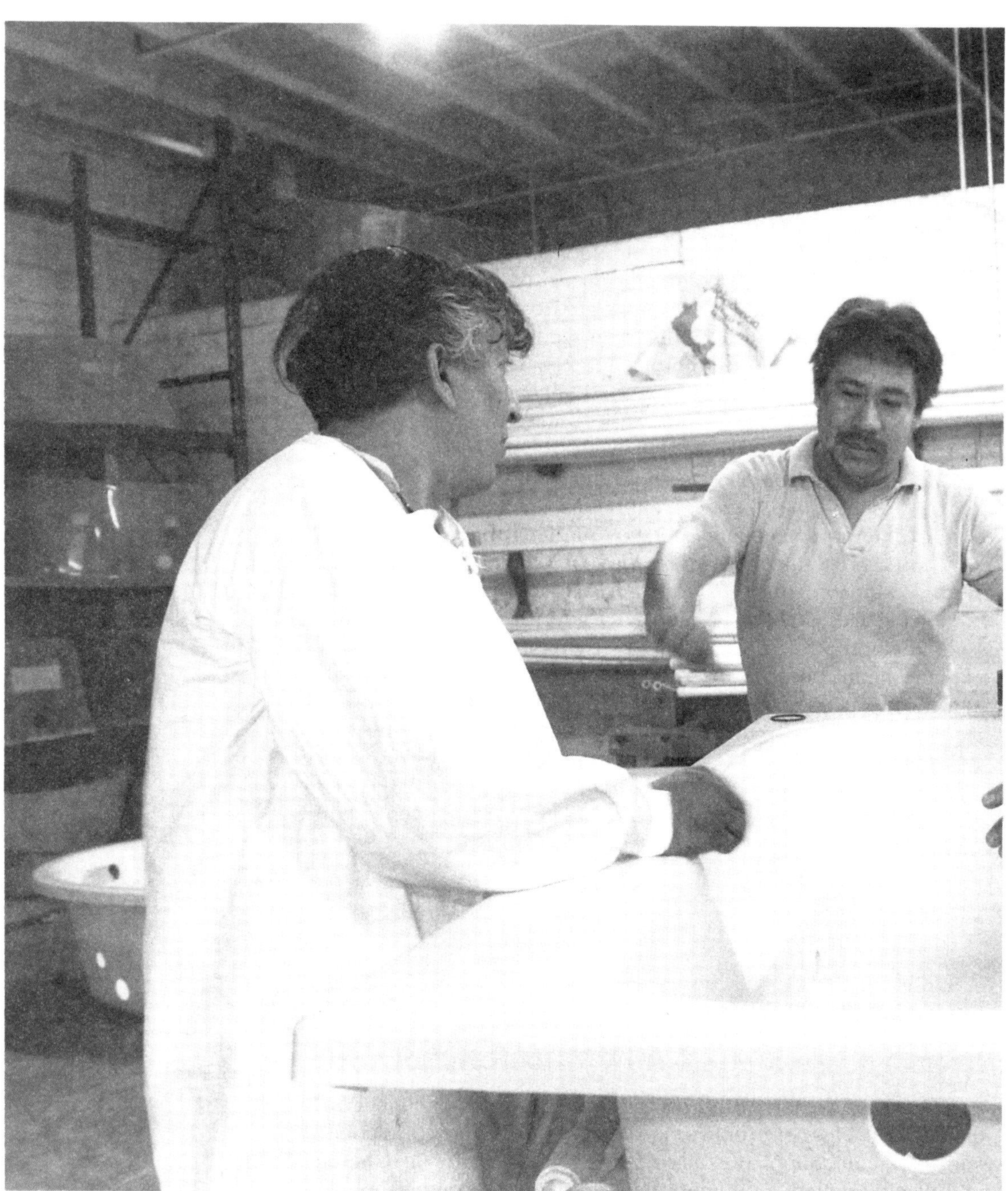

Chapter 16

The Problem Employee and the Nature of Discipline

Criticism without courtesy can make a passive person feel put down and defensive, or even create the desire for revenge.
—Johanna Hunsaker, Educator

Learning Objectives

When you finish this chapter, you should be able to:

1. Recognize how employee problems are actually disguised opportunities.
2. Discern the types of personality problems that employees may experience.
3. Perceive the types of behavioral problems that employees may experience.
4. Review the key elements of the disciplinary process.
5. Improve your effectiveness in disciplining employees.
6. Employ the essential ingredients associated with discharging employees.

Employee to a supervisor: *"I know you told me I'm supposed to wear safety goggles when I work. But I can't stand those darned things. They hurt my nose, they sometimes fog up while I work, and they get so much dust on them I can't even see what I'm doing half of the time. How can you expect me to do the work the way you want if I can't even see what I'm doing?"*

Different employee to a supervisor: *"You're absolutely right. I should be wearing my safety goggles when I work. I'm really sorry, but I completely forgot to put them on because I wanted to get this rush job out. I'll put them on right away. I think the company rule is a good one. I'm the last person who wants to have an eye accident."*

The above comments illustrate two distinct employee reactions to the same supervisory request—to wear safety goggles while working. One employee appears rebellious toward the company rule, and the other employee is earnestly willing to comply. Doesn't it seem that your leadership activities would be far less complex if all your employees behaved like the one in the second example? However, such expectations are akin to believing in a fantasyland not unlike Dorothy's in *The Wizard of Oz.* People are unique, and each employee comes to the workplace with a distinct set of wants, needs, emotions, and values. Each employee also has a distinct personality. Leaders have the challenge of attempting to adapt their own personalities to those of their employees. The task is difficult and requires a high degree of human understanding, patience, and perseverance.

Earlier chapters have already provided you with numerous examples on how to effectively lead and motivate employees. Special emphasis has been placed on the benefits of obtaining input from your associates for problem solving and decision making. Our primary concern in the current chapter turns to a less pleasant side of organizations: the *problem employee. Discipline* is a topic that goes hand in hand with the problem employee, both of which are of significant concern to most contemporary leaders.

What Employee Problems Can You Expect?

People problems, people problems, and *more* people problems. At times, it seems that all a supervisor really does is fill each day trying to resolve human resource-oriented problems. However, as most supervisors soon discover, dealing with employee difficulties is an activity that comes with the territory. Even the most experienced and skillful supervisors are unlikely to anticipate and resolve *every* problem in advance.

Aren't Problems Really Disguised Opportunities?

In Chapter 3 we defined a *problem* as a deviation from a preestablished standard. Your attitude toward employees with problems can significantly influence your effectiveness in dealing with them. Consequently, a more salutary manner of looking at employee problems might be as *disguised opportunities* or *challenges*, rather than as problems.

Not merely a play on words, an *opportunity,* as defined by *The American Heritage Dictionary,* is "a chance for progress or advancement."[1] Problems with employees can truly be converted into opportunities to utilize your leadership skills in a fashion that results not only in progress, but also in enhancing your own feelings of self-esteem. Resolving employee difficulties can be highly ego-gratifying for supervisors.

What Is a Problem Employee?

What do we mean, then, when we refer to a *problem employee*? A **problem employee** is one whose performance has *consistently* deviated from preestablished organizational standards. (Note the emphasis on the word *consistently.*) Any employee may periodically have a problem. Problem employees, however, are those who tend to take an inordinate amount of supervisors' time because of consistent substandard behavior. In our discussion of problem employees, we shouldn't assume that all behavior deviating from standards is harmful to an organization. Some of the most creative ideas that emerge from organizations are sometimes the result of unexpected behavior.

Problem employee: *A person who consistently deviates from organizational standards.*

What Types of "Challenges" and "Opportunities" Do Problem Employees Provide You With?

The scope of "challenges" that some employees bring to the work place is indeed extensive. Neatly categorizing specific types of employee problems is difficult because of their related and overlapping nature. Recognizing that the distinction is somewhat blurred, for purposes of convenience and simplification we'll examine problem employees from two general standpoints:

1. Personality problems
2. Behavioral problems

Each category, of course, includes various subcategories, which will receive separate treatment accompanied by suggested solutions in the sections that follow. Once again, recognize the individuality of each employee. A solution that might work perfectly with one employee may motivate another employee into resigning.

Some employees bring personal and behavioral problems to the workplace. What can a supervisor do about them?

What Personality Problems Might Exist?

On occasion, you may hear someone say something like, "What a deadhead Archie is. He's got *no* personality." Such a likelihood, however, is virtually impossible, since everyone has a personality. What a person making this type of statement frequently means is, "I don't like *his* personality."

Personality: *A person's psychological makeup and characteristic behavior as a whole.*

Personality has been defined as *the psychological makeup and characteristic behavior of the person as a whole.*[2] You can see from our definition that everyone qualifies to have a personality. Unfortunately, personality problems sometimes get in the way of employee performance and can create an uncomfortable working environment for department members.

In this section we examine some of the types of personality difficulties that you, as a supervisor, may have to confront. These include:

- Negative attitudes
- Hostility and anger
- Hypersensitivity
- Eccentricity

What Can You Do About Negative Attitudes?

What do you perceive when the gas gauge on your car is halfway between full and empty—a tank *half full,* or one *half empty?* You may at times find yourself with an employee who tends to perceive everything from a negative point of view. The gas tank is always half empty; sandwiches contain Swiss cheese with too many holes and not enough solid cheese; the weather is never right, always too cold or too hot, too dry or too humid, too windy or too torpid.

The negative-type person tends to be the same on the job. Reasons always exist as to why goals can't be reached, new equipment won't work properly, and new techniques are doomed to failure. The phrases, "But that won't work" or "We won't be able to do that" eternally emerge from the employee's mouth before you get the opportunity to even half complete your sentence.

Attitudes like these are not easy to change. Often such employees were raised in households where they were "fed" an unnourishing diet of continual "No No's." Children raised by parents who provided them with little in the way of encouragement and positive reinforcement frequently find themselves subconsciously behaving in a similar fashion with other people. What can you, as a supervisor, do about chronic negativism in employees?

Of utmost importance, you should personally *set a good example* with your associates. You, as their leader, significantly influence the departmental climate or culture. If, for example, you are generally negative in the presence of your associates each time a directive comes from your boss, can you really expect them to develop positive responses to your directives?

In addition, the continual application of the *Pygmalion effect* discussed in Chapter 12 may result in a more positive acceptance of your ideas. By conveying the attitude that you *expect* the employee will accept your ideas, you may find your expectation to be self-fulfilling. Of course, this technique does not produce miracles, but its use tends to be more effective than conveying to the employee a built-in negative expectation of rejection.

In cases where you can't seem to get the nonreceptive employee to develop a positive reaction to your directives, you might *ask the person to suggest a better alternative.* This approach sometimes helps the employee realize that your idea may not be so bad after all. In any case, the initial use of a participative style of leadership to develop acceptable ideas might have the effect of eliminating or reducing negative employee resistance.

What Can You Do About Hostility and Anger?

Some employees have personality disorders in which they easily become angry or display hostile attitudes toward others. Sometimes employees with this difficulty seem virtually to lose control of their behavior during explosive outbursts of anger. Such conduct can be highly disruptive, not only to you but also to other members of the department. What can you do about the employee who becomes angry?

Attempting to carry on a rational conversation while a person is highly emotional is essentially futile. The angry individual generally needs to release tension before being ready to communicate. Arguing with the person will only sever the lines of communication. Instead, *listen empathetically and attempt to understand* why the employee is disturbed.

An occasional employee flare-up is excusable. However, the continual disruption of the workplace by a particular employee can hardly be tolerated. You will have to convince the employee that his or her hostile behavior must change. In some cases, such employees should be referred to a company counselor or a professional therapist. However, the disruptive employee should be made aware that if change is not forthcoming, dismissal may be your only alternative, cruel as it may seem. A later section of this chapter discusses methods of discipline, such as the *progressive disciplinary approach,* which can be applied and accompanied by a commitment to change from the employee.

What Can You Do about Hypersensitivity?

Hypersensitivity: *Excessive susceptibility to the attitude of others; quick to take offense.*

Employees who suffer from low self-esteem sometimes have difficulty accepting criticism from others, even when the critic's intention is constructive. Employees with **hypersensitivity** tendencies may react in a defensive, offended, or even depressed manner when you make comments about their work. What may surprise you is that some employees even overreact to *compliments,* believing that you are actually attempting to deceive them with praise. They may think to themselves, "I know she doesn't mean it; she's just saying that to make me feel better."

How should you react to oversensitive employees? Try your best to avoid comments that tend to deflate their self-images. When there is a need for constructive criticism, instead of focusing on the negative you might say something that begins like this:

> *"Jerry, I really appreciate the effort you put in on the Jensen file. There's one thing, however, that I would appreciate your modifying. Would you mind changing. . . .?"*

Of course, as with any employee, hypersensitive employees need positive reinforcement and feedback regarding their work. Try to provide all of your associates with regular sincere reassurance regarding their performance.

What Can You Do about Eccentricity?

We've already defined a *problem* as a deviation from a preestablished standard or norm, and a *problem employee* as one whose performance has consistently deviated from preestablished organizational standards. **Eccentricity** is defined as departing or deviating from the conventional or established norms, and a person with an **eccentric personality** is one who departs from established norms. The meanings of the terms *problem employee* and *eccentric personality* appear to be remarkably parallel, don't they? Does this mean, therefore, that the employee who engages in unconventional or odd behavior is a problem employee? Not necessarily. Frequently, it is the highly creative individual who behaves in a less-than-standard fashion.

Eccentricity: *The condition of departing or deviating from conventional or established norms.*

Eccentric personality: *Characteristic of individuals who typically depart from established norms.*

For example, usual business standards of dress are practically nonexistent at Microsoft, a high-tech company that created and produces the operating system software that controls the inner workings of more than 30 million IBM PCs and compatible computers. Dress at Microsoft is informal: jeans, polo shirts, Hawaiian prints—anything but suit and tie. Some employees even go barefoot and have pizza delivered to their work stations. Profits don't seem to have suffered. Between 1982 and 1990, revenues of Microsoft surged more than 30-fold and profits swelled by double that rate.[3]

You may find the employee with eccentric behavior a real challenge to lead. Unfortunately, if the eccentric employee happens also to be a creative one, you run the danger of stifling the flow of original and useful ideas through traditional methods of supervision. Creative people tend to prefer making decisions themselves and are typically not good at taking orders. They usually need the latitude to explore their thoughts without interruption. You and your department can gain substantially from the creative employee's flow of ideas.

How should you supervise the creative employee who behaves in an eccentric manner? Should different standards of supervision be applied to such persons? Should they be able to behave in any manner they like regardless of their effect on others? Not really. Allowing any type of eccentric behavior, unfortunately, runs the risk of other employees becoming resentful or envious. It also might convey to them the erroneous impression that odd behavior is the best way to receive rewards. Your leadership will usually be more effective if your associates realize that you intend to treat all of them in a similar but equitable fashion, and that you expect results, not oddball behavior. Eccentric behavior, even in the name of creativity, is of little value when it creates a disruptive or unsafe work environment.

What Behavioral Problems Might Exist?

Employee behavior influences results. Since supervisors are responsible for attaining results, behavioral problems are one of their major concerns. The types of behavioral problems that can be found in organizations are considerable. However, we'll restrict our discussion of these problems to the following:

- Procrastination
- Excessive absences
- Alcohol and drug abuse
- Noncompliance with company rules

What Can You Do About the Employee Who Procrastinates?

Procrastination: *The tendency to postpone activities until a later period.*

"Why do today what you can put off until tomorrow?" That's not exactly the way the old saying goes, but—based on the behavior of some employees—it seems to be the preferred interpretation. **Procrastination**, the act of putting tasks off until a future time, appears to be a way of life for some employees. Some individuals are consistently late in completing projects, attending meetings, and fulfilling most of their commitments. Such behavior can become a tremendous burden on you and other members of your department, especially when various projects are dependent on the procrastinating employees's input for completion. Such conduct can also damage relations with customers when employees delay resolving their urgent problems.

What can you do about the employee who consistently procrastinates? Your first task is to try to understand why the particular employee postpones doing certain tasks. Many procrastinators don't necessarily want to put off doing things; in fact, doing so often causes them to become uncomfortably distressed and anxious. Their postponement, however, is sometimes the result of a low self-image and the fear that they will be unable to do a satisfactory job. They harbor doubts about the outcome of their efforts—that is, they fear *failure*—so they put off the "day of reckoning," so to speak. Any of the following guidelines may be effective with employees who tend to fall into the category of procrastinator:

1. Provide regular reassurance and encouragement.
2. Be certain employees realize how dependent you are on their efforts. For example, the timely completion of a project may hinge on their completing a component of the total. You might say something like, "Horatio, I really need your help. We won't be able to meet the deadline on the Field-Marshall Department Store account until I receive the final artwork from you. I'm really counting on you, Horatio; please don't let me down."
3. Try to show employees how they can gain positive feelings of self-satisfaction from successfully completing a project.
4. Make certain employees have received adequate training and developed the necessary skills to perform the tasks properly.
5. Establish a mutual agreement on deadlines; that is, get a commitment from employees as to when tasks will be completed. You might ask something like, "Harriet, when is a reasonable time for me to expect you to complete this project?" Make certain that the employee has estimated enough time for completion of the task. Recognize, of course, that a delay could be caused by circumstances that are beyond an employee's control.

What Can You Do About Excessive Absences?

In some organizations there exists the problem employee who is absent from work more often than what is considered to be the company norm. Excessive absences are a financial burden to an organization and frequently result in costly bottlenecks and delays in production.

Of course, a certain amount of absenteeism is unavoidable because of sickness, family crises, and other legitimate reasons. However, absenteeism that follows a particular pattern, such as the days immediately preceding and following weekends, before and after holidays, and after paydays, could be an indication of an attitudinal problem. There is the strong probability that anyone regularly absent on those days could be feigning illness.

Why do people avoid going to work when they know they should be on the job? In some instances, they may be experiencing some of the symptoms of *burnout* and simply dread having to face the responsibilities of their jobs. *Satisfaction may be missing from their work.* In other cases, they may *lack a sense of direction* and feel that they work solely for spending money. Such persons may not yet have become career oriented. Chronic absenteeism could also be a indication of *personal problems off the job,* such as marital or financial difficulties, or drug or alcohol abuse. Whatever the

What can the supervisor do about the employee who consistently has poor attendance?

cause, it is important for you to motivate the employee into reducing his or her absenteeism. Employee assistance programs (EAPs) were discussed in Chapter 11 as a possible referral source for employees with suspected personal problems.

What can you do about excessive absenteeism? In some cases, *dismissal* may be the only answer. However, before taking such severe action, you should *provide the employee with the opportunity to improve his or her behavior. Coaching* or referring the employee to a *counseling service* might also be helpful. Be certain to stress to the employee *how important his or her presence is to the functioning of the department.* You might further point out that *dependable employees are the ones who typically keep their jobs* when economic conditions are slack and layoffs become necessary. You might also require a *complete explanation* from the employee after each absence or even ask for a *doctor's signature.* You must be careful, however, that your requests or action are not in conflict with companywide policies and regulations, or you could be accused of discriminatory practices by your employees. You also must comply with the terms of a collective bargaining agreement if your company is unionized.

Some organizations maintain programs or policies designed to discourage unjustifiable absences. For example, your company may have a policy that allows employees to *use portions of their vacation time in one-day segments,* which could be applied to excessive absences. Although some employees don't like to use their vacation in this manner, the technique has been used with some success in reducing the amount of unwarranted absences.

Well pay:
A program that offers financial incentives for maintaining attendance standards.

Bonus days off:
A program that rewards employees with time off for putting in a given number of days without being absent.

Another novel approach to the problem of excessive absenteeism is the offering of **well pay,** or **bonus days off.** *Well pay* is a plan that provides financial incentives to employees who maintain certain attendance standards. A *bonus days off* plan provides an added incentive by rewarding workers with an extra day off after they have put in a given number of days without being absent.[3] It may seem strange at first to give an employee a day off for not taking days off. However, doing so provides you, the supervisor, with greater flexibility, since the bonus days off can be scheduled for periods when the work load is slack.

Another approach used by some organizations is to *post attendance records.* Employees with good attendance receive positive recognition from this approach, possibly even awards. One company even sticks gold and silver stars beside the employees' names as a form of recognition. Although some employees have "pooh-poohed" the approach, they usually have been among the first to make certain they've received their rightfully earned stars! The high profile of the posting approach plus the effect of peers tend to have a positive influence on those with a tendency for high absenteeism. The competitive nature of this approach likewise has the effect of improving overall employee attendance.

There are some instances when high absenteeism is related to the job itself. We've already mentioned that some employees may be lacking job satisfaction. If so, the application of some of the morale and job enrichment concepts discussed in Chapter 11 could result in improved employee attitudes toward their jobs. Employees who like their jobs and feel some degree of responsibility toward them tend to have lower absenteeism. Utilizing the participative approach and asking for employee input on how jobs might be redesigned and enriched could be a way of reducing absenteeism.

In certain instances your good intentions and painstaking efforts may have little effect on some employees, and disciplinary measures may become necessary. Various disciplinary techniques will be discussed shortly.

What Can You Do About Alcohol and Drug Abuse?

A question exists as to whether an employer has the right to become involved with employee use of alcohol or drugs off the job. There is, of course, a significant distinction between the occasional off-the-job *use* of substances and their chronic *abuse*. There is little doubt that supervisors must be concerned when the *abuse* of alcohol or drugs results in *changes in employee work performance and dependability.* Legislation known as *The Drugfree Workplace Act of 1988* has placed even greater burdens on supervisors related to substance abuse problems. More on this act will be discussed in Chapter 19.

Habits Can Be Costly. The employee who abuses alcohol or drugs can be a significant challenge to a supervisor. **Substance dependency** can be a costly habit, especially with drugs. To support drug habits, dependent workers sometimes become "pushers," and may even *induce fellow employees* into narcotics addiction. Addicts frequently support their expensive habits by *stealing* property from organizations and individuals, frequently their own employers. Addicted employees tend to experience *higher turnover rates,* which result in increased personnel costs for employers. The *job performance* of employees who abuse alcohol and drugs tends to fluctuate widely. Substance abuse knows no class boundaries and can affect workers from any educational background.

Substance dependency: *A situation in which an individual habitually lacks the ability to control his or her intake of drugs or alcohol.*

Detection. In addition to a decline in job performance, there are a number of other signs and symptoms of alcohol and drug abuse that exist, such as the *need to drink before facing certain situations, accidents due to impaired judgment,* and *distorted perceptions of space and time.* If you suspect that a particular employee is abusing substances, you should avoid accusing him or her of being an alcoholic or drug addict. You might first want to discuss your suspicions with your manager, who may provide you with some insights on how to deal with what is usually a delicate situation.

Documentation, Discussion, and Commitment. What can you, as a supervisor, do if you suspect substance abuse on the part of an employee? Of paramount importance is your consistently *documenting in writing* any incidents of substandard employee behavior. You should meet with the employee soon after discovering a pattern of behavioral problems. During your meeting you should review documented records with the employee, obtain a mutual agreement on the existence of performance problems, and secure a commitment from the employee related to future improved performance. Both you and the employee should also attempt to agree on a specific timeframe for improved performance rather than leaving the goal open-ended and indefinite.

The Need for Professional Counseling. Although you must be careful not to appear to be probing into the personal life of the employee, you should attempt to detect any personal problems the employee might have that are causing a substance abuse problem. For example, let's assume an employee had a child who committed suicide late last year. The employee has had difficulty adjusting to the reality of the incident. You could encourage that employee to seek the aid of a professional counselor. The employee may not be receptive to the idea at this time, but you have at least laid some positive groundwork for your follow-up session. Frequently, people reconsider such advice, especially when they know that their jobs may depend on their following it.

Following Up. As with any plan or decision-making activity, you certainly should follow up to ensure that the employee has kept his or her promises. In some instances an employee may conceal drug or alcohol problems, refuse to see a counselor, but assure you that performance will improve. You should follow up to ensure that performance has changed for the better and continue to document any ongoing deficiencies.

If performance does not improve within an agreed-on timeframe, you may have to engage in what has been termed "constructive coercion." Another meeting becomes necessary, at which session you might take a more direct approach, perhaps saying something like:

> *"Gil, you assured me that things would be different, that your work would improve. You and I both know it has continued to be below expectations. I think you're well aware that we just can't go on like this. Consequently, I'm going to send you to see our company counselor (or doctor), and unless you're able to work out the problem, I'm afraid that your future with our organization looks bleak."*

In other words, you must tell the employee that either he or she obtains professional help, or you will have to ask for his or her resignation. Many supervisors have learned that the shock effect of this approach, coupled with the desire by most employees to keep their jobs, is one of the most effective techniques for motivating them to seek help and modify their behavior. Table 16–1 summarizes a set of specific guidelines for supervisors to follow when they believe an employee is abusing alcohol or drugs.[4]

TABLE 16–1
Supervisory Guidelines Related to Suspected Employee Substance Abuse

- *Do* learn to recognize the symptoms of alcohol or drug abuse.
- *Do not* attempt to diagnose the employee's problem. Instead, show a genuine concern for the employee's problem and attempt to refer him or her to a company specialist qualified in such matters.
- *Do not* discuss drinking or drug problems with the employee; instead, focus on *job deficiencies* and *corrective action.*
- *Never* (repeat, *never*) accuse an employee of using drugs or being an alcoholic. If you do, you may open yourself and the company to a slander or defamation of character lawsuit.
- *Do not* feel guilty about referring an employee to staff specialists. Doing so is not an admission of failure in the way you manage your department.
- *Do* follow up after an employee both begins and completes rehabilitation to ascertain that he or she is following prescribed recommendations.
- *Do not* dismiss a previously satisfactory employee for deteriorating performance before giving the employee ample opportunity to seek assistance.

What Can You Do About the Employee Who Does Not Follow Rules?

A company rule, in a sense, is akin to a law. It is expected to be followed for the purpose of providing the organization with a certain degree of order and predictability. A rule that is out of date or not applied should be revised or removed, since many rules frequently outlive their useful lives. Unfortunately, some employees subscribe to the hackneyed phrase, "Rules were made to be broken." The employee with such a philosophy creates additional challenges for the supervisor. What can you do to encourage employees to follow rules?

Some organizations make certain that each employee receives an organizational manual that spells out (albeit not always *clearly*) the rules and policies of the company. Several organizations even require their employees to sign a document indicating that they have read the material. Unfortunately, merely signing a paper indicating that they've read a rule doesn't guarantee that employees will necessarily understand or abide by the rule.

Since you are responsible for making certain your employees comply with rules, you have the responsibility to make certain that rules have been clearly communicated and are being followed. If an employee does break a rule, you should first try to determine if he or she had a reasonable opportunity to become familiar with it. In addition, did the employee understand the rationale behind the rule? If the employee had sufficient opportunity to become familiar with the rule but failed to comply with it, then *discipline,* which is covered in the following section, should go into play.

What Should A Supervisor Know About Discipline?

What do you think of when you hear the word *discipline*? Something negative, unpleasant, and dreaded by employees? Or a positive activity that would be readily accepted and appreciated by them? Discipline—an extremely important supervisory concern—is another one of those terms that has different meanings for different people. In the past, the word typically had negative connotations, frequently representing various types of punitive activities.

Although punishment as a form of discipline *is* sometimes necessary, a more effective concept of disciplinary measures involves the attempt to modify, improve, or correct substandard behavior. Discipline generally takes place as a result of a problem. We've already suggested that a problem is a deviation from a preestablished standard. What, then, should your principal goal actually be? To *punish and harm* employees whose behavior is substandard, or to *correct and modify* their behavior so that it meets the standards of your organization?

In this section, we examine the important aspects of discipline that supervisors should become familiar with, along with some suggestions for improving the effectiveness of disciplinary measures when they must be applied.

"Rest assured, Fenston, that should we start cutting back *you* will be one of the first to know."

Source: Reprinted from *The Wall Street Journal* by permission of Cartoon Features Syndicate, ©.

What Is Discipline?

Before we delve too deeply into the topic of discipline, it would be a good idea for us to develop a working definition of the term. First, let's shake loose any preconceived notions we might have that discipline is *always* equated with punishment. Sometimes it is; frequently it isn't. For our purposes, **discipline,** which stems from the Latin meaning *teaching* or *learning,* can be defined as a managerial activity intended to *correct* work-related behavior that deviates from established standards. It can also be used as a tool for *employee development.*

Discipline: *Leadership activity intended to correct undesirable employee behavior.*

Self-Discipline. Discipline can actually take a variety of forms. For example, one type of discipline is termed **self-discipline,** which is a *self-imposed* form of control or influence over one's own behavior. Employees certainly can influence their own behavior. When they fail to influence their behavior in an acceptable manner, they are said to lack self-discipline, which can lead to a variety of organizational problems. For instance, a sales representative who works alone in the field must have self-discipline in order to manage his or her territory effectively. It takes self-discipline for the salesperson to awaken at a reasonable time in the morning, plan an itinerary, call on disgruntled customers, and learn about customers' needs, product features, and competitors' activities without a manager directing all of these moves.

Self-discipline: *Self-imposed control or influence over one's own behavior.*

Of course, as a supervisor you also need self-discipline. You might, for example, feel like "chewing out" an employee for a flagrant abuse of one of your directives. You will, however, do a more effective job of dealing with the employee if you maintain control of your emotions, especially in front of other employees. Any type of discipline, therefore, is a form of *control.* Consequently, our first way of looking at discipline is as an *internally imposed activity.* Self-disciplined employees tend to display a far greater commitment to organizational objectives than those who lack self-discipline.

Punishment. A second, more traditional way of perceiving discipline is as a form of **punishment.** This form also relates to rules and standards of performance. Punitive measures are sometimes necessary for supervisors to take, especially when other efforts to motivate employees to comply have failed. Examples of punishment include:

Punishment: *A penalty imposed for improper behavior.*

- Suspension without pay
- Dismissal
- Assignment to less desirable activities
- Reduced promotional opportunities
- Oral/written reprimands

Numerous fire departments, for example, have strict rules related to reporting to work drunk. If a firefighter abuses the rule, the disciplinary act is one of immediate dismissal. This type of discipline, therefore, tends to take the form of a *penalty.* It is a negative consequence that occurs after the fact—that is, after an employee has deviated from an established standard. The rule has the effect of discouraging firefighters from being intoxicated during working hours.

Some employees may refuse to perceive any necessity or right for punitive discipline to be applied. They may even react in an overemotional, sometimes threatening, and, in extreme cases, violent fashion. For example, instances have been reported in which disgruntled workers have actually opened fire after being told of their dismissals, killing and wounding participants during company disciplinary meetings.

When imposing punishment as discipline, any supervisor should strive to make the *reason* for the action clear to the *employee* being disciplined. Punitive discipline should not really come as a surprise to the employee who has been given proper warnings. Supervisors who mishandle punitive discipline may open themselves up to grievances, lawsuits, or, as we've seen, even physical threats or actual violence. Keep in mind that most people don't like to feel that they are being pushed. As one manager once said, "I don't mind being pushed as long as I can steer." When employees feel that they aren't being permitted to "steer," they tend to react emotionally.

Guidance and Correction. A third, and more modern, concept of discipline is to perceive the activity as one intended to *guide* and/or *correct* the behavior of an employee. For example, an effective supervisor, like a successful football coach, can create a disciplined environment—one in which team members feel an allegiance to the organization and its standards. Employees in such settings have been informed as to the reasons for organizational standards and, therefore, recognize the need to comply with them. When employees have deviated from preestablished standards, they generally have not done so as a deliberate, malicious act. Supervisors who employ positive discipline attempt to guide or counsel employees and assist them in performing up to existing standards.

Documentation: *Maintaining written records of employee behavior necessary for backing up disciplinary action and employee appraisals.*

Incident file: *A record of examples of favorable and unfavorable employee behavior.*

Why Is Documentation so Important?

It can't be overstressed that full **documentation** of any disciplinary action must be performed as a means of protecting you and your organization against false allegations by a disgruntled employee. Some supervisors also maintain an **incident file.** This file is used to record examples or incidents of deviations from standards as well as citations of favorable employee performance. Since remembering every incident that occurs in your department is no mean feat, an incident file can also serve you usefully as a memory jogger when preparing employee performance reviews.

What Is the Nature of Progressive Discipline?

A number of leaders today employ what is commonly referred to as **progressive discipline.** The philosophy behind this approach is that the severity of disciplinary measures should increase each time an employee must be disciplined. Typical stages of progressive discipline, as illustrated in Figure 16–1, are:

Progressive discipline: *Tactic where the severity of disciplinary measures increases after each repetition of unacceptable employee behavior.*

1. Oral warning
2. Written warning
3. Layoff without pay
4. Discharge

Each step is discussed below.

The first step in progressive discipline is to give an *oral warning* to the employee who has deviated from acceptable standards. The hope is that employees will be willing to alter their behavior on their own after being made aware of the problem. Even a oral warning is noted in the employee's personnel file to prevent the likelihood of the employee later denying that the oral warning was ever given.

If the employee's behavior isn't modified as agreed on during the oral warning, the next step is applied—*a written warning,* a copy of which is placed in the employee's personnel file and recorded in the supervisor's incident file.

If the previous two steps have little or no effect on motivating the employee to correct his or her behavior, then progressive discipline calls for increasingly severe measures. The third step—sort of a "shock treatment"—may go into play, a *disciplinary layoff without pay.* Some employees will be jolted into reality by such measures; others will return to work harboring deep feelings of resentment and hostility. Certain employees may even quit, which in some instances might benefit your organization, especially if the

FIGURE 16–1
Typical Stages of Progressive Discipline

selection process had been improperly administered. In any case, the employee should be clearly informed both orally and in writing as to the reasons for the discipline and be made aware that the next step in progressive discipline is discharge.

The ultimate in discipline—*discharge*—is the final step in the progressive discipline process and usually should be considered only as a last resort after all other reasonable attempts at correction have failed. Having to recruit, interview, and train a replacement employee is expensive. Also, many more persons than the fired employee may be affected; for example, his or her family may also suffer, or coworkers of the dismissed employee may react negatively to what they might perceive as unjust punishment. In some instances, workers have even engaged in a **wildcat strike** (a walkout not sanctioned by a union contract) in sympathy for a coworker who they thought had been unjustly fired. Of course, in the case of unionized operations, you must comply with the terms of the collective bargaining agreement when discharging employees. More will be covered on the important topic of discharge in a later section of this chapter.

Wildcat strike: *Employee work stoppages not sanctioned by collective bargaining.*

What Is the "Red-Hot Stove Rule"?

Have you ever heard about the days before gas, electric, and microwave ovens were so prevalent, when many people had wood- or coal-burning stoves? Once upon a time, many households had such devices that were used for cooking and/or comfort. Imagine what ordinarily happened when a person touched a red-hot stove. You guessed it! He or she would doubtlessly be burned. One doesn't have to be a physicist or dermatologist to realize that human skin and a glowing stove mix even less favorably than oil and water. A well-known disciplinary concept was developed from the awareness of the hazards of burning stoves, a concept referred to as the **red-hot stove rule**.

Red-hot stove rule: *Disciplinary measures equated with touching a glowing hot stove.*

Follow the red-hot stove rule, and visualize how it relates to discipline:

- A person approaching a red-hot stove receives *ample warning*—the red glow of the stove—as to the consequences of carelessly touching the stove. (Employees should receive ample warning regarding the consequences of breaking a rule.)
- If touched, the stove will provide *immediate feedback*—the feeling of being burned. (The supervisor should not delay the application of the disciplinary process or it will lose its effectiveness.)
- The discipline is *consistent*—a burn takes place each time the stove is touched. (The supervisor invariably applies disciplinary measures each time they are necessary.)
- The response of the stove is *impersonal*—the severity of the discipline depends on behavior (i.e., how much the person touched the stove), not on the person. (The supervisor will treat all employees in a similar fashion, not disciplining some persons more than others for the same substandard behavior.)

How Can You Improve Your Disciplinary Track Record?

Having to discipline employees is usually not one of a supervisor's favorite pastimes; at times, the task seems insurmountable for the less-experienced supervisor. However, an awareness and application of certain proven suggestions and guidelines should improve your own track record in the activity of applying disciplinary measures.

In the section that follows you will learn some of the major reasons why disciplinary efforts sometimes fail, discover how to conduct disciplinary interviews, and recognize the important guidelines for applying positive disciplinary measures to employees.

Why Do Disciplinary Efforts Sometimes Fail?

Most employees are not particularly surprised when they are disciplined for known infractions of rules or deviations from expected standards. Yet many attempts at disciplining employees fail. Efforts at disciplining have often backfired and have frequently been challenged by some employees and union representatives because the person administering the discipline has not avoided certain pitfalls. Let's briefly look at some main reasons for these failures:

- *Insufficient warning.* Is it fair to discipline employees for an infraction of rules with which they had no way of becoming familiar? All rules should be both in writing and a part of any orientation and training program your employees are involved in.
- *Vague rules.* Rules should be specific and clearly stated. Rules that are vague are likely to be interpreted differently by different managers and therefore applied unequally to various employees.
- *Prejudicial application.* Supervisors who apply discipline on the basis of personal prejudices or dislikes for a particular employee are likely exposing themselves to a discrimination lawsuit. For example, never fire a person for filing a grievance.
- *Inadequate proof.* Discipline often fails when it is based on feelings, hunches, and inadequate information. Be certain that you can factually substantiate the reasons for your disciplinary actions. Have you remembered to carefully document all incidents related to disciplinary action?
- *Unfair punishment.* Punishment out of proportion to the behavior of the employee is likely to be challenged. Make certain that your punishment relates to the actual employee situation. For example, never punish a person for joining a union.

What Can a Supervisor Do to Improve Disciplinary Interviews?

There's much that a supervisor can do to achieve better results during disciplinary interviews. The following are some useful suggestions (these are summarized in Table 16–2).

TABLE 16–2
Guidelines for Conducting Effective Disciplinary Interviews

- Interview in private.
- Avoid creating a hostile environment.
- Clearly explain your view of the problem.
- Focus on behavior, not the person.
- Focus on positive ways to improve the situation.
- Get a commitment from the employee.
- Close the interview in a friendly manner.
- Follow up (to ensure commitments are being fulfilled).

Interview in Private. A disciplinary interview may take place in a variety of settings, ranging from your office to the employee's work place. In general, disciplinary interviews tend to be more effective when they take place out of the earshot of others. Criticizing an employee in front of his or her peers can have a devastating effect on the employee's self-esteem, so try to select a setting for a disciplinary interview that will be most suitable in aiding you in accomplishing your goals.

Although most managers go along with the suggestion that you "criticize in private and praise in public," the policies of some companies and the contracts of some labor agreements require that a third party be present during any disciplinary interview. In the case of company policy, the purpose is to provide a witness in the event that the employee makes false accusations at a later time. Some union officials feel that a third-party witness who is a union member also helps to protect the employee against unfair treatment.

Avoid Creating a Hostile Environment. During the disciplinary interview, try your best to avoid causing the employee to become excessively emotional or angry by making him or her feel pushed or embarrassed. Try not to let an employee do the same thing to you. Instead, make every effort to maintain a calm, positive, and friendly atmosphere, even if you perceive the employee to be behaving in an excessively hostile manner.

Clearly Explain Your View of the Problem. There will be little motivation on the part of the employee to correct his or her behavior unless both of you agree on the nature of the problem. By first *stating your understanding of the problem,* and then *listening to the employee's response* to your views, you will be in a far better position to develop an *agreement* as to the nature of the problem and possible solutions.

Focus on Behavior, Not the Person. Your disciplinary interview is more likely to succeed if you focus your discussion on the specific *behavior of the employee* rather than on the person him- or herself. Remember that you want to *help the employee correct specific behavior,* not *attack the employee.*

Focus on Positive Ways to Improve the Situation. Build on the *strengths* of the employee rather than being excessively critical and picky. Gain the employee's confidence by pointing out how you are generally pleased with his or her work. Then stress that once the behavior for which discipline is being applied is corrected, he or she will once again be considered a satisfactory employee. Try as much as possible to encourage and guide the employee into developing solutions to the problem that resulted in the disciplinary interview.

Get a Commitment from the Employee. Attempt to get a firm commitment from the employee related to specific behavioral improvements. Be certain to let the employee know what consequences are likely if behavior doesn't improve.

Close the Interview in a Friendly Manner. Once you have covered everything that you've intended to discuss, end the interview in a cordial way. Be friendly and attempt to show that you truly believe that the problem will be corrected. Don't hold a grudge against the employee's past behavior.

Follow Up. Be certain to regularly monitor the employee's performance to make sure that he or she is fulfilling the commitment to change. If improvement doesn't occur, you may have to engage in further disciplinary measures.

A Special Problem—Firing—Oops! Make That *Terminating*—Employees?

Firing employees is one of the most difficult tasks supervisors have to face, one that places undue strain on leadership skills. Firing is so difficult that many leaders have eliminated the word *firing* from their vocabularies and instead use less emotion-charged words as *separation, termination, dehiring, outplacement,* and even *disemployment.* But as a pragmatic philosopher once said, "If it looks like a duck and walks like a duck and quacks like a duck, it probably is a duck!" So it doesn't really matter what it's called; there are circumstances when leaders must face the unpleasant task of firing employees.

Why Might Satisfactory Employees Have to Be Discharged?

In recent decades, large numbers of employees were discharged not for inadequate performance but because of economic reasons. On numerous occasions, firms were taken over by so-called corporate raiders, whose goal was to make the acquired organizations "lean and mean" by cutting costs substantially. Some employees who had served long and faithfully were suddenly terminated. In 1988, for example, mass layoffs—involving 50 or more workers for at least 31 days—affected more than 450,000 workers in 42 states, according to the Bureau of Labor Statistics.[5] (The BLS study excluded 8 states, among which were California, Illinois, Maryland, and Michigan.)

How Can You Avoid the Problem of Wrongful Discharge?

There are a variety of reasons why an employee may be fired, such as for unsatisfactory performance or serious rule violations, including the possession of illegal drugs or weapons, falsifying employment records, and stealing or willfully destroying company property. A danger associated with the dismissal of employees, however, is that a disgruntled employee may take the employer to court on the basis of **wrongful discharge,** that is, termination without just cause. In some cases, courts have ruled that a dismissal constituted discrimination and, therefore, was in violation of civil rights legislation.

Wrongful discharge: *The termination of an employee without just cause.*

How can you protect yourself from accusations of wrongful discharge? You will lessen your chances of having difficulties in this area if you follow the sound concepts previously discussed in relation to disciplinary action. We've already emphasized the importance of documenting unsatisfactory performance. In addition, employees should be informed of their substandard performance and given a reasonable opportunity to correct their behavior. Of course, you should apply disciplinary measures in the same manner to all employees who fail to comply with company standards.

How Can Organizations Ease the Transition for Fired Employees?

In some cases, organizations have assisted discharged employees in obtaining employment elsewhere by inviting prospective employers to job fairs for the purpose of interviewing the employees. Some firms have even hired temporary counselors, called **outplacement consultants,** who aid discharged employees. Although, as we've already stressed, firing employees is an unpleasant task, the guidelines cited in Table 16–3 can make separation easier on dismissed employees.

Outplacement consultants: *Persons who assist discharged employees in obtaining new employment.*

TABLE 16–3
Guidelines for Dismissing Employees
(*Continued on next page*)

- *Come directly to the point.* Don't strain so hard to be tactful that the employee doesn't know what you're up to. Some employees actually thought they were going to be informed of a promotion, not discharge, because of the supervisor's manner.
- *Watch your timing.* The bad news of dismissal will probably be less traumatic if given to the employee late in the working day. Choose a proper setting for the announcement to save the employee unnecessary embarrassment. Could your decision be postponed in the case of a serious illness existing in the employee's family?

TABLE 16–3
continued

- *Tell the employee the reason for the dismissal.* Self-doubt often follows a firing. Perhaps the dismissal is for economic reasons, not employee performance. Knowing this may help to ease the pain of discharge. If the employee is discharged for substandard behavior, he or she may benefit by being aware of behavior to avoid on the next job.
- *Remain calm during the interview.* Losing your temper may invite hostile retaliation on the part of the employee.
- *Discharge the employee soon after the decision is made.* Even if two-weeks' notice is required, immediate dismissal with salary paid to the employee for the two weeks not worked may be more beneficial for all involved. Employees tend not to be particularly productive during their last days and may spread discontent among other employees.

Summary

Most supervisors have to deal occasionally with what could be considered the *problem employee.* Problems could be considered *disguised opportunities* to improve the working environment. Two types of difficult employees discussed in this chapter were those with *personality problems* and those with *behavioral problems.*

On the personality side were *negative attitudes, hostility and anger, hypersensitivity,* and *eccentricity.* On the behavioral side were *procrastination, attendance, alcohol and drug abuse,* and *not complying with company rules.* Supervisors should consider referring employees with difficult problems to *professional counselors.*

Discipline, although often perceived as a negative activity, can be viewed as positive if it achieves the desired results. A more modern view of discipline is that of *guiding and/or correcting certain types of employee behavior. Documentation* is an important part of disciplinary activities.

A fairly typical approach to discipline is what is termed *progressive discipline,* which increases the severity of disciplinary measures each time an employee must be disciplined. The *red-hot stove rule,* an analogous guide to disciplinary action, was also discussed in the chapter.

Among the reasons why disciplinary efforts sometimes *fail* include *insufficient advance notice, ambiguous rules, prejudice, insufficient evidence,* and *unfair punishment.* Following *proven disciplinary interviewing techniques and guidelines* can aid substantially in avoiding unnecessary conflict between the supervisor and disciplined employees.

One of the most unpleasant tasks supervisors must do is *fire* employees. Following certain *guidelines,* as cited in the chapter, can make the activity less formidable.

Questions for Discussion

1. What is meant by the statement, "A more salutary manner of looking at employee problems is as *challenges* or *disguised opportunities*"?
2. What can a supervisor do to attempt to encourage *negative types of employees* to develop more *positive attitudes*?
3. What is a recommended approach to take when confronted by a highly *emotional, angry* employee?
4. What do *hypersensitive* employees seem to need?
5. Should organizations tolerate employees who are nonconforming *eccentrics*?
6. What can a supervisor do to attempt to discourage employees from *procrastinating* on the job?
7. Evaluate the following statement: "There's not much a supervisor can do about *excessive absenteeism.* Some employees are just programmed to miss more workdays than others."
8. Why should supervisors neither attempt personally to diagnose *alcohol or drug problems* nor counsel individuals about them?
9. What can a supervisor do about the employee who *fails to comply with rules*?
10. Why is *discipline* considered a form of *control*?
11. Why is *documentation* an important part of any disciplinary action? How does an *incident file* relate to documentation?
12. Why is *progressive discipline* referred to as "progressive?"
13. How does the *red-hot stove rule* relate to disciplinary activities?
14. What are *five reasons* discussed in the chapter as to why disciplinary efforts sometimes *fail*?
15. Why is it generally considered undesirable to criticize an employee *in front of others*?
16. Why do some managers feel that a fired employee should be *discharged as soon as possible* after the decision to fire has been made?

Can You Define These Terms?

Instructions: Write a definition for each of the following terms. You may check your definitions with those provided in the end-of-text Glossary.

problem employee
personality
hypersensitivity
eccentricity
eccentric personality
procrastination
well pay
bonus days off
substance dependency
discipline
self-discipline
punishment
documentation
incident file

progressive discipline
wildcat strike
red-hot stove rule
wrongful discharge
outplacement consultants

Supervision In Action

16–1 "But You Said We Were Friends!"

About three months ago, Kevin Nardinelli was promoted to a supervisory position in the industrial model-making department of Stereolithographic Technology Company's Beaverton division. Before his promotion, Kevin had always been one of the gang, so to speak, and quite popular with his peers. He was especially good friends with one of his coworkers, Patrick Olkowski. Both Kevin's and Patrick's families socialized regularly, and both men attended athletic events together.

After Kevin's promotion, he wondered if he could still be close friends with Patrick without appearing to show favoritism. Kevin thought to himself, "There's nothing really wrong with continuing to socialize with Patrick as long as I treat all the members of my department fairly. Besides, I've always liked Patrick as a friend."

Recently there has been a change in one of Patrick's habits. Twice in the past month he was late for work. Kevin didn't say anything to Patrick the first time he was late. There happens to be a companywide progressive discipline program in effect that requires a manager to give an oral warning after the first tardiness. A written notice with an entry into the employee's personnel file is to be given for the second offense. A third offense results in a half-day's suspension without pay.

This morning Patrick was a half-hour late, his third tardiness in recent weeks. Kevin decided to have a discussion with Patrick, which went as follows:

Kevin: Patrick, this is the third time you've been late in two weeks. I'm going to have to give you a written notice this time and make an entry into your personnel records.

Patrick: Come on, old buddy. Don't do that. I promise I'll try to improve my punctuality. I've been having troubles with my Toyota recently.

Kevin: I can appreciate that you might be having some car problems, Patrick, but I have to treat you the same as I treat anyone else. You know I had Bernard's pay docked about a month ago for excessive tardiness, don't you?

Patrick: I'm really not concerned about Bernard; I gotta worry about *numero uno*—and that's *moi*! For crying out loud, Kevin—don't you remember that we've been good friends? You can let it slip by this time. It's not going to hurt anyone. Besides, what are friends for? Oh yeah, *mon ami,* are you and Carla still coming to our barbecue this Sunday?

Questions

1. Can a person who has been promoted risk continuing to be

friends with is or her former peers? Explain your position.

2. How would you handle this disciplinary problem if you were Kevin? Demonstrate your approach by role playing the situation, with another person taking the role of Patrick.

16–2 A Switch in Time

Hayward Koo is a supervisor with the electroplating department of the SimpCo Corporation located in Catonsville. He is in charge of 15 day-shift and 11 second-shift employees.

Melanie Mosley was hired by SimpCo about three weeks ago and assigned to Hayward's department. Melanie was pleased to have been selected for a day-shift position because of her family situation. She has a young son, Jeffrey, who is seven years old and in the second grade. Her husband, Forest, is able to get Jeffrey ready for school in the morning. The day shift at SimpCo begins at 7:00 A.M. and ends at 2:30 P.M., which enables Melanie to be home in time for Jeffrey's return from school. (The second-shift hours are 2:15 P.M. to 9:45 P.M.) If it hadn't been for the day-shift hours, Melanie would not have taken the position. In fact, Hayward assured Melanie at the time she was hired that she would be able to work the day shift on a permanent basis.

An unexpected increase in demand for SimpCo's line of products recently necessitated an expansion of the second-shift's crew. Hayward's boss, Kristi Guelzo, informed Hayward yesterday (Thursday) that starting this upcoming Monday three of his personnel should be transferred to the second shift because three new employees had been hired and assigned to the day shift. Melanie is one of the three employees whom Hayward has selected to transfer to the night shift. He had the lead person, Edward, who assists him in supervising the crew, relay the information to the three persons.

When Melanie learned the news from Edward, she just about hit the ceiling. In fact, she was emotionally and quite visibly upset when she stormed up to Hayward's desk, where the following discussion took place:

Melanie: Mr. Koo, I've got to see you in private. I'm really upset about something.

Koo: Listen, Melanie, if you've got any gripes, you can tell me right here. I don't have time to leave my desk.

Melanie: But Mr. Koo, I'm really disturbed about something and would prefer not to talk to you in front of all the other employees.

Koo: Geez, another one of those working mothers. You know, I thought you were going to be trouble from the day personnel assigned you to me.

Melanie: (shouting): Damn it, Mr. Koo! You haven't even let me explain to you what I'm upset about.

Koo: Well, I've seen your type before. You working mothers think the world owes you a special living!

Melanie: (shaking with emotion): You are without a doubt one of the most lousy, no-good s.o.b.'s I've ever worked for. I don't have to take your. . . .

Koo: (interrupting): You don't have any choice, little girl. And watch your fowl mouth. Women don't talk that way in this plant! One more word out of you and you're fired.

Melanie: Listen here, Koo, all I came in here to tell you was. . . .

Koo: That's it—pack up your gear and go home; you're through, sweetheart!

Melanie: (throwing up her arms and walking out): I give up!

The next Monday morning, the union steward, Frieda Fairmont, called Koo on the telephone and said, "Koo, I'll be by to see you at 9:30 this morning to discuss a grievance that one of your employees, Ms. Melanie Mosley, filed with me on Friday afternoon. Her side of the story indicates a gross mishandling of a complaint she tried to discuss with you last Friday. I will be bringing with me another employee who overheard all of the discourse between you and Melanie."

Questions

1. What *specifically* was wrong with the manner in which Koo handled Melanie's complaint?

2. Develop a set of recommendations for handling employee complaints that could relate to the Mosley/Koo confrontation.

Endnotes

1. *American Heritage Dictionary* (New York: Houghton Mifflin, 1985), p. 892.
2. Gardner Lindzey, Calvin S. Hall, and Richard F. Thompson, *Psychology* (New York: Worth Publishers, 1976), p. 773.
3. Brenton R. Schlender, "Meanwhile, Back among the Fir Trees at Microsoft. . . .," *Fortune* (International Edition), October 9, 1989, p. 44.
4. Gene Dent, "Absenteeism Solution Must Deal with Many Factors," *World of Work Report,* August 1986, pp. 3, 4.
5. Stan Kossen, *The Human Side of Organizations,* 5th ed. (New York: Harper, Collins, 1991), Ch. 12.
6. "Layoffs in '88 Affect 450,000, BLS Study Omits Some Key States," AFL-CIO News, August 19, 1989, p. 10.

Chapter 17

The Art of Managing Your Boss

You don't have to like nor do you have to hate your boss. You do have to manage your boss so he or she becomes your resource for achievement, accomplishment, and personal success.

—Peter F. Drucker, Management Philosopher

The most effective managers are those who can exert influence not only downward but also upward in their organizations, thereby enabling their work group to get the support it needs to attain its goals.

—Warren Keith Schilit, Educator

Learning Objectives

When you finish this chapter, you should be able to:

1. Apply techniques for maintaining and improving your relationship with your boss.
2. Avoid counterproductive relationships with your boss.
3. Utilize proven techniques for selling ideas to your boss.

Much of what we've discussed to this point has revolved around the relationship between you—a supervisor—and the people accountable to you. But that is only one of the important relationships that you must be concerned with; another is the relationship that exists between you and your boss.

As a leader, you may spend considerable time in developing programs designed to aid you in working more effectively with your associates. A sadly neglected area, however, one that is possibly even more important to your future achievement, accomplishments, and personal success: the development of techniques for working more effectively with and through your boss.

Bosses, as you've surely noticed, are also human beings. And as with any human being, bosses too have human needs, feelings, and sentiments. Most of the sound leadership concepts related to dealing with associates also can be applied to your relationship with your boss. Should working effectively with your boss really be important to you? You bet it should! Your boss directly influences your organizational existence. He or she regularly appraises you, and those appraisals can affect your *future salary, future job assignments,* and *career path.*

Your boss also needs your support, since his or her successes are also tied directly to the types of relationships he or she has with associates, peers, and other bosses. So it should be fairly apparent that both you and your boss need each other. You both significantly influence each other's present job satisfactions and future job opportunities. Learning how to relate to your boss, therefore, can create a working environment for you that is far more enriching than one in which conflict and stress perpetually exist.

In this chapter, then, we'll explore some of the significant ways in which you can *maintain and improve your relationship with your boss.* We'll also study some specific types of *supervisor-boss relationships that you would be wise to avoid.* We'll conclude with an examination of some ways in which you may increase your effectiveness in *"selling" ideas to your boss.*

How Can You Maintain and Improve Your Relationship With Your Boss?

The influence that your boss has on both your present job satisfaction and your future career opportunities should be fairly apparent. The application of some basic and sound supervisor-boss relationships could assist you considerably in maintaining and improving your association with your boss. Let's now examine some specific guidelines and suggestions designed to aid you in interacting with your boss.

Supporting one's own boss with positive reinforcement tends to reap positive benefits.

Are You Supportive of Your Boss?

Supervisors who have regular contact with their bosses often view them in a light that others may never see. Some people who have little exposure to managers may perceive them as invincible, god-like creatures who are never supposed to make mistakes. You, however, may easily see that bosses are nothing like that, but instead have insecurities and other human weaknesses just like everyone else. Seeing your boss make occasional mistakes could cause your confidence level to sag, a condition that might make you less supportive of him or her.

Are you any more likely, however, to have a perfect boss than you are to have perfect employees reporting to you? Are *you* perfect? As Weller's Law states, "Nothing is impossible for those who don't have to do it themselves." We sometimes expect the impossible from others, such as bosses, when we ourselves could never live up to these expectations.

Do you remember the *Pygmalion effect* discussed in Chapter 12? It suggested that your expectations influence the results you are likely to attain. Your boss has the need for recognition and self-esteem, as do you and your associates. The higher anyone goes in an organization, the lonelier it may become. Even presidents of corporations need regular reassurance and support from their employees. Supporting your boss with positive reinforcement, as you do with your own employees, will tend to reap benefits for you. Showing support for your boss is likely to make him or her reciprocate and show far more support for you. Furthermore, by working hard to enable your boss to be promoted, you are at the same time making a space for your own promotion.

Your boss needs you—and you need your boss. Why not focus, then, on his or her positive traits and accomplishments? You both are on the same team, so why not be supportive of your boss just as you would hope and expect your employees to be supportive of you? Since you're unlikely ever to have the perfect boss, you may as well try to adapt to the one you have—or be miserable on your job.

Do You Listen to Your Boss?

We learned in Chapter 13 how listening to employees can really pay off for supervisors. The concepts of active listening are just as applicable when you are dealing with higher management. We needn't repeat here the concepts discussed earlier. You might want to review them at this time and consider how they could apply to your interpersonal relationships with your boss.

An important factor that warrants reemphasis is this: Listening to your boss, or to anyone else, is like giving the other person a compliment. Bosses, too, have their tensions, stresses, and problems that they would like to get off their chests. The higher that managers rise in an organizational hierarchy, the narrower the pyramid becomes, and thus the fewer peers they may have to relate to. Bosses sometimes simply need an "ear to bend," an empathetic person who is willing to listen as a means of helping them reduce tensions. And finally, another basic but highly important reason for listening to your boss is that doing so can help to reduce misunderstandings between the two of you.

Should You Ever Argue or Disagree With Your Boss?

As a leader, with whom do you prefer to deal—employees who maintain *positive* relationships with you or those who are perennially *negative*? Of course, you probably prefer the positive. Similar feelings generally hold true for your boss. He or she is also likely to prefer positive relationships.

A sound guideline for maintaining a constructive supervisor-boss relationship, therefore, is to avoid arguments with your boss. When inclined to argue, you might ask yourself, "Am I really likely to ever *win* an argument with my boss?" You probably won't. If you do win the argument, you might also "win" the opportunity for a transfer or a demotion.

This isn't to say that you should never have healthy and constructive differences of opinion. Of course, there will be some occasions during which you may—and probably should—disagree with your boss. As we'll see in a later section, most effective bosses don't particularly care for a *"Yes, sir/Yes, ma'am"* relationship with their associates. You'll probably gain far more respect, however, if you learn how to disagree without arguing.

Conflict situations provide good opportunities for drawing on your communication skills. Before airing any disagreement you might have with your boss, be certain to weigh the benefits versus the costs of expressing opposing views. You can often sense your boss's reaction, so why push a rejected idea to the point of lowering your esteem in the boss's eyes? As one manager bluntly said, "A safe course of action is this: When the presentation of different points of view is permitted, argue to the point of decision, and then either accept the boss's decision or go to work somewhere else!"

The purpose of your actions should be to try to accomplish or change something. If you're not going to be better off as a result of your actions, then there is little purpose in complaining (other than getting things off your chest). Arguing with your boss merely to release your personal tensions could be an unwise move that leads to undesirable consequences. If you sense an argumentative feeling coming on, you should try to recall the words adapted from a prayer by Reinhold Niebuhr:

> *God grant me the serenity to accept the things I cannot change; the courage to change the things I can; and the wisdom to know the difference.*[1]

If the Reverend's prayer doesn't help, you might try some form of physical activity (such as running or biking) as a stress release.

Do You Make Selective Use of Your Boss's Time?

Bosses, if they're "earning their salt," tend to have their days jam-packed with scheduled activities. Although effective bosses tend to allow for those omnipresent surprise factors that creep into virtually every workday, they don't particularly relish having their activities unnecessarily interrupted.

Do you remember the *exception principle* from Chapter 8? To refresh your memory, it states that regular, recurring activities and decisions should routinely be delegated to and handled by employees, and unusual, nonrecurring decisions should be referred to a higher level. We previously discussed the concept as it relates to you and your employees. The exception principle, like many concepts, can also apply to your relationship with your boss.

Just like you, your boss has only so much time, and probably doesn't want to be continually interrupted. Whenever you draw on his or her time, you are using time that your boss probably has scheduled for something else. Consequently, you should become familiar with the boundaries of your decision-making authority, and make routine decisions within the scope of your authority without continually running to your boss about minor matters. Once again, keep your manager informed of your activities, but try to be somewhat selective in your use of his or her time. Consuming it for relatively trivial matters that you can adequately handle yourself may result in your boss neglecting other affairs that require his or her immediate attention. Excessively interrupting your boss to discuss trivial matters may also lower your esteem in his or her eyes.

Should You Admit Your Blunders?

There's a natural tendency for supervisors to be embarrassed by personal mistakes, especially those supervisors who suffer from the misconception that *leaders aren't supposed to make mistakes.* Rather than trying to cover up your mistakes, or "passing the buck" by blaming your associates, peers, or bosses for your actions, you're far more likely to gain your boss's respect by admitting when you're wrong or when you don't know something. Someone once said, "Doctors are luckier than leaders; doctors can bury their mistakes!" Most people don't expect you to be superhuman, so they're not going to be especially shocked when they see you make an occasional error. When you do err, apologize sincerely and move on to correct the mistake so that you can resume normal working relationships.

Must You Discuss Mini-Problems?

A pet phrase of advertising agencies is, "It pays to advertise." Advertising certainly gets results, but sometimes not the results that are desired. Here's an amusing example of some unwanted results:

> *Two businesspersons are talking. One says: "Is your new advertising getting results?"*
> *"It sure is," answers the second. "Last week we advertised for a night security guard, and the next night we got robbed!"*

Let's assume that you have a few minor problems that you know can be solved easily. Unexpected reactions sometimes erupt when you "advertise" small problems to your manager. Because of your manager's concern and attitude of responsibility, he or she may feel that your problem is far more critical than it actually is.

Of course, you're likely to have some small problems that arise now and then, some of which may increase in scope, but most of which you can probably handle on your own with little difficulty. Your manager is likely to periodically ask you how things are going. If you respond with, "Well, there's this problem I'm working on . . . ," your manager may become overconcerned. Before you can take another breath, you have *another* problem—one with your manager. There's no need to waste the manager's time with a lot of trivial or routine problems that you can handle quite well by yourself.

When your manager asks "How are things going?" you can say something like, "Fine, thanks," unless, of course, you have exceptional problems that require his or her awareness or attention. Naturally, you should always keep your manager informed of things that he or she needs to know. But for routine problems that you can easily handle by yourself, there is no particular need to waste your manager's time.

Do You Avoid Credibility Gaps?

We now come to an important recommendation, which ignoring can be extremely hazardous to your future organizational health: *Avoid activities that create credibility gaps between you and your boss.* If you deceive your boss, the chances are quite good that you'll ultimately be caught, which will be likely to create a situation in which your manager will not trust your future statements.

Related to making intentional false statements is making promises that you don't fulfill. By keeping track of your commitments and setting goals for their completion, you're more likely to inspire the type of personal image that you'd like your boss to have of you. Be certain to let your boss know in advance if you'll be unable to fulfill a prior commitment.

What Types of Supervisor-Boss Relationships Should You Avoid?

A great deal of tension and conflict seem to exist between some supervisors and their bosses. Such strained relationships are frequently the result of the ways in which supervisors interact with their bosses. Let's now turn to some specific examples that highlight the select ways in which some supervisors deal with their bosses—and generally attain *counterproductive results* in the process. An understanding of these negative approaches should help you to recognize why they should be avoided in your interpersonal relationships with your own boss.

What Is the "Yes, Sir/Yes, Ma'am" Relationship?

Some supervisors believe that they must do everything possible to please their bosses. As a result, they develop what could be called a **Yes, sir/Yes, ma'am relationship** to virtually everything the boss says, always responding in a fawning manner. Is it likely that you would gain respect from your boss by such behavior? Probably not. You may not appear to be too secure in your boss's eyes. You likewise could be perceived in a negative light, unless your boss shortsightedly prefers the "Yes, sir/Yes, ma'am" type of subordinate. Usually, though, you would probably *lose* rather than *gain* the respect of your manager through such behavior.

Yes, sir/Yes, ma'am relationship: *A servile, condescending way of interacting with those of higher authority.*

Problems other than the loss of respect can also result from a "Yes, sir/Yes, ma'am" relationship with bosses. For example, this author has observed a supervisor in the publishing industry who seemed to develop near-panic whenever higher-level managers walked into his department. He appeared to feel that the way to show respect to the higher-level managers was to drop everything he was working on and give the manager his undivided attention. A major shortcoming inherent in this approach was that the supervisor was usually working with a chemical process requiring his full attention. Neglecting the chemical process in order to provide instant service to the manager often resulted in the costly destruction of the entire project he was working on. Regardless, the supervisor repeatedly acted this way whenever a higher-level manager was present.

The supervisor who acts in a submissive way toward his or her boss may not have developed a sufficient amount of self-confidence or feeling of security with those in positions of authority. Any supervisor should try to keep in mind that bosses really are human too. They put on their shoes the same way you do—one shoe at a time. Bosses have the same types of frailties, the same types of insecurities, and many of the same types of needs that you have. You would be well advised to try to avoid the demeaning "Yes, sir/Yes, ma'am" relationship with your boss.

What Is the "Hotliner" Relationship?

An agreement was made between the Soviet Union and the United States at the Geneva Disarmament Conference in 1963 to establish a so-called "hotline" between Moscow and Washington D.C. Its primary purpose was to provide a direct-line teletype communication system between the chiefs of state of both countries for use during critical emergencies. It was first used in 1967 during an Israeli-Arab conflict. Various crises hotlines also exist throughout the United States to enable callers to obtain information, be counseled, or talk confidentially with sympathetic listeners.

Hotliner relationship: *Behavior characterized by bypassing normal chains of command.*

A less favorable offshoot of this concept—one that relates to the scalar principle of organization discussed in Chapter 8—is what can be termed the **hotliner relationship** between a supervisor and higher levels of management. A "hotliner" is the type of person who bypasses official lines of communication and talks "out of school," so to speak, to senior management about other personnel and their activities. Virtually anything the hotliner's boss, peers, or associates do or say immediately shoots right up to higher levels of management.

As a supervisor, you may be assuming unnecessary risks by communicating directly with the "top" rather than either confronting a situation yourself or recognizing those things that you have little control over. Take, for example, the case of a young supervisor—let's call him Ernest—whose father happens to be the president of the company. Ernest is a conscientious person who wants to see the plant run efficiently, especially since he has family ties to the firm. Ernest feels that the plant manager, Sophie, does an inefficient job of running the plant and managing people. Because of his vested concerns, Ernest "hotlines" all of his feelings to his father about the way Sophie is running the plant.

Although Ernest may feel that he has every right to inform his father about all the problems he sees in other personnel, he runs the risk of alienating others who may find out that he is the organization "stool pigeon." He may even find out that others begin to hesitate confiding in or communicating with him for fear that everything they say will be transmitted directly to his father. Ernest, like any supervisor, needs the confidence of others. He should weigh the risks of revealing certain types of information to others that could create more harm than good for him and the organization.

What Is the "Stab-in-the-Back" Relationship?

There are some supervisors who, for a variety of reasons, intentionally attempt to make their bosses look bad. Their association with their bosses is what can be called the **stab-in-the-back relationship.** Supervisors, like some employees, may have a subconscious resistance toward authority. Some supervisors, even though they too are managers, may either resent being in a subordinate relationship to someone else or may harbor deep-seated feelings of animosity toward their bosses for specific past incidents. Furthermore, supervisors usually want to look good in the eyes of their associates. Certain supervisors may feel that one way to make themselves look good in their associates' eyes is to criticize their own bosses. In some cases, some supervisors may try to make their boss look bad because they want his or her job.

Stab-in-the-back relationship: *Behavior intended to make one's own manager look bad.*

Some supervisors may also have personal problems that affect their on-the-job performance. Other supervisors may be just plain frustrated about some aspect of their lives or work. For example, perhaps they feel their bosses have imposed unrealistic deadlines on them, which has caused stress and frustration. People react in a variety of ways when they are frustrated, ranging from increased absenteeism to missing deadlines and sabotaging work processes. Persons who try to make their bosses look bad may have serious psychological problems and could be in need of professional counseling. Their actions could be a subconscious reaction to their own problems and frustrations.

What Is the "Boot Ensign" Relationship?

There is a situation in the military that has its parallel in civilian organizations, one that could be termed the **boot ensign relationship.** In the U.S. Navy, for example, a boot ensign is a person who has completed officers' training school and recently arrived at a first assignment with little in the way of practical experience.

Boot ensign relationship: *Attempting to effect too much change before gaining the confidence of others.*

The new officer may see activities and processes that, based on past formal education and recent training, appear to be inefficient. The inexperienced officer may impatiently feel that changes have to be made soon and may complain to his or her superior about the sad state of organizational affairs that exist in the work unit. Or the officer may make unilateral changes that affect enlisted personnel who usually are much older and have been in the military considerably longer. In some instances, the affected personnel may have served for 15 to 20 years, while the ensign has served for only a matter of months.

A problem often arises when a young officer starts exercising authority without drawing on the backgrounds and experiences of older staff, or starts telling his or her boss how to handle an established set of work activities. Such behavior may cause oldtimers to develop a resentment of the newcomer. Consider how you would feel, for example, if you were a manager and a new supervisor said something to you that came across like: "Everything's wrong around here! I frankly don't see how you were able to function before I got here!"

You may find yourself in the "boot ensign" position one day. If so, try not to come on too aggressively with either your boss, your peers, or your associates. You may see situations that seem to be in dire need of changing. To avoid a serious morale problem and possible conflict between you and your boss, peers, or associates, wait until you've gained their confidence before making or even suggesting a lot of changes. Although your intentions are doubtlessly honorable, you may come across as a "know-it-all" who isn't really concerned about the feelings and ideas of others.

What Is the "Two-Faced" Relationship?

Two-faced relationship: *Behavior critical of the manager in front of employees and critical of employees in front of the manager.*

Another type of relationship some supervisors experience with their bosses and other individuals is what can be called the **two-faced relationship.** This involves the type of supervisor who is continually putting others down, criticizing workers when with management and criticizing management when with workers. This is a negative sort of relationship that you should actively strive to avoid. The two-faced approach can have a significantly demoralizing effect on organizational members. In addition, you'll probably lose the respect of your boss *and* your associates.

It's not very satisfying to work around people who are continually negative, constantly criticizing things rather than attempting to build them up. Morale in an organization is likely to be much better if a positive climate is maintained in the workplace. As a supervisor, you strongly influence the organizational climate and culture. If you're a gossip who continually faults everything and everyone in the organization, you're likely to find that your associates are going to react similarly. People, as we know, tend to follow as they're led.

What Is the "Work-Overload" Relationship?

Work-overload relationship: *Situation in which a manager assigns excessive amounts of tasks to a supervisor.*

Some supervisors have a veritable stress-inducing relationship with their bosses termed the **work-overload relationship.** This is the situation in which your boss doesn't seem to recognize how busy

Good lines of communication can help avoid work-overload relationships between supervisors and their managers.

you already are, or how long tasks actually take for completion, and, instead, keeps piling more and more projects on you. Such a relationship can be frustrating and discouraging, especially if you seldom feel that you are on top of your work.

What can you do if you find yourself in this sort of a relationship, where you are asked to take on new tasks and responsibilities that you know can't be worked into your already overcrammed schedule? Be honest with your boss, who might be like some bosses who genuinely don't realize they are overloading their supervisors. Point out that you would sincerely like to take on the project, but that your present workload prevents you from being able to do a satisfactory job on it. You might also indicate that, rather than to do a lousy job, you'd rather not take on any additional responsibilities at this time. Isn't it unlikely that your boss would want you to do a slipshod job on an important task?

A different approach you might take is to say something like:

"You mentioned earlier that the Fisher and Lassen accounts were red-hot priority jobs. If I take on this additional project, one of those two will have to be delayed. Which one would you recommend I put aside?"

In some instances, you might maintain a better personal image by indicating that you'd like to give the request careful consideration before deciding to take it on. Then, within two or three days, contact your boss again and explain that your present schedule doesn't allow you to take on any additional responsibilities. Don't let too much time elapse, however, between the request and your response. If you do, you might begin to develop guilt feelings that could interfere with your normal working activities.

W. H. Weiss recommends that you not succumb to the temptation of pointing out how much you are already doing in relation to another supervisor. You may put your manager in the defensive position of having to justify his or her actions regarding the other supervisor, and your assignments will probably not change.[2]

In some cases, it may be better for you to merely grin and bear it, so to speak, especially where there are "political" implications associated with your turning down a new task or opportunity. In some instances, your career path might be damaged if you fail to make certain adjustments in your schedule to show your boss that you are willing to accept additional assignments. Therefore, it might be better to take on the additional task without comment, which you could later use as evidence as to why you should qualify for a pay raise or promotion.

Do Bosses Have to Be Sold?

Some people react negatively to the concept of selling. The word *salesperson* evokes negative images in their minds. They envision a fast-talking, quick-stepping, high-pressure huckster, wildly beating on their doors, overeager to take the money and run—to extract as much as possible from prospective customers' hard-earned paychecks.

But all selling activities don't necessarily fall into such common stereotypes. Selling is a skill, and like any skill it can be either used or abused. From our point of view, however, selling is the art of influencing and persuading others to "buy" a particular point of view.

Virtually everyone engages in sales or persuasion activities of some sort, even if they're not actively concerned with promoting and marketing goods and services. Children try to sell their parents on a variety of things. Husbands and wives also attempt to sell each other on various ideas or activities. And supervisors often find themselves in the position where they have to sell their bosses on ideas, concepts, or activities. Selling, therefore, doesn't have to be an invidious activity unless, of course, your goal is to be underhanded. As a supervisor, you *have* to be a salesperson from time to time if you are going to motivate others to act on your ideas. You should realize that many of the concepts taught to salespeople apply significantly to the relationship you have with your boss. In this section, we'll explore a few basic selling concepts that you can apply to that relationship.[3]

What Is the FUN-FAB Approach?

In training salespeople, one of the things sales managers usually discourage is focusing on a product's *features* during the sales presentation. For example, salespeople are advised to use a sales approach that is referred to as the **FUN-FAB approach.** The *FUN* in FUN-FAB stands for *f*irst *u*ncover *n*eeds. The *FAB* stands for *f*eatures, *a*dvantages, and *b*enefits. Let's see if we can shed some light on this alphabet soup.

FUN-FAB approach: *Acronym symbolizing a method for selling ideas or products, first uncover needs; then relate features, advantages, and benefits.*

Imagine for the moment that you are a salesperson trying to sell a product to a customer. Assume that your product is a videocassette recorder/player. Should you begin your presentation by stressing the *features,* such as the black color of the equipment's casing? Or should you begin by stressing the specific *advantages* this recorder/player has over others, such as the ability to operate videocassettes manufactured in France and the Netherlands, where different video broadcasting systems exist? Actually, you should begin with neither. First you should carefully try to determine what the customer *wants* or *needs*—that is, what is important *to him or her,* not to you. Then you can put the three parts of FAB together and show your customer how your product's *features, advantages,* and *benefits* relate to his or her wants and needs.

What are you overlooking when you extol the virtues of the black color of the videocassette recorder/player's casing? Perhaps a black color isn't the least bit important to your prospective customer. Merely because *you* think that the black color is great doesn't mean that your customer does. You should try to find out if color is even important to the prospective buyer before stressing the desirability of a color that you prefer.

The same concepts can apply when you're trying to sell your boss on an idea. You should relate your idea to how your boss or the organization is going to *benefit*—that is, focus on those factors that will satisfy his or her wants and needs.

If, for example, you are attempting to sell your boss on giving you a pay raise, would you necessarily be persuasive by pointing out what a great person you are and, therefore, talk primarily about your own personal characteristics? Not necessarily. You'd probably be far more effective pointing out how the *organization* has benefited and will continue to benefit from your performance. You might show your boss statistics that indicate improved results in your department, such as reduced scrap rates or absenteeism. You can show him or her how you willingly took on added assignments when you were already overburdened. Your own personal wants, such as the desire to buy a weekend cabin in the mountains or to send your child to medical school, are far less important to your boss than knowing how you have been satisfying the needs of the organization.

A similar situation exists when you are vying for a promotion. Knowing and stressing your strong points *and* relating them to the needs of the organization will be far more persuasive than merely talking about yourself and your own personal needs. Don't be like the girl scout attempting to sell cookies door-to-door by saying something like, "If *you buy* these cookies, *I get to go* on a one-week trip to Pismo Beach, all expenses paid." Are you really concerned about the vacation to Pismo Beach the child might win? You might be, but wouldn't her approach be more direct if she appealed to *your* tastes and needs?

How Can AIDA Aid You?

AIDA approach: *Symbolizes four steps related to influencing others: attention, interest, desire, and action.*

Another technique often used by professional salespeople is the **AIDA approach.** The use of AIDA involves four specific steps, each of which are goals related to a person's attempts at influencing another person. These steps are:

1. Obtain *a*ttention.
2. Arouse *i*nterest.
3. Arouse *d*esire.
4. Obtain *a*ction.

The first letter of each goal makes up the acronym *AIDA.* When applying this approach, you are, in effect, guiding your boss through the four steps in order to persuade him or her to decide on something of interest to you.

Step one involves getting the boss's *attention,* which should take place as early as possible during the interview. You can't get very far in selling the boss an idea unless you have his or her attention. Obtaining undivided attention is going to be difficult if your boss's mind is preoccupied with something else or burdened with problems or pressures. If you sense that you can't readily obtain the boss's attention at a particular time, maybe you'd better make an appointment for another time when he or she will be more receptive.

After you get your boss's attention, the second step in AIDA is to try to arouse his or her *interest* in the meaning of your message. You can gain interest through a sound choice of words, or maybe through graphic means, such as charts or other types of visual aids. Once again, focusing on organizational needs, interests, and desires is more apt to secure his or her attention.

The third step in AIDA is attempting to get your boss to have a *desire* to do something related to your proposal. Without a desire—that is, the feeling of wanting something—the final step, *action,* is unlikely to follow. And it is *action*—a *decision*—that you're attempting to influence your manager into making. In summary, you've got to get the *attention, interest,* and *desire* of the person you're trying to sell something to so that you can get that person—in this case, your manager—to engage in *action* of some sort.

Trial balloon approach: *Technique intended to test reactions of other people to ideas.*

Should You Try a Balloon?

A fairly soft-sell approach that is often very effective in selling ideas to your boss is the **trial balloon approach.** For example, to employ this technique you might say something to your boss like, "The other day I got an idea I'd like to share with you. . . ." After briefly discussing the idea you might quickly back off, not even referring to the idea again during the current conversation.

You've just planted a seed, so to speak, in your boss's mind that very likely could grow and blossom. You have not forced him or her into an immediate decision or defensive position. People often develop initial negative attitudes toward new ideas that require adjustments in their thinking or behavior. After a chance to mull them over in their minds without the feeling of being "up against the wall," bosses often become far more receptive.

Here's another more specific example of the trial balloon approach: Assume there's a temporary assignment at another branch of your company that you are interested in taking. To sell your boss on the idea of assigning you to the position, you might merely express an interest in the position but not actually ask your boss to make a decision at this time. Doing this might enable you to know immediately how receptive your boss is to the idea. At the same time, you might also uncover some clues as to what you will have to emphasize when you actually ask your boss for a decision. A boss may have an immediate negative response to a new idea or proposal, but if given lots of space—that is, ample time to think about the idea—his or her resistance is more likely to fade.

An offshoot of the trial balloon approach is the **trial offer approach.** This technique assumes that to make a fairly large "sale," you are willing to settle for less at first in order to convince the "client" on the merits of your idea. For example, assume that you want to sell your boss on the idea of obtaining five new pieces of relatively expensive equipment for your department. You have fairly valid reasons to believe that your boss is going to reject the request because of the high cost. However, you might suggest that the department buys and tries one machine so that you can develop concrete evidence related to how cost effective the equipment is. The boss is likely to be more receptive to purchasing additional equipment when factual information related to the cost savings of the first piece of equipment is readily available.

Trial offer approach: *Technique intended to gain acceptance of ideas by suggesting that someone try a small segment of the idea.*

What Is a Third-Party Reference Approach?

Another technique for selling ideas to your boss is the use of the **third-party reference approach.** With this technique, you use the names of other concerned parties in the organization who support your ideas. Your boss is likely to be more supportive of your efforts if other leaders in whom he or she has confidence also show their support. Your reference to them may serve as sort of a *peer effect* that will influence your boss positively.

Third-party reference approach: *The use of names of other concerned parties to support ideas during efforts to sell a manager on the ideas.*

Contacting others in the organization who are likely to be affected by your proposals is also considered common courtesy. Frequently, the success of your plans will depend on their support, so you have a headstart on selling your boss if other managers in the organization are already sold. Of course, this technique is less effective if your boss feels that you lack authority to contact others to gain support for your ideas before obtaining his or her prior approval. Try your best to discern what approach will most effectively appeal to your boss.

How Critical Is Timing?

Whenever attempting to sell your boss on ideas, you should try to be sure that your *timing* is right. It's hard to be absolutely certain when the "right" time is, but by being alert you can frequently recognize those times that would be unsatisfactory for trying to persuade your boss on matters that are important to you.

Attempt to assess your boss's present mood before trying to sell him or her on something. Also, be sure to do your homework before you have a conference with your boss. For example, if your request is going to involve substantial financial outlays, be certain to check in advance on the current state of the budget.

In many situations, optimum timing is as important as your choice of words. A good rule to follow is to convey important messages *when your message is competing least with other communications or situations attempting to gain the attention of your audience.* Remember, too, that your message is also more likely to be considered and listened to when it provides a *benefit* or a *solution to a problem* affecting the receiver.

"Timing is everything."

Source: Reprinted from *The Wall Street Journal* by permission of Cartoon Features Syndicate, ©.

Summary

Much of this text has focused thus far on the subject of developing more effective managerial techniques and skills for working with and through subordinates. Many of these concepts apply with equal importance to the *relationships a supervisor has with his or her boss.*

This chapter focused on some specific methods for *maintaining* and *improving* your relationship with your boss. It also dealt with the types of supervisor-boss relationships that should be *avoided.* Handling a boss effectively requires a certain amount of *selling ability.* We discussed some of the proven techniques for selling to others, with special stress placed on relating to the *needs and benefits* to your boss of accepting your ideas.

The selling approaches examined included *FUN-FAB, AIDA, trial balloon, trial offer,* and the *third-party reference.* We concluded with the suggestion that you be concerned with *timing* when attempting to approach and convince your boss to accept your ideas.

Questions for Discussion

1. Why do some people tend to have greater—but sometimes less realistic—expectations regarding their *boss's performance* than they do for their own performances?
2. What are some of the benefits that can result from your *listening actively and empathetically* to your boss?
3. Paraphrase in your own words the following statement: "You can seldom become the real victor in an argument with your boss."
4. Why is the *selective use of your boss's time* so important?
5. Evaluate the following statement: "When you are in a situation in which you fear making a mistake, the best approach is to avoid making decisions altogether."
6. According to the chapter, is it advisable to keep your boss *informed of every problem* that crops up in your department?
7. What is frequently the unfavorable result of *not fulfilling commitments*?
8. Evaluate the following statement: "I frankly prefer having the *'Yes, sir/Yes, ma'am'* type of supervisors reporting to me in my position as general manager. Those types of supervisors enable me to get my job done more effectively because they are obedient, respect my ideas and wishes, and enable me to achieve my goals with fewer disruptions."
9. In what ways might the *hotliner* type of supervisor create problems for him- or herself?
10. Why might some supervisors adopt a *stab-in-the-back relationship* with their bosses? Are they likely to gain from such an approach? Explain.

11. What advice might you give to a *"boot ensign,"* that is, a new supervisor, who feels that the many good ideas he or she offers to the staff are unreasonably rejected?
12. Describe the *two-faced relationship* that some supervisors employ. Why should it be avoided?
13. What can you do if your boss has the tendency to *overload you with tasks*?
14. In what ways should supervisors consider themselves *"salespeople"*?
15. Develop a specific example of how you might employ the *FUN-FAB technique* of selling your boss on an idea.
16. What is the significance of the *AIDA approach* to selling your boss on ideas?
17. How might the *trial balloon approach* assist you in getting your ideas across to your manager? How does it relate to the *trial offer approach*?
18. Why is the *timing* of any proposal to your manager so critical to its likely acceptance?

Can You Define These Terms?

Instructions: Write a definition for each of the following terms. You may check your definitions with those provided in the end-of-text Glossary.

Yes, sir/Yes, ma'am relationship
hotliner relationship
stab-in-the-back relationship
boot ensign relationship
two-faced relationship
work-overload relationship

FUN-FAB approach
AIDA approach
trial balloon approach
trial offer approach
third-party reference approach

Supervision In Action

17–1 "Have I Got a Boss!"

"My name is Sycamore Morrison. I'm a supervisor of the accounts payable section of one of the largest banks in town. I've been in this position for about 18 months. I used to get considerable satisfaction from my job. I've generally had a good relationship with my employees. Recently, however, I haven't had such good feelings. Let me explain why.

"About three months ago, I got a new boss, Hyman Kaustic. I'm no psychologist, but I personally feel that Mr. Kaustic doesn't feel too secure in his situation—either that, or he doesn't understand much about professional management. I'm not pretending I'm an expert on management, but I have been taking courses at Navarro Community College during the past year and a half, and Mr. Kaustic seems to me to be the perfect example of what we were taught not to do as supervisors.

"For example, Mr. Kaustic continually bypasses me in dealing with my employees. He gives them direct orders, which sometimes are contrary to what I've told them to do. This undermines my authority.

"Something else Mr. Kaustic does that really bugs me is to override my decisions and criticize me in front of my associates. This really embarrasses me and affects my credibility with them.

"Also, I've always tried to improve things in my department. I've heard through the grapevine, however, that Mr. Kaustic has been taking credit for some of the new procedures that I've developed.

"As I mentioned, I really liked working here in the past. I thought I had a good future with the company, and I hoped to rise in the organization. Now, quite frankly, I'm frustrated. I'm not sure what to do. I'm about ready to start looking for a different job in another company."

Question

What are some specific alternatives that Morrison might consider to reduce or eliminate the frustrations she is currently facing?

17–2 "But, Boss! None of the Other Sups Are Doing It!"

About a month ago, your boss, Reginald Cook, requested that you and the other supervisors in your office enforce the 10-minute coffee break rule. During the previous six months, the enforcement of the rule was generally ignored and most employees were taking 15- to 20-minute breaks.

You told each of the employees in your department that breaks were not to exceed 10 minutes, but apparently not all of the other supervisors followed suit. A number of your employees have complained that it's grossly unfair for them to be restricted to only 10 minutes when not everyone else is.

A few of your employees have started taking longer breaks again. Production demands and workloads have been somewhat slack recently so you are not really certain if you should enforce the 10-minute break rule or not.

Questions

1. Of what use is a rule if it is not enforced?
2. What should you do now?

17–3 Is It Now or Later?

"My name is Reggie Johnson. I am a training supervisor assigned to the training department of a large electronics firm, and I am responsible for ensuring that company supervisors receive adequate training. About a month ago I developed a new training program for supervisors on the topic of time management. It is a terrific program that should really help supervisors make far more effective utilization of their time.

"I've really hesitated, however, to request approval from my manager, since there will be some costs associated with the program that were not allowed for in the originally forecasted training budget for this year. However, I'm sure that the program could be funded with some minor budgetary juggling. Over this past weekend I decided that I am not going to put off approaching my manager any longer. Monday will be the day I will attempt to get her approval. I will go into her office first thing Monday morning. The one possible hitch, however, is that my manager seems to have developed an aversion as of late to "messing around" with the budget. Oh, well, *asi es la vida*. I'm going to give it my best shot anyway.

"It is now Monday morning and I am approaching my manager's office. What's this? Oh, no! She looks upset about something. I hear her ranting and raving to one of her other associates, Joe Babcock, about something. It sounds as though Joe misplaced an important document. Darn it! I've been wanting to talk to her for a month about my program. I'm not sure what I should do now."

Questions

1. Would now be the optimum time for Reggie to present his proposal? Why or why not?

2. What advice discussed in the chapter should Reggie probably follow right now?

3. Assume that you are Reggie, and that you are discussing your new training program with your manager during a receptive period. Develop a "sales talk" intended to get her to buy your ideas.

Endnotes

1. As cited in Bill W. [no last name], "The AA Way of Life," *Selected Writings of AA's Cofounder* (New York: AA World Service, March 1962), P. 20.
2. W. H. Weiss, *The Supervisor's Problem Solver* (New York: American Management Associations, 1982), p. 112.
3. Adapted from selling ideas presented in Stan Kossen, *Creative Selling Today,* 3rd ed. (New York: Harper & Row, 1989), Ch. 10.

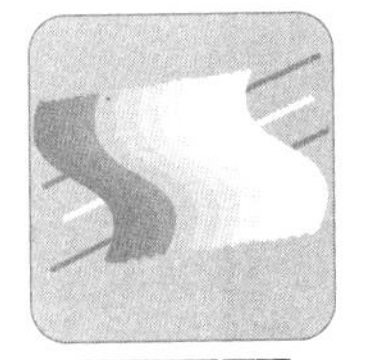

Part Six

Special Employment Concerns

206

Part Six

Special Employment Concerns

206

Chapter 18

Special Employment Concerns—

Equal Employment Opportunities

Once special employment groups have achieved their rightful place in the American economy, their members will no longer need special consideration because the problems of special employment groups will no longer be special problems.

—S. Prakash Sethi, Author

Learning Objectives

When you finish this chapter, you should be able to:

1. List the groups that are considered special employment concerns of organizations.
2. Apply acceptable techniques for handling special employment groups.
3. Trace the changes that have affected women in the work force.
4. Understand the methods for more effectively supervising older and younger employees.
5. Direct the activities of the knowledge worker with less difficulty.

"Try to put yourself into my body and soul, mi amigo. *Would you like to have been raised in a household in which your papa was continually turned down for decent jobs? He studied accounting in school because he wanted a job his family would be proud of. The only work he was ever offered was cutting the grass at a motel for the minimum wage. My mama had to work night and day cleaning rich people's houses so that my sisters and I would have enough food to eat and clothes to wear. I don't want the same to happen to me or my kids. Would you?"*

What is your reaction to the above words? To some readers it may seem exaggerated and overmelodramatic. To others it may come exceedingly close to home. If you've never been on the receiving end of prejudice and discrimination in employment, it may be difficult to imagine what the experience really feels like.

Today's organizational world, however, is vastly different from the one that existed prior to 30 years ago. Contemporary organizational leaders are expected to practice a greater degree of responsibility than they did in the past. A host of various legislation now exists that protects **special employment groups** and affects the hiring practices of organizations. Such protected groups are considered to consist of individuals who have been treated differently principally because they are members of a special group and not for reasons related to their employment situations.

Special employment groups: *Individuals treated differently because they are considered members of a special group, such as the elderly.*

The topics included in this and the following chapters are especially important to today's leaders. Many companies and supervisors have been charged with discrimination, and various lawsuits have been initiated against them by employees. Others have been investigated by government agencies for discriminatory practices. Today supervisors must be aware of the responsibilities and obligations necessary to ensure fair employment practices in an increasingly more diverse work force. A supervisor has to recognize that all employees must be treated in an equitable manner. (Be certain to read and take the short quiz in Supervision in Action 18–1 at the end of this chapter, to see if you might unknowingly be practicing job discrimination.)

The concepts of supervision discussed prior to this chapter apply equally to anyone in organizations. This chapter emphasizes the need to apply leadership concepts to special employment groups, which include racial and ethnic minorities, women, older and younger workers, and the knowledge worker. Chapter 19 will examine the supervision of individuals with disabilities, including physical, intellectual, and drug or alcohol dependency.

Isn't Everybody Prejudiced?

If you were asked if you are prejudiced, what would be your response? Some people might answer with a well-meaning "No," yet even those who harbor no ill will toward the members of any group probably have some types of prejudices. For example, they may have never tried one yet be prejudiced *against* eating a freshly cooked snail *(escargot)*, a slow-moving gastropod mollusk perceived by some as a very discriminating type of delicacy and *hors d'oeuvre*. Or people may be prejudiced *in favor* of a particular wine to be drunk with meat and another with fish or fowl. Prejudice against food and drink is one thing, but prejudice that results in unfair discrimination against other human beings is altogether another matter.

What Are Prejudice and Discrimination?

Prejudice and *discrimination* are two words bandied about quite regularly. Each has its own distinct meaning. **Prejudice** is, by definition, the act of *prejudging*. It is an *internal feeling* or *attitude* toward things or people based on incomplete information and resistance to any information to the contrary. After you understand and are reasonably well acquainted with something or someone, then, in effect, you are not *pre*judging.

Prejudice: *An attitude of making prejudgments with insufficient evidence.*

Discrimination, on the other hand, is *external*—overt—and is usually the *result* of a prejudiced attitude. It is an *action* directed either *against* or *in favor* of something or someone.

Discrimination: *Actions directed either against or in favor of something or someone.*

We must make some prejudgments or assumptions in our daily activities in order to function. Time pressures often do not permit us to search for every infinitesimal shred of evidence. We should be on guard, however, when we make judgments based on incomplete data. We should leave at least some room for changing our minds or direction when results differ from our expectations. We should also try to withhold our judgments until after we have examined the best available evidence.

Who Are Members of Special Employment Groups?

Many members of special employment groups have been discriminated against. Whom are we talking about when we refer to *special employment groups*? The list of groups who have been treated unfairly in employment is amazingly numerous and includes those listed in Table 18–1.

How Should Members of Special Employment Groups Be Supervised?

As can be viewed from Table 18–1, a wide variety of special employment groups have received unfair employment treatment in the past. Federal legislation, executive orders, and court rulings have influenced the manner in which special employment groups are to be treated. Today's supervisor must be familiar not only with his or her

FIGURE 18–1
Attitudes can lead to prejudice, which may lead to discrimination.

TABLE 18–1
A Partial List of Special Employment Groups

- African Americans
- Asians
- Eskimos
- Hispanics (Spanish-speaking subgroups, such as those of Mexican, Puerto Rican, Cuban, and Central and South American descent)
- Homosexuals (gays and lesbians)
- Immigrants (especially those with "foreign" accents or "foreign-sounding" names)
- Individuals with AIDs
- Individuals with disabilities
- Middle-Easterners
- Native Americans (American Indians)
- Religious group members
- Substances abusers (drugs and alcohol)
- Vietnam veterans
- Whites ("reverse discrimination")
- Women
- Young and aging individuals

Affirmative action program (AAP): *An organizational program intended to ensure fair recruitment, hiring, and promotion practices.*

organization's employment policies and **affirmative action program (AAP),** but also with the legislation that protects members of special employment groups. Table 18–2 summarizes the major legislation that affects employment in the work place.

Supervisors play a key role in the success or failure of any program designed to ensure equitable treatment of members of any special employment group. The following section suggests some ways to help you be a more effective supervisor of members of protected classes of employees.

Do You Avoid Mental Set?

Less-experienced supervisors sometimes have their minds already made up about certain types of people. For example, they approach minorities with a built-in bias, expecting them to behave substantially differently from the way non-minority employees would in the same situations. Try to shake off any long-held myths or stereotypes that you may hold. Preset negative attitudes, unfortunately, can produce an unhealthy organizational climate. Supervisors whose minds are made up in advance may unwittingly help to create the very problems they are set to see. Continually remind yourself of the *Pygmalion effect* (or self-fulfilling prophesy) discussed in Chapter 12. Your negative expectations of a minority member assigned to you are likely to be sensed by the person and significantly influence his or her future job performance.

TABLE 18–2
An Overview of Major Employment Legislation
(*continued on next page*)

Legislation	Purpose	Employers Covered
Civil Rights Act of 1866 and 1970	Prohibits race discrimination in hiring, placement, and continuation of employment	Private employers, unions, employment agencies
Equal Pay Act of 1963 (a part of Fair Labor Standards Act of 1938), amended by the Fair Labor Standards Amendments of 1974	Requires employers to provide equal pay for substantially equal work regardless of sex	All employers and labor organizations
Title VII of the Civil Rights Act of 1964, as amended by the Equal Employment Act of 1972	Prohibits employment discrimination based on race, color, sex, religion, or national origin	Private employers with 15 or more employees, governments, unions, employment agencies
Executive Order 11246 (1965), as amended by E.O. 11375, E.O. 11478, and E.O. 12086	Prohibits discrimination based on race, color, religion, sex, or national origin (affirmative action required)	Federal contractors and subcontractors, federal government
Age Discrimination in Employment Act of 1967 (amended in 1978)	Prohibits discriminatory employment practices related to persons age 40 and over	Private employers with 20 or more employees, unions with 25 or more members, employment agencies
Rehabilitation Act of 1973 (amended in 1980)	Prohibits discrimination based on a physical or intellectual handicap (affirmative action required)	Federal contractors, federal government
Vietnam Era Veterans' Readjustment Assistance Act of 1974 (amended in 1980)	Prohibits discrimination against veterans with disabilities and Vietnam era veterans (affirmative action required)	Federal contractors, federal government

TABLE 18–2
continued

Age Discrimination Act of 1975	Prohibits age discrimination	Employers receiving federal financial assistance
Civil Rights Attorney's Act of 1976	Provides that courts may allow the prevailing party a reasonable attorney's fee in actions to enforce the Civil Rights Act	All employers
Pregnancy Discrimination Act of 1978	Prohibits discrimination in employment on the basis of pregnancy, childbirth, and related conditions	Private employers with 15 or more employees, governments, unions, employment agencies
Civil Service Reform Act of 1978	Specifically incorporates Title VII of the 1964 Civil Rights Act, which mandates a federal government "workforce reflective of the nation's diversity"	Federal government
Drug-Free Workplace Act of 1988	Requires contractors and grantees of federal agencies to certify that they will provide drug-free work places as a precondition for receiving a contract or grant	Private employers and individuals
Americans with Disabilities Act of 1990	Prohibits discrimination based on a physical or intellectual handicap (affirmative action required)	Private employers with 25 or more employees

Should Legislation-Protected Groups Be Treated Differently?

There are many well-meaning supervisors who are anxious to "do the right thing" with members of special employment groups. Some supervisors attempt to prove that they are not prejudiced by figuratively bending over backwards and giving *more than equal treatment* to certain employees. Although you should always try to maintain flexible attitudes, don't bend the rules for certain employees because of their ethnic background or sex. You won't gain the respect of any of your employees by ignoring rule infractions with some individuals and enforcing rules with others. Even employees to whom you give special treatment may question your motives. You will obtain better results by maintaining the same fair and consistent treatment with members of special employment groups as you should with any employees.

Should You Talk Openly About Your Problems?

Suppose you have a problem with a member of a minority group. Should you share your negative feelings with other employees in the organization? Although you may feel the need to discuss your feelings with others as a means of releasing your tensions, you may find that doing so only compounds your problem, making it even more difficult to resolve. Negative feelings about an employee that you gossip about to others are likely to become known by the talked-about employee. The employee could even develop the self-conscious feeling that everyone else is against him or her. If you must discuss the problem with others, you probably should limit your audience to your manager or the company human resource specialist.

How Important Is Training?

Training all employees is important and at times can be especially so in the case of members of minority groups. In some instances, individuals may have come from disadvantaged backgrounds where success didn't come easily because of economic barriers. By providing adequate training to any employee who is unfamiliar with processes and procedures, you are reducing their chances of failure.

Will Discussing Performance Problems Discourage the Employee?

Some supervisors hesitate to discuss performance problems with minority employees for fear that such conversations will either appear prejudiced or possibly have a discouraging effect. However, all of your employees need to know how they are performing. You would do them a real disservice if you didn't provide them with regular, accurate feedback. Performance problems are not likely to be overcome unless the employee receives guidance from you regarding improvement. The performance review, as discussed in Chapter 10, can provide you with an excellent opportunity to provide such guidance to employees.

What Is Reverse Discrimination?

In recent decades, minorities and women were sometimes hired instead of white males because of the organization's quota systems. In some instances, a white male may have been equally or better qualified than the person actually selected. The courts have sometimes ruled

Reverse discrimination: *Applying preferential treatment toward minorities and women over white males related to conditions of employment.*

Proportional employment: *A hiring practice that attempts to match percentages of particular groups in the local work force.*

Title VII of the Civil Rights Act of 1964: *A law that prohibits employers, labor unions, and employment agencies from discriminating in employment practices.*

Equal Employment Opportunity Commission (EEOC): *An agency created by Title VII to administer civil rights legislation and investigate complaints.*

such practices to be **reverse discrimination** and, therefore, unlawful hiring practices. A fairly recent example occurred in June 1989, when the Supreme Court ruled that white firefighters in Birmingham, Alabama, could challenge an affirmative action program aimed at increasing the number of African Americans on the force—even years after the program had been approved by a lower court.[1]

To avoid the problem of reverse discrimination and to create greater equity in hiring, many organizations now utilize an affirmative action program known as **proportional employment,** which is a hiring practice that attempts to maintain a proportion of employees in an organization that approximately matches the percentages of particular groups in the local work force. For example, if 15 percent of the local supply of workers were Hispanic, then a firm would attempt to have 15 percent Hispanic employees.

The selection process has always been a challenge. A major challenge relates to your need to attempt to make every reasonable effort to apply equitable hiring practices toward all groups. Supervisors who don't may find themselves on the receiving end of lawsuits alleging unfair employment practices.

What Should You Do if You Are Accused of Discrimination?

Title VII of the Civil Rights Act of 1964 prohibits private employers with 15 or more employees from discriminating in employment based on race, color, sex, religion, or national origin. The 1964 act was amended by the Equal Employment Act of 1972 to create the **Equal Employment Opportunity Commission (EEOC).** Congress granted the EEOC authority to investigate and conciliate grievances alleging racial, religious, national origin, or sex discrimination. As a supervisor, you are expected to comply with the act to avoid the likelihood of discrimination charges against you and your organization.

One of the most unpleasant work-related experiences you might have is to be accused of discrimination or harassment by a minority employee. In some cases the charges may arise out of a misunderstanding. Above all, try not to overreact to the accusations. Treat the charges as you would most any grievance. First, try to understand the reasons for the complaint. Second, find as much specific information as you can related to the incident. Third, try to resolve the problem with the employee. In the case of a misunderstanding, apologize. Be certain the employee understands that you didn't intend to offend or discriminate. Be sure to keep your boss informed of the situation, especially if the employee intends to pursue the charge in spite of your efforts to resolve the problem.

What Has Changed for Women in the Work Force?

The U.S. work force has changed considerably since 1923, when a group of militant suffragettes (women who advocated that political voting rights be extended to females in the United States), after long-awaited success in obtaining for women the basic right to vote, presented a bill to Congress designed to make women first-class citizens under the U.S. Constitution. Although the bill remained in hiding for *49 years* under the care, custody, and control of the House Judiciary Committee, it was finally passed by Congress in 1972. Known as the **Equal Rights Amendment (ERA),** it never received ratification by the required three-quarters of the states to become law.

Equal Rights Amendment (ERA): *A bill passed by Congress in 1972 to amend the U.S. Constitution, outlawing discrimination based on sex; never ratified by enough states to become law.*

The long-term trend of female participation in the labor force has been steadily upward. As can be viewed in Figure 18–1, only about 18 percent off the total female working-age population was in the civilian labor force in the early part of this century. By 1950, the percentage was almost 30 percent, and by 1990, the total female participation rate had risen toward 60 percent.

How Should a Supervisor Supervise Women?

Sound techniques of leadership should be employed in supervising all employees—both women and men. Supervisors must avoid the unconscious use of double standards and remember that all employees are entitled to common courtesies. (Note that both male and female supervisors can fall into the double-standards trap.)

Avoid being more critical of a woman than you would of a man for making similar types of mistakes. Guard against the tendency to expect *more than adequate* performance from a female (or minority) worker. Unfortunately, some male supervisors are conditioned to feel that when a woman makes a mistake, it's "because she is a woman." When a man makes a mistake, however, it's "merely

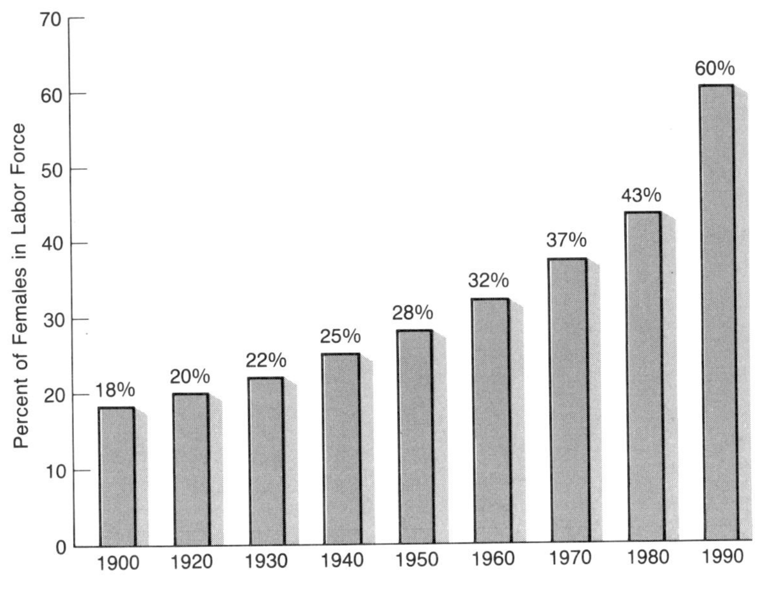

FIGURE 18–2
Female Participation in the Labor Force (selected years)

a human error." Try your best to avoid applying separate standards for men and women.

Remember, also, that women have names. Although less common than in the past, some male supervisors still have the tendency to call women employees such names as "sweetie," "honey," "dear," or to refer to their secretaries as "my girl" or "gal." An upcoming section discusses the nature of *sexual harassment.*

How about opening doors and helping with coats? Why not? People of *either sex* tend to respond favorably to politeness and courtesy. Some male supervisors also still feel a bit awkward regarding who should pay the bill when a female peer invites them out to lunch. One guideline is for the person who did the inviting to offer to pay. If you are a male supervisor, don't insist on paying when the other person invited you. Instead you might say something like, "Okay, I'll catch it next time."

What Is a Woman Worth Compared to a Man?

Equal Pay Act of 1963: *A bill requiring employers to provide equal pay to women and men for performing substantially similar work.*

What is your reaction to the heading of this section? It might be one of indignation, since all reasonable people would agree that a qualified woman performing the same work as a qualified man should receive the same rewards. However, equal pay for equal work was not required until Congress passed the **Equal Pay Act of 1963.** The law requires employers "to provide equal pay for substantially equal work regardless of sex."

How about instances where women work in traditionally female-dominated occupations, performing tasks that require *comparable,* but not identical, *skills, training, responsibilities,* and *effort* as are performed by men in male-dominated occupations? Should women

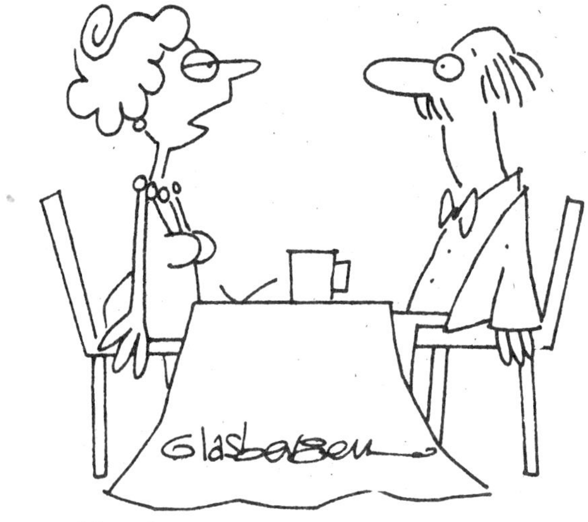

"Jim, just because I'm a liberated woman, it doesn't mean I have to pick up the check *every* time."

Source: Reprinted from *The Wall Street Journal* by permission of Cartoon Features, ©.

who work in such fields as elementary school teaching, nursing, and secretarial work be paid as much as men in other occupations that make similar demands on the employee? Yes, according to those who support the concept of **comparable worth.** Some states and cities have enacted comparable worth legislation. Opponents feel that such laws will raise wages and salaries and thus price traditionally female occupations "out of the market," thereby harming women in the longer run. What's your opinion?

Comparable worth: *The belief that occupations requiring comparable skills, training, responsibilities, and effort should command comparable pay.*

What Should You Know about Sexual Harassment?

Accusations of *sexual harassment* have created problems for some supervisors in organizations. Consequently, an understanding of what constitutes sexual harassment is the first step to avoiding future complications. Some supervisors who mean no particular harm are unaware when they cross over the thin line into the region of a potentially unlawful act.

What is **sexual harassment**? As defined by the EEOC, it is any "unwelcome sexual advances, requests for sexual favors, and other verbal or physical conduct of a sexual nature that unreasonably interferes with an employee's work performance or creates an intimidating, hostile or offensive work environment."[2] Management professor James Ledvinka, University of Georgia, suggests that management develop some clear, specific program steps to discourage the likelihood of sexual harassment. These steps are:[3]

Sexual harassment: *Actions, suggestions, or propositions with sexual overtones that tend to transgress normal working relationships.*

1. Issue a *specific written policy* against sexual harassment.
2. Establish a *grievance system,* a specified procedure that individuals claiming to be victims of sexual harassment can follow to present their claims, have them investigated by management, and secure compensation if the investigation indicates that the claim was justified. Of course, employees must have confidence in the grievance system for it to be effective.
3. Maintain *training and controlling procedures,* which are necessary to implement the policy. Training can enable supervisors and other employees to become more aware of the legal requirements for eradicating sexual harassment. Controlling includes applying disciplinary steps for violations of the policy.

Avoid any activities that can be interpreted as verbal or physical sexual harassment. Sexual harassment can be considered a continuum and may range from verbal suggestions to leering to friendly pats to kisses to indecent propositions with job-related threats to force sexual relations.

The EEOC has ruled that employers are even responsible for *acts by nonemployees that affect employees.* An example is an outside male salesperson who sexually harasses your female assistant. The salesperson is not an employee of your company. However, EEOC guidelines suggest that employers "have the responsibility to make their workplace free from harassment." You, therefore, could be held responsible for the salesperson's actions if you did nothing to prevent them.[4]

How Should Older and Younger Workers be Supervised?

The older worker and the younger worker are members of two more groups that modern supervisors should strive to understand in order to be more effective in their leadership positions. Let's take a brief look at each group.

Do Older People *Need* to Work?

A 65-year-old medical doctor retires after practicing medicine for 35 years—and within two months takes a job as a low-paid clerk at a blood bank. A self-employed businessperson retires at age 68—and before the ink is dry on her first social security check takes a job as a social director of a senior citizens home. Why would a "retired" person do such a thing? Why not sit idly in a rocking chair contemplating past achievements? The answer to these questions relates to the concept of needs.

The topic of needs was covered in Chapter 11. Older people, too, have needs similar to anyone else's, especially the needs for belongingness, self-esteem, and security, much of which they derive from their work. The benefits are not one-sided; the work force benefits from the maturity, wisdom, and experience that many older employees bring to the workplace. In addition, older people are helping to fill the labor shortage caused by declines in birthrates. The position of older people in the work force was reinforced by the passage of the *Age Discrimination Act of 1967,* which protects persons age 40 and over from unfair employment practices.

What Is an "Older Worker?"

Age Discrimination Act of 1967: *Legislation prohibiting employers from discriminating against a person age 40 and over.*

Aging is an uneven process. Although the **Age Discrimination Act of 1967** refers to people over 40, some people seem old at age 30, while others are strong and alert at age 75. A variety of factors influence the aging process, especially ***heredity, past dietary and health habits,*** and ***attitudes.*** The ***nature of a particular job*** and the ***industry itself*** significantly influence how "old" a person is for a specific job.

For example, at age 42 Ted Williams slammed a home run in his last official time at bat. Golda Meir was 71 when she became prime minister of Israel. George Bernard Shaw was 94 when one of his plays was first produced. And that "finger-lickin'" colonel, Harland Sanders, who founded the Kentucky Fried Chicken fast-food chain, remained with the KFC Corporation as a consultant until he died at age 90.

As with any special employment group, there are a number of myths associated with older employees. For example, contrary to popular belief, older employees have lower than typical absenteeism and lateness rates, and they tend to have fewer, rather than more, accidents. Turnover rates also tend to be lower among older employees, who often are more loyal to their supervisors and organizations. Further, older workers are able to bring to the work place a wealth of experience and judgment that may not yet have been acquired by younger employees.

Although some older workers may be physically weaker than their younger counterparts, many older people have led active lives and continue to be strong enough for many jobs. In instances where an employee does lack sufficient strength for a particular job, some concerned managers have either *reassigned the person* to a different job within the organization, or *redesigned the job* to enable a physically weaker person to perform it.

In other instances, some older workers may develop a low self-image when they lack the physical agility and stamina to take part in such company activities as playing on departmental softball teams. Perhaps they could be encouraged to assist the team in other useful ways such as by coaching, maintaining equipment, or participating in activities that are important to the team's success.

What Are Younger Workers Like?

Younger workers also have needs, although often they exist with different intensities than in older people. We will arbitrarily define *younger workers* as those employees under age 25. In general,

Older workers can add a great deal to an organization. How can you, as a supervisor, take advantage of their maturity, experience and wisdom?

younger workers seem to lack patience. "They want everything right now," is a common accusation aimed at them. Yet young people often feel that their elders show little patience with them.

Younger workers, in general, have more years of education than their predecessors. For example, the percentage of the work force having earned college diplomas rose from 20 percent in 1978 to 25 percent in 1988. The numbers also increased for those with one to three or more years of college—from 16 percent in 1978 to 20 percent in 1988. Workers with less than a high school education dropped from 24 percent to 15 percent during the same years.[5] Unfortunately, many young people hold jobs that don't require as much education as they have acquired; as a result, a number of them have trouble relating to their jobs. In certain instances, the reverse exists: The skills of some younger employees do not reflect their attained level of education.

Supervisors should attempt whenever possible to relate to the needs of younger employees. For example, younger workers tend to have fairly strong needs for *self-esteem* and *self-actualization.* They frequently respond favorably, for example, to sincere praise, encouragement, and the awareness that they are doing something significant.

What Are Some Guidelines for Supervising Older and Younger Employees?

Tables 18–3 and 18–4 provide some specific suggestions for supervising older and younger employees. Many of the guidelines should be applied equally to other employees as well.

● What Is the Supervisor's Role Related to the Knowledge Worker?

Traditionally, workers have been stereotyped by being placed into two broad classifications: white collar (generally salaried employees or professionals whose work does not involve manual labor) and blue collar (generally wage-earners whose work is typically manual). Because of the increase in employment in the services sector, white-collar jobs are currently growing much more rapidly than blue-collar, and a more precise breakdown of the white-collar

TABLE 18–3
Guidelines for Supervising Older Workers

- Recognize the *individual differences* among older employees.
- Utilize *selective placement* where possible (i.e., place an older person in a position that matches his or her capabilities).
- *Support the ego needs* of older employees by drawing on their expertise wherever possible.
- Evaluate the older employee on the basis of performance, not age (i.e., *avoid stereotyping*).

TABLE 18–4
Guidelines for Supervising Younger Workers

- Avoid treating a young adult as though he or she were a child.
- Don't "talk down" to younger employees.
- Learn the aspirations of your younger employees, and assist them in career development.
- Recognize and learn to cope with some younger employees' lack of respect for authority.
- Learn what motivates each of your younger employees.
- Try to gain the respect of younger employees by being open and honest, and by following through with your commitments (as you should with all employees).

segment has developed as it has grown. A subgroup of white-collar employees is the *knowledge worker.*

What Is a Knowledge Worker?

Knowledge worker: *An employee with a high level of education and characterized by an independent nature and achievement orientation.*

A **knowledge worker** is a type of employee that typically has attained a fairly high level of education and a low level of tolerance for authority. This category of employee includes researchers, computer programmers, engineers, economists, accountants, nurses, chemists, teachers, financial experts, and managers. The value of knowledge workers is not in their physical strength or manual dexterity, as is the case with manual or clerical employees. Instead, their principal strength lies in their ability to apply the knowledge they've acquired to the job.

It might seem at first that knowledge workers should be relatively easy to supervise, since they tend to be well paid and perform more varied and interesting tasks than production and other white-collar workers usually do. However, reality suggests otherwise.

How Do You Direct the Activities of the Knowledge Worker?

The traditional Theory X style of management discussed in Chapter 12 got results when used on production workers until workers collectively demanded more equitable treatment and working conditions. Fear did, as it sometimes still does, motivate the production worker, though the risks associated with the use of fear as a motivating technique are great. The knowledge worker, however, tends to operate within even a different, far more independent, framework than does the production worker.

Though all knowledge workers are individuals, a study by management philosopher Peter F. Drucker identified certain characteristics they have in common. Two important characteristics that supervisors must recognize are the *independent nature* and *achievement orientation* of knowledge workers.[6]

Because of their relatively ***independent nature,*** knowledge workers are less motivated by fear or traditional styles of leadership. Their specialized knowledge is usually in high demand, so their tolerance of an unfavorable work atmosphere is slight. When dissatisfied with jobs, knowledge workers seldom hesitate to look elsewhere for a new position. The output of knowledge workers is more difficult to measure than that of production or clerical workers. Several months, or even years, can elapse between the beginning and completion of a knowledge worker's project.

Knowledge workers tend to be ***achievement oriented.*** Achievement, as we discovered in our earlier studies of Herzberg's motivational theories, tends to be a ***motivating factor.*** Supervisors should recognize this factor when directing knowledge workers. Such workers also tend to need ***recognition*** for their achievements and typically prefer tasks that are ***challenging,*** with opportunities for ***growth*** and ***personal satisfaction.***

Supervisors, of course, should always recognize the individual nature of every employee. However, their are certain guidelines, as presented in Table 18–5, that can aid you in directing the activities of knowledge workers.

TABLE 18–5
Guidelines for Directing the Activities of Knowledge Workers

- Select and place knowledge workers carefully. Try to place qualified people in positions where they can best accomplish and blend their personal goals with those of the organization.
- Provide knowledge workers with the opportunity to apply their creativity wherever possible.
- Try not to underemploy knowledge workers (i.e., place them in positions below their capabilities) or they are likely to become bored with their jobs. Knowledge workers tend to prefer challenging, rather than routine, work.
- Develop goals and objectives jointly with knowledge workers (the MBO process), being certain to follow up for control and recognition purposes.
- Provide regular feedback related to the knowledge worker's performance and company operations. Knowledge workers tend to be highly interested in information concerning the company and the job.
- Eliminate activities that tend to block the progress of knowledge workers, such as unnecessary meetings, reports, and paperwork. Occasionally ask knowledge workers what might be impeding their progress.
- As with any employee, watch for warning signs of poor morale. Organizations typically have made substantial investments in knowledge workers. Irreversible damage can often result if problems are not resolved as early as possible.

Summary

The word *prejudice* means to *prejudge.* It is related to an attitude typically based on insufficient facts, or sometimes none at all. *Discrimination* goes beyond attitude; it is action directed *against* or *in favor of* something or someone.

The list of those who have received unfair treatment in employment is amazingly long. Supervisors are responsible for recognizing the rights of *special employment groups.* Today's leaders must also be aware of the key types of employment legislation that protects many classes of employees. You should also know what to do if you are accused of discrimination by an employee.

Women have increasingly entered the work force in recent decades for a variety of reasons. Supervisors should avoid applying double standards related to male and female employees. Supervisors should also be familiar with what constitutes *sexual harassment.*

The impending shortage of skilled labor coupled with an aging U.S. population will result in a greater need for supervisors to understand the needs and feelings of *older workers.* Specific legislation also protects workers 40 years and over.

Supervisors should also strive to understand how the needs and motivations of *younger workers* and *knowledge workers* may differ from other employees.

Questions for Discussion

1. What is the difference between *prejudice* and *discrimination*?
2. Evaluate the following statement: "You have to supervise members of *special employment groups* completely differently from the way you would other employees."
3. Is it desirable to discuss with your other associates a problem you are having with a member of a *minority group*? Explain. Would your answer be any different if the employee were a white male?
4. What is the problem of *reverse discrimination*?
5. What should you do if you are accused of *unfair employment practices* by an employee?
6. Evaluate the following statement: "Most *women* don't have to work. They only do it for the extra spending money."
7. What is the difference in meaning between the concepts of *equal pay for equal work* and *comparable worth*?
8. What is considered to be *sexual harassment*? Could a male employee justifiably accuse a female manager of it? Explain.
9. How would you describe an *older worker*?
10. What are some ways in which supervisors can be more effective in dealing with *younger workers*?
11. What are *knowledge workers*? What should a supervisor attempt to recognize when directing them?

Can You Define These Terms?

Instructions: Write a definition for each of the following terms. You may check your definitions with those provided in the end-of-text Glossary.

special employment groups
prejudice
discrimination
affirmative action program (AAP)
reverse discrimination
proportional employment
Title VII of the Civil Rights Act of 1964
Equal Employment Opportunity Commission (EEOC)
Equal Rights Amendment (ERA)
Equal Pay Act of 1963
comparable worth
sexual harassment
Age Discrimination Act of 1967
knowledge worker

Supervision In Action

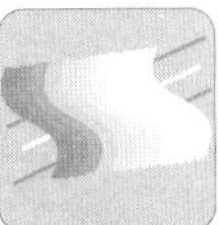

18–1 Could You Be Practicing . . .?

The following exercise was excerpted from a questionnaire provided by the Equal Employment Opportunity Commission to stress the importance of understanding current antidiscrimination laws related to hiring, firing, promotion, and pay.

COULD YOU BE PRACTICING ILLEGAL JOB DISCRIMINATION—AND NOT EVEN KNOW IT?

The answer is *yes.* Due to outdated policies or failure to understand the law, many employers do discriminate in the way they hire, fire, promote, or pay.

Take this short test and see where you stand.

An employer . . .	True	False
1. Can refuse to hire women who have small children at home.	____	____
2. Can generally obtain and use an applicant's arrest record as the basis for nonemployment.	____	____
3. Can prohibit employees from conversing in their native language on the job.	____	____
4. Whose employees are mostly white or male can rely solely on word of mouth to recruit new employees.	____	____
5. Can refuse to hire women to work at night because it wishes to protect them.	____	____
6. May require all pregnant employees to take a leave of absence at a specified time before delivery.	____	____
7. May establish different benefits—pension, retirement, insurance and health plans—for male employees than for female employees.	____	____
8. May hire only males for a job if state law forbids employment of women for that capacity.	____	____
9. Need not attempt to adjust work schedules to permit an employee time off for a religious observance.	____	____
10. Only disobeys the Equal Employment Opportunity laws when it is acting intentionally or with ill motive.	____	____

Answers: The answers to 1 to 10 are false. The Equal Employment Opportunity Act makes it against the law for an employer to discriminate on the basis of race, religion, color, sex, or national origin.

Endnotes

1. Tony Mauro, "Court Cuts Anti-Bias Remedies," *USA Today* (International Edition), June 13, 1989, p. 1.
2. David P. Twomey, *A Concise Guide to Employment Law: EEO & OSHA* (Cincinnati: South-Western Publishing Co., 1986), p. 21.
3. James Ledvinka, *Federal Regulation of Personnel and Human Resource Management* (Boston: Kent Publishing Co., 1982), p. 68.
4. "EEOC Acts on Apprenticeship Age Rules, Sex Harassment and Religious Options," *The Wall Street Journal,* September 24, 1980, p. 8.
5. "USA Snapshots—More Workers Have More Education," U.S. Department of Labor, *USA Today* (International Edition), December 10–12, 1988, p. 1.
6. Peter F. Drucker, *People and Performance: The Best of Peter Drucker on Management* (New York: Harper & Row, 1977), pp. 271, 275.

TDC

Chapter 19

Special Employment Concerns—

Disabilities, AIDS and Substance Abuse in the Workplace

Helping people to work is in the short- and long-term interest of society as a whole.

—Jay Rocklin, Director President's Committee On Employment of People with Disabilities

Drug abuse is an economic hemorrhage on the business community.

—Mark de Bernardo, Director, Institute for a Drug-Free Workplace

Learning Objectives

When you finish this chapter, you should be able to:

1. Recognize who is considered a person with disabilities.
2. Recall the various legislation that applies to persons with disabilities.
3. Apply proven techniques for more effectively supervising employees with disabilities.
4. Explain how you should deal with AIDS in the workplace.
5. Identify the symptoms and effects of substance abuse.
6. Restate the supervisor's responsibility related to substance abuse.

If you've never been in the body of a person with disabilities, it's far more difficult to imagine some of the ways in which persons without disabilities—even well-intentioned ones—might act toward you. Evan Kemp, selected by President George Bush to chair the Equal Employment Opportunity Commission (EEOC), knows. In 1989, at the second hearing on the *Americans with Disabilities Act (ADA),* Kemp provided the following personal insight:

> *After I completed law school, I was rejected by every company where I applied for work. I finally went to work for a federal agency, where, because of a refusal to provide a* reasonable accommodation, *I fell and eventually had to use a wheelchair.*
>
> *Individuals without disabilities assume that if you use a wheelchair you don't work at all, or if you do work, it's merely part time.*
>
> *Once a person I met said to me, 'Oh, you're an EEOC Commissioner? I didn't know those were part-time jobs.'*[1]

Individuals with disabilities, including persons who abuse alcohol or drugs and individuals with AIDS, are also members of special employment groups with whom supervisors must be concerned. This chapter focuses on the role of the supervisor in working with individuals with disabilities.

What Is the Supervisor's Role Towards Persons with Disabilities?

Persons with disabilities generally experience difficulty in the job market. As evidence, U.S. Census Bureau 1988 data indicates that while 75 percent of men *without* a work disability were employed full time, only 23 percent of men *with* a work disability were employed full time. Women had it even worse: As you can see in Figure 19–1, whereas 47 percent of women *without* a work disability were employed full time, only 13 percent of women *with* a work disability were employed full time.[2] In reality, since many individuals with disabilities receive training from state departments of rehabilitation, they actually perform some jobs better than persons without disabilities. Perhaps a more fitting term for them is *persons with physical or intellectual challenges.*

Individual with disabilities: *Person who has or is regarded as having physical or mental impairments that substantially limit one or more major life activities.*

Who Are Persons with Disabilities?

The U.S. Department of Labor Employment Standards Administration defines an **individual with disabilities** as "any person who has a physical or intellectual impairment that substantially limits

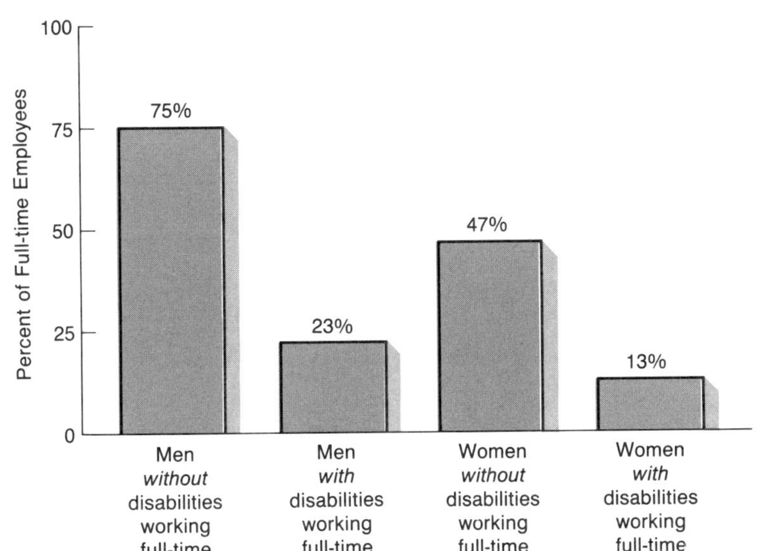

FIGURE 19–1
Percentages of Men and Women Employed Full Time, without and with Work Disabilities (1988)

one or more of the major life activities of such individual, has a record of such an impairment, or is regarded as having such an impairment."

The majority of physically and intellectually challenged people, however, are capable of working and are referred to as *qualified individuals with disabilities.* A **qualified individual with a disability** is a person with a disability who, with or without reasonable accommodation, is capable of performing the essential functions of the employment position. Table 19–1 lists the types of persons considered to have disabilities under the *Rehabilitation Act of 1973* and expanded in scope by the *Americans with Disabilities Act of 1990.* These limitations can result from a variety of causes. For example, some limitations are present at or caused by *birth.* Others can result from *accidents* or *diseases.* They also can be a result of *cultural* or *environmental deprivation* or the *aging process.*

Qualified individual with a disability: *A person with a disability who, with or without reasonable accommodation, is capable of performing the essential functions of a position.*

What Laws Apply to Persons with Disabilities?

Legislation requires organizations to hire and advance qualified individuals with disabilities. Laws also require employers to provide such persons with "reasonable accommodation." The hiring of persons with disabilities first became regulated under the **Rehabilitation Act of 1973.** The act authorizes financial grants to states for vocational rehabilitation services. The act also tells employers with federal contracts the steps they must take to recruit, train, and employ persons with disabilities. The regulations further require certain federal contractors to draw up affirmative action plans for seeking out, hiring, and promoting persons with disabilities, and to report each year on their results.

Rehabilitation Act of 1973: *An act that requires federal contractors to take affirmative action to hire and advance persons with disabilities.*

TABLE 19–1
Persons Considered to Have Qualified Disabilities

Individuals with the following functional limitations:

- Motor (loss of limb, paralysis)
- Sensory (vision, hearing, deaf/blind, speech)
- Neurological functioning (mentally retarded, mentally ill, heart disease)
- General bodily systems (allergies, diabetes, heart disease)
- Multiple limitations (muscular dystrophy, multiple sclerosis, cerebral palsy)
- Dependency on alcohol or drugs (when they do not pose a direct threat to property or the safety of others in the work place)
- Disease or infection (when it does not pose a health or safety risk to themselves or coworkers)

Vietnam Era Veterans' Readjustment Assistance Act of 1974:
An act that prohibits discrimination against veterans with disabilities and all Vietnam era veterans.

Americans with Disabilities Act of 1990 (ADA):
Legislation that extends the Rehabilitation Act of 1973 to include private employers as well as government contractors.

The **Vietnam Era Veterans' Readjustment Assistance Act of 1974** has a section that protects individuals with disabilities as well as other veterans of the military. The act requires that employers holding government contracts over a certain value to establish affirmative action programs that cover all veterans with service-connected disabilities rated at 30 percent or more, plus all veterans, whether disabled or not, of the Vietnam era.

The **Americans with Disabilities Act of 1990 (ADA)** broadened the scope of the Rehabilitation Act by extending to individuals with disabilities the same protection against discrimination as provided by other civil rights legislation. The *Equal Employment Opportunity Commission (EEOC)* is responsible for carrying out the intent of the ADA.

Why Is Hiring Persons with Disabilities a Sound Business Practice?

Hiring those with physical and intellectual limitations makes sound business sense. Often such people are trained workers who have been assisted in acquiring job-related skills by state departments of rehabilitation; hiring them could thus reduce the organization's training costs.

Furthermore, because of their appreciation for the opportunity to work, and because suitable jobs are often difficult for them to find, individuals with disabilities tend to have lower turnover and absenteeism rates. Many persons with disabilities are especially motivated to perform their tasks well.

How Should You Supervise Persons with Disabilities?

As with any employees, certain techniques of supervision tend to obtain more positive results. Below are some specific suggestions for supervising individuals with physical or intellectual limitations.

The workplace can usually be adapted at relatively low cost to accommodate qualified individuals with disabilities.

Make Reasonable Accommodation. In general, your responsibility is to select a person whose skills or potential relate to the job opening. In the case of individuals with disabilities, the law requires you to make **reasonable accommodation,** which means an adaptation of the workplace, the equipment, or the job itself that enables the person to do a particular job for which he or she is qualified in training and abilities. You are not required to make an accommodation where it would create an "undue hardship" for the operation of your program or for the conduct of your organization's business.

Reasonable accommodation: *The adaptation of the workplace, equipment, or job to enable a person with disabilities to do the job for which he or she is qualified in training and abilities.*

In most instances, accommodating the employee is not costly nor does it require you to alter your procedures substantially. A Department of Labor study revealed that 51 percent of the reported accommodations cost nothing, an additional 30 percent cost less than $500, and only 8 percent cost more than $2,000.[3] In some cases, a slight modification in duties or machine controls could make a job safer and more suitable. For example, a lever could be changed from a right- to left-hand operation or from hand to foot control (or vice versa).

Prepare the Individual with Disabilities for the Job. All employees need to get off to a good start in a new job, and this is especially true for a person with a disability. Be certain that the new employee is properly trained and knows what is expected.

Proper preparation makes adjustment to the new position easier and aids the new employee in building confidence.

Maintain a Normal Relationship. Supervisors are often uncertain about the best approach to take when dealing with a person with disability. Experienced rehabilitators suggest that supervisors should neither overemphasize the disability nor be overprotective toward the employee.

Try your best to treat the person as you would any other employee. Also, prepare the workgroup so that they will treat the new employee as a typical team member. Too frequently, well-meaning employees are overprotective of persons with disabilities, which can damage the challenged employee's self-esteem. Persons with disabilities are usually aware of their own strengths and weaknesses and generally prefer not to be singled out as someone strange or different.

Be Candid with the Employee. Find out from the employee with a disability if he or she has any limitations that would make the job more difficult. Encourage the employee to be candid about his or her limitations. A self-conscious attempt by the employee to conceal the condition tends to accentuate it. Rehabilitators generally recommend that the challenged person attempt to clear the air by explaining what he or she can't do.

How Should You Handle AIDS in the Workplace?

Acquired Immune Deficiency Syndrome (AIDS): *A disease that destroys the body's immunity system; transmitted by an exchange of certain bodily fluids.*

We now come to a difficult subject—the problems associated with an applicant for employment or an employee who has the illness **Acquired Immune Deficiency Syndrome (AIDS).** A wide variety of beliefs surround the disease, which has reached epidemic proportions in parts of the world. Most doctors contend that it is primarily a *sexually transmitted disease (STD),* and is *not* transmitted through casual contact with persons with AIDS. In addition to *unsafe sex,* the principal ways in which the disease is transmitted is through *shared hypodermic needles* and by *infected mothers to their unborn babies.*

Individuals with AIDS are legally considered persons with disabilities under both the *Rehabilitation Act of 1973* and the *Americans with Disabilities Act of 1990.* You are expected to follow the same EEOC guidelines as you would with substance abusers. You do not have to retain persons with AIDS *if* they pose a direct threat to the health or safety of other individuals in the workplace. Because of some abiguity in the law, you should obtain competent advice from your boss and a human resource specialist when in doubt about a decision regarding an employee with AIDS.

We began with the suggestion that the subject of AIDS is a difficult one, and it truly is. Assume, for example, that you find out that one of your employees, let's call him Tracy, has AIDS. Let's also assume that Tracy is fully capable of carrying out his duties in a satisfactory manner. You are knowledgeable about the disease and know that Tracy poses no health risks for you or any other organizational member, but your departmental associates have fears related to Tracy's continuing to work near them. What can you do?

First of all, it is important for you to recognize that you are legally required to maintain Tracy on the job. Some legal advisors might suggest that you deal with the challenge by attempting to persuade and educate your associates with a reasonable approach and *not* by discharging Tracy. As a part of the informational program, you could request a medical expert to speak to your associates to assist in allaying their fears. If you have the tendency to want to "get rid of" Tracy, keep in mind that well-worn expression, "There but for fate go I." It could happen to you. Remember that the disease is not restricted to any special group of people—it has spread to mainstream America and, indeed, to people all over the world.

What Should Supervisors Know about Substance Abuse?

Substance abuse occurs when individuals are unable to control their intake of alcohol or drugs. Substances, in effect, are any ingested matter that have an altering effect on the body or mind. A survey of executives reported that *substance abuse* is their most critical workplace issue.[4] Another survey, commissioned by the Institute for a Drug-Free Workplace, indicates that one in four U.S. workers have personal knowledge of coworkers using illegal drugs on the job, and that one in three workers is using illegal drugs before and after work.[5]

Substance abuse: *The inability of individuals to control their intake of alcohol or drugs.*

The use and abuse of substances has become increasingly the concern of supervisors, especially since the U.S. Attorney General's office ruled that people with histories of alcoholism and drug abuse are considered individuals with a disability and, accordingly, are covered under the *Rehabilitation Act of 1973,* which bans discrimination against individuals with disabilities. (The act was amended, however, to *exclude* substance abusers whose *current* use of alcohol or drugs prevents them from performing the duties of the job or whose employment constitutes a direct threat to the property or safety of others.)

What Is an Alcoholic or Drug Addict?

What is an *alcoholic*? A person could experience some isolated examples of drinking problems without necessarily being an alcoholic. The term **alcoholic** generally refers to the person who habitually lacks self-control in using alcoholic beverages, who drinks to the extent that his or her health is adversely affected, or whose social or economic functioning is significantly disrupted.

Alcoholic: *A person who habitually lacks self-control in the use of alcoholic beverages.*

What is a *drug addict*? Similar to our definition of an alcoholic, a **drug addict** is a person who habitually lacks the ability to control his or her intake of drugs. Many people in our society take drugs

Drug addict: *A person who habitually lacks the ability to control his or her intake of drug substances.*

in various forms. In fact, television advertising heavily promotes the taking of "ethical," over-the-counter drugs. Unfortunately, far too many individuals lose their self-control and begin to consume excessive amounts of drugs on a regular basis.

What Are the Job-Related Side Effects of Alcohol and Drug Abuse?

The National Institute on Drug Abuse estimates that as much as one quarter of a company's work force suffers from alcohol or drug addiction or has a family member with a substance abuse problem. Substance abuses create tremendous challenges for organizational managers.

Related to substance abuse in industry, the National Institute on Drug Abuse reports that substance abusers are:

1. Late to work three times more often than the average employee
2. Three times more likely to take sickness benefits
3. Four times more likely to be involved in on-the-job accidents
4. Five times more likely to file compensation claims
5. Sixteen times more likely to be absent from work[6]

Drug addiction tends to produce added hazards. To support drug habits, dependent workers sometimes become "pushers" and may sometimes even induce fellow employees into drug addiction. Ad-

Alcohol and drug abuse has become a costly challenge for American industry.

dicts also often support their expensive habits through the *theft* of property from organizations and individuals, frequently their own employers. A survey of 130 retail companies indicated that 40 percent of the retailers say drugs caused employees to steal from them in a recent year and 41 percent say customers arrested for theft were frequently high on drugs, carried drugs, or showed other signs of drug abuse.[7] Addicted employees tend to experience *higher turnover rates,* which result in increased personnel costs for employers. The *job performance* of employees who abuse drugs or alcohol likewise tends to fluctuate widely; U.S. companies lose about $35 billion annually because of impaired employee ability.[8]

Can You Recognize the Symptoms of Substance Abuse?

Many organizations have shown their growing concern for substance abuse problems by taking an active interest in attempting to reduce the prevalence of the two costly afflictions: drug addiction and alcoholism. A growing number of firms, such as IBM, Union Carbide, and Standard Oil, have turned to their *employee assistance programs (EAPs)* for help. (EAPs will be discussed in the following chapter.) Organizations that can't afford their own programs have attempted to counsel employees into seeking treatment from outside agencies. Modern organizations have also established formal policies and guidelines related to substance abuse.

As they do with many other activities, supervisors determine the success or failure of a substance abuse program. Supervisors should learn to recognize the major symptoms of substance abuse. However, because no one symptom is necessarily conclusive proof of a person's dependency on alcohol or drugs, a supervisor shouldn't accuse an employee of being an alcoholic or a drug abuser. Doing so could create some legal complications. Tables 19–2 and 19–3 provide some of the more common signs and symptoms of alcoholism and drug dependency. Read them carefully and refer to them again when you notice observable changes in an employee's work performance.

When you detect changing job performance that you suspect may be related to substance abuse, consider discussing your suspicions with your manager. He or she may provide you with some insights on how to deal with what is usually a delicate situation. In addition, document in writing any changes in job performance that you become aware of.

What Is Your Responsibility Related to Substance Abuse?

Supervisors generally have four principal responsibilities related to substance abuse among their employees. These are to:

1. Communicate policies and rules
2. Recommend professional assistance
3. Follow up
4. Discipline when necessary

TABLE 19–2
Signs and Symptoms of Alcoholism[9]

- Decline in work performance
- Occasional complaints about the employee from customers of the company
- Hand tremors
- The need to drink before facing certain situations
- Frequent drinking and intoxication
- Absenteeism, especially on Monday mornings and after holidays
- Frequent denial of drinking
- The occurrence of blackouts
- Poorly explained lapses in fulfilling responsibilities
- Occasional sloppy personal appearance on the job
- Hangovers on the job
- Occasional moving violations or automobile accidents
- Steady increases in the amount of alcohol consumed
- Family quarrels and disruptions over drinking
- Early morning drinking
- Drinking alone

Communicate Policies and Rules. One of your primary responsibilities in relation to substance abuse is to make certain that your employees are familiar with related policies and rules. You should also inform them about the availability of counseling services through your company's EAP program or various outside agencies. Clearly explain to your employees what circumstances will bring about their immediate dismissal for substance abuse.

Recommend Professional Assistance. You should discuss any noticeable changes in job performance with the employee and attempt to make him or her aware of the necessity for improved performance, possibly by seeing a professional counselor. As discussed in Chapter 16, be certain to *document* any relevant facts related to the employee's behavior. Informally, you could ask the employee about any personal problems that might be affecting job performance. Even though the employee may not admit to a problem, and may possibly reject the suggestion that he or she see a professional counselor, the idea has been planted in the employee's mind. Frequently people reconsider such advice, especially when they know that their jobs may depend on following it.

Follow Up. As with any planning or decision-making activities, you certainly should follow up to ensure that the employee has kept his or her promises to you. In some instances, an employee may conceal a drug or alcohol problem, refuse to see a counselor, but assure you that his or her job performance will improve. You should follow up to ensure that performance has really changed for the better and continue to document any deficiencies.

TABLE 19–3
Signs and Symptoms of Drug Dependency[10]

- Anxiety reactions and states of panic
- Accidents due to impaired judgment and distorted perceptions of space or time
- Attitudes of paranoia or excessive suspicion of others
- Mental confusion, loss of contact with reality, and lapses of memory
- Indifferent, apathetic, and sometimes compulsive behavior
- Dilated pupils, a flushed face, and a feeling of being chilly
- Chronic sniffles
- Occasional convulsions
- A deterioration of values
- Falling asleep on the job (i.e., drowsiness)
- Abscesses, needle marks, and "tracks" (discolorations along the course of veins in the arms and legs)
- Regularly wearing dark sunglasses indoors (to protect dilated pupils)
- An unhealthy appearance because of poor diet and personal neglect

If performance doesn't improve, you must take further action. Another meeting becomes necessary, at which you might take a more direct approach, perhaps saying something like:

Roger, you assured me that things would be different and that your work would improve. You and I both know it has continued to be below expectations. I think you're well aware that we just can't go on like this. Consequently, I'm going to send you to see our company counselor (or doctor), and unless you and the counselor work out your problem, I'm afraid that your future with our organization looks bleak.

A condensed version with a similar objective could be: Roger, I'm going to have to ask you for your resignation (pause), if you don't seek help related to your performance problems.

A direct approach like the second example above may seem contrary to our discussion of empathy and concern for employees, but it really isn't. Experienced supervisors have learned that the desire of employees to keep their jobs is one of the most effective factors for motivating them to seek help and modify behavior.

Be certain to *follow up* after the employee both begins and completes rehabilitation to ascertain that the prescribed recommendations are being applied.

Discipline when Necessary. An employee should be given the opportunity to seek treatment and improve his or her performance.

However, if the employee is unwilling to seek help, or is involved with the illegal trafficking of drugs, you have little choice but termination. You should also be on guard against what has been referred to as the **sham approach,** in which an employee gives lip service to his or her intention to seek professional counseling, but, in reality, is not convinced of the benefits of doing so.

Sham approach: *An employee giving only lip service to his or her intention to seek professional counseling.*

Can a Workplace Be Drug Free?

A growing concern has developed about substance abuse, especially the use of hard or illegal drugs. As a result, the U.S. Congress enacted the **Drug-Free Workplace Act of 1988.** This law requires contractors and all organizations who receive grants from the federal government to certify that they "will maintain drug-free workplaces." In the case of individuals, they must certify that their "conduct of grant activity will be drug free." Making the required certification is a precondition for receiving a contract or grant from a federal agency. Organizations or individuals in violation of the Drug-Free Workplace Act may be barred from receiving government funds for up to five years if they violate the workplace legal requirements. Figures 19–2 and 19–3 are examples of certification forms that are used to certify that a *grantee* provides a drug-free workplace.

Drug-Free Workplace Act of 1988: *Legislation requiring federal government contractors and grantees to certify a drug-free workplace before receiving a contract or grant.*

FIGURE 19–2 Drug-Free Workplace Certification for Organizations

Certification Regarding Drug-Free Workplace Requirements

Grantees Who Are Individuals

This certification is required by the regulations implementing the Drug-Free Workplace Act of 1988, 34 CFR Part 85, Subpart F. The regulations, published in the January 31, 1989 Federal Register, require certification by grantees, prior to award, that their conduct of grant activity will be drug-free. The certification set out below is a material representation of fact upon which reliance will be placed when the agency determines to award the grant. False certification or violation of the certification shall be grounds for suspension of payments, suspension or termination of grants, or governmentwide suspension or debarment (see 34 CFR Part 85, Sections 85.615 and 85.620).

The grantee certifies that, as a condition of the grant, he or she will not engage in the unlawful manufacture, distribution, dispensing, possession or use of a controlled substance in conducting any activity with the grant.

Organization Name (As Appropriate) PR/Award Number or Project Name

Printed Name

Signature Date

FIGURE 19–3 Drug-Free Workplace Certification for Individuals

Certification Regarding Drug-Free Workplace Requirements Grantees Other Than Individuals

This certification is required by the regulations implementing the Drug-Free Workplace Act of 1988, 34 CFR Part 85, Subpart F. The regulations, published in the January 31, 1989 Federal Register, require certification by grantees, prior to award, that they will maintain a drug-free workplace. The certification set out below is a material representation of fact upon which reliance will be placed when the agency determines to award the grant. False certification or violation of the certification shall be grounds for suspension of payments, suspension or termination of grants, or governmentwide suspension or debarment (see 34 CFR Part 85, Sections 85.615 and 85.620).

The grantee certifies that it will provide a drug-free workplace by:

(a) Publishing a statement notifying employees that the unlawful manufacture, distribution, dispensing, possession or use of a controlled substance is prohibited in the grantee's workplace and specifying the actions that will be taken against employees for violation of such prohibition;

(b) Establishing a drug-free awareness program to inform employees about--

(1) The dangers of drug abuse in the workplace;
(2) The grantee's policy of maintaining a drug-free workplace;
(3) Any available drug counseling, rehabilitation, and employee assistance programs; and
(4) The penalties that may be imposed upon employees for drug abuse violations occurring in the workplace;

(c) Making it a requirement that each employee to be engaged in the performance of the grant be given a copy of the statement required by paragraph (a);

(d) Notifying the employee in the statement required by paragraph (a) that, as a condition of employment under the grant, the employee will--

(1) Abide by the terms of the statement; and
(2) Notify the employer of any criminal drug statute conviction for a violation occurring in the workplace no later than five days after such conviction;

(e) Notifying the agency within ten days after receiving notice under subparagraph (d)(2) from an employee or otherwise receiving actual notice of such conviction;

(f) Taking one of the following actions, within 30 days of receiving notice under subparagraph (d)(2), with respect to any employee who is so convicted--

(1) Taking appropriate personnel action against such an employee, up to and including termination; or
(2) Requiring such employee to participate satisfactorily in a drug abuse assistance or rehabilitation program approved for such purposes by a Federal, State, or local health, law enforcement, or other appropriate agency;

(g) Making a good faith effort to continue to maintain a drug-free workplace through implementation of paragraphs (a), (b), (c), (d), (e) and (f).

____
Organization Name PR/Award Number or Project Name

____
Name and Title of Authorized Representative

____
Signature Date

ED 80-0004

Summary

A person without *disabilities* may find it hard to imagine what a life might be like with them. However, most disabled individuals do not seek sympathy. They want to be treated as *normally* as possible, especially from the standpoint of *economic opportunities*.

Three important laws related to individuals with disabilities are the *Rehabilitation Act of 1973*, which relates to firms that contract with the federal government; the *Vietnam Era Veterans' Readjustment Assistance Act of 1974*, which prohibits discrimination against veterans with disabilities and all Vietnam era veterans; and the *Americans with Disabilities Act of 1990 (ADA)*, which provides individuals with disabilities the same protection against discrimination as provided by other civil rights legislation.

Reasonable accommodation, generally a low-cost adaptation of the workplace, equipment, or job, can frequently enable individuals with certain disabilities to readily perform most tasks. Individuals with disabilities also tend to perform better with *proper training*, when *peers maintain normal relationships*, and when *the supervisor and employee are candid toward each other*.

AIDS as well as *alcohol* and *drug abuse* have become significant concerns of employers. Individuals affected by these problems are also considered to have a disability and therefore have legislative rights comparable to others with disabilities.

Questions for Discussion

1. Why is hiring persons with *physical and intellectual limitations* considered to make "sound business sense"?
2. How do you feel about the concept of *reasonable accommodation* related to individuals with disabilities?
3. What is a major distinction between the *Rehabilitation Act of 1973* and the *Americans with Disabilities Act of 1990?*
4. What are some of the ways in which a supervisor can reduce the chances of *frustration* for a newly hired person with disabilities?
5. Do supervisors have any legal responsibilities toward carriers of the disease *AIDS?* Explain.
6. What are some of the signs and symptoms of *alcoholism* and *drug dependency?* Does the presence of any one of them provide absolute certainty of a substance abuse problem?
7. How should a supervisor handle suspected cases of *drug* or *alcohol abuse* among employees?

Can You Define These Terms?

Instructions: Write a definition for each of the following terms. You may check your definitions with those provided in the end-of-text Glossary.

individuals with disabilities
qualified individual with a disability
Rehabilitation Act of 1973
Vietnam Era Veterans' Readjustment Assistance Act of 1974
Americans with Disabilities Act of 1990 (ADA)
reasonable accommodation
Acquired Immune Deficiency Syndrome (AIDS)
substance abuse
alcoholic
drug addict
sham approach
Drug-Free Workplace Act of 1988

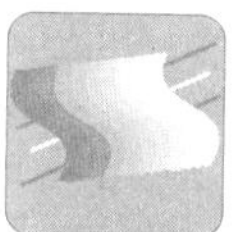

Supervision In Action

19–1 "Why Can't I Use a Pencil, Too?"[11]

Tina Singer was injured in an automobile accident that left her with *quadriplegia*, a condition of paralysis from the neck down. Eight years later she was hired by the United Telephone & Telegraph Company to be a long-distance operator working at the electronic consoles that have replaced cord switchboards.

Tina has no problems of mobility with her wheelchair since she was assigned to an office that is fully accessible. However, her boss, Herman Heinz, was somewhat concerned when Tina first reported to him. He wondered how she would be able to operate the consoles.

Tina has limited use of her arms and little use of her fingers. A metal hand splint is required to support her right hand. She is able to operate the console by picking up a pencil with the thumb and forefinger of her left hand, place it in a clasp on the hand splint, and then use the eraser end of the pencil to depress the keys of the console.

There is an office rule that operators are not to use pencils to depress keys because of the belief that fingers are more sensitive and the use of pencils could cause more errors.

United Telephone and Telegraph has contracts with the federal government, and, as a result, Sections 503 and 504 of the Rehabilitation Act of 1973 applies to its employment practices. Sections 503 and 504 stipulate, in effect, that for any contract in excess of $2,500, the party contracting with the U.S. government owes an obligation to persons with disabilities if they are qualified for a job and are able to do the particular job "with *reasonable accommodation* to their disability." The human resource director advised Herman that allowing Tina the use of pencils could be considered a reasonable accommodation and would not, therefore, be considered a violation of the department rule prohibiting their use.

Recently, two of Tina's coworkers, Harriet Jacobs and Bill Glass, approached Herman and said:

> Herman, we think the rule against the use of pencils at the consoles is completely ridiculous! Tina uses a pencil and has few problems. We once overheard you say to a visitor that you would have no problems if you had "a room full of Tinas." We don't have any disabilities, so we should be able to do at least as well as, if not better than, Tina. We think you should change the rule.

Questions

1. If you were Herman Heinz, what would you say to Harriet and Bill?
2. Would you change the rule? Why or why not?

19–2 A Case of AIDS

Jamahl Richards is the office manager of an accountancy corporation located in downtown Fresno, California, where he is responsible for supervising 10 employees.

Last Friday at quitting time Richards received some news that shocked him. Kevin O'Sullivan, an employee with the firm for six years, asked to talk to Richards privately. They went into Richards' office where the following conversation took place:

O'Sullivan: Jamahl, I really find it difficult to discuss this with you, but I've been feeling a bit strange recently and so I decided to have a physical examination. The doctor told me. . . .
(O'Sullivan began to cry uncontrollably.)

Richards: Kevin, what's wrong?
(O'Sullivan regained his composure and began to talk again.)

O'Sullivan: Well, the doctor told me that . . . eh, that . . . I have Acquired Immune Deficiency Syndrome.

Richards: You don't mean AIDS, do you?

O'Sullivan: I'm afraid I do.

Richards: You don't expect to be able to continue working here, do you?

O'Sullivan: I have to continue working here. I've got a family and loads of financial responsibilities. I also have some heavy medical expenses now. Besides, my doctor said that there is no risk that I will transmit the disease to anyone working with me. He said that I can probably continue working for several years, and that perhaps a cure will be developed before my health forces me to quit. The doctor also told me that there are laws that provide me with the right to continue working.

(Richards thinks, "Ye gads! How in the world am I going to handle this one?")

Questions

1. What legal rights does O'Sullivan have?
2. Outline specifically how Richards should handle this situation, both with O'Sullivan and with the other employees.

Endnotes

1. Legislative update prepared and distributed by the President's Committee on Employment of People with Disabilities, House Americans with Disabilities Act Hearings, September 15, 1989, p. 2.
2. Ibid.
3. "A Study of Accommodations Provided to Handicapped Employees by Federal Contractors," prepared for the U.S. De-

partment of Labor, submitted by Berkeley Planning Associates, Berkeley, California, June 17, 1982, p. 2.

4. "USA Snapshots: Workplace Worries," a 1989 survey by Jackson, Lewis, Schnitzler, and Krupman (a labor law firm), *USA Today* (International Edition), December 7, 1989, p. 1.
5. Jack Kelley, "Poll: On-Job Drug Use Is 'Significant,' " *USA Today* (International Edition), December 14, 1989, p. 1.
6. "Drugs in the Workplace," *USA Today* (International Edition), October 12, 1989, p. 16.
7. "Stores: Drugs Behind Thefts," *USA Today* (International Edition), November 29, 1989, p. 16.
8. Shelley Liles-Morris, "More Firms Help Workers Kick Addiction," *USA Today* (International Edition), October 12, 1989, p. 16.
9. Stan Kossen, *The Human Side of Organizations,* 5th ed. (New York: Harper Collins, 1991), Chapter 12.
10. Ibid.
11. Adapted from a true incident reported in the Legislative Update from the President's Committee on Employment of People with Disabilities, as presented to the House Subcommittee on Select Education of the Education and Labor Committee, September 13, 1989, pp. 13, 14.

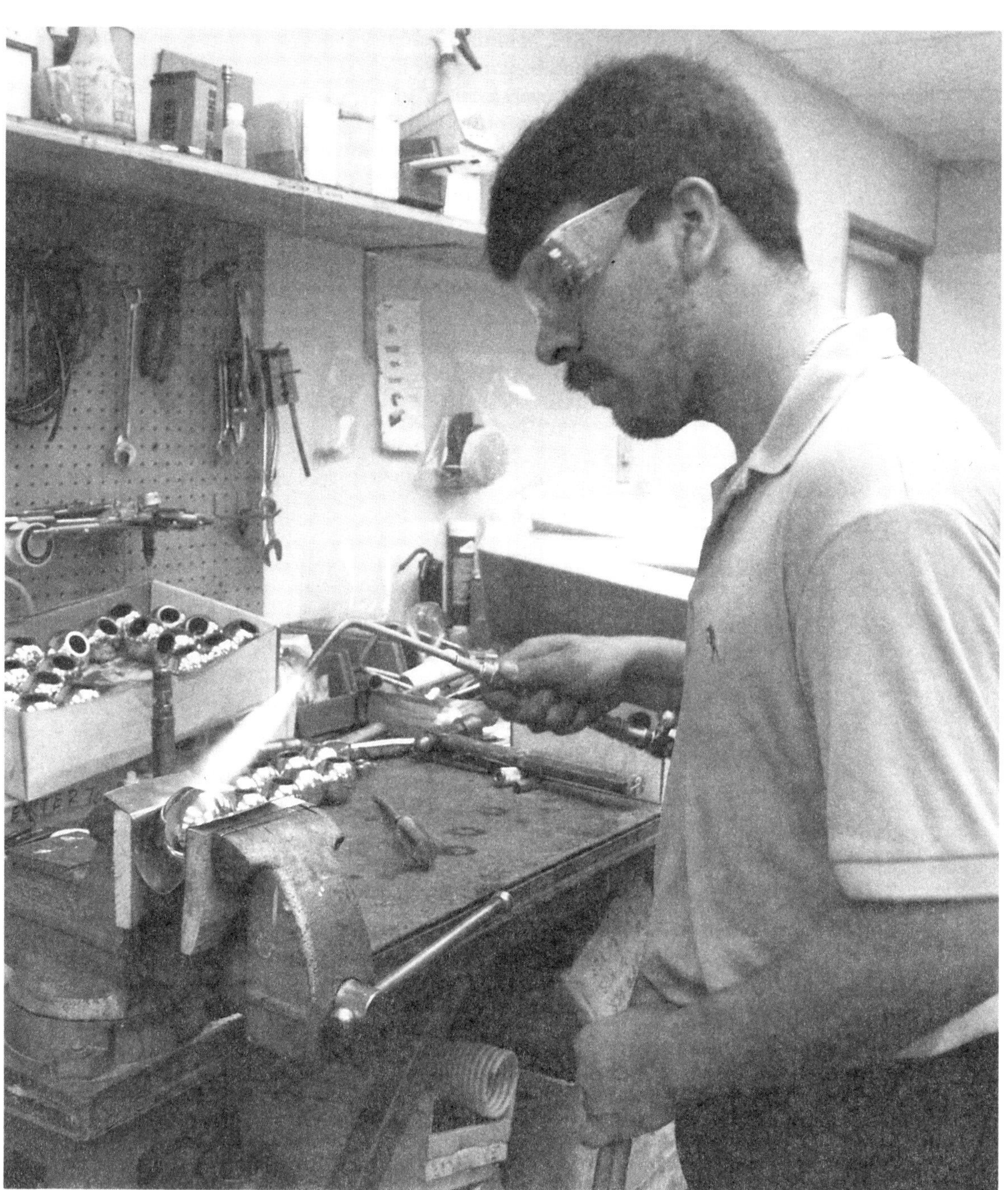

Chapter 20

Special Employment Concerns—

Organizational Health and Safety

The quest for improved technology must not blind us to the importance of combating occupational disease. It would be a tragic irony if technology advancement took the lives of those workers who made progress possible.
—Howard Metzenbaum, Politician

Learning Objectives

When you finish this chapter, you should be able to:

1. Summarize the various legislation that affects safety and the workplace.
2. Reduce or prevent the frequency of on-the-job accidents.
3. Relate the purpose of employee physical examinations and wellness programs.
4. Explain how toxic hazards can affect the health of employees.
5. Summarize the supervisor's role related to employee assistance programs.

At social gatherings, people are often asked what they do for a living. For some employees the "living" part of the question is a misnomer, because about 10,000 American workers are accidentally killed on the job each year. More than 25 million workers are exposed to toxic and cancer-causing substances at their jobs. Tens of thousands of employees die from the long-term effects of occupational diseases. The construction industry alone experiences more than 2,500 fatalities and 275,000 serious injuries each year.[1]

Accidents are costly in terms of medical expenses and time lost from work. Work-related accidents cost business about $35 billion a year. Who is responsible for preventing all of this tragedy? Larger firms may employ full-time safety professionals to develop and promote safety programs. In reality, however, everyone in an organization has a responsibility to ensure that a concern for sound safety standards and health practices exist. Accidents, by definition, are not deliberate; they usually result from negligence. Many of them can be eliminated through sound planning and other accident prevention activities.

Our focus in this chapter is on occupational safety and health management. We will first explore the major legislation that influences occupational safety practices. We will then examine how on-the-job accidents may be prevented, along with the supervisor's role in this endeavor. We will also look at the health maintenance activities and responsibilities of supervisors and their organizations. And finally, we will see how employee assistance programs can help with problems of employee physical and mental health.

What Legislation Affects Safety and the Workplace?

As a supervisor, you have a legal responsibility to maintain safe working areas. State workers' compensation laws and federal safety and health legislation affects your supervisory activities. As a result, you should be familiar with the major types of legislation that affects the workplace. We shall examine three principal types of legislation in this section:

1. Workers' compensation laws
2. Occupational Safety and Health Act (OSHA)
3. States' "right-to-know" laws

What Are Workers' Compensation Laws?

Employers' Defenses. In the early days of the Industrial Revolution, employees had little recourse toward their employers after occupational accidents or illnesses occurred. Common law seemed more on the side of employers than injured employees because of the legal defenses employers could apply. For example, when an employee was injured, the employer could plead that the *employee's negligence* contributed toward the accident, or that a *coworker was responsible,* or that the *employee assumed the risk* of injury by accepting the position in the first place.

Workers' Compensation Laws. With the assistance of muckraking journalists attacking business practices, in 1911 several states passed **workers' compensation laws,** which required most employers to obtain workers' compensation insurance. Every state now has such laws. The insurance pays part of an employee's wage or salary plus medical expenses, and any necessary rehabilitation, retraining, job placement, or counseling if a worker is accidentally injured on the job or contracts an industrial disease. Employers usually pay into a state insurance fund or, in some states, pay premiums to a private company. Some states allow companies to self-insure or to join a self-insurance fund maintained by a trade association, although most firms opt to purchase insurance from insurance companies or a state agency.

Workers' compensation laws: *Legislation requiring employers to obtain insurance to indemnify employees who are accidentally injured or contract a disease in a job-related incident.*

Determination of Premiums. Workers' compensation insurance costs employers billions of dollars each year in premiums. The cost of the insurance is significantly influenced by an organization's accident and illness record. Therefore, the difference between a good and a bad record can be costly for the company. Employers can save themselves substantial sums of money by adopting stringent risk-reduction measures, especially employee safety programs. The supervisor plays a key role in ensuring that employees comply with such safety standards. Workers' compensation insurance premiums are based on three factors:

1. The organization's accident and illness record
2. The number of employees on the organization's payroll
3. The degree of hazard or risk inherent in the positions

What Role Does OSHA Play in Safety Management?

During the 1960s, the public became increasingly aware of dangers in the workplace. Annually, over 14,000 workers were killed, and more than 2 million were injured in industrial accidents. Another 300,000 workers became ill with occupational diseases each year. By 1970, the political climate was right for the passage of preventive legislation. An act that became effective in early 1971 was the *Williams-Steiger Act,* more commonly known as the **Occupational Safety and Health Act (OSHA).** The legislation applies to virtually every business with one or more employees. Exempt are farmers with fewer than 10 employees and federal or state governments as employers, which are covered by other legislation. The intent of the act is "to assure so far as possible every working man and woman in the Nation safe and healthful working conditions and to preserve our human resources."[2]

Occupational Safety and Health Act (OSHA): *Legislation that requires most employers to create and maintain safe, healthful working conditions.*

The Nature of the Act. The Occupational Safety and Health Act contains two important requirement clauses, the first a *general* and the second a *specific* duty clause. The act states:

> *Each employer—(1) shall furnish to each of his employees employment and a place of employment which are free from recognized hazards that are causing or are likely to cause death or serious physical harm to his employees; (2) shall comply with occupational safety and health standards promulgated under this Act. . . .*

Employees are also required to comply with the standards established by the act. However, employers are still considered legally responsible even when employees fail to comply with the safety and health regulations. No provision was made in the act to penalize employees who failed to fulfill their duties.

An interesting sidelight of the act is that employers have been held responsible for injuries to their own employees caused by *outside* contractors (such as in the construction field). OSHA's reasoning is that the employer has the ability and duty to remove the hazardous working conditions and is therefore responsible even though it did not directly create the situation. Can you see how you, as a supervisor, might be affected by this interpretation?

Occupational Safety and Health Administration (OSHA): *A federal agency responsible for administering the provisions of the Occupational Safety and Health Act.*

The Administration of the Act. Three federal agencies were created by the act to carry out its provisions. These are:

- **Occupational Safety and Health Administration (OSHA).** The primary agency created by the act. A part of the Department of Labor, it is responsible for promulgating standards, conducting on-site inspections, and seeking enforcement of the law.
- **National Institute of Occupational Safety and Health (NIOSH).** A center of occupational health research, it recommends standards for adoption by OSHA.
- **Occupational Safety and Health Review Commission (OSHRC).** An agency operating autonomously from OSHA, it hears and settles cases involving safety and health violations. OSHA only recommends penalties to OSHRC, which then determines the penalties. OSHRC decisions can be appealed at Federal Circuit Courts of Appeal.

National Institute of Occupational Safety and Health (NIOSH): *A federal health research center that recommends health standards for OSHA adoption.*

Occupational Safety and Health Review Commission (OSHRC): *A federal agency responsible for settling cases involving safety and health violations.*

Inspection of Premises. OSHA staffs compliance officers or inspectors whose responsibility it is to call on the businesses covered under the law and, as necessary, impose fines of up to $10,000 for deliberate violations of the Occupational Safety and Health Administration's health and safety standards.

Inspectors were originally allowed to make surprise visits under a **no-knock provision** of the act; however, such form of entry is no longer permitted. Although most employers voluntarily allow inspectors to enter their premises, they are not required to do so unless the inspector first obtains a warrant. Under the general clause

No-knock provision: *A currently prohibited activity that enabled OSHA to inspect an employer's property for safety abuses without a warrant.*

of the act, however, *ex parte* warrants have been relatively easy to obtain. An ***ex parte* warrant** is a judicially granted right to search an employer's premises without prior notification or permission.

Ex parte warrant: *A judicially granted right for OSHA inspectors to search an employer's premises without prior notification or permission.*

What Are States' "Right-to-Know" Laws?

The majority of states have enacted **"right-to-know" laws** in recent years. The purpose of such legislation is to require employers to inform employees if any hazardous substances exist in the workplace. Most of the laws also allow for local fire and public health officials to discover if regional employers are using hazardous substances that could pose health or safety problems to the community.

"Right-to-know" laws: *Acts enacted by the majority of states that require employers to inform employees if any hazardous substances exist in the workplace.*

Although the laws may vary to some degree by state, common features of "right-to-know" laws generally include the following:[3]

- Employers have an obligation to post notices on bulletin boards in the work area advising employees that they have the right to request information about toxic substances in the workplace. These notices commonly require the employer to state that no reprisals will be taken against employees who exercise their right to request information.
- In some states, employers have an obligation to inform prospective and current employees of hazards that could cause reproductive problems. For example, employees must be told if radioactive materials are used in the workplace.
- In some states, employers have an obligation to put warning labels on containers of toxic substances.
- In some states, employers must conduct training programs for employees. These programs inform employees about the properties of the toxic substances in the work place, train employees how to safely handle toxic substances, and instruct employees in emergency treatment for overexposure to such substances.

Taking its cue from the states' "right-to-know laws," in 1986 OSHA published the **OSHA Hazard Communication Standard (HCS)** on chemical hazards. The standard requires companies to identify hazardous substances they produce, distribute, or use. Companies also are required to identify the nature of the hazards of these substances, and to tell employees what they can do to protect themselves. Firms must also make all this information available to employees. They must also label containers of hazardous substances with appropriate warnings, and they must train and educate employees about the hazards.

OSHA Hazard Communication Standard (HCS): *An OSHA promulgation that is patterned after states' "right-to-know" laws.*

What Sort of Records Must the Supervisor Maintain?

As a supervisor, you may be responsible for maintaining certain records related to occupational accidents or illnesses. Some managers feel that supervisors should investigate and document *all* known accidents, even if the information isn't required by OSHA.

Doing so often aids in preventing reoccurrences of the same problem and can help to reduce future legal complications.

After an accident, you may be expected to investigate its nature and causes. Your organization may utilize a preprinted form on which you merely check off relevant items related to physical causes, unsafe activities, and personal factors.

Accident frequency rate: *A formula-created ratio that reveals the incidence of accidents per 100 full-time employees.*

Accident severity rate: *Determined from number of lost-time cases, lost workdays, and deaths, related to total hours worked per 100 full-time employees, and compared to industrywide rates.*

Frequency and Severity Records. For accidents and illnesses requiring medical treatment, **accident frequency rate** records (how often they happen) and **accident severity rate** records (how many workdays the employee misses) are typically kept. Your human resources (or personnel) department typically requires such records for health and workers' compensation insurance purposes.

OSHA's Recordkeeping Requirements. OSHA also requires the maintenance of certain records. Any employer with 10 or more employees is required by OSHA to maintain records of various occupational accidents and illnesses. (Smaller firms that have an unfavorable history of job-related deaths or frequent hospitalization injuries or illnesses may have to complete OSHA's basic reporting document, Form 200.) Table 20–1 summarizes occupational injuries or illnesses that *must* be recorded.

Right to See Records. Employees, inspectors, and representatives of employees have the right under OSHA to *request to see records related to exposure to toxic or harmful physical agents upon request.* Employees also have the right to *report to OSHA any violations related to safety standards.* Section 11(c) of the act protects employees from retaliation in the event they exercise these rights.

How Are On-the-job Accidents Prevented?

Accident prevention is one of the most important responsibilities that a manager has. Any successful accident prevention program

TABLE 20–1
OSHA Recordkeeping Requirements

Any occupational accident or exposure must be recorded if it results in:

1. Death
2. Illness

Any occupational accident must be recorded if it involves:

1. Medical treatment (other than first aid)
2. Loss of consciousness
3. Restriction of work or motion
4. Transfer to another job

An injury or illness need not be recorded if it does not result:

1. From a work accident
2. From an exposure in the work environment

must have *a senior management that is committed and communicates its support throughout the organization.* In addition, the workplace must receive *proper safety engineering,* and employees need to receive *adequate safety training and indoctrination.* As a supervisor, you must also serve as a *role model to employees* for safety programs to really work. *Regular safety inspections* and *employee discipline* when necessary will also assist in minimizing on-the-job accidents and industrial diseases.

What Is Safety Engineering?

As supervisor, one of your major responsibilities in the area of accident prevention is **safety engineering,** which primarily is identifying workplace hazards and designing jobs and the workplace in a manner that reduces the risk of accidents and industrial disease. Depending on the size and structure of your organization, there may be a safety specialist assigned to the human resource management department who can assist you in safety engineering.

Safety engineering: *Identifying workplace hazards and designing jobs and workplaces to reduce risk of accidents and industrial disease.*

Among the concerns of safety engineering include planning your department's safety needs and making certain that such items as hard-toe shoes, hard hats, or other protective clothing are available for employees as needed.

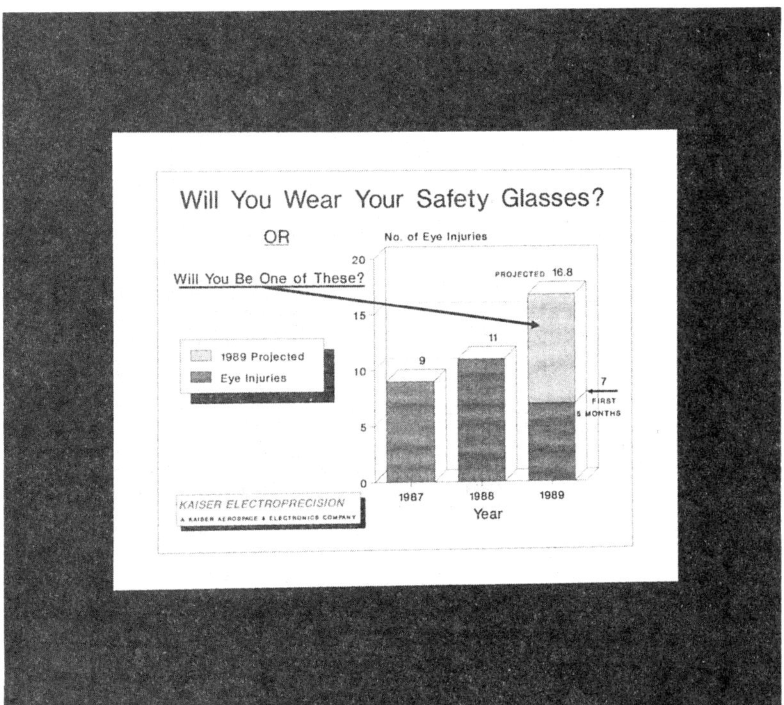

Safety prevention is an ongoing process. Employees need a continual reminder of the need for safe work habits.

Ergonomics:
Designing products and workplaces to make jobs more suitable and safe for employees.

A related area of safety engineering is termed **ergonomics,** which is designing products and workplaces in a way that makes the job more suitable for employees. Examples include designing handles of tools so that fatigue is lessened during their use, designing chairs that reduce back strain, providing employees with computer monitors that ease eyestrain, and installing proper lighting and ventilation equipment.

What Is the Nature of Safety Education and Training?

Since far more reported accidents are caused by unsafe acts by employees than by mechanical failure, a fairly apparent method for dealing with this problem is providing employees with adequate **safety education and training.**

Safety education and training:
Providing employees with information and skills intended to reduce the incidence and severity of accidents and industrial illness.

One might assume that everyone in a department would be supportive of sound safety practices, but this is not always the case. For example, some employees resist the use of safety equipment because they feel encumbered by it. To have to put on safety goggles each time they operate a machine may seem bothersome. Unfortunately, many employees have learned the hard way about the importance of utilizing safety equipment (See Supervision in Action 20–1 at the end of this chapter for a true example.)

Merely lecturing employees on the importance of practicing safe working habits is seldom sufficient to make them safety conscious. A more effective approach is to involve your associates in developing and promoting safety programs. They are likely to identify with and support a program far more enthusiastically when they have a feeling of involvement with it. Regular safety meetings can also be conducted in which your employees are responsible for making presentations on specific safety topics.

When training employees on safety concerns, be certain that they are aware of the specific hazards associated with their jobs. You might occasionally show some films or videos that graphically portray the injurious effects of employee negligence.

Some organizations place safety posters on walls to reenforce safety concepts. However, some observers contend that posters ultimately end up like old fixtures. Employees become accustomed to them so that they are hardly observed, something like the cautionary notice on the side of a pack of cigarettes. That is not to say that posters should never be used, but a more effective approach is to change or rotate the location of posters on a regularly scheduled basis so that "fresh" ones are more likely to attract the attention of passersby.

Safety training is akin to selling, and as with any professional selling, the salesperson should point out how the *customer* will benefit. For example, pointing out to the employee how much accidents cost the company has far less impact than pointing out *what the employee will lose* as a result of personally experiencing a disabling accident.

How Does Serving as a Role Model Help?

"People tend to follow as they are led," is an oft-heard cliché. The statement's implications are extremely important related to accident prevention. It is essential that you serve as a **role model** to your employees from the standpoint of following sound safety practices. Can you reasonably expect your associates to comply with safety rules if you don't set a good example?

Role model:
Someone who serves as a model in a particular behavioral role for another to emulate.

Why Are Safety Inspections Essential?

You needn't wait for the OSHA inspector to knock on your door before engaging in inspection activities. Instead, you might find it worthwhile to develop a *checklist* of items that should be inspected on a regularly scheduled basis. Would you be likely to want to fly on an airplane from San Francisco to Chicago if you learned that the airline had not established a plan for inspecting its flying equipment? Periodic safety inspections are essential for the prevention of accidents.

How Important Is Discipline?

Safety standards and rules will be meaningless to employees when ignoring them has no recognizable consequences. Always follow up immediately when you discover a deviation from established safety standards. The discipline concepts discussed in an earlier chapter are especially important in relation to safety regulations. For example, reinforcement techniques can be used for motivating employees.

Some organizations provide regular rewards and positive recognition to employees who maintain accident-free records for certain periods of time. Company publications often proudly announce the number of days an organization has been accident free. Providing positive incentives can be a highly effective method for maintaining a sound accident prevention program.

What Is the Nature of Organizational Health?

Health, another important organizational topic, is the nonidentical twin of safety. **Health** can be defined as a general state of physical, mental, and emotional well-being. Organizations have a logical concern for the overall well-being of their employees, since employee performance is no less related to health maintenance than it is to accident prevention.

Health:
The general state of physical, mental, and emotional well-being.

Supervisors typically play a lesser role in an organization's employee health program than they do in the area of safety, although they may be expected to administer parts of the program. Supervisors may also be expected to encourage employees to participate in company-sponsored activities related to health maintenance.

Why Provide Employee Physical Examinations?

Some organizations provide their employees with regular physical examinations. Such activity is akin to inspecting equipment regularly to ensure its continued safe operation. As with machinery, early detection of potentially harmful symptoms can frequently eliminate or reduce problems before conditions become irreversible.

How Do Toxic Hazards Affect Health?

Many organizations use various hazardous substances in their production processes. Thousands of workers in the United States are incapacitated each year as a result of improper exposure to toxic hazards. Acting on a worker's complaint, for example, an OSHA inspection at one company found work surfaces covered with mercury, with no protective gear provided for the workers. Even the area where the employees ate lunch was contaminated. OSHRC fined the company $1,400.[4]

Since it is unlikely that industry is going to stop producing or using hazardous substances, it is essential that adequate precautions be taken to minimize the risk of employee exposure to them. Enlightened, safety-conscious engineering is essential to organizational health maintenance. Ensuring that employees have available to them specialized articles of clothing can reduce risk. For example, rubber gloves should be available for people whose hands must touch toxic chemicals and hygienists who clean teeth. Employees working around airborne chemicals or dust should be provided with face masks.

What Are Wellness Programs?

Wellness programs: *Employer-sponsored fitness programs for maintaining and improving employees' physical health and sense of well-being.*

Many organizations, recognizing the benefits associated with maintaining a healthy work force, have developed fitness programs referred to as **wellness programs.** Such organizations recognize that employees who are physically and mentally fit tend to enjoy more positive attitudes toward their jobs, have higher productivity, engage in less absenteeism, and experience substantially less stress.

Such programs vary by company, but may include on-premises fitness facilities, such as basketball, tennis, and/or volleyball courts; running tracks; exercise equipment; plus showers and locker rooms. Other organizations pay all or a portion of membership fees in an outside fitness center.

How Can EAPs Assist with Problems of Employee Health?

Employee assistance programs (EAPs): *Organizational programs for aiding employees with personal problems that affect job performance.*

As briefly mentioned in an earlier chapter, some firms have developed an adjunct to the human resource or personnel department designed to assist employees with personal problems that can include health, self-identity, marriage, finance, and alcohol or drug dependency. Often called **employee assistance programs (EAPs),** such activities can substantially benefit an organization's health maintenance program when they have the full support and commitment of all levels of management. Some employers, rather than establish their own EAP departments, establish a liaison relationship with a social service counseling agency. Employee counseling costs are typically paid for by the employer in full or an amount up to a preestablished limit.[5]

What Is the Supervisor's Role Related to EAPs?

You, the supervisor, can't be expected to diagnose the problem employee's physical health, emotional, or other personal difficulties, since you're not a medical doctor or professional therapist. Your principal task is to detect when problems are serious enough to require professional counseling. Then you should display a friendly but firm concern about the employee's need to seek help. In the case of serious health problems, such as substance abuse, the employee should be informed that if he or she refuses to accept help, and performance continues to be unsatisfactory, his or her future with the company will be in jeopardy. The employee must make a choice.

What Are Some Cautionary Measures the Supervisor Should Take Related to EAPs?

Attempting to refer an employee to an EAP department is sometimes a delicate matter. Some employees may take offense at the very suggestion of it. Here are a few guidelines that can make referring the problem employee to an EAP easier:[6]

- Do emphasize that all aspects of the EAP are confidential.
- Don't try to diagnose the problem yourself.
- Don't discuss the employee's problem with anyone except those associated with the EAP program.
- Don't be misled by sympathy-evolving tactics, at which the alcohol or drug dependent person may have become expert.
- Don't cover up for the employee, even if he or she is a friend. Misguided "kindness" can lead to a serious delay in his or her obtaining real help. Many employees have literally been *killed* by this sort of kindness.

Summary

Safety and *health* are major concerns of organizational leaders today because of their *high costs* in terms of *injuries, loss of human life, medical care, lost worker days,* and *damage to property.* As a result, many organizations spend a great deal of time, effort, and money on *accident prevention.* Through effective *safety engineering, training,* and *control*, accident frequency and the incidence of industrial disease can be reduced. The supervisor's role is especially important in serving as a *good example* before employees, along with *training* and *disciplining* employees when necessary.

A supervisor should be familiar with the requirements of *state workers' compensation laws, the Occupational Safety and Health Act (OSHA),* and *states' "right-to-know" laws.*

Many organizations are committed to a concern for employee physical and mental health. They may influence health by offering *regular physical examinations,* sponsoring *wellness programs,* and maintaining *employee assistance programs (EAPs).*

Questions for Discussion

1. Why did state legislators believe that *workers' compensation insurance* was a necessary requirement for employers to provide for their employees?
2. What were the typical common legal defenses employers could draw on prior to the passage of *workers' compensation laws*?
3. What factors typically determine the cost of workers' compensation insurance premiums? Do employers have any influence over these factors? Explain.
4. What is the expressed intent of the *Occupational Safety and Health Act (OSHA)*? Do you agree with its purposes? Explain.
5. Can employers be held responsible for *acts committed by individuals who are not their employees*? Explain.
6. Name and describe the primary functions of the *three federal agencies* responsible for carrying out the provisions of the Occupational Safety and Health Act.
7. What is the major purpose of *states' "right-to-know" laws*?
8. Who has the right under OSHA rules to see *employer records* related to worker exposure to toxic or harmful physical agents?
9. Describe the nature of *safety engineering.*
10. How effective are *posters* when used for *accident prevention*?
11. How does *discipline* relate to accident prevention?
12. What is the purpose of a company *wellness program*?
13. How does an organization's *EAP* relate to employee health?

Can You Define These Terms?

Instructions: Write a definition for each of the following terms. You may check your definitions with those provided in the end-of-text Glossary.

workers' compensation laws
Occupational Safety and Health Act (OSHA)
Occupational Safety and Health Administration (OSHA)

National Institute of Occupational Safety and Health (NIOSH)
Occupational Safety and Health Review Commission (OSHRC)
no-knock provision
ex parte warrant
"right-to-know" laws
OSHA Hazard Communication Standard (HCS)
accident frequency rate
accident severity rate
safety engineering
safety education and training
ergonomics
role model
health
wellness programs
employee assistance programs (EAPs)

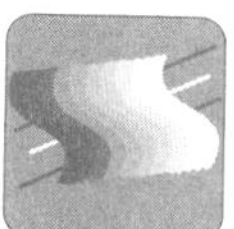

Supervision In Action

20–1 More Efficient? Maybe. Safer? Never!

Albert Foster was a bindery worker in a large printing plant. His responsibility was to work at a machine that cuts large sheets of 35 × 45-inch paper into smaller sheets of 8½ by 11 inches. Albert was considered to be a hard worker, but he usually resisted the use of safety devices on his machine.

The paper cutter was designed with a safety clutch so that both of Albert's hands were supposed to be involved gripping the cutter's two handles as the large guillotine-shaped blade rapidly sliced through large stacks of paper. Albert, however, contended that he had to disengage the clutch by tying it so that his left hand would be free to pat the sides of the paper to prevent sheets from sliding outward on the cutter.

One evening a shrill scream bellowed out from Albert's work station. Four fingers on his left hand had been amputated at the knuckles by the machine's sharp blade.

Questions:

1. Since Albert believed that he could not do an effective job of cutting paper unless the clutch was tied, was he justified in altering the safety equipment? Explain.
2. Who is to blame for the accident? Why?

20–2 "But I'll Give You a Ride Home"[7]

About an hour before the usual quitting time, Shane Owen, a male supervisor in the production department, approached Jenny Millstone, one of his female employees, and the following conversation took place:

Shane: Jenny, I wonder if you would be willing to work two hours overtime today.

Jenny: Ordinarily I would be happy to, Mr. Owen, but if I did I would miss my vanpool that leaves in about an hour. If I worked I wouldn't have a way to get home.

(Company rules prohibit employees from working overtime without a supervisor on premises.)

Shane: Jenny, I have to be here anyhow during those overtime hours, so I'll be able to give you a ride home. It won't be any inconvenience for me since you live in the same part of town I do.

(Jenny agreed to work the overtime hours.)

It was already dark when they left work, and the roads were coated with ice. Shane's car went into a skid, slid off the road, and came to a gentle stop. The sudden shift in the car's direction, however, pushed Jenny over into Shane's arms. Shane became a bit "familiar" with Jenny who became angry and wrenched Shane's arm, dislocating it at the shoulder, which kept him off the job for six weeks. Shane filed a workers' compensation claim against his employer for lost pay and medical expenses.

Questions

1. In your opinion, should workers' compensation insurance cover Shane's loss of income and medical expenses as a result of the injury caused by Jenny? Why or why not?
2. Do you feel that an employer should ever be responsible for injuries that occur off the premises of the company?

20–3 "Here's How Our Company Will Benefit"

Maria Payton, a supervisor in a manufacturing facility, was told by her boss, Jayne Campos, to try to instill a "safety-first" attitude among her employees. Campos pointed out to Maria that reduced frequency and severity of accidents would help to lower the company's workers' compensation insurance premiums, since they are affected significantly by the company's accident rates.

Activity

Assume that you are Maria, and you have decided to discuss the concept of safety at your bimonthly department meeting. Prepare one or two paragraphs that illustrate how you would attempt to motivate your associates into being more safety conscious.

20–4 "We Want All of You There"

The Glasgal Company has had mediocre sales success in the sneaker manufacturing business until recently. About a year ago it developed a $200 basketball shoe called "Power" that has taken off phenomenally in sales. "Power" has become a fad item throughout the United States and Canada, with many people actually wearing them as they work in their offices.

Glasgal directors decided to show their appreciation to employees for the outstanding financial results the company has enjoyed during the past year, so they arranged a weekend company celebration at a summer resort in the nearby Copituc Mountains. Wanting the party to be a success, the directors announced that attendance at the party was compulsory for all employees.

A softball game was arranged during the party, and one of the employees, Jack Palermo, broke his collarbone while sliding into home plate. Palermo became a quadriplegic, and was paralyzed from the neck down.

Palermo decided to sue Glasgal, the employer, for $2 million dollars on the grounds that the surface of the playing field was uneven and therefore excessively unsafe and unduly hazardous. His attorney further charged that the employer engaged in "gross, willful, reckless, and wanton misconduct" for arranging an activity it "knew or should have known was exceedingly dangerous." As their defense, Glasgal directors countered that the outing was "work related," and the injury, therefore, should be covered under workers' compensation insurance. (An employee does not have the legal right to sue if an injury is deemed to be work-related and covered under workers' compensation laws.)

Questions

1. Do you feel that an employer can be held responsible for injuries that occur off the premises during social events?

2. How would you rule if you were a judge: (1) the injured party should be covered under workers' compensation insurance or (2) the injured party must litigate to recover damages? Why?

Endnotes

1. Howard Metzenbaum, "Inform Workers about Job Perils," *Contra Costa Times,* August 17, 1986, p. 19A; and "Job Safety & Health," *AFL–CIO News,* August 20, 1988, p. 1.
2. "All About OSHA," U.S. Department of Labor, Occupational Safety and Health Administration, OSHA Pamphlet No. 2056 (Washington, D.C.: Government Printing Office), p. 3.
3. David P. Twomey, *A Concise Guide to Employment Law: EEO & OSHA* (Cincinnati: South-Western Publishing Co., 1986), p. 133.
4. "Workplace Criminals 'Get Away With Murder,'" *AFL–CIO News,* October 15, 1988, pp. 1, 6.
5. Robert L. Mathis and John H. Jackson, *Personnel: Human Resource Management,* 5th ed. (St. Paul, Minn.: West Publishing Co., 1985), p. 480.
6. Adapted from a program instituted by Kemper Insurance Company, as reported in Kenneth N. Wexley and Gary P. Latham, *Developing and Training Human Resources in Organizations* (Glenview, Ill.: Scott, Foresman and Company, 1981), pp. 225, 226.
7. Adapted from Russell L. Greenman and Eric J. Schmertz, *Personnel Administration and the Law,* 2nd ed. (Washington, D.C.: Bureau of National Affairs, 1979), p. 201, as reported in James Ledvinka, *Federal Regulation of Personnel and Human Resource Management* (Belmont, Calif.: Kent Publishing Co., 1982), p. 137.

Glossary*

ABC Priority System A method for prioritizing work activities for the purpose of making more effective use of time. (6)
Acceptance An employee reaction that exists when an employee feels virtually no threat connected with a proposed change. (14)
Accident frequency rate A formula-created ratio that reveals the incidence of accidents per 100 full-time employees. (20)
Accident severity rate Determined by figuring the number of lost-time cases, the number of lost workdays, and the number of deaths, relating them to total hours worked per 100 full-time employees, and comparing them to industrywide rates. (20)
Accountability The *answerability* that organizational members have to their managers; sometimes used interchangeably with *responsibility*. (8)
Accountability-for-results principle A principle asserting that managers are still held answerable for results even when the authority needed to achieve objectives has been assigned to their subordinates. (8)
Acquiescence An employee reaction that exists when an employee passively complies with a change without protest. (14)
Acquired Immune Deficiency Syndrome (AIDS) A disease that destroys the body's immunity systems; transmitted by the exchange of certain bodily fluids. (19)
Action plan Specific recommendations for resolving a problem. (3)
Activities management Virtually the same as *time management.* (6)
***Ad hoc* committee** A body of persons formed to handle a specific, temporary situation. (3)
Adequacy-of-authority principle A principle asserting that any authority assigned to managers should be sufficient to enable them to achieve expected results. (8)
Administrative skills The ability to see the whole picture, conceptualize, and think in the abstract. (2)
Administrators A typical classification of senior managers in governmental organizations. (1)
Affirmative action program (AAP) An organizational program intended to ensure fair recruitment, hiring, and promotion practices. (18)

*The number following each definition indicates the chapter in which it is discussed.

Age Discrimination Act of 1967 Legislation prohibiting employers from discriminating against a person over age 40. (18)
AIDA approach Symbolizes four steps related to influencing others: *a*ttention, *i*nterest, *d*esire, and *a*ction. (17)
Alcoholic A person who habitually lacks self-control in the use of alcoholic beverages. (19)
Americans with Disabilities Act of 1990 (ADA) Legislation that extends the Rehabilitation Act of 1973 to include private employers as well as government contractors. (19)
Application forms Forms designed to provide the interviewer with basic information about an applicant for a position; serves as a record of the applicant's interest in securing employment; becomes a part of the applicant's permanent personnel file if employed. (9)
Appraisal cycle A five-step process related to evaluating the performance of employees. (10)
Appraisal interview A conference between the supervisor and an employee to discuss the employee's past performance and plans for improvement. (10)
Apprentice training Training that generally involves both classroom (off the job at a trade or vocational school) and on-the-job or vestibule training; commonly used for persons entering a trade or craft. (10)
Arbitration Use of impartial third party to develop binding decisions during management/labor disputes. (15)
Asch conformity studies A study conducted by Solomon Asch that illustrated the apparent need people have to conform to group standards. (11)
Attitude surveys An approach used to uncover employee attitudes and opinions in some depth. (11)
Authority The *right* (or power) of people in an organization to make decisions, act, and direct others to act; flows down the organizational hierarchy. (8)
Authorization cards Cards signed by employees to indicate their desire to vote for union representation. (15)
Autocratic (authoritarian) leadership A style of leadership in which managers keep decisions and controls to themselves. (12)

Basic needs See *Needs, physical.* (11)
Binding outside arbitration The use of an outside party to settle disputes in nonunion organizations. (15)
Bona fide occupational qualification (BFOQ) A

provision of the Civil Rights Act of 1964 that permits employers to discriminate against employees in hiring practices in certain instances when reasonably necessary to the normal operation of a particular enterprise. (9)

Bonus Additional money paid to employees as an incentive for performing more effectively; typically relates to improved results in the areas of production, sales, or cost reduction. (9)

Bonus days off A program that rewards employees with time off for putting in a given number of days without being absent. (16)

Boot ensign relationship Attempting to effect too much change before gaining the confidence of others. (17)

Brainstorming A nonjudgmental group problem-solving and idea-generating activity encouraging the free-flow of ideas. (3)

Budget Typically a financial plan that allocates operating funds for a particular period of time; serves as a control device for providing feedback. (5)

CAD/CAM process Symbolizes the terms *c*omputer-*a*ided *d*esign and *c*omputer-*a*ided *m*anufacturing. (3)

Cafeteria-styled benefit programs Employee benefit schemes in which employees can choose a combination of insurance and other options based on their personal desires rather than on a predefined basis. (9, 15)

Certification election Election officially recognizing union as legal bargaining representative of employees. (15)

Chain of command The route, or channel, in the formal organization through which authority is passed and policies are transmitted to lower levels for implementation. (8)

Change Any variation in conditions that previously existed. (14)

Civil Rights Act of 1964—Title VII Legislation that prohibits employers, labor unions, and employment agencies from discriminating against persons on the basis of color, religion, sex, or national origin. (9)

Closed questions Questions that typically can be answered with only a yes or no. (9, 13)

Collective bargaining Negotiation between management and labor representatives to establish a written agreement. (15)

Commission Compensation, generally paid to salespeople, on the basis of a percentage of the purchase price of each unit sold. (9)

Committees A group formed to study, act, or report on issues related to an organization; also referred to as *task forces*. (3)

Communication A two-way process resulting in the transmission of information and understanding between individuals. (13)

Comparable worth The belief that women should be paid as much as men for doing tasks in occupations requiring comparable skills and effort. (18)

Computer-aided design The use of computers in designing parts and products. (3)

Computer-aided manufacturing The use of computers in linking design computers with manufacturing computers. (3)

Contingency leadership Applying a style of leadership that is called for by the particular situation. (12)

Contributory pension plan A program in which both the employee and the employer contribute to a retirement fund that is placed in reserve for later distribution to employees. (9)

Control sharing Involving employees wherever possible in the development of control standards. (5)

Control standards Predetermined goals and objectives that are expected to be met. (5)

Controlling A management function that involves the regular and systematic comparing (monitoring) of actual results with planned objectives to determine if goals are being accomplished or if corrections must be made. (5)

Cost control A systematic activity intended to ensure that actual financial outlays are in line with projected expenditures. (5)

Cost-benefit analysis Comparing costs and benefits associated with a specific decision. (3)

Crisis management Management style where decisions are made after critical problems develop, often a result of poor planning. (3)

Current problem A time-oriented problem that already exists. (3)

Customer departmentation Organizing departments according to type of purchaser. (8)

Daily activities summary log A time management tool that can assist supervisors in keeping track of how their time has been expended on a daily basis. (6)

Daily planner A form on which a supervisor can list all of his or her planned daily activities and the specific times they are to be performed. (6)

Data Facts and figures that by themselves have little to do with managerial decisions. (3)

Decertification election Election resulting in elimination of a union as the legal bargaining representative of employees. (15)

Decision That part of a manager's activities requiring a choice to be made between two or more alternatives. (3)

Decision-assisting MIS Nonprogrammed decisions arrived at through the utilization of MIS systems. (3)

Deep sensing The attempt by senior managers to find out face-to-face what is on the minds of rank and file employees. (13)

Delegating (delegation) The act of giving rights or assigning responsibilities to another person; an activity that frees the delegator for other important tasks and helps to develop the delegatee. (2, 8)

Delphi method Group decision making in which each participant works independently of others, then views the others' results and revises original recommendations. (3)

Department The specific location or set of activities for which managers are responsible; can include activities called sections, divisions, and branches. (8)

Departmentation Organizing jobs, tasks, responsibilities, and activities into subunits, or departments, for the purpose of improving efficiency of operations. (8)

Derived X Theory (I've-been-burned theory) A negative attitude toward employees held by some managers who believe themselves to be positively oriented but who have had negative experiences (real or imagined) that caused a shift in their assumptions. (12)

Descriptive questionnaire A survey of employee attitudes that asks open-ended questions. (11)

Desktop appointment calendar A device that serves as a written guide to, and record of, a supervisor's daily activities. (6)

Developmental goals Specific goals intended to improve some part of the organization, such as the goal to develop personnel through training. (4)

Discipline Leadership activity intended to correct undesirable employee behavior. (16)

Discrimination Actions directed either against or in favor of something or someone. (18)

Distress A negative type of stress that, if not managed properly, can lead to a variety of diseases and mental depression. (7)

Documentation Maintaining written records of employee behavior necessary for backing up disciplinary action and employee appraisals. (16)

Do-nothing approach A decision, made either consciously or unconsciously, to let a problem work itself out. (3)

Downsizing A form of restructuring that results in laying off employees; closing less efficient plants, departments, or product lines; and attempting to operate more efficiently. (2)

Downward communication Communication that conveys messages from higher to lower levels of an organization, such as from a supervisor to workers. (13)

Driving forces Factors that prevent a problem from being worse. (3)

Drug addict A person who habitually lacks the ability to control his or her intake of drug substances. (19)

Drug-Free Workplace Act of 1988 Legislation requiring contractors and grantees of the federal government to certify a drug-free workplace as a precondition for receiving a contract or grant. (19)

Dual command The situation in which one subordinate is accountable to more than one manager; an abuse of the unity of command principle. (8)

Eccentricity The condition of departing or deviating from conventional or established norms. (16)

Eccentric personality Characteristic of individuals who typically depart from established norms. (16)

Ego need See *Needs, ego.* (11)

Empathy The attempt to feel something as another person feels it. (13)

Employee assistance programs (EAPs) Organizational programs for aiding employees with personal problems that affect job performance. (11, 20)

Employee benefits Also termed *fringe benefits*; considered to be nonfinancial rewards provided to employees beyond their regular compensation. (9)

Employee compensation The rewards provided to employees for performing their job responsibilities. (9)

Employee counselors Staff individuals who assist employees with their problems and complaints. (15)

Employee orientation (induction) program A planned introduction of new employees to the organization and other pertinent information related to employment. (9)

Employee performance evaluation system (performance appraisal, performance review) A set of activities designed to determine how well employees are carrying out their duties, tasks, and responsibilities; a useful tool for guiding the direction of employee performance. (10)

Employee referral plan A system that rewards existing employees with a finder's fee for bringing in successful job candidates. (9)

Employee stock ownership programs (ESOPs) Programs that grants employees stock at little or no cost. (9)

Employment interview A screening procedure intended to aid in determining the suitability of an applicant for a particular position. (9)

Employment process The staffing function of management; includes the various activities necessary to recruit and select qualified individuals for employment. (9)

Employment requisition A formal written request for additional labor, one that initiates the recruitment process. (9)

Employment tests A screening device intended to measure a person's acceptability for a particular position; attempts to measure such factors as ability, intelligence, aptitude, interests, and personality; must be carefully designed to avoid charges of discrimination. (9)

Equal Employment Opportunity Commission (EEOC) An agency created by Title VII to administer civil rights legislation and investigate complaints. (18)

Equal Pay Act of 1963 A bill requiring employers to provide equal pay to women and men for performing substantially similar work. (18)

Equal Rights Amendment (ERA) A bill passed by Congress in 1972 to amend the constitution to outlaw discrimination based on sex; not ratified by enough states to be incorporated into the Constitution. (18)

Equilibrium In force field analysis, the location of the current state of the problem. (3)

Equity theory The theory that individuals are motivated by their perception of how fairly or unfairly they are being treated compared to their efforts and to others. (11)

Ergonomics Designing products and work places to make jobs more suitable for employees. (20)

Espirit de corps An attitude of enthusiasm, support, and loyalty that members of a group have toward the workgroup. (2)

Esteem needs The desire to be respected as human beings. (11)

Ethics Standards of conduct or morals established by the current and past attitudes and moods of a particular society. (7)

Eustress A positive and necessary type of stress that enables one to function and accomplish goals. (7)

***Ex parte* warrant** A judicially granted right for OSHA inspectors to search an employer's premises without prior notification or permission. (20)

Exception principle The assertion that regular and recurring decisions should be delegated to employees and than nonroutine decisions be handled at a higher level. (8)

Executives A typical classification of senior managers in private organizations. (1)

Exit interviews Sessions with departing employees, especially those who resign, to determine reasons for leaving and to uncover possible organizational problems. (11, 13)

Expectancy theory The theory that individuals will be motivated by their belief that specific behavior on their part will lead to a desired outcome. (11)

External compensation discrepancy A misalignment of compensation relative to what similar positions are paid by other organizations in the geographical area. (9)

External placement The selection of candidates for open positions from sources located outside the hiring organization. (9)

Faulty translations The misinterpretation of communications because of ineffective listening, mental set, or other causes of misunderstanding. (13)

Federal Labor Relations Council (FLRC) Federal agency that coordinates federal policy in labor relations; becomes involved with impasse disputes in the federal sector after negotiation and mediation have failed. (15)

Feedback The process through which one learns of the response to his or her message. (13)

Feedback control A process that attempts to return conditions to previously established standards after a deviation has taken place; may involve revising original goals. (5)

Feedforward control A process that attempts to anticipate deviations from planned objectives or standards for the purpose of modifying activities and procedures before a deviation actually takes place. (5)

Filter factor The straining out of ingredients that are essential to the understanding of messages as they rise up to management levels. (13)

Finder's fee A cash reward paid to existing employees for bringing in successful job candidates, "bounties" ranging from $25 to in excess of $1,000; typically withheld from the referring employee until the new person proves to be satisfactory. (9)

First-line managers The first level of management; generally referred to as *supervisors* or, in some goods-producing organizations, *foremen,* who are responsible for making certain that organizational policies and procedures are carried out. (1)

Flexible working hours A condition in which employees may, usually with prior approval of their supervisors, alter their usual working hours. (4)

Flextime (flexible working hours) A program in which employees have the freedom to choose, within certain limits, what time they begin and quit their jobs each day. (11)

Force-field analysis A problem-solving technique useful for identifying forces that impede and foster goal achievement. (3)

Foreman The traditional term for first-line management in goods-producing industries; *supervisor* is currently more common. (1)

Formal communication Official communication that is transmitted through the structured organizational network. (13)

Formal organization The planned structure; relates to the official lines of authority, responsibility, and accountability ranging from the board of directors and chief executive officer to the operative workers. (8)

Four C's of written communication A device for remembering the four essential elements of written communication: *c*omplete, *c*oncise, *c*orrect, and *c*onversational. (13)

Free-rein (laissez-faire) leadership A style of leadership in which the leader serves more to facilitate rather than to directly lead the group, which works out its own techniques for accomplishing organizational goals. (12)

Full flextime A program that permits employees to decide each day without prior notice to their managers what time they will arrive and depart; employees typically leave eight hours after they started. (11)

Functional authority relationship An authority structure that allows for specialists to exert direct authority over certain line activities. (8)

Functional departmentation Organizing departments around major activities (functions), such as finance, marketing, personnel, and manufacturing. (8)

FUN-FAB approach Acronym symbolizing a method for selling ideas or products; *f*irst *u*ncover *n*eeds; then relate *f*eatures, *a*dvantages, and *b*enefits to those needs. (17)

Gantt charts A planning and controlling tool that utilizes a bar graph format for graphically presenting the time relationships among the various tasks involved in a production plan. (5)

GIGO In computer jargon, symbolizes "garbage *i*n, garbage *o*ut"; i.e., inadequate input results in inadequate output. (3)

Goal Objectives, or ends, toward which activity is directed. (4)

Goal-setting A process that aids in clarifying the activities necessary to accomplish specific tasks. (4)

Goods-producing industries Firms directly involved with the production of tangible products, such as construction, mining, and manufacturing. (1)

Grapevine The network of informal relationships through which facts, half-truths, and rumors are transmitted. (3, 13)

Grievances Disputes over interpretation of the labor-management agreement; complaints by employees who feel they have been treated unfairly. (15)

Groupthink The deriving of negative results from group decision making efforts. (3)

Health The general state of physical, mental, and emotional well-being. (20)

Hearing officers Human resource management specialists who listen to and rule on employee grievances. (15)

Hierarchy of needs A concept that suggests each level of need must be satisfied to some extent before the next level assumes importance. (11)

High-impact problem A problem that, if gone unsolved, tends to have severe consequences on the organization. (3)

Horizontal communication Communication that takes place between departments or people on the same level in an organization. (13)

Hostile (unfriendly) takeovers When one firm is unwillingly acquired by another. (2)

Hotliner relationship Behavior characterized by bypassing normal chains of command. (17)

Human relations approach An approach to management that believes that employees desire to participate in decision making and be treated with dignity and respect. (2)

Human resource control The establishing and monitoring of standards related to employee performance and behavior, such as absenteeism, theft, and accidents. (5)

Human resource director Also known as a *personnel manager*; a staff specialist who generally has the major responsibility to assist the various departments of an organization with personnel needs, such as staffing. (9)

Human resource-oriented problems Deviations from standards involving employees and requiring decisions. (3)

Human skills The ability to motivate, communicate, and influence others in a positive way. (2)

Hypersensitivity Excessive susceptibility to the attitudes of others; quick to take offense. (16)

Incident file A record of examples of favorable and unfavorable employee behavior. (16)

Individuals with disabilities Persons who have or are regarding as having physical or mental impairments that substantially limit one or more of their major life activities. (19)

Informal communication Unofficial communication that supplements information transmitted through the formal network. (13)

Informal organization The natural self-grouping of individuals according to their personalities and needs rather than to any formal plan. (8)

Information Data that have been processed to aid in decision making. (3)

Internal compensation discrepancy A misalignment of compensation amounts in a particular department relative to what comparable positions and individuals receive in other departments. (9)

Internal placement The selection of candidates for open positions from sources located within the hiring organization. (9)

Intuition Arriving at conclusions on the basis of feelings and hunches, rather than on the basis of logic or available facts. (3)

Inventory control Balancing the need to have materials on hand with the costs of purchasing, handling, and storing such materials. (5)

JIT (just in time) Purchasing materials from vendors under a prearranged delivery schedule so that parts or supplies arrive just in time to be used by the purchaser. (5)

Job analysis A systematic approach to gathering, evaluating, and organizing information about a job. (9)

Job description Also known as a *position description*; a document that summarizes the principal duties and responsibilities inherent in a particular job; an aid for determining the type of person needed for an available position. (9)

Job enlargement The process of increasing the complexity of a job to appeal to the higher-order needs of employees. (11)

Job enrichment A form of changing or improving a job to create a more motivating work environment. (11)

Job evaluation A method of comparing and ranking each job in an organization as a means of determining its relative worth. (9)

Job opportunity announcement (JOA) Also termed *job posting*; a formal announcement within the organization of the opening of positions; in a sense, an invitation to employees to throw their hats into the ring. (9)

Job rotation Shifting employees from one job to another for the purpose of reducing boredom and increasing skills. (11)

Job satisfaction (morale) The atmosphere created by the attitudes of the members of an organization. (11)

Job sharing An approach to job enrichment in which two employees share a full-time position; also termed *twinning*. (11)

KISS approach The notion that communications should be delivered in an understandable fashion; an acronym that symbolizes either *k*eep *i*t *s*imple, *s*tupid or *k*eep *i*t *s*hort and *s*imple. (13)

Knowledge worker An employee with a high level of education and low level of tolerance for authority. (18)

Landrum-Griffin Act (Labor Management Reporting and Disclosure Act of 1959) Act restricting use of union funds by union officials. (15)

Leadership The use of developed skills to influence or change the behavior of others in order to accomplish organizational, individual, or personal goals. (12)

Letters of recommendation Letters solicited by job applicants from friends, acquaintances, former teachers, and past employers as an aid in obtaining employment; not highly valued by many employers. (9)

Leveraged buyouts (LBOs) When one firm borrows heavily for the purpose of acquiring the assets of another. (2)

Line authority The rights of individuals who generally are directly responsible for achieving the organization's objectives. (8)

Line organization A structure in which individuals are engaged in activities intended to directly accomplish the primary goals of the organization. (1)

Listening responses Various methods for showing interest in what a speaker is saying. (13)

Long-range plans Broader, more general organizational intentions, formulated for five to twenty years or more. (4)

Low-impact problem A problem that tends to have minor consequences on the organization. (3)

Maintenance goals Specific goals related to the ongoing and routine operations of an organization; goals that are intended to keep an organization on an even keel. (4)

Maintenance (hygiene) factors Factors, according to Frederick Herzberg, that tend to have a neutral effect on the work environment but are likely to cause dissatisfaction if not met; they include salary, employee benefits, interpersonal relationships, working conditions, company rules and policies, and job security. (11)

Management The process of combining resources to achieve organizational goals. (1)

Management attitude A belief in and a willingness to carry out the goals and objectives of an organization. (2)

Management by objectives (MBO) A management activity whereby a supervisor and his or her subordinates jointly establish goals and objectives; involves regular follow-up and appraisal activities to see if objectives have been accomplished or are in need of modification. (10)

Management information system (MIS) A computer-based information system that assists managers in their planning and controlling functions. (3, 13)

Managerial functions Activities that aid in achieving organizational goals, such as planning, organizing, staffing, directing, and controlling. (2)

Managerial Grid A device for dramatizing the various concerns—either for production, people, or combinations of both—that managers have. (12)

Managers Those who blend resources—human, material, and financial—to achieve organizational goals. (1)

Material resource-oriented problems Deviations from standards involving things rather than people and requiring decisions. (3)

Matrix authority relationship An authority structure organized around specific projects, programs, or products, rather than along traditional lines; in effect, the matrix structure overlays the basic organization and is usually disbanded after a project is completed. (8)

Mediation Use of an impartial third party who assists opposing sides in reconciling a dispute. (15)

Mental set The tendency to see or hear what we want or are set to see regardless of reality. (13)

Middle management The next level of management above the supervisory level (plant managers, superintendents, and department heads). (1)

Mission A general type of organizational goal that relates to the philosophical objectives of an organization. (4)

Mission goals General goals that relate to the philosophical objectives of an organization, such as "to offer to the consuming public a quality product at a reasonable price." (4)

Modified flextime A program that permits employees to decide on an eight-hour frame of working time falling between predetermined hours, such as 7:00 A.M. and 9:00 P.M. (11)

Motivation The feelings or factors that drive a person toward achieving a particular objective. (11)

Motivational factors (satisfiers) Factors, according to Frederick Herzberg, that tend to motivate and cause job satisfaction, such as achievement, recognition, challenging work, growth and advancement possibilities, and responsibility. (11)

Motivation-maintenance model A theory developed by Frederick Herzberg that describes two sets of factors in the work place, one set tending to motivate employees and the other tending to create dissatisfaction if withdrawn. (11)

Multiple interviews An interviewing technique in which several managers have the opportunity to observe, challenge, and pool their impressions of a job candidate. (9)

National Institute of Occupational Safety and Health (NIOSH) A federal health research center that recommends health standards for OSHA adoption. (20)

National Labor Relations Board (NLRB) Government agency established to enforce the Wagner Act. (15)

Need The feeling of deprivation; that which motivates a person into action designed to obtain relief or satisfaction. (11)

Needs, ego See *Needs, psychological.* (11)

Needs, physical Basic factors vital to human survival, such as food, drink, sleep, oxygen, and acceptable climate. (11)

Needs, primary Basic physical needs. (11)

Needs, psychological Personal desires concerned with self-realization and self-esteem, such as feelings related to titles, status symbols, and the accomplishment of significant goals; higher-order needs related to a person's ego needs. (11)

Needs, safety and security Personal desires concerned with feelings of safety and security, such as union membership, seniority rights, and retirement programs. (11)

Needs, secondary Social and ego needs. (11)

Needs, self-realization The need to feel accomplishment. (11)

Needs, social Feelings that are usually learned, such as the desire to belong and to enjoy peer acceptance. (11)

No-knock provision A currently prohibited activity that enabled OSHA to inspect an employer's property for safety abuses without a warrant. (20)

Nonprogrammed decisions Nonroutine decisions that are a result of analyzing computer-generated data and information, also termed *decision-assisting MIS.* (3)

Nonverbal language Forms of communication other than the spoken or written word, such as voice tones, facial expressions, gestures, body posture, and the use of time. (13)

Norris-LaGuardia Act of 1932 An act of Congress that outlawed the yellow-dog contract and greatly restricted the conditions under which court injunctions against labor unions could be used. (15)

Objective A specific statement of results that individuals or organizations want to achieve. (4)

Objective questionnaire A survey of employee attitudes that asks multiple-choice, rather than descriptive, questions. (11)

Obsessive-compulsive personality Behavior characterized by the presence of anxiety, with persisting, unwanted thoughts (obsessions) and/or the felt need to repeat certain acts over and over (compulsions). (7)

Occupational Safety and Health Act (OSHA) Legislation that requires most employers to create and maintain safe, healthful working conditions. (20)

Occupational Safety and Health Administration (OSHA) Established in 1971, a governmental agency that requires organizations to provide their employees with safe and healthful working conditions; responsible for administering the provisions of the Occupational Safety and Health Act. (5, 20)

Occupational Safety and Health Review Commission (OSHRC) A federal agency responsible for settling cases involving safety and health violations. (20)

Off-the-job training Training that is conducted away from the regular work place setting; could include taking evening courses at nearby colleges, programmed instruction, and correspondence courses. (10)
Ombudsperson An objective third party who assists employees with grievances. (15)
One-way communication A message flowing in one direction with no feedback or certainty of understanding involved. (13)
Ongoing (standing) committee A body of persons formed to handle a situation on a standing or long-term basis. (3)
On-the-job training (OJT) Training that takes place on the premises of the organization and may be conducted by specialists or the trainee's supervisor or coworkers; the new employee is partially productive during the training period. (10)
Open-door policy The practice by some managers of permitting others to drop by their offices without appointments. (13)
Open-ended meetings Meetings that do not have a definite cut-off time. (6).
Open-ended questions (open questions) Questions that cannot be answered with a simple "yes" or "no" response; intended to elicit greater response from an interviewee. (9, 13)
Operating employees Employees other than those in management positions. (1)
Organization A group of individuals structured by specialized activities and levels of authority for the purpose of effectively accomplishing a firm's goals. (8)
Organization chart A formal document that shows the chain of command and the titles that have been officially assigned to managers. (8)
Organization manual A guidebook that provides employees with information on authority relationships and attempts to clarify formal policies, procedures, and rules. (4)
Organizing The activity of coordinating human, material, and financial resources for the purpose of achieving preestablished standards and goals. (8)
OSHA Hazard Communication Standard (HCS) An OSHA promulgation that is patterned after states' "right-to-know" laws. (20)
Outplacement consultants Advisors employed by organizations to assist discharged employees in obtaining new employment. (16)

Participative (democratic) leadership A style of leadership that involves employees in decision making that affects them; develops greater employee commitment toward organizational goals. (12)
Pay grades Compensation categories that express the monetary value for each position in the job hierarchy; a range of compensation often exists within each grade level so that raises can be provided without promotions. (9)
Peer decisions Solutions to grievances recommended by a jury of employees and managers. (15)
Pension plan A fund set aside by the employer for distribution to employees after they retire. (9)
Performance appraisals A set of activities designed to evaluate how well employees have been carrying out their tasks and responsibilities. (10)
Person specification Also termed *job specification*; a form that summarizes the personal qualifications needed in the person who is to fill the job; provides the basis for selecting the individual who best fits the available position. (9)
Personality A person's psychological makeup and characteristic behavior as a whole. (16)
PERT (program evaluation and review technique) A planning and control technique for graphically presenting the time and paths that events take in the production process. (5)
Physical needs See *Needs, physical*. (11)
Piecework rate A compensation system that pays employees according to the number of units they produce. (9)
Pilot study A trial period intended to analyze and enhance the acceptance of change. (14)
Planned agenda A predetermined set of activities to be presented and discussed during a meeting; serves to reduce the amount of time wasted during a meeting. (6)
Planning A management function that establishes organizational goals and objectives and determines the means for accomplishing them. (4)
Pocket-sized appointment book An item that provides a supervisor with a portable and handy reference to, and record of, appointments and planned activities. (6)
Policies Guides to decision making and action for organizational employees. (4)
Potential problem A time-oriented problem that is likely to occur in the future. (3)
Preemployment medical examination A procedure sometimes used in the employment screening process to determine an applicant's physical or mental fitness for employment; sometimes used to detect substance abuse. (9)
Prejudice An attitude of making prejudgments with insufficient evidence. (18)
Primary needs See *Needs, primary*. (11)
Problem A deviation from a preestablished standard. (3)
Problem employee A person who consistently deviates from organizational standards. (16)

Problem-solving goals Goals that are intended to correct deviations from previously established standards or plans. (4)

Problem-solving teams Groups usually consisting of volunteers from different areas of a department who meet one or two hours each week to discuss and solve problems associated with their work activities; see also *Quality circles.* (11)

Procedures A system that details specific steps to be followed to achieve a particular objective. (4)

Procrastination Putting off doing something until a future time. (16)

Product departmentation Organizing departments along product lines; an insurance company, for example, could have life insurance, health insurance, business insurance, and personal lines insurance all organized into different departments. (8)

Production control A set of procedures for coordinating materials, machines, and labor into a smooth-flowing production process. (5)

Production dispatching A control activity that involves providing information to production workers regarding when work on a job is to begin, what machines are to be used, and which materials and tools are to be made available. (5)

Production inspection Following up production sequences and operations to make certain that scheduling and quality standards have been met. (5)

Production planning Determining future needs and activities for the purpose of making optimum use of materials, labor, and facilities. (5)

Production routing Determining the order or sequence in which various operations are performed throughout a plant. (5)

Production scheduling Setting up timetables showing when and how long each operation in the production process should take. (5)

Profit sharing An incentive-type of compensation that relates solely to the profitability of the firm and distributes a certain percentage of annual profits to employees. (2, 9)

Programmed decisions Computer-generated decisions made automatically after the occurrence of certain variables. (3)

Progressive discipline The severity of disciplinary measures increases after each repetition of unacceptable employee behavior. (16)

Project Management Software Programs Computer applications designed to assist management in planning and controlling activities. (5)

Proportional employment Hiring practice that attempts to match percentages of particular groups in the local work force. (18)

Psychological distance The mental attitudes of supervisors toward their associates regarding the closeness of the working relationship. (8)

Psychological needs See *Needs, psychological.* (11)

Punishment A penalty imposed for improper behavior. (16)

Pygmalion effect (self-fulfilling prophecy) Concept suggesting that the expectation of an event or certain types of behavior can actually cause the event or behavior to occur. (12)

Qualified individual with a disability A person with a disability who, with or without reasonable accommodation, is capable of performing the essential functions of a position. (19)

Quality circles (QCs) A method used for attempting to improve the quality and quantity of output; consists of rank-and-file employees with a common concern who form a team to exchange information for mutual improvement; QCs typically consist of 5 to 10 members and a leader to guide each team. (11)

Quality control A part of the inspection process intended to determine if the product meets the established standards of quality; may be on a sample (spot) or a 100 percent basis. (5)

Quality control specialist One who checks output to verify that product quality meets standards. (3)

Quality of work life (QWL)/human resource approach A concern for how effectively the job environment meets the needs and expectations of employees. (2)

Quantitative approach An approach to management that extensively utilizes mathematics for decision making. (2)

Reasonable accommodation The adaptation of the workplace, equipment, or job to enable a person with disabilities to do the job for which he or she is qualified in training and abilities. (19)

Recruiting An activity intended to obtain qualified applicants to fill available positions. (9)

Red-hot stove rule Disciplinary measures equated with touching a glowing hot stove. (16)

Refusal An employee reaction that exists when organization members disapprove of a change and, therefore, attempt to avoid complying with it. (14)

Rehabilitation Act of 1973 Act that requires federal contractors to take affirmative action to hire and advance persons with disabilities. (19)

Reliability A condition that exists if the results of an employment test are the same when administered repeatedly under identical conditions. (9)

Resistance Employee reaction that may appear to accept a change while engaging in activities intended to sabotage its objectives. (14)

Responsibilities Specific tasks or duties that have been assigned to an organizational member. (8)
Responsibility The obligation that organizational members have to perform assigned work or to make certain that someone else performs it in a prescribed way. (8)
Restraining forces Factors that cause a problem to exist. (3)
Restructuring Especially after hostile takeovers, reorganizing an acquired firm for the alleged purpose of more efficient operations. (2)
Results-centered leadership A technique of leadership that generally informs the employee of the goals of the organization and department and suggests that the employee work with the supervisor in deciding how those goals will be achieved. (12)
Resumé A short account of a person's career and qualifications, typically prepared by an applicant for a position. (9)
Reverse discrimination Applying preferential treatment toward minorities and women over white males related to conditions of employment. (18)
"Right-to-know" laws Acts passed by majority of states that require employers to inform employees if any hazardous substances exist in the work place. (20)
"Right-to-work" laws State laws prohibiting requirement that employees join a union or pay union dues to obtain a job. (15)
Role model Someone who serves as an example in a particular behavioral role for another to copy. (20)
Rules Statements of precisely what activities or conduct are or are not to be engaged in; rules generally relate to disciplinary action. (4)
Rumors Information transmitted through the grapevine, usually without a known authority for its validity. (13)

Safety and security needs See *Needs, safety and security.* (11)
Safety control Establishing and monitoring safety standards to prevent and reduce accident frequency and severity. (5)
Safety education and training Providing employees with information and skills intended to reduce the incidence and severity of accidents and industrial illness. (20)
Safety engineering Identifying work place hazards and designing jobs and the work place to reduce risk of accidents and industrial disease. (20)
Salary Compensation paid to employees based on a specific period of time, such as a month or year, rather than on an hourly basis. (9)
Scalar principle The assertion that authority and accountability in an organization should flow in a clear unbroken line between the point of ultimate authority (the manager at the top) and the workers at the bottom of the hierarchy. (8)
Scientific management approach An approach to management in which technical efficiency and productivity are all-important. (2)
Screening process A set of activities intended to determine whether a candidate has the necessary qualifications for the available position. (9)
Secondary needs See *Needs, secondary.* (11)
Selective reception A condition that exists when a person hears or sees the information he or she is set to hear or see and tunes out much of the rest. (13)
Selective X-Y Theory An approach that assumes that attitudes toward employees are not fixed but may vary with a person's past experiences and current prejudices. (12)
Self-concept The manner in which a person perceives him- or herself or status. (7, 11)
Self-discipline Self-imposed control or influence over one's own behavior. (16)
Self-managing teams Groups who are allowed to take over various managerial duties, including selecting compatible workmates for their group, scheduling work and vacations, and ordering materials; members may be authorized to set up their own job and work rotation assignments. (11)
Self-realization needs See *Needs, self-realization.* (11)
Senior (top) management The top of the management hierarchy—the administrative level—which includes senior executives, vice-presidents, and the president; individuals who determine the broad objectives and basic policies of the organization. (1)
Serendipity Making unexpected discoveries by accident. (3)
Service-producing industries Groups of firms or organizations not directly involved in the manufacturing of products, such as public utilities, insurance, and banking. (1)
Seven-step system A logical procedure for more effective decision making and problem solving. (3)
Sexual harassment Actions, suggestions, or propositions with sexual overtones that tend to transgress normal working relationships. (18)
Sham approach An employee giving lip service to his or her intention to seek professional counseling. (19)
Shop steward A union representative who is also employed by a firm. (1)
Short-range plans Fairly detailed organizational intentions designed to assist in accomplishing day-to-day objectives. (4)

Situational thinking Drawing on similar past experiences when analyzing present problems, recognizing that each situation is unique and may require a distinct solution. (3)
Social need See *Needs, social.* (11)
Spaced repetition Training materials presented with time intervals between each repetition rather than in uninterrupted doses; results in greater trainee retention of information and skills. (10)
Span of supervision (span of control; span of management) A principle that asserts that, in general, the larger the number of employees reporting to one manager, the more difficult it is for him or her to supervise effectively. (8)
Special employment groups Individuals treated differently because they are considered members of a special group, such as older employees. (18)
Specialization and division of labor The process of dividing up tasks and responsibilities among individuals, departments, divisions, or regions for the purpose of increasing organizational effectiveness and productivity. (8)
Special-purpose teams Groups generally consisting of both operating employees and management representatives who participate in decision making at various levels of the organization. (11)
Stab-in-the-back relationship Behavior intended to make one's own manager look bad. (17)
Staff authority Individuals whose main responsibility is to provide assistance, advice, services, or to solve specialized problems for line personnel. (8)
Staff specialists Those whose responsibility is to assist the basic line organization. (1)
Strategies Carefully thought-out decisions that aid in developing an action plan for achieving the end results desired by management. (4)
Stress Pressures and demands from one's environment that, when not controlled, can cause physical and psychological disorders; may be either positive (eustress) or negative (distress). (7)
Stress management The ability to influence, control, and adapt to the forces that create pressure in one's life. (7)
Stressors Events or factors that cause stress. (7)
Substance abuse An activity by persons who lack the ability to control their intake of alcohol or drugs. (19)
Substance dependency A situation in which an individual habitually lacks the ability to control their intake of drugs or alcohol. (16)
Suggestion system A feedback mechanism used to encourage upward communication in organizations. (13)
Supervision The art of motivating and coordinating resources to accomplish organizational goals; generally applied to the first level of management. (1)
Supervisor Similar to other managers but generally applied to first-level of management. (1)
Surprise factors Those unexpected, yet ever-present, interruptions that continually upset plans made by supervisors. (6)
Swiss-cheese method A time and activities management technique that involves doing something regularly on a project, regardless of how little is accomplished. (6)
Synergism The interaction of two or more independent parts resulting in an effect of which each is individually incapable. (3)

Taft-Hartley Act (Labor Management Relations Act of 1946) Legislation prohibiting unions from engaging in certain unfair labor practices. (15)
Technical skills The ability to apply techniques, utilize processes, and understand procedures necessary for carrying out specific tasks. (2)
Territorial (geographic) departmentation- Organizing departments by geographic location; locating plants or service facilities in various parts of the country or world. (8)
Theory X Developed by Douglas McGregor; a traditionally negative set of assumptions held by some managers toward employees. (12)
Theory Y Developed by Douglas McGregor; a positive set of assumptions held by some managers toward employees. (12)
Theory Z See *Z theory*. (11)
Third-party reference approach Using names of other concerned parties to support ideas during efforts at selling a manager on an idea. (17)
Time control Monitoring time-related activities for the purpose of improving effectiveness in the use of time. (5)
Time departmentation Organizing departments on the basis of time, such as day, 2nd, and 3rd shifts. (8)
Time management An activity that involves analyzing past and current activities, setting realistic goals, and coping with ever-present potential time wasters for the purpose of making more effective utilization of time. (6)
Time-oriented problems Deviations from standards that relate to present and future time frames. (3)
Title VII of the Civil Rights Act of 1964 A law that prohibits employers, labor unions, and employment agencies from discriminating in employment practices. (9, 18)

Tolerance The allowable leeway, or deviation, from a control standard. (5)
TRAF A time and activities management acronym that represents *t*hrow it away, *r*efer it to someone else, *a*ct on it, or *f*ile it. (6)
Training Providing instructional opportunities intended to systematically enable employees to acquire skills, understand rules and concepts, and modify attitudes for the purpose of improving performance on the job. (10)
Transfer of training A condition that exists when what is learned can be transferred from the training site to the job itself. (10)
Trial balloon approach Technique intended to test another person's reaction to ideas. (17)
Trial-offer approach Technique intended to gain acceptance of ideas by suggesting someone try a smaller segment of the idea. (17)
Tuition aid programs An employee benefit that reimburses employees for certain expenses incurred while attending classes off the premises. (10)
Two-faced relationship Behavior critical of the manager in front of employees and critical of employees in front of the manager. (17)
Two-tiered wage system A double standard wage system in which new employees are paid at lower wage and benefit rates than existing employees are for the same work. (2, 9)
Two-way communication A necessary ingredient of communication that helps to ensure that understanding has taken place. See also *Feedback.* (13)
Type A personality A characteristic of persons afflicted with a tendency toward work addiction and an obsession with time and achievement. (7)
Type B personality A characteristic of individuals who tend not to experience work addiction traits. (7)

Union An association of workers that has as its major objective the improvement of conditions related to employment. (15)
Union shop Agreement requiring all employees to join a union within a specified period of time. (15)
Union (shop) steward A delegated employee who assists other employees with unresolved complaints. (15)
Unionization process Activities associated with organizing nonunion employees and bargaining for union employees. (15)
Unity of command The assertion that since instructions or orders from two or more managers may conflict, no employee should be accountable to more than one manager. (8)
Unity of direction The assertion that each group of activities with the same goal should have only one head and one set of plans; focuses on process rather than personnel. (8)
Universality of management A term denoting that all managers engage in a similar set of functions. (2)
Upward communication The type of communication that flows up the organizational structure, including suggestion systems, open-door policies, employee grievances, labor news publications, attitude surveys, exit interviews, listening, and observation. (13)
Upward Pygmalion effect The influence that an employee's expectations have on the behavior of his or her manager. See also *Pygmalion effect.* (12)

Validity A condition that exists if it can be proven that a test consistently measures what it purports to measure, that is, predicts potential job performance. (9)
Verbal symbols Words that are used in either oral conversations or written messages. (13)
Vested A provision in some pension plans that allows employees who resign or are terminated prior to their retirement to receive a lump-sum settlement. (9)
Vestibule training A form of training that simulates the actual work situation utilizing sample equipment; provides a learning situation at a relatively small risk, since the environment is mock rather than real. (10)
Vietnam Era Veterans' Readjustment Assistance Act of 1974 An act that prohibits discrimination against veterans with disabilities and Vietnam era veterans. (19)

Wage A type of compensation in which employees receive wages according to the number of hours they work during a given time period. (9)
Wagner Act (National Labor Relations Act of 1935) Act providing employees with the right to engage in collective bargaining. (15)
Weekly activities summary log A time management tool used to summarize daily activities over a week for the purpose of analyzing how effective past utilization of time has been. (6)
Weekly planner A form that provides a supervisor with an overview of planned activities for an entire week. (6)
Well pay A program that offers financial incentives for maintaining attendance standards. (16)
Wellness programs Programs sponsored by employers for the purpose of maintaining and improving employees' physical health, sense of well-being, and productivity. (7, 20)
"What if?" analysis Decision-making technique that compares alternative outcomes by applying various inputs. (3)
Wildcat strike Employee work stoppage not sanctioned by collective bargaining. (16)
Work distribution charts Control devices that aid

the supervisors in assigning and controlling employee work assignments. (5)

Workaholism A compulsive type of behavior inherent in persons who experience withdrawal or guilt feelings when they are not working; also termed *work addiction.* (7)

Worker teams Groups of employees organized to work together. (11)

Workers' compensation laws Legislation providing financial benefits to employees unable to work as a result of physical injuries, disease, or mental disorders caused by job-related conditions; also requires most employers to obtain insurance to indemnify employees seeking such benefits. (5, 20)

Work-overload relationship Situation in which a manager assigns excessive amounts of tasks to a supervisor. (17)

Wrongful discharge Discharging an employee without good cause. (16)

Yellow-dog contract Forced agreement prohibiting employees from joining a union as a condition of employment. (15)

Yes, sir/Yes, ma'am relationship A servile, condescending way of interacting with those of higher authority. (17)

Z theory A concept developed by William G. Ouchi, refers to the ideal combination of characteristics of typically Japanese firms (Type J) and American firms (Type A); Theory Z organizations tend to maintain formal explicit control mechanisms, believe in formal planning, employ management by objectives, and utilize sophisticated information and accounting systems. (11)

Zero defects (ZD) A production control standard concept that strives to achieve no flaws or errors, that is, zero tolerance. (5)

Index